Positive Psychology

CW01667370

SECOND LANGUAGE ACQUISITION

***Series Editors*: Professor David Singleton**, *University of Pannonia, Hungary* and Fellow Emeritus, *Trinity College, Dublin, Ireland* and **Dr Simone E. Pfenninger**, *University of Zurich, Switzerland*

This series brings together titles dealing with a variety of aspects of language acquisition and processing in situations where a language or languages other than the native language is involved. Second language is thus interpreted in its broadest possible sense. The volumes included in the series all offer in their different ways, on the one hand, exposition and discussion of empirical findings and, on the other, some degree of theoretical reflection. In this latter connection, no particular theoretical stance is privileged in the series; nor is any relevant perspective – sociolinguistic, psycholinguistic, neurolinguistic, etc. – deemed out of place. The intended readership of the series includes final-year undergraduates working on second language acquisition projects, postgraduate students involved in second language acquisition research, and researchers and teachers in general whose interests include a second language acquisition component.

Full details of all the books in this series and of all our other publications can be found on http://www.multilingual-matters.com, or by writing to Multilingual Matters, St Nicholas House, 31-34 High Street, Bristol BS1 2AW, UK.

SECOND LANGUAGE ACQUISITION: 97

Positive Psychology in SLA

Edited by

Peter D. MacIntyre, Tammy Gregersen and Sarah Mercer

MULTILINGUAL MATTERS
Bristol • Buffalo • Toronto

Library of Congress Cataloging in Publication Data
A catalog record for this book is available from the Library of Congress.

Names: MacIntyre, Peter D., 1965– editor. | Gregersen, Tammy, editor. | Mercer, Sarah, editor.
Title: Positive Psychology in SLA/Edited by Peter D. MacIntyre, Tammy Gregersen and Sarah Mercer.
Description: Bristol, UK; Tonawanda, NY: Multilingual Matters, [2016] | Series: Second Language Acquisition: 97 | Includes bibliographical references and index.
Identifiers: LCCN 2015044276| ISBN 9781783095353 (hbk : alk. paper) | ISBN 9781783095346 (pbk : alk. paper) | ISBN 9781783095360 (ebook)
Subjects: LCSH: Second language acquisition – Psychological aspects. | Positive psychology. | Psycholinguistics.
Classification: LCC P118.2 .P676 2016 | DDC 418.001/9 – dc23 LC record available at http://lccn.loc.gov/2015044276

British Library Cataloguing in Publication Data
A catalogue entry for this book is available from the British Library.

ISBN-13: 978-1-78309-535-3 (hbk)
ISBN-13: 978-1-78309-534-6 (pbk)

Multilingual Matters
UK: St Nicholas House, 31–34 High Street, Bristol BS1 2AW, UK.
USA: UTP, 2250 Military Road, Tonawanda, NY 14150, USA.
Canada: UTP, 5201 Dufferin Street, North York, Ontario M3H 5T8, Canada.

Website: www.multilingual-matters.com
Twitter: Multi_Ling_Mat
Facebook: https://www.facebook.com/multilingualmatters
Blog: www.channelviewpublications.wordpress.com

Copyright © 2016 Peter D. MacIntyre, Tammy Gregersen, Sarah Mercer and the authors of individual chapters.

All rights reserved. No part of this work may be reproduced in any form or by any means without permission in writing from the publisher.

Typeset by R. J. Footring Ltd, Derby, UK

Contents

Contributors

Ana Maria F. Barcelos is Associate Professor of English at Federal University of Viçosa, Brazil. She holds a PhD from the University of Alabama, Tuscaloosa, AL, USA. Her main research interests include beliefs about language learning and teaching as related to emotions and identities. She has co-authored and edited, among others, *Beliefs About SLA: New Research Approaches* (Kluwer, 2003), *Narratives of Learning and Teaching EFL* (Palgrave Macmillan, 2008) and, more recently, *Identity in Foreign Language Learning and Teaching* (Palgrave Macmillan, 2015), with Paula Kalaja, Mari Aro and Maria Ruhothie-Lyhty. She has presented papers and given workshops for teachers in Brazil, Mexico, Argentina, the USA and Canada.

Linnea P. Belnap is a registered nurse and has extensive experience in settings involving cognitive-behavioural therapy, including group processing and mindfulness training. An All-American volleyball player, her background of working with coaches, athletes, stress and maximising performance adds an important dimension to the Project Perseverance team. She has coached struggling students in study abroad programmes in Amman, Cairo, Jerusalem and Tangier, and just completed six years of working as a volunteer with a 12-step addiction recovery programme.

R. Kirk Belnap is Professor of Arabic in the Department of Asian and Near Eastern Languages at Brigham Young University. He served for 13 years as director of the National Middle East Language Resource Center and now heads the Project Perseverance team. His research interests include second language acquisition, language policy and planning, and the history of Arabic. He has been running intensive language programmes since 1989 and since 2007 has directed intensive STARTALK Arabic summer camps for high school students that have helped hundreds of students develop proficiency in Arabic and grow in confidence in their academic abilities.

Jennifer Bown is Associate Professor in the Department of German and Russian at Brigham Young University. Her articles on affect and self-regulation in language learning have appeared in such journals as *Language Teaching, Foreign Language Annals* and *Modern Language Journal.* She is co-author of two textbooks and an edited volume on teaching language at professional proficiency levels.

Hilda Simone H. Coelho is Assistant Professor of English at the Federal University of Viçosa, Brazil. She holds a PhD from the Federal University of Minas Gerais, in Brazil. Her work on teacher education has mainly concerned language teaching in public schools. She is a member a government project to improve the quality of education in schools in Brazil. Her research focus is on understanding emotions and beliefs in language learning and teaching, with the biology of cognition as the main theoretical framework. She has presented papers in applied linguistics and education in Brazil and co-edited *Emoções, reflexões e transformações de alunos, professores e formadores de professores de línguas* (Pontes, 2010).

Éva Czimmermann graduated from Eötvös Loránd University, Budapest, as a psychologist and an English teacher in 2011. In her MA thesis, she connected psychology and applied linguistics through a study of 'flow' in language learning. Currently working as a psychologist in a special education school for children with physical disabilities, she supports a learning environment that builds on individual differences and creativity as a principle. Besides working with children, she helps teachers and parents realise the potentials of positive psychology and health promotion in the complex development process of students.

Jean-Marc Dewaele is Professor of Applied Linguistics and Multilingualism at Birkbeck, University of London. He is interested in individual differences foreign language acquisition and use. He is Vice-President of the International Association of Multilingualism, Convenor of the AILA Research Network Multilingualism, and former president of the European Second Language Association. He is General Editor of the *International Journal of Bilingual Education and Bilingualism*. He won the Equality and Diversity Research Award from the British Association for Counselling and Psychotherapy (2013) and the Robert C. Gardner Award for Outstanding Research in Bilingualism (2016) from the International Association of Language and Social Psychology.

Dan P. Dewey, Associate Professor of Linguistics at Brigham Young University, received a PhD in Second Language Acquisition from Carnegie Mellon University. His research focuses largely on language acquisition in settings other than the classroom (residence/study abroad, internships, autonomous online learning, etc.). He is specifically interested in social networks and language learning, motivation and a variety of affective factors. He also conducts research on second language assessment.

Joseph Falout is an Associate Professor at Nihon University, College of Science and Technology, Tokyo, Japan. He has authored or co-authored over 40 papers and book chapters about language learning affect, motivation and group dynamics. He received awards for publications and presentations from the Japan Association of Language Teaching (JALT). He edits for JALT's *OnCUE Journal* and the *Asian EFL Journal*. His collaborations include creating the theoretical and applied foundations of critical participatory looping, present communities of imagining, and ideal classmates. He has taught rhetoric and composition, public speaking, and ESL at colleges in the USA.

M. Carmen Fonseca-Mora is the head of ReALL (Research in Affective Language Learning) group and Professor in the Department of English Philology at the University of Huelva, Spain, where she has been also Vice-Chancellor for Lifelong Learning Programmes and Innovation. Her main research interests are applied linguistics and language teacher training. Her work has appeared in academic journals and edited volumes, as well as scientific journals. She has lectured in Germany, Portugal, France, Italy, Great Britain, Sweden, Peru, the United States, Austria and Spain. She is currently co-editor of the English Edition of *Comunicar* journal, a media education research journal.

Candy Fresacher has been teaching at various vocational colleges in Vienna for the past 25 years. In 2006 she received her PhD in American Studies from the University of Vienna. In the past 10 years she has become involved in teacher training as part of her position on the board and as chair of TEA (Teachers of English in Austria). She has also edited its *ELT News* and published a number of articles, including, for example, in the online site Humanizing Language Teaching. In 2015 she received the Pannonia Award from the University of Pannonia in Hungary.

Tammy Gregersen has a PhD in Linguistics from Valparaiso, Chile. She began her teaching and researching career in a university in the Atacama Desert in the North of Chile and is now a professor of TESOL and teacher educator at the University of Northern Iowa (USA). She is the author, with Peter MacIntyre, of *Capitalizing on Language Learners' Individuality* (Multilingual Matters, 2014) and is currently working on another book with him on non-verbal communication in the language classroom. She has published extensively on individual differences, teacher education, language teaching methodology and non-verbal communication in language classrooms. She is passionate about travelling and has presented at conferences and graduate programmes across the globe.

Marc Helgesen is Professor in the Department of Intercultural Studies, Miyagi Gakuin Women's University, Sendai, Japan. He also teaches positive psychology in ELT in the MA-TESOL programme, Nagoya University for Foreign Studies. He is author of over 150 ELT articles, books and textbooks and has been an invited speaker at conferences on five continents. In addition to positive psychology, he is interested in extensive reading and neuroscience in ELT. He is chair of the Extensive Reading Foundation (www.ERFoundation.org). He is working on a book of positive psychology activities for ESL/EFL which will be published in 2017 by ABAX ELT. Websites: www.ELTandHappiness.com and www.HelgesenHandouts.weebly.com.

Phil Hiver is a lecturer in the Department of English Language Teaching at the International Graduate School of English, Seoul. His research interests include L2 learner psychology in instructed second language acquisition, research methods for SLA using a complexity theory framework, and L2 teacher identity and cognition. Along with several chapters in edited volumes on these topics, he has recently authored articles in journals such as *Applied Linguistics* and *Language Teaching Research*.

Zana Ibrahim is a PhD researcher in the School of English, University of Nottingham. He is a former recipient of the Fulbright Scholarship and obtained his master's degree in TESOL from the Indiana University of Pennsylvania. He has worked in the field of foreign language teaching and translation. His research interests include directed motivational currents, positive affect and dynamic systems theory.

J. Lake, PhD, is a lecturer at Fukuoka Jo Gakuin University. He has taught at universities in Japan for over 20 years. His research interests include language learning motivation, psychological and educational assessment, and positive psychology.

Francisco Herrero Machancoses is Lecturer in the Department of Developmental, Educational and Social Psychology and Methodology, Jaume I University, Castellón (Spain) and a visiting professor at University of Huelva (Spain). His main research interest is applied statistics in human processes and behaviour. He has been involved in evaluation methods of teacher quality and has participated in the testing of many research projects since 2000. During the last 13 years, he has been involved in several projects, including psychometric applications and advanced methodological issues. He has lectured in Mexico and Spain. He is also a member of the editorial board of the *Spanish Journal of Drug Addictions*.

Peter D. MacIntyre received his PhD in psychology from the University of Western Ontario (now Western university) in 1992 with R.C. Gardner and is now Professor of Psychology at Cape Breton University. His research examines emotion, motivation and cognition across a variety of types of behaviour, including interpersonal communication, public speaking and learning. The majority of his research examines the psychology of communication, with a particular emphasis on second language acquisition and communication. He is co-author of *Capitalizing on Language Learners' Individuality* with Tammy Gregersen (Multilingual Matters, 2014) and co-editor of *Motivational Dynamics in Language Learning* with Zoltan Dörnyei and Alastair Henry (Multilingual Matters, 2015).

Sarah Mercer is Professor of Foreign Language Teaching at the University of Graz, Austria, where she has been working since 1996. Her research interests include all aspects of the psychology surrounding the foreign language learning experience, focusing in particular on self. She is the author, co-author and co-editor of several books in this area, including *Towards an Understanding of Language Learner Self-Concept* (Springer, 2011), *Psychology for Language Learning* (Palgrave, 2012), *Multiple Perspectives on the Self in SLA* (Multilingual Matters, 2014) and *Exploring Psychology in Language Learning and Teaching* (Oxford University Press, 2015).

Margarita Meza is a psychology student at the University of Northern Iowa, where she has been involved in positive psychology research and has plans to pursue her passions in Bio/Neuro-Psych. She has been involved in refugee and immigrant support and empowerment as well as working with international students on campus. Her mentoring/teaching has included working with first-year undergraduate students who are making the transition into university life.

Tim Murphey has a PhD from the Université de Neuchâtel, Switzerland. He is TESOL's Professional Development in Language Education series editor, co-author with Zoltan Dörnyei of *Group Dynamics in the Language Classroom* (Cambridge University Press, 2003) and author of *Music and Song* (Oxford University Press, 1992). He researches Vygotskian socio-cultural theory (SCT) with transdisciplinary emphasis on community, play and music at Kanda University, Japan. His most recent books are *Teaching in Pursuit of Wow!* (Abax, 2012), *Meaningful Action – Earl Stevick's Influence on Language Teaching* (Cambridge University Press, 2013), co-edited with Jane Arnold, and a critical novel on the Japanese entrance exams in Italian, Japanese and English, *The Tale that Wags* (Perceptia, 2010).

Rebecca L. Oxford is Professor Emerita and Distinguished Scholar-Teacher, University of Maryland, where she focused on language education and culture. Her Lifetime Achievement Award states that her 'research on learning strategies has changed the way the world teaches languages'. She is currently an adjunct professor of psychology and English language teaching at two branches of the University of Alabama. On topics such as language learning strategies, positive psychology in language learning, language and peace, peace cultures, and spirituality and education she has published approximately 250 articles and chapters, 12 books (several of which were translated into Japanese, Korean and Arabic) and eight journal special issues, as well as giving approximately 475 addresses (keynotes, plenaries and other presentations) in 42 countries. In the past she initiated and co-edited the 'Tapestry Program', a global book series for English language learning (Heinle/Thomson), and she is currently co-editing two other book series, 'Transforming Education for the Future' (Information Age Publishing) and 'Spirituality, Religion, and Education' (Palgrave Macmillan). She served as a tenured professor and programme chair at the University of Alabama, Teachers College at Columbia University, and the University of Maryland. She was also department chair and associate dean at the University of Alabama.

Katalin Piniel is Assistant Professor in the Department of English Applied Linguistics at Eötvös University, Budapest, where she obtained her PhD in language pedagogy. She is particularly interested in conducting research on the dynamic interrelationship of individual differences in foreign language learning, with a special focus on language anxiety. Currently, she is a member of a research team exploring the motivations, beliefs and strategies of deaf foreign language learners.

Patrick R. Steffen is Professor of Psychology at Brigham Young University and is the director of the doctoral programme in clinical psychology. His research interests lie in the areas of clinical health psychology, stress reduction, and biofeedback, with specific interests in culture, spirituality and health. He is particularly interested in the Hispanic Paradox and how disadvantaged groups display resiliency and positive adaptation in spite of significant stressors. He is on the editorial boards of *Annals of Behavioral Medicine*, *Journal of Behavioral Medicine* and *Frontiers in Psychology*, and on the board of directors of the Association for Applied Psychophysiology and Biofeedback.

1 Introduction

Tammy Gregersen, Peter D. MacIntyre and Sarah Mercer

A hand making ripples in the water struck us immediately as an embracing and suitable image for our book on positive psychology in applied linguistics. For us, water represents an ever-moving and changing environment in which we can be fully immersed. As individuals, we can influence our environments, we have agency and exercise it at times by extending a hand to others. We can cause perturbations in our surroundings, sending ripples from the slightest action that might expand to create waves from even the smallest of actions. It is this interaction of context and individual, their complete symbiosis with the potential for human agency that so captures how we feel about socially situated views of human psychology in language practice. The positivity flows fluidly from the inherent hope in having agency to be able to affect our lives and those of others, as well as how we think and feel about them.

In their seminal article outlining positive psychology, Seligman and Csikszentmihalyi (2000) each wrote about a source of inspiration for them. That idea appeals to us as well, as we write about positive psychology in SLA. As editors, we have each taken one element from our cover image (hand, ripple, water) to tell our personal story about a source of inspiration that describes why positive psychology appeals to us, stories that we would like to share with readers.

When Tammy saw the hand causing ripples in the water, her mind was immediately drawn to another famous pair of hands that acted as agencies of positive change, reaching out in a most sacrificial of ways to literally 'pay it forward'. The story is of the Dürer brothers, Albrecht and Albert, who grew up in 15th-century Nuremberg. Both were incredibly gifted artists; both wanted to pursue their talents in art school. As two of 18 children, their goldsmith father had to labor 18 hours a day to feed the family. The boys understood that their parents could never afford to finance either of them to study. After many long conversations, the brothers came to the decision that they would leave their fates to the flip of a coin. The winner would attend the academy, while the other earned money in the depths of the nearby mines. Upon completion of art school, the winner would finance the other's art education either through artwork sales or, if need be, by toiling in the mines. Albert lost the toss, and slogged away in the dangerous mines. Albrecht, the winner, attended school, financed by his brother. His etchings and woodcuts became an immediate sensation, netting sizeable sums for his commissioned art. After four years, the young artist's homecoming was a festive affair with a family meal full of music and laughter. At dinner's end, from his honored place at the head of the table, Albrecht rose to deliver a toast to his beloved brother's long years of sacrifice. He extolled Albert's good will and told his cherished brother that it was now his turn to go to Nuremburg to pursue his dream. Albert, tears streaming down his face, slowly shook his head from side to side and sobbed, telling his brother that he could not go. Holding his hands close to his face he softly lamented that it was too late, that four years in the mines had ruined his hands. Every bone in every finger had been broken at least once, and his arthritis was so bad that he could not even return his brother's toast, much less use his hands to make the delicate motions demanded by parchment or canvas. Several years later, to honor Albert for everything he had forfeited, Albrecht Dürer meticulously drew his brother's battered hands, palms together and fragile fingers stretched skyward. He called his powerful drawing simply *Hands*, and, after 450 years, many are now familiar with only that one famous piece of Dürer's work.

Tammy continually challenges her pre-service language teachers by asking whether there is a more poignant reason for becoming a teacher than to 'pay it forward'. She is inspired by the symbolism of the hands in this story because it suggests that no one ever accomplishes treasured dreams alone, that it is in the context of community that important goals are achieved.

Peter's inspiration is related to the notion of ripples; it comes from a story by Art Buchwald, who was a fascinating American satirist and humorist. Buchwald's humor skewers the wealthy and privileged and his sentiments have always appealed to Peter, but one story in particular touched his heart. 'Love and the Cabbie' tells of Buchwald's harrowing taxi ride through the busy streets of New York with one of his most optimistic friends. When the driver delivered his passengers safely to their destination, the friend gave a genuine, unexpected compliment to the driver along with a nice tip. After some convincing that the praise was both genuine and well earned, the driver accepted the compliment and went about the rest of his day. A small seed had been planted. The driver was now going to have a slightly better day than he otherwise would have, and maybe he will be a little nicer to his next passengers, who, being just a little happier themselves, would be a little nicer to their family and friends. In this way, one small random act of kindness might reach 1000 people in a single day.

Peter has used this story during workshops on teaching and with his positive psychology students for several years. For him, the meaning of the story continues to grow. Peter sees in the story the ways that teachers can affect students in positive ways through even the smallest gestures – a compliment on an otherwise dismal paper, a casual conversation about the student's hopes for the future, or a few days' extension on a project when the student would rather not say why it is needed. As the ripples grow, students touch each other, their family, friends and, potentially, strangers. With growing language ability, they can communicate their humanity to more and more people, even in the smallest of ways; this is how learning a language helps make the world just a little better than it otherwise would have been. Positive psychology, to Peter, is all about the little ripples of positivity that spread, often without anyone noticing. But what a thing it is when you start to notice those little ripples! The chapters of this anthology provide an abundance of ways of both noticing and appreciating the little ripples, and creating new ones.

For Sarah, water is her favorite element. She grew up on boats and around water, lakes, seas and the ocean. She learned to have a deep respect for water in all its forms. Sarah loves swimming, preferably outdoors in open water, whether lakes, rivers or the sea, although she is keen to point out that she is most definitely an amateur who typically enjoys a 10-minute paddle or a soothing float rather than any strenuous swimming. Recently, Sarah had the opportunity to take part in a charity swim and she jumped at the chance. It was an excellent way for her to get fitter, spend more time in her favorite element and do something worthwhile for a good cause. She trained for a year, some days more, some days less, and all too soon the day itself arrived. Despite some initial nerves, Sarah was just keen to get on with it and enjoy the experience, which she truly did. The atmosphere featured people, many much more out of their comfort zone than she, all challenging themselves in various ways and almost exclusively for the benefit of others; it is an experience she will never forget.

Sarah profited in so many ways from that swim, sharing the challenge with others, engaging with a meaningful purpose that inspired their collective action, watching as others pushed themselves to their limits. Sarah witnessed first-hand how we are capable of so much more than we sometimes believe but, with the right mindset, we can reach beyond the limits of our own minds. This is what positive psychology is about for her. It has the potential to dramatically alter how we cope with things, how we look at life, what we believe about ourselves and others, and how we go about living. Over time, and with cooperation among people, we can change our circumstances and even the physical conditions in which we live.

Like water, human psychology is powerful, precious and needs to be treated with great respect and care. It too is constantly shifting and moving, intimately connected with others in a complex ecology that can cover an incredibly diverse range of emotions and forms, and, ultimately, can be both powerfully constructive and destructive. While much research in psychology has examined how to cope with and manage the destructive forces, less attention has been paid to the positive powers and aspects of psychology that allow us to flourish, even in the most barren settings. In this collection, our focus is on the positive dimensions of psychology, on how we can make the most of our potential as humans; we explore the strengths we have, how we can build on these, how we can promote positive relationships within our ecologies with others, and how we can foster positive nurturing environments.

In this volume, readers will have the opportunity to explore evidence concerning the strengths that enable both language learners and teachers to thrive individually and in communities. Authors of the chapters in this collection consider what makes language learning meaningful and fulfilling. Rather than focusing on the traditional, often negative concerns that we have had in applied linguistics milieus (e.g. aptitude problems, non-native-like speech, subtractive bilingualism, high anxiety, demotivated students), colleagues in this volume focus on strengths and building upon the assets of learners and teachers. Without neglecting the importance of previous work or making a caricature of it, we attempt to demonstrate the importance of positive psychology concepts such as positive emotion, empathy, love, engagement, hope, enjoyment, meaning and relationships, among others.

Rebecca Oxford's chapter is a thorough introduction to positive psychology that helps to organize familiar themes in applied linguistics as well as introduce concepts that have not yet been studied in this area. Oxford uses Seligman's (2011) description of the PERMA paradigm as a base, expanding its applications to language learning and teaching. Her innovative vision, referred to with the acronym EMPATHICS, is an exhaustive exploration of the pivotal attributes that empower some language learners and teachers to achieve success, while, at the same time, it provides insight into why and how others struggle. The chapter offers a comprehensive explanation of the crossroads where positive psychology meets applied linguistics and will surely be a well cited contribution.

Following Oxford's contribution, we have divided the remaining contributions into three parts: theoretical, empirical and applied. Sarah Mercer opens Part 1, 'Theoretical', with a call for greater understanding of empathy in language learning and teaching. She discusses the importance of empathy from both learner and teacher perspectives. For learners, empathy fosters an appreciation and understanding of other cultures, and demands interaction with diverse others through a foreign medium, as well as understanding of peers in class. For teachers, empathy provides the tools for positive group dynamics and a facilitative learner-centered classroom experience. Mercer takes both social relationships and interpersonal skills as central concerns in studying empathy.

Joseph Falout's chapter draws readers' attention to the need to appreciate, investigate and cultivate learners' past selves in juxtaposition to their future selves. He carefully explores the similarities and connections between remembered past selves and imagined future selves, and demonstrates how past selves can help or hinder language learning. He establishes the importance of past selves in L2 learning and provides ways for learners to reconstruct their own and their classmates' past L2 selves for the purposes of nurturing positive emotions and greater engagement in their present, experiencing selves, which results in superior guidance, adaptation and self-consistency in language learning.

The final chapter in Part 1, by Ana Barcelos and Hilda Coelho, addresses the seemingly 'forbidden emotion' of love in applied linguistics literature. The authors begin their argument by discussing some myths and misrepresentations about love in education and then present several different definitions of love that can be found in education and social sciences. They conclude by highlighting the interrelationship of love, language learning and teaching as they reflect on how this intersection can instill a better quality of life in the classroom for teachers and students.

In the opening chapter of Part 2, 'Empirical', Tammy Gregersen, Peter MacIntyre and Margarita Meza suggest that some techniques for fostering one's positive emotions may be more effective than others. Using a mixed-methods approach, they trace the emotional growth of five learners of academic English over the course of a 12-week, one-on-one mentoring program. The effects of positive psychology exercises (including music, exercise, animals, laughter, gratitude and altruism) were tracked using a self-report Likert-type scale whereby participants rated their moods at various times within each session. Respondents also wrote journals at the conclusion of each of the meetings. The authors suggest that building 'social capital' (a network of relationships that provide resources) and the individualization of the positive psychology activities were the most important factors in the success of the mentoring program.

Phil Hiver examines novice language teachers' struggles to find hope. He creates a strong case for examining the seemingly hopeless demands of first-year professionals from a supportive perspective. Based on the data he collected, Hiver argues that making sense of hope sometimes requires despair. However, not all novice teachers continue past their first few months in the profession – some feel futility and hopelessness, ironically reinforced by their supervisors, and cannot extract themselves from the downward spiral. Yet, for others, although it might decline initially, hope can be regained by generating goals and forging pathways to those goals that establish a sense of control over life events. These agentic feelings are associated with treating hardships as problems that can be solved, rather than insurmountable obstacles. Hiver's evidence suggests that hope and hardiness interact adaptively to provide positivity to novice teachers, allowing them to anticipate ebbs and flows in their careers. He concludes that the intimate link between a hopeful teacher's sense of purpose and the process of developing hope within one's teaching persona will ultimately help novice teachers thrive in the profession.

Éva Czimmermann and Katalin Piniel offer data suggesting that flow experiences in the language classroom are characterized by optimal levels of task difficulty, together with concentrated engagement in a motivating activity that offers manageable challenges over which the participant perceives an adequate level of control. Their study tested advanced Hungarian language learners' classroom and task-specific flow as well as anti-flow (boredom, apathy and anxiety). Using a variety of quantitative measures, their results show that the majority of the participants experienced both classroom and task-specific flow. Flow and anti-flow states in the language classroom were linked with particular tasks and situational characteristics, but not task modes. These results led Czimmermann and Piniel to encourage language teachers to plan for different ways to engage learners' attention by using a variety of relevant and interesting activities to enhance the positive language learning experience.

In a mixed-methods study, Jean-Marc Dewaele and Peter MacIntyre associated enjoyment and anxiety in the foreign language classroom with the left foot and the right foot of the language learner. Their results from a principal components analysis of 29 items given to over 1700 learners from around the world revealed three dimensions, labelled Foreign Language Classroom Anxiety, Foreign Language Enjoyment – Social, and Foreign Language Enjoyment – Private. Supporting the quantitative results is a series of excerpts from the participants who were asked to describe enjoyable episodes in the foreign language class. Surprisingly, some of the most enjoyable episodes involve what might be considered risky or even ill-advised teaching techniques, such as singling out students and making fun of errors in the classroom. Consistent with Csikszentmihalyi (2008), the authors highlight the risk that is inherent in episodes that learners report as being most enjoyable.

Using quantitative analytic techniques, J. Lake demonstrates how positive psychology constructs can be integrated with language learning motivation and self-related theories through structural equation models. Lake argues that the specificity of self-related constructs and their measurement need to be clarified and then modelled appropriately. He includes a global level, where positive self-concept references the whole person, a domain-specific level, where positive L2 self-references the person within the L2 domain, and even more specific concepts of L2 self-efficacy and proficiency. Lake's conclusions suggest that although focusing on content and communication has an important place in the language classroom, teachers may also want to consider helping learners develop positive identities for personal growth, which may contribute to a flourishing self.

Connecting innovative ideas about language learning motivation and positive psychology tenets, Zana Ibrahim used in-depth interviews to investigate the effect of Directed Motivational Current (DMC) experiences. DMCs are prolonged surges of intense motivation that occur when a combination of contextual and personal/group parameters come together at an appropriate time to create powerful momentum directed towards a valued goal/vision. DMCs are defined as having a self-propelling property. Ibrahim defined one of the focal features of a DMC as the positive emotionality that is linked with a learner's enjoyment and triggered by the realization that progress is being made towards potentially life-changing language-related goals. Ibrahim successfully argues that a steady presence of eudemonic happiness, fueled by future visions and anticipatory emotions, results in personal growth, self-realization and improved personal skills. He concludes that DMCs have the potential to alter the interpretation of negative emotions such as anxiety and boredom in light of feelings of happiness and prosperity that operate on a longer timescale.

The final chapter of Part 2, 'Empirical', marks a cross-over to Part 3, 'Applied'. R. Kirk Belnap, Jennifer Bown, Dan P. Dewey, Linnea P. Belnap and Patrick R. Steffen share initial results of 'Project Perseverance', a training program to prepare learners for success in intensive study. The aim of their intervention is to empower students to become effective self-regulating language learners, especially in those circumstances that generate intense negative emotions that challenge their identity, specifically study abroad. The authors report on 52 English-speaking students of Arabic who participated in pre-program training for an intensive semester-long program in Amman, Jordan. On-site in Jordan, learners were coached almost daily in group settings and met weekly with faculty or teaching assistant role models trained in reflective listening to discuss their experiences. Participants also kept weekly learning journals, which were used to tailor on-site training and provide some individualized feedback. Furthermore, learners met at the end of each week for a group processing session. Although participants had mixed views on the efficacy of some specific program elements, overall the results suggest that those who achieved high oral proficiency gains during study abroad were characterized by a high degree of satisfaction with their daily speaking experiences. Belnap *et al.* conclude their chapter with a series of short case studies that illustrate both successes and cases where students with impressive past histories of language learning failed to live up to their own and others' expectations.

In Part 3 of the book, on the practical applications of positive psychology, the authors introduce exciting and innovative ways to implement positive psychology in language classrooms. Marc Helgesen's chapter explains why positive psychology is more than a smiley face. He demonstrates how happiness can be combined with language through positive psychology strategies and explicit goals. Using Seligman's (2011) PERMA model, Helgesen takes each letter of the acronym in turn (Positive emotion, Engagement, Relationships, Meaning and Accomplishment) and provides explicit steps to classroom activities that result in positive outcomes for learners.

Tim Murphey proposes that we examine learner well-being less as a state and more as a process (which he calls 'well-becoming'). Murphey describes how getting students to teach other people outside of class not only helps them influence others in their wider networks of family and friends, but also embeds learning even more deeply in the students themselves, due to what he has dubbed 'the teaching/giving hypothesis'. Murphey's chapter shares results from 181 Japanese students learning English who, over a five-year period, taught English-language affirmation songs to people in their social networks. Students describe the 'teaching rush' they experienced and their pride in publishing their activities as individual case studies. In addition to songs, Murphey applies the student–teaching process to topics such as split-story narratives, eight ways to reduce stress, the power of sleep and ground-breaking neuroscience information about learning, among others. By integrating interesting content with a requirement for learners to teach other people in English, Murphey shows that learners are eager to pass on the positivity. He concludes by proposing that recasting 'task-based learning' as 'task-based teaching' (by students) offers a way to appreciate the value of what is being learned.

Candy Fresacher also shares teaching ideas that were inspired by positive psychology studies. She argues that an increase in positivity can provide resilience in language learners, making it easier for them to cope with difficult situations as well as making them more productive, creative and healthy. With an understanding that content in language classrooms has shifted from a strict focus on linguistic material to incorporating other subject matter, she proposes that interventions that have demonstrated efficacy in increasing positivity bring added value in language courses. Fresacher concludes that students with varying purposes for learning a language can improve their overall positive attitudes and continue using such interventions as they are increasing their language proficiency.

In the final chapter on the application of positive psychology, Maria del Carmen Fonseca-Mora and Herrero Machancoses advocate the use of melody and rhythm in language learning. They outline in detail the emotional and cognitive elements found in music that can improve the teaching and learning of language. Through a review of recent literature on the affective–cognitive cross-modal transfer between music and language, they suggest music benefits memory, increases attention and effort, induces both positive mood and deep concentration, and allows for a tighter connection to learners' inner selves. The authors argue that incorporating music in language teaching unlocks creativity and fosters a relaxed, motivating and productive classroom atmosphere for teachers and learners alike.

The concluding chapter, written by the editors, examines ways in which the present volume deals with issues that were identified in the area of positive psychology over a decade ago. It is argued that SLA is ready both to receive positive psychology and to advance it. In addition, the conclusion takes note of potential criticism of positive psychology and offers responses to it.

We hope that readers find inspiration among the themes, ideas, techniques and approaches that are present in this book. Together we hope the papers in this collection provide readers with a solid introduction to positive psychology in SLA. We hope that we can show exciting avenues of theoretical thinking, with claims supported by solid empirical research, and demonstrate that it is beneficial for language teachers to engage with positive psychology in their practice. We hope that readers find their own ways to make small, positive ripples in the lives of their students, and that the positivity returns in waves.

References

Csikszentmihalyi, M. (2008) *Flow: The Psychology of Optimal Experience*. New York: Harper Perennial.

Seligman, M.E.P. (2011) *Flourish: A Visionary New Understanding of Happiness and Well-Being*. New York: Free Press.

Seligman, M.E.P. and Csikszentmihalyi, M. (2000) Positive psychology: An introduction. *American Psychologist* 55 (1), 5–14.

2 Toward a Psychology of Well-Being for Language Learners: The 'EMPATHICS' Vision

Rebecca L. Oxford

1. Introduction

The 'EMPATHICS' vision in this chapter heralds the arrival of positive psychology to the language learning arena (see also MacIntyre & Mercer, 2014) and moves us toward a psychology of well-being for language learners. The term EMPATHICS is an acronym (see the Appendix to this chapter for details of its development) outlining important psychological forces that help learners achieve high well-being and progress rapidly, develop proficiency, and relish the language learning experience. At the same time, its components help explain why learners with low well-being crash on the rocks of frustration, anxiety or indifference. The letters in the acronym stand for ...

E **e**motion and **e**mpathy (dimension 1);
M **m**eaning and **m**otivation (dimension 2);
P **p**erseverance, including resilience, hope and optimism (dimension 3);
A **a**gency and **a**utonomy (dimension 4);
T **t**ime (dimension 5);
H **h**ardiness and **h**abits of mind (dimension 6);
I **i**ntelligences (dimension 7);
C **c**haracter strengths (dimension 8);
S **s**elf factors (**s**elf-efficacy, **s**elf-concept, **s**elf-esteem, **s**elf-verification) (dimension 9).

In the psychology of the language learner, the EMPATHICS factors are part of a complex dynamic system 'in the sense that high-level mental attributes and functions are determined by a complex set of interconnected components that continuously evolve over time' (Dörnyei, 2009c: 195–196). In such a system, no component works by itself; 'individual variation is not so much a function of the strength of any individual determinant ... as the way by which the complex system of all the relevant factors works together' (Dörnyei, 2009c: 195). This chapter indicates numerous connections within and across the nine EMPATHICS dimensions by means of bold print, as in 'we find or create meaning by being *responsible* in the current moment (see **agency and autonomy**)' and 'creating, imaging, innovating (see **motivation** and **character strengths**)'.

Many of the EMPATHICS themes, such as meaning, empathy, hope, optimism, time (in the sense of time perspective), hardiness, habits of mind, character strengths and self-verification, have not been addressed in our field. Certain other themes, such as resilience and intelligences, have rarely been discussed in relation to language learning. Even the familiar aspects, such as emotions, motivation, agency, autonomy, time (in the sense of possible selves), and three of the self factors, could benefit from further attention based on positive psychology. Therefore, this chapter opens up new vistas for theory and research, for language teaching practice and, of course, for language learning itself.

Positive psychology is important because it looks at positive elements and strengths in the human psyche and human experience, not at just the problematic, distressing aspects that have often been psychology's centerpiece (Lopez & Gallagher, 2011). Positive psychology, with its concentration on well-being, does not ignore human difficulties, but it faces them from the point of view of human strength rather than weakness. Positive psychologist Ed Diener (2011) noted that in one sense positive psychology has been with us for thousands of years, ever since ancient religious leaders and philosophers discussed virtues, happiness and the good life. Diener pointed out that in the last 100 years certain scientists have worked on positive subjects, such as effective coping. However, only in the last 15 years has positive psychology become a coordinated scientific field, with intensive idea-sharing and networking. As a new field, positive psychology is still 'finding itself' in terms of a deep theory, although 'the meta-theory of the person-centered [humanistic] approach ... provides a core basis for positive psychology theory development' (Linley *et al.*, 2011: 43).

2. Organization of this Chapter

This section outlines the structure of the chapter. Sections 3–11 address the nine dimensions. Some readers might be more interested in certain dimensions than others, and the structure of the chapter will help them find what they need. In this chapter, the respective sections differ substantially in length because there is more information available for some dimensions than for others. Due to page restrictions, I cannot explain the methods by which research has been conducted in all the dimensions, so I encourage readers to go to the original sources for further information. Section 12 summarizes the dimension-related hypotheses about the well-being of language learners. Section 13 is concerned what positive psychology might be missing in relation to language learners' well-being, and is followed by the conclusion (section 14), an appendix on the development of EMPATHICS to reflect well-being in language learning, and references.

3. Dimension 1: E = *E*motion and *E*mpathy

Hypothesis: Language learners with high well-being recognize their emotions, manage them effectively, and show empathy for others.

This section opens with emotion, because emotion 'functions as an amplifier, providing the intensity, urgency, and energy to propel our behavior' in 'everything we do' (MacIntyre, 2002: 61). In fact, MacIntyre (2002) suggested that emotion should be considered 'the primary human motive' (p. 61). The section then moves to a discussion of empathy, which is connected with emotion.

3.1. Emotion

The following exploration of emotion encompasses the emotional brain, duration of emotion, positive emotions and the 'broaden-and-build' theory, negative emotions and a possible silver lining, mixed emotions in certain language learner narratives, and emotional intelligence.

The emotional brain

The human brain is an emotional brain, creating relationships among thought, emotion and motivation (Le Doux, 1998). Emotions involve physiological arousal, such as changes in blood pressure, heart rate, body temperature and stomach sensations. Emotions are accompanied by conscious, subjective interpretations called feelings. In fact, theorists have developed approaches to emotion that are highly complex, containing multiple, interactive components. For instance, Lewis's (2005) theory includes four elements: arousal, action tendencies, attentional orientation, and affective feeling. Berry *et al.* (2002) argued in favor of a more detailed approach to emotion, containing the following constituents: antecedent events (situations eliciting an emotion), appraisal (evaluation of a situation or stimulus), subjective feelings, physiological reaction patterns, action readiness, behavioral expression, and regulation of this expression. Looking at the appraisal function alone, Schumann (1997) identified five stimulus appraisal dimensions: novelty, pleasantness, goal/need significance, coping potential, and self and social image. All of these help us calculate the emotional relevance of stimulus events, leading to emotional responses and emotional states.

Indeed, cognition and emotion are not separate: '[C]ognition and emotion were never two distinct systems at all… . [A] neuroscientific analysis finds them to be different aspects of a unitary phenomenon in which interpretation and relevance emerge together' (Lewis, 2005: 194; cited in Dörnyei, 2009c: 201). Emotions can be divided into two subsystems. The first is a primitive, automatic, visceral system that includes joy, interest, sadness, disgust, anger and fear, and is located in the brain's subcortical area (i.e. below the cerebral cortex), more specifically in the amygdala. By means of the amygdala, emotions help to shape cognition by modulating perception and attention, and conscious regulation of emotion by the second emotion subsystem can in turn influence the function of the amygdala (Dörnyei, 2009c: 222). The second subsystem is a more 'cognitive' one. Based on a person's developmental and experiential history, it is the link between emotions and attitudes, and is found in the cerebral cortex (MacIntyre, 2002). The second subsystem allows the person to experience emotion without a current, external prompt by merely reflecting on past or upcoming experiences (MacIntyre, 2002).

Because cognition and emotion are inseparable, emotion is an inherent part of learning (Arnold, 1999; Damasio, 1994; Le Doux, 1998). As explained by the world's most famous cognitive psychologist, Jean Piaget (1981), 'States of pleasure, disappointment, eagerness, as well as feelings of fatigue, effort, boredom, etc., come into play [in learning]… . [F]eelings of success or failure may occur' (p. 3).

Duration of emotion

Dörnyei (2009c: 222) noted that emotional experiences can vary dramatically in pervasiveness and duration on an 'emotional continuum'. Emotional states, or just 'emotions', are dynamic, continuously fluctuating processes that unfold in time. Moods are more prolonged and with less specific causes than emotions. Emotional traits (affective styles, temperament or emotional habits) are stable predispositions to emotional responding and are the most enduring emotional phenomena. Even infants have temperaments or ongoing emotional reactions. Rothbart (2007) described these as *surgency/extraversion*, or the tendency to approach new experiences positively, actively and energetically, rather than being inhibited or withdrawn; *negative affectivity*, or the tendency to be sad, anxious, easily frustrated and irritable; and *effortful control*, or the ability to focus and shift attention when desired and regulate one's emotions. Meaningful connections exist between temperament in infancy and personality later in life (Sigelman & Rider, 2012).

Positive emotions and the 'broaden-and-build' theory

Studies of positive emotions (Cohn & Frederickson, 2011; Frederickson, 2001, 2003, 2004) have resulted in Frederickson's 'broaden-and-build' theory. Frederickson cited happiness, curiosity, interest, pleasure and joy as positive emotions, while Seligman (2011: 17) added 'ecstasy, comfort, warmth, and the like'. Such emotions, according to Frederickson, broaden the individual's attention and build toward innovative thoughts and actions. This broadened range builds skills and psychological resources that are useful in the future. For instance, pleasure in interacting with someone else can build up friendship and social skills; joy in childhood's rough-and-tumble play can build up motor skills; and curiosity can build up searching skills. Positive emotions are valuable because they (a) 'trigger upward spirals toward emotional well-being' (Frederickson & Joiner, 2002: 172), (b) broaden the scope of attention (Frederickson & Branigan, 2005), (c) contribute to resilience (Frederickson *et al.*, 2003; Waugh *et al.*, 2008), and (d) speed up recovery from cardiovascular conditions related to negative emotions (Frederickson & Levenson, 1998). Dewaele and MacIntyre (2014) conducted a large-scale survey study concerning both foreign language enjoyment (enjoyment being an important member of a family of emotions surrounding the core emotion of joy) and foreign language anxiety (see 'Negative emotions and a possible silver lining', below). They discovered significant wells of language learning enjoyment among the participating students. Greater levels of foreign language enjoyment arose among individuals at higher levels of proficiency, among those who had learned more languages and among females compared with males (though females also had higher levels of anxiety). Thus, it is possible for the same person to experience both 'positive' and 'negative' emotions – high enjoyment and high anxiety – in relation to the learning of a foreign language. (See also 'Mixed emotions in certain language learner narratives', below.)

Positive emotions such as 'pride and satisfaction with one's efforts' contribute to language learners' self-regulation (Schunk & Ertmer, 2000: 631) and autonomy (Benson, 2011; Oxford, 1990, 2015a) and have a significant role to play in cognition (see **motivation** and 'Intrinsic motivation, flow and hot cognition' in section 4.2). Positive psychologists often view happiness as a prime positive emotion, and some detractors of positive psychology and even some proponents used to call the field 'happiology'. However, rather than describing happiness as a positive emotion, we could just as easily – and perhaps more accurately – depict it as a skill that can be developed. Matthieu Ricard (2003), a biochemist turned Buddhist monk who wrote *Happiness: A Guide to Developing Life's Most Important Skill*, argued that happiness includes acceptance of both pleasant and painful emotions. He stated, 'We so often confuse genuine happiness with merely seeking enjoyable emotions', but happiness is more about acceptance, or learning how to 'reduce the gap between appearances and reality' (pp. 26, 23; cited in North & Swann, 2011:

471). Acceptance of all of one's emotions, including joys and sorrows, means acceptance of oneself. For Ricard, happiness should not be about reframing all emotions as positive ones. North and Swann stated that we should not try to shoehorn

> all experiences into positive ones.... [A]cceptance is essential to enduring happiness at both an intrapsychic and interpersonal level, but it is often overlooked in the definition and measurement of happiness.... [A] more expansive definition of happiness ... is needed to reflect a richer understanding of the nature and origins of the construct. (North & Swann, 2011: 472)

Negative emotions and a possible silver lining

Neither Frederickson nor Seligman had much good to say about negative emotions. According to Frederickson (2001, 2003, 2004), negative emotions narrow the individual's response options to survival behaviors. Seligman (2011) stated that '[n]egative emotions warn us about a specific threat: when we feel fear, it is almost always preceded by a thought of danger' (p. 139), such as sadness being preceded by a thought of loss, or anger being preceded by a thought of trespass. He cautioned that anxiety leads to the restrictive fight-or-flight response, a set of behaviors used for survival. '[T]he negative, firefighting emotions ... identify, isolate, and combat external irritants' (Seligman, 2011: 66) rather than broadening and building anything.

Learning a language is sometimes considered 'a profoundly unsettling psychological proposition' (Guiora, 1983: 8). In the language learning field, Pavlenko's (2006) research participants suffered with guilt, insecurity, sadness and confusion. Much emotion research in language learning concerns negative emotions, especially learner anxiety, which has 'insidious' effects (Dewaele & MacIntyre, 2014: 238) that relate to the narrowing effects of negative emotions (Frederickson, 2001). Results of anxiety or insecurity include, but are not limited to, reductions in cognition, self-confidence, personal agency, control, willingness to communicate and ability to express and recognize emotions (Dewaele, 2010; Dewaele & MacIntyre, 2014; Horwitz, 2001, 2007; Horwitz & Young, 1991; MacIntyre, 2002; see **agency**). It is possible for language learners to transform negative emotions into positive emotions by means of humor (Vaid, 2006), but most practitioners likely would agree that when language learners are in a state of anxiety they tend not to engage in humor.

Considering all this, one would expect that negative emotions have only bad consequences. However, there is potentially a bright side to negative emotions – a possible silver lining. For instance, anticipatory anxiety can have utility when it stimulates language learners (Marcos-Llinas & Juan Garau, 2009), keeping them on their toes. My research (e.g. Oxford, 2014;

Oxford *et al.*, 2005, 2007) discovered that anger or sadness can sometimes serve as a helpful wake-up call to change something in a harsh situation, thus stimulating resilience (see **perseverance**). Similarly, Dewaele and MacIntyre (2014) argued that anxiety offers the benefit of generating a focus that calls learners to specific action, though these researchers also stated that positive emotions should ideally be more frequent than negative emotions in a language learner's emotional mix. We need to understand that positive and negative emotions serve different functions and are not merely two different ends of a seesaw.

Mixed emotions in certain language learner narratives

Certain narrative studies of language learners have unfolded a combination of positive and negative emotions. For instance, a study of Japanese women learning English identified emotions of longing, disappointment, sadness, powerlessness and occasional confidence (Piller & Takahashi, 2006). My colleagues and I (e.g. Kao & Oxford, 2014; Ma & Oxford, 2014; Oxford, 1996, 2014; Oxford & Cuéllar, 2014; Oxford *et al.*, 1996, 2005, 2007, 2014) discovered learners' positive emotions, such as excitement, pleasure, pride, contentment, satisfaction, joy and love, as well as their negative emotions, including anxiety, anger and shame. Thus, narrative research shows that a language learner's emotional response to the language and/or the learning situation is often complex; it cannot always be simplified to one or two emotions.

Emotional intelligence

Emotional intelligence is 'the ability to understand feelings in the self and others and to use these feelings as informational guides for thinking and action' (Salovey *et al.*, 2011: 238). A four-branch model of emotional intelligence includes the ability to do the following: perceive emotions in self and others; use emotions to facilitate cognition; understand emotions; and manage emotions in self and others (Salovey *et al.*, 2011). It is possible to transform negative emotions into positive emotions by developing greater emotional intelligence and increasing resilience-related personal and social supports (Oxford, 2015b). Emotional intelligence has been shown to reduce stress, anxiety and conflict; improve relationships; and increase achievement, stability, self-motivation, social awareness and harmony (Goleman, 2005). Emotional intelligence overlaps with intrapersonal intelligence and interpersonal intelligence, two of the multiple intelligences described by Howard Gardner (see **intelligences**; section 9.1). Intrapersonal (introspective) intelligence gives access to one's emotional life and allows the expression of feelings, while interpersonal (social) intelligence involves, at a minimum, being alert to others' emotions and needs.

Emotional intelligence is an important factor in language learning, according to Dewaele *et al.* (2008; also Dewaele, 2013), who found that adult multilinguals with higher emotional intelligence had generally lower levels of foreign language anxiety. These researchers discovered that during communication, individuals with higher emotional intelligence, compared with those with lower emotional intelligence, perceived themselves as more capable of (a) gauging the emotions of their interlocutor, (b) controlling their own stress and (c) feeling self-confident.

3.2. Empathy: Not a single emotion

Positive psychologists place a high value on empathy, which is formally defined as an 'other-oriented emotional response elicited by and congruent with the perceived welfare of someone else.... [It] is not a single, discrete emotion but includes a whole constellation of feelings ... [such as] sympathy, compassion, soft-heartedness, tenderness, and the like' (Batson *et al.*, 2011: 418). The word 'congruent' refers to the valence of the emotional response (Batson *et al.*, 2011); it is positive when the other person is feeling positive (e.g. we feel empathic happiness when the other person is has received good news) and it is negative when the other person is feeling negative (e.g. we feel empathic sadness and concern when the other person is distressed). Empathy is situational rather than being a disposition or a personality trait. 'There may well be [trait-like] individual differences in the ability and inclination to experience empathic emotion ... but attempts to measure these ... seem suspect at best' (Batson *et al.*, 2011: 419).

It is possible for us to feel happiness, sadness and concern for *ourselves*, but that is not empathy; in empathy, such feelings are always in relation to another person. We are cautioned by Batson *et al.* (2011) to perceive empathy as not merely inferring, intuiting, imagining, assuming or projecting something about another person's internal state: it is also necessary to be in tune to the welfare of that person. Mercer (in Chapter 3 of this volume) underscores the important links between the cognitive and emotional components of empathy.

Regarding a situation when the other person is struggling, sad or otherwise in need, antecedents of empathy include perceiving the other as being in need, valuing of the other's welfare, and being alert to situations that influence that welfare. As a result of such valuing, some people spontaneously adopt the other's perspective (Batson *et al.*, 2011). This perspective-taking can lead to altruistic motivation and behavior to help the other. Although it could be argued that altruism is merely a guise for instrumental, egoistic motives (e.g. the desire to get rewards for helping the other, or to reduce one's own discomfort, or to maintain one's self-concept, or to avert punishment or guilt for not helping the other), research does not support such theories (Batson *et al.*, 2011).

Empathy is clearly relevant to language teaching and learning. Skilled language teachers are empathetic, recognizing the needs and emotional states of their students and having compassion and tender-heartedness toward them, while keeping the students' welfare in mind. Language learners can empathize with other students, with teachers and with others, and this can build relationships, situation by situation. In circumstances of need in language learning, empathy can lead to altruism. See Mercer (Chapter 3) for more details, particularly on the cognitive aspects of empathy.

4. Dimension 2: M = *M*eaning and *M*otivation

Hypothesis: Language learners with high well-being seek and create meaning, which helps them be motivated.

Without meaning in our lives, we might as well give up or give in. Meaning is roughly described as personal relevance and significance that give purpose to life. For well-being to occur, it is important to have 'goals and beliefs that affirm sense of direction in life and feel that life has a purpose and meaning' (Keyes, 2011: 91). Positive psychology additionally suggests that 'human beings are intrinsically active and goal-seeking, constantly constructing meaning and a sense of purpose in their lives' (Linley *et al.*, 2011: 40) – although I would add that some individuals, compared with others, are much more active in this effort. For example, in contrast to less successful language learners, more successful ones seek learning contexts, tasks and materials that are meaningful. Also, they create meaning by assigning relevance and significance to contexts, tasks and materials in an agentic way (Lantolf & Thorne, 2006) (see **agency**) that serves to motivate them. This section therefore focuses on aspects of meaning and then discusses motivation, which would not exist without meaning.

4.1. Meaning

Positive psychology tells us that a sense of meaning is crucial to human life (see Keltner, 2009). Here I examine the meaning of meaning; the meaning-based work of Viktor Frankl, Gertrude Moskowitz and Earl Stevick; meaning in learner narratives; and meaning in inspired consciousness, peak experiences and self-actualization.

The meaning of meaning

'[M]eaning in life refers to people's belief that their lives are significant and that they transcend the ephemeral present' (Steger, 2011: 680). Meaning is also defined as 'the extent to which people comprehend, make sense of, or see significance in their lives, accompanied by the degree to which they perceive themselves to have a purpose, mission, or overarching aim in life' (Steger, 2011: 682). Meaning 'enables people to interpret and organize their experience, achieve a sense of their own worth and place, identify the things that matter to them, and effectively direct their energies' (Steger, 2011: 680). Meaning and wisdom are closely linked, because wisdom is the expert, highly valued knowledge that deals with fundamental, existential problems related to the meaning and conduct of life (Baltes & Kunzmann, 2003).

Making meaning involves establishing mental images of expected relationships that join together components of the external world with components of the self (Heine *et al.*, 2006). Though opinions differ about where meaning comes from, most theorists would probably agree that (a) meaning is enhanced when people engage in important pursuits while recognizing their own worth, abilities and qualities; and (b) 'meaning is most fully achieved when people actively engage in pursuits that transcend their own immediate interests ... [relationships, religion, culture]' (Steger, 2011: 683).

Meaning is important because people who believe they have meaning or purpose in their lives are happier, have greater well-being and life satisfaction, are more engaged in their work, and experience less depression, anxiety, suicidal ideation, workaholism, substance abuse and need for therapy (Steger, 2011). Those who have experienced traumatic events and have found meaning in them report better outcomes than those who have experienced such events as meaningless (Steger, 2011). I contend that successful language learners are those who have found meaning in learning the language – those for whom the language itself, not just getting a good mark in a language course, has some compelling meaning for them.

Frankl and the will to meaning

Viktor Frankl, the great Viennese existentialist psychiatrist who lost his whole family in the gas chambers of Auschwitz, discovered that his own horrific suffering as an Auschwitz prisoner could be transmuted by maintaining a sense of meaning. He helped others in the concentration camp to recognize meaning in their lives, and he developed logotherapy (meaning therapy) to enable people in general deal with the issue of meaning in their lives. My comments about Frankl and meaning come from his book *Man's Search for Meaning* (1984). For Frankl, the human search for meaning is the primary motivation in life. A person's meaning is 'unique and specific in that it must and can be fulfilled by him [or her] alone; only then does it achieve a significance which will satisfy ... [the] *will* to meaning' (Frankl, 1984: 105; original emphasis). Frankl cited a survey conducted by Johns Hopkins University involving nearly 8000 students at 48 colleges. Of these students, 78% said their primary goal at that time was finding a purpose and meaning to their lives (p. 105). Existential frustration can occur when one's will to meaning is frustrated.

For a given individual, 'the meaning of life differs ... from day to day and from hour to hour. What matters, therefore, is not the meaning of life in general but rather the specific meaning of a person's life at a given moment' (Frankl, 1984: 113). We should not search for an abstract meaning, because each person has 'a specific vocation or mission in life to carry out a concrete assignment which demands fulfillment.... [E]ach situation in life represents a challenge to [a person] and presents a problem for him [or her] to solve' (p. 113). Importantly, we find or create meaning by being *responsible* in the current moment (see **agency and autonomy**), with the object of that responsibility – 'the option for what, to what, or to whom'– being decided by ourselves (p. 114). Through emphasizing responsibility and meaning, logotherapy helps people gain a realistic picture of the world. 'The logotherapist's role consists of widening and broadening the visual field of the patient so that the whole spectrum of potential meaning becomes conscious and visible' (p. 115).

The meaning of life can be discovered through responsibility in various ways, all of which can be applied to language learning. One way is by creating a work or doing a deed, that is, by achievement of some kind. Any small or large achievement (e.g. acing a language test, writing a good paper, having a good conversation in the language, or going on a study-abroad trip) that the learner creates can contribute to meaning. Another way to find meaning through responsibility is by experiencing something special and valuing it. Frankl mentioned goodness, truth, beauty, nature or culture as things to be experienced that offer meaning; for language learners, encounters with the language itself and with other cultures can provide meaning. According to Frankl, yet another way to reach meaning is through encountering another human being, and especially loving that person. In this regard, language learners can collaborate closely and help each other, can get to know people from other cultures, and can generate and share love and friendship. In narrative studies (e.g. Oxford & Cuéllar, 2014), language learners spoke of their love for their teachers. Barcelos and Coelho (in Chapter 5 of this volume) describe how loving and teaching are interrelated actions.

A final way to discover meaning is by having a positive attitude in the face of suffering. Frankl contended that suffering typically occurs when we feel we are in a hopeless situation, which has not been changed despite our best efforts. When the circumstances are beyond repair, we may 'transform a personal tragedy into a triumph, ... turn [the] predicament into a human achievement. When we are no longer able to change a situation ... we are challenged to change ourselves' (p. 116) by altering our attitude. Clearly, language learners are not usually in a completely hopeless situation, but occasionally they might feel that way. If all else fails, they can deal with seemingly intractable problems by transforming themselves through a good attitude and a sense of dignity.

Specific concepts and techniques in logotherapy have utility for language learners. For instance, when learners combat their own boredom and thus find meaning, this process can alleviate what is known as the existential vacuum (see Frankl, 1984). Recognition of the dangers of hyper-intention (i.e. excessive intention) and hyper-reflection is valuable to language learners. Hyper-intention, such as the overwhelming determination to do a great job on a particular language task, can make the learner feel overwhelmed and cause the individual to fail. Too much gloomy attention to, or hyper-reflection on, oneself and especially one's failures or difficulties will not help language learning either. Finally, the technique of 'paradoxical intention' can be useful, particularly for students with very strong anticipatory anxiety. It involves inviting oneself to focus precisely on that which one fears and to make a paradoxical wish, for example resolving to fail the upcoming language test or deciding to become a blithering idiot when talking to the next native speaker one encounters. Paradoxical intention gives the learner a capacity for self-detachment and humor. Language teachers can teach learners to combat boredom, avoid hyper-intention and hyper-reflection, and try paradoxical intention.

We have seen that Frankl's existentialist thinking can aid language learners by promoting meaning. Let us now consider the meaning-based contributions of humanistic language teaching.

Meaning in humanistic language teaching: Moskowitz and Stevick

Humanistic educators Gertrude Moskowitz and Earl Stevick made a significant impact on language education. According to Moskowitz (1978), author of *Caring and Sharing in the Foreign Language Classroom: A Sourcebook of Humanistic Techniques*, humanistic education is concerned with making learners more fully human and more accepted by themselves and others. Given that learners often feel detached or isolated and are searching for their identities, humanistic educators focus on teaching the whole person, including intellectual and emotional aspects (Moskowitz, 1978; also Oxford, 1990; see **emotion**). In the view of Moskowitz, following Carl Rogers (1961), humanistic educators help learners self-actualize, that is, fulfill their greatest potential by getting in touch with their real selves. Self-actualizing people have special characteristics: they experience pleasurable feelings in everyday life; are creative, natural and spontaneous; accept themselves and others; lack prejudice; have empathy and affection for others; and seek meaning by looking to themselves for their own growth, having a mission in life, and being responsible (cf. Frankl, 1984).

Meaning is also a key to Stevick's work. In *Humanism in Language Teaching*, Stevick (1990) depicted humanism as emphasizing 'some *uniquely human attributes* of the learner', affirming and promoting 'human *freedom*' and contributing 'to the *dignity* of the learner' (p. 131, original emphasis).

Stevick analyzed these aspects in detail regarding two instructional approaches, Curran's Counseling-Learning Approach and Gattegno's Silent Way, as well as mentioning these elements in relation to a host of other language teaching methods. In the same book, he emphasized the sacramental, and hence deeply meaningful, nature of life's activities in the language classroom and outside. In that book and in *Memory, Meaning, and Method* (Stevick, 1976), he highlighted the personal and cognitive depth that is crucial to language education and showed deep concern about what goes on *within* and *between* people in the language classroom. In *Teaching Languages: A Way and Ways* (Stevick, 1980) he stated, 'I have begun to suspect that the most important aspect of "what goes on" is the presence or absence of harmony – it is the parts working with, or against, one another ... within and between the people in a language course' (p. 5; see also Kristjánsson, 2013). With Stevick's pervasive concern for meaning, responsibility, freedom and harmony in the language classroom, no wonder Arnold and Murphey (2013) chose to edit the spectacular collection of papers entitled *Meaningful Action: Earl Stevick's Influence on Language Teaching.*

Meaning in learner narratives

Learner narratives are powerful conveyors of meaning. A narrative recounts events and experience. It is a cognitive and emotional structure for retrospectively making sense of the world and our place in it (Bruner, 1998; Herman, 2009; Oxford, 2011a; Porter Abbott, 2002) – in other words, for giving meaning to our lives. 'Stories identify, unify, give meaning to. Just as music is noise that makes sense, a painting is color that makes sense, so a story is life that makes sense' (Martel, 2011: 15). Narrative is 'the primary scheme by which human existence is rendered meaningful' (Polkinghorne, 1988: 1). Narrative helps both the teller and the receiver to make sense of the teller's experiences – to hear with new ears, see with new eyes and grasp meaning with a new heart and mind. People without narratives do not exist (Polkinghorne, 1988). To paraphrase Jean-Paul Sartre, people are always tellers of tales, living surrounded by stories and trying to live life as if telling a story (in McAdams, 1993). A narrative meaningfully reflects identity, 'who I am, how I came to be, and where my life is going in the future' (McAdams, 2005: 241). Turning to a new subtheme, we now discuss meaning in terms of particularly meaningful moments.

Meaning in inspired consciousness, peak experiences and self-actualization

Learner narratives (e.g. Oxford & Cuéllar, 2014) demonstrate that meaning can occur through inspired consciousness and peak experiences. Inspired consciousness consists of superior states, such as intuitions, flashes of insight, visions and sudden ecstasy, rapture or recognition (Silo, 2006).

Ecstasy is accompanied by movement and generalized energy, *rapture* is marked by powerful positive emotion, and *recognition* involves a sense of comprehending everything in an instant (Silo, 2006). Inspired consciousness is a dynamic perturbation or shaking up of ordinary consciousness that allows the feeling of comprehending everything in a single moment. The word 'inspiration' comes from the Latin *inspirare*, 'to inspire, inflame, blow into' the heart and mind (Harper, 2013). In inspired consciousness, the mind operates with tremendous coherence, achieves immediate intuitions of reality and flashes of insight, and organizes groups of experiences without resorting to deductive or discursive thought. Inspired consciousness involves the self-organization of thoughts and feelings in service to a higher value. Inspired consciousness can respond to either a present (focused, attention-filled) intention or to a co-present (out-of-awareness) intention (Silo, 2006).

Mystics, philosophers, poets, novelists, artists and musicians often attain inspired consciousness, but Silo (2006) argued that ordinary individuals can also reach such consciousness when they have successful hunches, fall in love, experience dreams and intuitions, suddenly comprehend a complex situation, or instantaneously solve a problem. Language learners can experience inspired consciousness, particularly when they are intrinsically motivated (see **motivation**).

Peak experiences overlap with inspired consciousness. Peak experiences are especially joyous, exciting, ego-transcending moments of self-actualization involving sudden feelings of intense happiness, ecstasy, creativity, well-being, wonder, awe, love, empathy and timelessness (Maslow, 1970, 1971). Maslow (1971) described a peak experience as 'a great and mystical experience, a religious experience if you wish – an illumination, a revelation, an insight ... [leading to] "the cognition of being", ... the cognition that Plato and Socrates were talking about; almost, you could say, a technology of happiness, of pure excellence, pure truth, pure goodness' (p. 169). In peak experiences, the person feels simultaneously more powerful and also more helpless than ever before (Maslow, 1970). Maslow (1971) indicated that 'most people, or perhaps all people, have peak experiences, or ecstasies' (p. 168). Peak experiences can also occur through intense relationships and interactions, as with a very special teacher. There are countless meaningful triggers for peak experiences, such as meditation, art, music and nature (Maslow, 1970, 1971) – and especially positive experiences of language learning. (Compare peak experiences with 'flow', which is discussed in the next section, under **motivation**.)

It is likely that people who experience inspired consciousness and have peak experiences are becoming self-actualized people, whose lives are rich with meaning. Self-actualization refers to being all that one is meant to be (Maslow, 1962, 1968, 1970). Maslow's hierarchy of human needs, often displayed in the shape of a pyramid, shows physiological needs for survival and safety and physical security needs as the two bottom levels, which he viewed as deficiency-based motives. Higher levels, which include love and belongingness, esteem and self-actualization, are growth-based motives, and self-actualization is the highest level. Self-actualizing people are efficient and accurate in perceiving reality and unwilling to accept purely rationalistic, dichotomizing perceptions (Maslow, 1971). They accept themselves, other people and nature; ask important philosophical questions; show healthy autonomy; appreciate ordinary events but also experience transcendent feelings; feel linked with humanity; are creative and inventive; and have a sense of humor (Carver & Scheier, 2012; Maslow, 1968).

4.2. Motivation

According to Dörnyei (2009c), 'motivation refers to a cumulative arousal, or want, that we are aware of' (p. 209). In my view, meaning is inextricably linked with motivation, because a goal must be meaningful for the person to be motivated. Below I explore (a) intrinsic motivation, flow and hot cognition; (b) self-determination theory; (c) functional self-determination theory; and (d) theories of motivation related to possible selves.

Intrinsic motivation, flow and hot cognition

A particularly important kind of motivation is intrinsic motivation, which is the desire to do something for its own sake due to interest, enjoyment and challenge (Ryan & Deci, 2001), which point to personal meaning. Another definition of intrinsic motivation is the 'undertaking of activities because of their own appeal and not because of external rewards and punishments' (Peterson, 2006: 73), again focusing on personal meaning.

> Intrinsically motivated learners are deeply concerned to learn things well, in a manner that is intrinsically satisfying and that arouses a sense of optimal challenge appropriate to their current level of skill and competence. Compared to their extrinsically motivated counterparts [or to unmotivated learners], … such learners are likely to display much higher levels of involvement in learning, engage in more efficient and creative thinking processes, use a wider range of problem solving strategies, and interact with and retain material more effectively. (Ushioda, 2008: 21–22)

Intrinsic motivation is integral to learners' self-determination (Benson, 2011; Deci & Ryan, 2000; Ryan & Deci, 2001; see below). Self-determination is one of the possible criteria for flourishing and well-being.

Flow is a subjective combination of intrinsic motivation (described as autotelism) and confidence that comes from complete immersion in a task (Csikszentmihalyi, 2008). Flow also includes an optimal balance between challenge and competence (the task is neither too easy nor too hard), a merging of action and awareness without distractions, heightened control (security and lack of worry about failure), effortlessness, lack of self-consciousness, and an altered perception of time (slowing down or speeding up; see **time**). Csikszentmihalyi (2008) and Nakamura and Csikszentmihalyi (2011) asserted that the best times of our lives – moments of flow – are not marked by passive relaxation but instead occur when our body or mind is stretched to its limits, particularly while we are trying to do something worthwhile but difficult. A sense of flow, along with a peak experience, was evident in a learner narrative (Oxford *et al.*, 1996) when Greg, a native English speaker new to Spain, shoved aside his anxiety in order to order a ham sandwich in a Spanish bar and mingle for the first time in the *movida* (street scene). He compared this experience to jumping out of a helicopter for the first time.

Hot cognition is cognition or thought that is sparked by emotion and/or intrinsic motivation. William James, writing in 1910, described volition as the 'hot' merger of personal desire, excitement, will and tension, creating a higher level of energy (see James, 1987). Building on the work of James, researchers Pintrich *et al.* (1993) rejected a 'cold', overly rational and affect-free version of learner cognition and emphasized the need for hot cognition, that is, learning in which multiple levels of cognition are sparked by motivation and emotions in lively sociocultural contexts. They found that transformation of identity, self-worth or attitude is linked to hot cognition (Pintrich *et al.*, 1993). Lack of a strong tie to the learner's emotions can result in 'cold cognition', lacking 'motivational potency' (MacIntyre *et al.*, 2009: 47; cited in Dörnyei, 2009c: 226). Some earlier learner narratives exhibited hot cognition, as described by Oxford (2013). For instance, after Greg (see above) threw himself into using Spanish consistently, 'miraculous changes occurred' reflecting hot cognition: 'he was able to understand far more, quickly became much more fluent, moved in with Spanish friends, and was happy to feel socially accepted almost everywhere' (Oxford, 2013: 98; see also Oxford *et al.*, 1996). Hot cognition also emerged for Yaru, a young Chinese woman with a terror of speaking in English:

> She suddenly intuited that if she communicated in English, the visiting evaluator who was observing her English teacher would think the teacher was successful. Out of compassion for the teacher, Yaru took the first opportunity to stand and – in a flash of competence, pleasure, and excitement – spoke at length in perfectly understandable English. This event saved the teacher and permanently rejuvenated Yaru's faith in her own language ability. (Oxford, 2013: 98–99; see also Oxford *et al.*, 2007)

She is now successfully teaching English as an associate professor at a highly ranked Chinese university.

Self-determination theory

Self-determination theory or SDT (Deci & Ryan, 1985, 1991, 2000; Ryan & Deci, 2001) focuses on two types of motivation: intrinsic, which is seen as generally superior, and extrinsic. In SDT, intrinsic motivation also requires supportive self-perceptions in the areas of autonomy (capability of self-regulating one's thoughts, learning, actions and interactions; see **autonomy**), competence and relatedness to others. In SDT, extrinsic motivation is the desire to 'carry out activities for reasons other than their intrinsic interest (e.g., for external reward) or because ... [of] external or internalized pressure' (Benson, 2011: 84). In this theory, forms of extrinsic motivation include: external regulation (i.e. doing something because of a requirement while feeling controlled, alienated and uninterested, and hence putting in little effort); introjected regulation (contingent self-esteem – anxiously doing something that is required to assuage guilt, avoid failure, demonstrate ability or bolster self-worth); identified regulation (i.e. effortfully doing something based on consciously valuing someone else's goal and accepting it as personally important); and integrated regulation (i.e. effortfully doing something when the formerly external goal has been fully assimilated and brought into congruence with one's own values and needs). It is possible for the learner to move from extrinsic motivation to intrinsic motivation 'by willfully "taking an interest" in language learning' (Benson, 2011: 84), thereby enhancing personal meaning.

In a study based on the theory of self-determination propounded by Deci and Ryan, intrinsically motivated students described learning a language for the enjoyment of finding out new things, for the pleasure experienced when grasping something difficult, and for the 'high' experienced when learning or using the language (McIntosh & Noels, 2004).

Functional self-determination theory

Wehmeyer (1996, 2001, 2005) and Wehmeyer *et al.* (2011) proposed a theory of functional self-determination that conceptualizes self-determination as a disposition based on the function (purpose) a behavior serves for the individual. Though functional self-determination theory (fSDT) has often been used with those with disabilities, it also holds promise for those who do not have disabilities (see for example research by Shogren *et al.* 2006). 'Self-determined behavior' constitutes 'volitional actions that enable one to act as the primary causal agent in one's life and to maintain and improve one's quality of life' (Wehmeyer, 2005: 117; see **agency**). According to fSDT, self-determined actions have four characteristics: the person acts autonomously (see **autonomy**), the behavior is self-regulated, the person initiates and responds to the relevant event(s) in a psychologically empowered manner, and the person acts in a 'self-realizing' (purposeful, personally meaningful) manner (see **meaning**) (Wehmeyer, 2005: 258). For more on fSDT, see Wehmeyer *et al.* (2011). Working with adolescents, Shogren *et al.* (2006)

studied interrelationships among self-determination and other positive psychology constructs, such as **hope**, well-being and life satisfaction.

Theories of motivation related to possible selves

Motivation, imagination and possible selves interact, and they are related to time perspective (see **time**). Imagination helps us in 'defining a trajectory that connects what we are doing to an extended identity, seeing ourselves in new ways' (Wenger, 1998: 185; cited in Murray, 2011: 85) – as possible or imagined selves. Imagination is thus 'a process of expanding our self by transcending our time and space and creating new images of the world and ourselves' (Wenger, 1998: 176; cited in Murray, 2011: 76). 'It is through imagination that we see our own practices as continuing histories that reach far into the past.... By taking us into the past and carrying us into the future, it can recast the present and show it as holding unsuspected possibilities' (Wenger, 1998: 178; cited in Murray, 2011: 87). Thus, imagination helps to create identity (Pavlenko & Blackledge, 2004) while serving a motivational function.

We often generate inner representations of the self outside of our current context, enabling us to project images of ourselves into the future and to anticipate reactions of ourselves and others. Imagining is thus a form of 'mental simulation' (Ryan & Irie, 2014: 109, 111). Defining identity as one's sense of self in relation to a certain context or community of practice, Ryan and Irie asserted that the imagination is a key site for identity negotiation. People are storied selves in the midst of an ongoing, dynamic, complex narrative with many simultaneous plot lines. 'Goals within a possible-selves framework represent a form of self-definition, an essential part of who one is, rather than some distant, desired future outcome' (Ryan & Irie, 2014: 115). Imagination can help us productively focus on the process of a goal pursuit, rather than the outcome. However, mental simulations can sometimes lead down the primrose path of fantasies ungrounded by reality. 'For the workings of the imagination to have meaningful behavioural consequences, there must be some expectation that a vision may be realized. The notion of plausibility in future-oriented visions of the self is crucial' (Ryan & Irie, 2014: 115).

Possible selves are not just in the future but also in the past and present, as explained by Ryan and Irie (2014). How we see ourselves is related to how we interpret our past experiences. We use mental simulation to interpret past events and form theories about our current self. Our interpretations of past events are constantly changing. Meanwhile, using these interpretations we make attributions (internal explanations) for our perceived failures and successes, and these attributions help us develop self-efficacy (Bandura, 1997), that is, our current assessment that we can succeed at a given task in a particular context (see **self-efficacy**).

Agency, the power to act volitionally to influence outcomes (see **agency**), is a primary characteristic of possible selves (Erikson, 2007). According to

Ryan and Irie (2014), Erikson (2007) cautioned that possible selves must be adequately close or relevant to the individual's current self-concept and must have a degree of experiential meaning (see **meaning**). Experience is helpful in imagining oneself acting effectively (Williams, 1995; cited in Maddux, 2011). Possible selves are more than mere representations of ourselves in some future state; they contain an element of experiencing ourselves in that future state' (Ryan & Irie, 2014: 113).

Markus and Nurius (1986) described three 'possible selves': what the individual might become, what he or she would like to become (ideal self), and what he or she is afraid of becoming (feared self). Higgins (1987) focused on two self-guides: the 'ideal self', or hoped-for attributes; and the 'ought self', the representation of attributes that the person believes he or she ought to possess, based on someone else's sense of obligations or duties. The ought self is a more extrinsic, and hence less internalized, type of instrumental motivation. In Higgins's view, motivation involves the person's desire to behaviorally reduce the discrepancy between the actual self on the one hand and the future-oriented ideal and ought selves on the other hand. The motivational salience of the ideal and ought selves depends on: (a) the availability of a vivid future self-image, (b) the perceived plausibility of these two selves, (c) harmony between these selves, (d) activation or priming of the self-image through reminders and relevant events, (e) accompanying procedural strategies, and (f) the balance brought about by the feared self, which offsets the desired possible self (Dörnyei, 2009c).

Dörnyei (2009b, 2009c) adapted Higgins's ideas to the language learning field to develop the L2 (second language) Motivational Self System. This system 'has emerged to accommodate the multiple possible drives of learners who participate in increasingly interconnected, multilingual and multicultural communities from across the globe' (Mercer, 2011a: 58–59). In this system, the primary constituents are two future self-guides – the ideal L2 self (the L2-specific aspect of the person's ideal self) and the ought-to L2 self (corresponding to Higgins's ought self and thus more extrinsic, instrumental motives to learn the L2) – and the L2 learning experience. The learning experience deals with 'situated, "executive" motives related to the immediate learning environment and experience (e.g. the impact of the teacher, the curriculum, the peer group, or the experience of success)' (Dörnyei, 2009c: 218). The two future self-guides, ideal and ought-to, are powerful attractors, the first centered on internal desires and the second on social pressures from significant people. In addition, the learning experience itself serves as a powerful attractor. Each one of these subsystems can serve as a coordinating influence on behavior, but 'if the three [sub]systems are in harmony, that will have an increased, cumulative effect' (Dörnyei, 2009b: 218). Gregersen and MacIntyre's (2014) text offers several options for language learners to explore their possible selves.[1]

5. Dimension 3: P = *P*erseverance

Hypothesis: Language learners with high well-being persevere in their learning.

Perseverance is defined as continued effort to do or achieve something despite difficulties, failure or opposition; the action or condition or an instance of persevering; steadfastness (*Merriam-Webster Dictionary*, 2015). Perseverance is important to language learning. Robert Gardner (2001) identified persistence (closely related to perseverance) as one of the three key elements in language learning motivation, along with enjoyment in learning and the desire to achieve a goal. I argue that perseverance involves, at a minimum, three factors: resilience, hope and optimism. I contend that this set of factors propels language learners toward task completion and proficiency. Confidence relates to all three elements, resilience, hope and optimism. 'People confident about an eventual outcome will persevere even in the face of great adversity' (Carver *et al.*, 2011: 303).

5.1. Resilience

Masten *et al.* (2011) said that resilience consists of '*patterns of positive adaptation during or following significant adversity or risk*' (p. 118, original emphasis), while Truebridge (2014) emphasized an ability or capacity: 'the self-righting and transcending capacity within all youth, adults, organizations, and communities to spring back, rebound, and successfully adapt in the face of trauma, adversity, and/or everyday stress' (pp. 12–13). Seligman (2011) asserted that resilience is akin to 'psychological fitness' (pp. 127, 240). In an international, multi-case study, my colleagues and I found that successful language learners demonstrated resilience in particularly difficult situations (Oxford *et al.*, 2007). Severely anxious Yaru, mentioned above, in the discussion of hot cognition, exemplified great resilience when she spoke in public to help her teacher and discovered she possessed great talent in English.

Risk factors and protective factors

Risk factors are stressful life events, adverse situations, or difficulties that threaten good adaptation (Masten *et al.*, 2011). Some research emphasized personal traits, or personal protective factors, which aid in developing resilience in the face of risk factors. These personal traits include outgoing and adaptable personalities, ability to enlist support, achievement-oriented competence, self-efficacy, self-esteem, belief in the future, a sense of purpose and meaning in life, anticipation, goal-directedness, a positive outlook, talents valued by self and society, hardiness, educational aspirations, general attractiveness to others, humor, and other social, emotional and moral/ spiritual qualities (Benard, 1991; Masten *et al.*, 2011; Masten & Obradovic,

2006; Truebridge, 2014; Werner & Smith, 1992; see **meaning**, **motivation**, **hardiness**, **habits of mind**, **character strengths**, **self-efficacy** and **self-esteem**). Despite these stellar personal traits associated with resilience, Masten *et al.* (2011) argued that resilience arises from ordinary psychological and biological processes, rather than from any 'rare or special qualities' in the individual (p. 129).

Assets and environmental (social) protective factors

In addition to personal protective factors, the dynamic process of resilience includes *assets* (resources or promotive factors), defined as 'human, social, and material capital' (Masten *et al.*, 2011: 120) and environmental protective factors (social protective factors), such as: (a) strong, warm, caring, compassionate and supportive relationships; (b) messages that convey high expectations and focus on strengths, not just challenges; (c) opportunities for meaningful participation, contribution and responsibility; and (d) positive schools and institutions (Luthar *et al.*, 2000, 2006; Masten *et al.*, 2011; Truebridge, 2014).

Fostering resilience

There are several ways to foster resilience (Masten *et al.*, 2011): (a) providing assets, which in our field might be language books, computers, materials, interesting and exciting lessons, and opportunities to use the language; (b) mobilizing protective factors, such as attachment relationships with language teachers or mastery experiences that increase language learners' self-efficacy; and (c) removing or reducing risks, such as embarrassment or failure for language learners, but without reducing an appropriate sense of classroom challenge.

Let us now move to hope, the second element of perseverance.

5.2. Hope

Hope is a powerful force that helps generate motivation and resilience in language learning. Hope is broader than optimism (Diener, 2011; see below). It is not a foolish pipedream, nor is it the same as a wish[2] or a fantasy (Clarke, 2003), which is by definition not grounded in reality. Hope is not 'false hope' – that which does not stand a chance of fulfillment. Instead, hope is 'desire accompanied by (reasonable) expectation' (Clarke, 2003: 164; also see Schrank *et al.*, 2008; Snyder *et al.*, 2011).

Diverse views of hope

Vaillant (2008) wrote that hope reflects the capacity for 'one's loving, lyrical, limbic memory of the past to become attached to the "memory of the future"' (p. 102). Menninger (1959) described the hopes we develop as a measure of our maturity. For Marcel (1962), hope is the oxygen of the soul. Emily Dickinson poetically wrote that 'Hope is the thing with feathers,/That perches on the soul' and never stops singing (quoted in Vaillant, 2008: 112). For developmental psychologist Erik Erikson, '[h]ope became the very foundation block of all human development.... Hope seems essential to almost all of the eight stages of Eriksonian development' (quoted in Vaillant, 2008: 110). However, some researchers caution that hope has a negative potential, sometimes being a denial of reality (Breznitz, 1986) or a source of possible disappointment.

Where does hope come from? Vaillant (2008) said that hope comes through our earliest experiences with care. However, when one's earliest experiences with care – or later experiences in living – are overly turbulent and filled with loss, hope can be hard to maintain. The opposite of hope/hopefulness is hopelessness, which is quite often linked with negative distortions of reality (Clarke, 2003) and with despair (Vaillant, 2008). 'Suffering equals hope destroyed, and suffering is more than pain; it is loss of control, it is despair, it is the loss of hope.... Suffering is the loss of autonomy' (Vaillant, 2008: 103). Thus, hopelessness is a despairing lack of self-regulation and autonomy (see **emotion** and **agency and autonomy**), a lack connected to demoralization. The hallmarks of demoralization are helplessness, hopelessness and a subjective sense of incompetence (Clarke, 2003: 166). 'There is treatment for demoralization, and it involves the restoration of hope' (Clarke, 2003: 167).

Components of hope: A research review

Schrank *et al.* (2011) proposed the following components of hope based on a major review of the literature in psychology, psychiatry and nursing (Schrank *et al.*, 2008): (a) time, including both past experience and, of course, the future reference of hope (see **time**); (b) goals, either broad or specific; (c) control, which can be internal (personal activity) or external (contextual/environmental); (d) relations, such as spirituality, partnerships, or a sense of life purpose and a belief that the world makes sense (see **meaning**); (e) personal characteristics (e.g. motivation, inner strength and energy to pursue the goals; see **motivation**); (f) reality reference (the goals must be perceived as feasible); and (g) negative or positive spur to hope (i.e. hope can arise from either a negative or a positive starting point).

Hope: Emotion-based or not?

For Vaillant (2008) and Lazarus (1999), hope is primarily emotion-based. As Vaillant (2008) stated, 'Real hope is rooted in heart and song as well as in cognition.... Hope is *not* cognitive; hope is *not* reasonable' (pp. 105, 110, emphasis added). Schrank *et al.* (2011) argued against such theories because of their vagueness and because they failed to consider that hope can be a means of maintaining or improving an already positive condition.

A number of cognitive definitions of hope exist. Breznitz (1986) contended that hope is the cognitive expectation of goal attainment. Averill *et al.* (1990) cognitively defined hope as being appropriate when goals are (a) at an intermediate level of difficulty and thus relatively attainable, (b) under control, (c) perceived as important, and (d) socially and morally acceptable. (See Schrank *et al.*, 2011, and Snyder *et al.*, 2011, for details.)

Snyder's hope theory

In positive psychology, one of the best-known hope theories, that of Snyder, is largely cognitive. Snyder and colleagues (Snyder, 1994, 2000, 2002; Snyder *et al.*, 1997) defined hope as a cognitive set including a person's beliefs in (a) his or her capacity to produce workable *pathways* to goals, which are mental targets or desired future conditions that guide actions; and (b) his or her *agency*, that is, ability and intention to initiate and sustain movement via pathways toward those goals (see **agency**). This theory asserts that human behavior is largely goal-directed. Goals can be expressed in words (e.g. for the language learner, 'I want to talk intelligibly in Spanish') or mental images (e.g. for the language learner, an image of himself or herself engaged in a spirited, fully intelligible discussion in Spanish).[3] Goals can be 'approach goals' (e.g. 'I will pass my Mandarin test') or 'avoidance goals' (e.g. 'I will try hard not to fail my Mandarin test') (see Snyder, 2002). Goals can be short term or long term. They can be conscious or, perhaps surprisingly, non-conscious (Chartrand & Cheng, 2002).

In this hope theory, *pathways thinking* involves the perceived competence to generate routes or pathways (Snyder sometimes called them strategies) leading to goals (Snyder, 2002). Pathways thinking is very important when original routes are blocked. When facing a stressor, higher-hope people, compared with lower-hope people, create more pathways for dealing with the stressor and express more agency, that is, have a greater probability of using these pathways in the goal pursuit (Snyder, 2000). Those with low hope are more likely to use avoidance as a coping strategy. If an original pathway to a goal is definitely blocked, high-hope people tend to use cognitive flexibility (Snyder *et al.*, 2002a; see **character strengths**) and positive self-talk (Snyder *et al.*, 1998) to find alternative routes, while low-hope individuals just ruminate about being stuck (Michael, 2000).

In Snyder's theory, as mentioned above, *agency* is the perceived ability and intention to use pathways (strategies) to reach goals, and *agency thinking* involves telling oneself positive statements about one's ability to start and continue movement along a pathway, as well encouraging oneself to act (see **agency**). An example is 'I can do this' (Snyder *et al.*, 1998). Agency thinking is especially important when a route to a goal becomes blocked, because it helps individuals find and move along an alternative pathway (Rand & Cheavens, 2011). '[T]hose who see themselves as having greater capacity for agency thinking also endorse energetic personal self-talk statements, such as

"I will keep going"' (Snyder *et al*., 1998; cited in Snyder *et al*., 2011: 185). In language learning, where small or large blockages toward goals occur with some frequency, it would be very useful to teach learners how to generate alternative pathways (strategies, routes) toward a particular goal and how to use positive self-talk for support.

Hopeful thinking thus involves both pathways thinking and agency thinking, or '*both* the perceived ability to generate routes to a goal *and* the perceived ability/determination to use those routes' (Rand & Cheavens, 2011: 324, original emphasis). Pathways thinking increases agency thinking, and agency thinking increases pathways thinking. Hope theory views these processes as cognitive rather than affective. Emotions are the results of goal-directed thoughts and behaviors (Snyder *et al.*, 2002a), but they are not the same as such thoughts and behaviors. Positive emotions come from perceiving progress toward or achievement of a goal, whereas negative emotions arise from a goal pursuit being blocked, impeded or halted (Rand & Cheavens, 2011). See Snyder's full hope model in Rand and Cheavens (2011) and in Snyder *et al.* (2011).

Hope is important to life generally. In a review of studies using Snyder's hope theory, Brown Kirschman *et al.* (2011) reported that: (a) adolescents at risk for dropping out of high school were less likely to do so if they had higher hope; (b) in a high-crime area, children with higher hope were less likely to believe they would die a violent death; and (c) children's hope level and types of coping behaviors were important to psychological adjustment to chronic illness. Researchers found that higher levels of trait hope (long-term hope) relate to greater academic success, such as higher grade point averages and higher graduation rates for college students, after controlling for intelligence, previous academic performance, college entrance-exam scores and self-esteem (Snyder *et al.*, 2002b). In various studies, high-hope college students reported being more energized, inspired, goal-oriented and confident than their low-hope counterparts (Snyder *et al.*, 1991), and they experienced greater self-worth and less depression (Snyder *et al.*, 1997). For older adults (average age 76 years), higher hope was tied to greater life satisfaction and better subjective well-being, regardless of physical health and ability (Wrobleski & Snyder, 2005). Feldman and Snyder (2000) demonstrated that trait hope was strongly related to several measures of meaning in life, thus indicating that hope's influence might operate through meaning (see **meaning**).

Hope-based interventions

According to Rand and Cheavens (2011), hope-based interventions are currently being tested on university campuses, and self-help texts based on hope theory have been written for adults. Applying that concept to language learning, there are many self-help books on how to learn a foreign language; in such books, the inclusion of a chapter on how to maintain hope, particularly when major challenges arise, might be helpful to struggling learners. The hope-enhancing self-help texts described by McDermott and Snyder (2000) could be adapted for language learners and those around them. Within the Snyder framework, Brown Kirschman *et al.* (2011) reported that hope scores were significantly higher for middle-school youth who participated in a hope intervention that included (a) identifying hopeful and unhopeful language, (b) working with 'hope buddies' who mutually communicated future goals, and (c) writing hope stories (Pedrotti *et al.*, 2008). It would be enlightening to use a discourse analysis of the interactions between teachers and students to identify which types of vocabulary, syntax, verbal images and body language promote hope or hinder it. Writing personal stories of hope and communicating goals to peers would seem to be very feasible in some language classrooms. The outcomes in terms of hope, achievement and proficiency could be dramatic.

Unconnected with Snyder-related hope interventions, Clarke (2003) provided a research-based system of interventions to ameliorate the demoralization that is linked with hopelessness. The system included offering reassurance and help, teaching problem-solving skills, being quietly supportive with the individual, and exploring meaning (see **meaning**). Clarke suggested that effective language teachers ordinarily use reassurance and help to hope-challenged learners but may not habitually enact the other possible interventions.

5.3. Optimism

Optimism and hope are variants on the theme of positive expectancy (Snyder *et al.*, 2000). In fact, Tiger (1979) wrote a book called *Optimism: The Biology of Hope*. However, Lopez noted a distinction between these two constructs, stating that 'hope doesn't come naturally; it takes effort. This might help explain why, according to Gallup surveys, 84 percent of the human population is "optimistic", but only 50 percent is "hopeful"' (University of Missouri at Kansas City, 2013). Lopez and Gallagher argued that we need to test theories and constructs 'in unison to determine, for example, the overlap or incremental value of optimism and hope when predicting changes in well-being over time' (Lopez & Gallagher, 2011: 5).

Confidence or doubt

Optimism and pessimism are broad versions of confidence or doubt pertaining to most situations in life (Carver *et al.*, 2011). A key definition of optimism is a pattern of generalized positive expectations for the future (dispositional optimism) (Carver *et al.*, 2011). Optimism is particularly linked to expectancy-value theories of motivation, which assume that behavior reflects the pursuit of goals (desired states or actions). People attempt to fit their behavior to attain the goal, and they have a certain expectancy or degree of confidence that the goal can be attained. Optimists are more likely than pessimists to believe they can achieve a valued goal, and they confidently persevere, even when facing adversity. In this way, optimists look much like resilient people (see **resilience**). Conversely, pessimists doubt that the goal can be reached and are therefore hesitant or reluctant when dealing with adversity (Carver *et al.*, 2011; for additional comments on culture and optimism, see Peterson, 2006).

Gauging optimism

It is possible to gauge optimism by asking people whether they expect outcomes to be positive or negative. Optimists anticipate good outcomes, despite difficulties, and this creates a rather positive mix of emotions, such as excitement and eagerness, whereas pessimists expect bad outcomes and experience more negative emotions, such as sadness, despair, anxiety and anger (Carver & Scheier, 1998) (see **emotion**). Some studies look at optimism and pessimism only after an adverse event, with the result that pessimists show more distress than optimists. Such a study does not show whether pessimists, compared with optimists, had more distress before the event (Carver *et al.*, 2011). Longitudinal studies give a clearer picture. In longitudinal studies of college students, stronger optimism at the start of college predicted less distress at the end of the first semester and greater development of friendship networks (Carver *et al.*, 2011). A number of longitudinal health studies noted by Carver *et al.* (2011) showed that optimism predicted lower distress both initially and later, as well as greater resilience.

Coping strategies

Optimists and pessimists use different coping strategies. According to Carver *et al.* (2011), pessimists revert to wishful thinking, denial, distractions, escapism and giving up, all of which reflect an attempt to distance themselves from the problem facing them. Optimists, in contrast, keep on trying to solve the problem at hand despite adversity. If the problem cannot be solved, optimists use other strategies, such as acceptance (restructuring their experience to come to grips with the reality of the situation, rather than merely giving up; see also acceptance in relation to **emotion**), positive reframing and humor. If the worst happens, optimists readjust themselves, look to the future and keep on going. 'Thus, optimists appear generally to be approach copers, and pessimists appear to be avoidant copers' (Carver *et al.*, 2011: 305). In language classrooms, it would be wise to help learners to deal optimistically and effectively with difficulty through realistic acceptance of the problem, reframing to gain a new perspective, and using humor (see affective strategies in Oxford, 1990, 2011b).

Research shows that optimists fare better than pessimists in subjective well-being during periods of adversity as well as in terms of proactive health behaviors, problem-solving, task-focused behavior, persistence in education, income and relationships (Carver *et al.*, 2010). Nevertheless, Brown Kirshman *et al.* (2011) argued that there are some advantages to pessimism in specific circumstances. For instance, optimists might tend to ignore a threat until it is too late, or might have a fragile worldview that could be shattered by trauma. Carver *et al.* (2011) dispensed with those anti-optimism, pro-pessimism arguments by noting that there is no sound research evidence to support them. I personally doubt that there can be such a thing as a too-optimistic language learner, except one who misuses optimism to avoid putting effort into studying.

Perfectionism

Occasionally people are pessimists because they are perfectionistic. For instance, some high-achieving language learners think they cannot meet their own extremely high standards. Their high aspirations cause them to demand perfection from themselves, and then they develop fears of being inadequate and doubts about succeeding. Pessimism follows. Rather than undergoing optimism training, such learners need help in setting realistic goals and disposing of goals that simply cannot be met (Carver & Scheier, 2003). I have met many learners who had unrealistically high goals and who could have benefited from help in goal-setting. Some books about how to become a better language learner include information about setting realistic goals (e.g. Oxford, 1996, 2011b).

Helping pessimists become optimists

It is possible to help pessimists become optimists through cognitive-behavioral therapy by changing negative thoughts. 'The therapies aim to make the cognitions more positive, thereby reducing distress and fostering renewed effort' (Carver *et al.*, 2011: 309). Techniques of cognitive-behavioral therapy, such as identifying the problem, determining the associated feelings and beliefs related to the problem, and adjusting dysfunctional feelings and beliefs, might be useful in the language learning situation, particularly when a pessimistic learner comes to the teacher complaining of a problem. However, merely reducing an individual's pessimistic thoughts through cognitive-behavioral therapy does not guarantee that person will become optimistic. To become an optimist, the person must learn to 'think in the ways optimists think and act in the ways optimists act' (Carver *et al.*, 2010).

See Gregersen and MacIntyre (2014) for language classroom activities to enhance optimism.

Optimism as an explanatory style

So far I have discussed optimism as a generalized expectancy. A different way to think about optimism is as an explanatory style, that is, the habitual way that people explain causes of events in their lives. Original sources of optimism as an explanatory style may be genetics, modeling by parents of explanatory styles, criticism from others, life experiences promoting either mastery or helplessness, safety and coherence of life during childhood, appropriate challenges to exercise control over the environment, the effects of good teachers, lower exposure to violence and negativity in the media, and fewer experiences with traumatic events (Peterson & Steen, 2011; Seligman *et al.*, 1995). Speaking of optimism and pessimism as explanatory styles, Peterson and Steen stated, 'we can assume neither that optimism is the simple opposite of pessimism nor that the determinants of optimism can be gleaned from the study of the determinants of pessimism' (Steen, 2011: 319).

Optimism as an explanatory style refers to how an individual considers an event's causality in terms of three dimensions: stability (permanent/stable versus temporary/unstable effects), globality (universal versus specific scope) and internality (internal cause = self versus external cause = others or environment).

> An explanatory style characterized by internal, stable, and global explanations for bad events has been described as 'pessimistic', and the opposite style – external, unstable [temporary], and specific explanations for bad events – has been described as 'optimistic'. (Peterson & Steen, 2011: 315)

Thus, for a pessimist, defeat seems permanent, destroys everything and appears to have been caused by the person himself or herself. For an optimist, defeat is viewed as temporary, restricted to a specific case and not his or her fault. For instance, a pessimist might say, self-disparagingly, 'I don't have an ear for languages', while an optimist might leave the door open for improvement and say 'I haven't yet developed my ear for languages'.

Compared with those who use a pessimistic explanatory style, people with an optimistic explanatory style perform better academically, have better physical and mental health, are more active, do not give up as easily and may live longer (Peterson *et al.*, 1988; Seligman, 1991, 2006). 'Invariably, those with an optimistic explanatory style fare better than those with a pessimistic explanatory style' (Peterson & Steen, 2011: 316). We can help language learners use a more optimistic explanatory style by enabling them to make more positive attributions of success and failure, that is, not viewing negative situations as permanent, widespread and having been caused by the learner.

To conclude this discussion, it is important to remember that resilience, hope and optimism are interconnected and related to confidence. Together they contribute to perseverance, or the ongoing effort to achieve something despite difficulties. Other factors tied to perseverance are agency and autonomy, discussed next.

6. Dimension 4: A = *A*gency and *A*utonomy

Hypothesis: Language learners with high well-being embody agency and autonomy.

The terms 'agency' and 'autonomy' have already been frequently mentioned in this chapter, but this section goes more deeply into their meaning in positive psychology and their application to language learning.

6.1. Agency

Agency has particular meanings within positive psychology. The basis of theories of human agency is that organismic aspirations drive behavior. 'An organismic perspective views people as active contributors to, or "authors" of[,] their behavior, where behavior is described as self-regulated and goal-directed "action" [and where] ... actions are defined as purposive and self-initiated activities' (Wehmeyer *et al.*, 2011: 357). Agency is 'the sense of knowing and having what it takes to achieve one's goals' (Little *et al.*, 2002: 390; cited in Wehmeyer *et al.*, 2011: 357). This subsection distinguishes between agentic and non-agentic people, mentions agency in a variety of positive psychology theories, and discusses agency in language learning research.

Agentic versus non-agentic

The agentic person is:

> [the] origin of his or her actions, has high aspirations, perseveres in the face of obstacles [see **perseverance**], sees more and varied options for action, learns from failures, and overall, has a greater sense of well-being. In contrast, a non-agentic individual can be a pawn to unknown extra-personal influences, has low aspirations, is hindered with problem-solving blinders, often feels helpless and, overall, has a greater sense of ill-being. (Little *et al.*, 2002: 390; quoted in Wehmeyer *et al.*, 2011: 357)

Agency in hope theory, functional self-determination theory and causal agency theory

As noted earlier, in Snyder's (1994, 2000, 2002) hope theory (see **perseverance**), agency is the ability and intention to initiate and sustain movement via pathways (strategies) toward desired goals. Agency thinking entails telling oneself that one has the ability to initiate and sustain movement along pathways (strategies) and the intention to use those pathways (Snyder *et al.*, 1998). Thus, agency embodies not only the ability to act by using strategies but the decision to do so (Rand & Cheavens,

2011). In functional self-determination theory (fSDT), mentioned above (see **motivation**), the agentic individual controls his or her behavior (self-determination), despite not having control over events and outcomes.

Causal agency theory (CAT; Wehmeyer & Mithaug, 2006) aims to explain how people become self-determined. CAT distinguishes between causal capability (mental and physical capability to cause something to happen, including knowledge and behavioral skills) and agentic capability (mental and physical capability to *direct* causal action, including self-regulatory self-management knowledge, goal-oriented skills, agentic perceptions, or beliefs about oneself that enable action). A third element in CAT is causal affects, which are the emotions, feelings and other affective components that regulate human behavior.

Agency in language learning research

In language learning, agency is defined as the 'capacity to act volitionally to affect outcomes' (Ryan & Irie, 2014: 113). Benson (2007) described agency as a 'point of origin for the development of autonomy' (p. 30; cited in Gao & Zhang, 2011: 27). Agency can also be defined as actively engaging in the 'terms and conditions' of one's own learning (Lantolf & Pavlenko, 2001: 145), voluntarily controlling behavior, and assigning relevance and significance to language learning as a whole and in specific events. As Lantolf and Thorne stated,

> [L]earning a language is necessarily the action of an intentional agent.... Agency, as we construe it, is about more than voluntary control over behaviour, although to be sure this is a critical component of what it means to be an agent. The concept also entails the ability to assign relevance and significance to things and events.... [Agents act within the constraints of] social groupings, material and symbolic resources, situational contingencies ... and so on. (Lantolf & Thorne, 2006: 142–143, 239)

In this way, agency is not only a point of origin for autonomy development as mentioned above, but it is also a starting point for learners' efforts in using learning strategies (Gao & Zhang, 2011). Agency and autonomy contribute to the use of learning strategies, but one might also say that learning strategies help build greater agency and autonomy (Oxford, 2003, 2008) (see **habits of mind**). Moreover, self-efficacy, the belief that one can do a particular task, is related to agency (see **self-efficacy**). However, as Dörnyei contended, 'the dynamic interaction among language, agent, and environment is rather undertheorized and underresearched' (Dörnyei, 2009a: 243). For more about that interaction, see van Lier's classic work on the ecology of language learning (2004).

6.2. Autonomy

This subsection explores 'behavioral autonomy', existentialist and Freirean perspectives on autonomy, Vygotsky on self-regulation, cognitive apprenticeship, and comments on autonomy from language learning theorists.

Behavioral autonomy

In one branch of positive psychology, functional self-determination, 'behavioral autonomy draws from two sources: autonomy as synonymous with individuation and autonomy as roughly synonymous with independence' (Wehmeyer *et al.*, 2011: 361). Individuation, or the process of forming one's individual identity, is a crucial part of social and personality development. Autonomy as independence refers to the outcome of a movement from (a) dependence for care and guidance to (b) self-care and self-direction.

Existentialist perspective on autonomy

Autonomy is more than just 'behavioral autonomy'; it a pervasive belief system and frame of mind. Key ideas about autonomy come from existentialist philosophers. Existentialist Viktor Frankl has been warmly accepted and widely quoted by positive psychologists. Likewise, other existentialist philosophers, psychiatrists and psychologists (Camus, 1983; Cooper, 2003; Sartre, 1984; van Deurzen, 2012; Yalom, 1989) have consistently recognized the chaos and stress human beings encounter in living. In the face of such difficulty, which can make the world seem meaningless, individuals have the freedom and the responsibility to create personal meaning in life (Frankl, 1984; see **meaning**). To create meaning, individuals must strengthen their autonomy. This is done in multiple ways: (a) developing and using skills or strategies for living well in the face of adversity (see **perseverance**); (b) becoming intrinsically motivated (see **motivation**); and (c) forging collaborative relationships (see **character strengths**) (van Deurzen, 2012). Existentially speaking, autonomy in one sphere of life can lead to autonomy in other spheres (van Deurzen, 2012). Applying these themes to language learning, I contend that learners can become more autonomous by exercising the freedom and responsibility necessary to make learning personally meaningful, developing and using helpful learning strategies, and strengthening intrinsic motivation.

Freirean perspective on autonomy

While Paulo Freire is not generally included in discussions of positive psychology, his ideas are highly positive and potentially relevant here. Freire was a sociopolitical philosopher who encouraged individuals to become autonomous by developing the capacity for freedom in any and all social contexts (Pennycook, 2001). Freire (2000) contended that freedom must be constantly and responsibly pursued and that it is indispensable for humanity. Freire wanted an education system in which teachers and students are free and equal and in which they learn together to think critically and create a more positive society. To build on Freire's ideas, we might say that autonomous language learners actively pursue freedom and use it responsibly. They engage in meaningful interactions in which they are treated as budding critical thinkers.

Vygotsky on self-regulation

Two main sources on positive psychology – *The Oxford Handbook of Positive Psychology* (Lopez & Snyder, 2011) and *A Primer in Positive Psychology* (Peterson, 2006) – do not mention Lev Vygotsky, the father of self-regulation, though Lopez and Snyder include a chapter (Wehmeyer *et al.*, 2011) largely focusing on self-regulation. I consider Vygotsky (1978, 1981) to be one of the most positive contributors to psychology and education in history, but he is ignored by positive psychology. The reason might be that his ideas were socially contextualized, a rare approach for positive psychology. He presented a social constructivist theory of stages of development of internal self-regulation, which is closely tied to autonomy and even to motivation. 'This Vygotskian perspective illuminates how motivation "from within" can be fostered through the formulation of shared intentions and purposes (rather than exclusively teacher-imposed goals)' (Ushioda, 2008: 25).

In Vygotsky's view, learning occurs within a sociocultural environment through the learner's dialogues with a more competent person, who might be a parent, a teacher or a more advanced peer and who: 'mediates' the learning; models higher thought processes, such as analyzing, synthesizing and evaluating (see **habits of mind**); and provides scaffolding or assistance as long as it is needed – but no longer than that. With mediation, the learner transits the 'zone of proximal development' or the distance that can be covered with assistance and cannot be traversed by the learner alone (Benson, 2011; Oxford, 2003; Vygotsky, 1978, 1981). Self-regulation is achieved by moving through three stages: (a) social speech – vocal interaction with the more capable person, who models higher-order thinking skills, such as cognitive and metacognitive strategies; (b) egocentric or private speech – overtly giving oneself instructions for applying higher-order skills; and (c) inner speech – mental self-guidance, a sign that the learner has completely internalized such skills. Vygotsky's theory implies a rather close relationship between the learner and the more capable person. However, in some cases the mediating function in learning involves books or the media rather than a separate, more capable person. Vygotsky (1978, 1981) also said that language itself plays a mediating role for the learner.

Cognitive apprenticeship

Another sociocultural form of mediation that moves the learner toward autonomy is cognitive apprenticeship, in which the learner again benefits from a more capable person. Cognitive apprenticeship is omitted by most positive psychologists, again probably because it is socially situated. However, I include it here because it is a positive theory that relates to autonomy. A cognitive apprenticeship occurs in a community of practice, that is, a learning community composed of people who share a common interest. Such an apprenticeship is a strategic, practical, learning-based relationship involving a novice who is allied with someone more expert than he or she is (Collins, 1988). A '[c]ognitive apprenticeship helps students to acquire, develop, and use learning strategies in authentic activities via interaction, social construction of knowledge, scaffolding, modelling, goal-setting, peer sharing, and learner reflection' (Oxford, 2011b: 29; see **habits of mind**). By observing, following and internalizing the performance of the expert or of more advanced peers, the learner gradually moves from an initial position of peripheral participation in the community of practice to a position of more central participation (Lave & Wenger, 1991). This process involves agency, which, as we have seen, is a starting point for the development of autonomy. In the context of sociocultural activity theory, which underlies the concept of communities of practice, agency is not a property of individuals but is instead relational – that is, it occurs in relationships between or among individuals (see **agency**).

Comments about autonomy from language learning theorists

Menezes (2008) identified autonomy as a key element in the complex dynamic system of language learning. Benson (2011) defined autonomy as follows: ' [A]utonomy best refers to the capacity to control or take charge of one's learning' (p. 14; similarly, see Little, 2007: 15). Oxford (2008) described autonomy as fundamentally 'taking responsibility' for one's own learning (p. 43). Learning strategies are directly tied to learner autonomy (Oxford, 1990). '[S]trategies are an important element of learner autonomy, since it is by using strategies that learners are able to become autonomous' (Griffiths, 2013: 31).

Nunan (1997) discussed increasing autonomy through stages. Farmer (1994), Farmer and Sweeney (1994) and Pierson (1996) described autonomy in terms of degrees. Little (2000) described autonomy as part of a spiral. In that image, the learner progresses to new levels of independence only by first moving through additional phases of interdependence with a teacher or others. Holec (1981) commented that the autonomous learner has the ability to take charge of every aspect of his or her learning, including decisions about objectives, content, progression, methods, techniques, monitoring procedures and evaluating outcomes. Dickinson (1987) also argued that the autonomous learner can make all decisions concerned with his or her learning, including implementation. However, Holec stated that most learners are not autonomous but are involved in the process of gaining autonomy. In a study of self-determination theory, researchers (Noels *et al.*, 1999, in Benson, 2011) found that when teachers supported learner autonomy, learners' sense of self-determination increased.

One of the most significant theoretical clashes of recent years in the language learning field has occurred between proponents of Western-style individual autonomy and what is called 'social autonomy'. Little (1999) argued that autonomy is more than just a Western cultural construct, and later (Little, 2007) he called for some fundamental reconsiderations of autonomy. Pennycook (1997) condemned what he saw as attempts to push the individual, competitive, Western version of autonomy onto non-Western societies, and he strongly encouraged awareness of cultural alternatives. Esch (2006) similarly critiqued the concept of individual autonomy and as a result promoted the idea of social autonomy, in which the person takes responsibility for learning in the context of the group and society as a whole. Some theorists (e.g. Benson, 2007) argued that social autonomy – a group-oriented approach – is a valid way by which Asians manifest autonomy. Holliday (2003) described the social autonomy approach as assuming the following: (a) the existence of different forms of autonomy in different sociocultural contexts; (b) the presence of autonomy in learners' social worlds, no matter what the culture; and (c) the need for us to look for and learn from the autonomous learning strategies that learners are already using while sharing other potentially useful learning strategies. In my view, this stance helps to preclude cultural and social insensitivity and unwitting attempts at dominance by Western 'experts' in autonomy and strategies. More recently, Murray *et al.* (2011) explored language learning identity, motivation and autonomy in many different settings, and Murray (2014) edited a book that emphasized the social aspects of language learning autonomy.

Holliday (2003) stated that we should *'presume'* that 'autonomy is *universal* until there is evidence otherwise …, thus treating people equally as people' (original emphasis). Learner autonomy is indeed diverse, difficult to pin down as a single entity, tightly embedded in varied sociocultural contexts, and located around the world, not just in Western societies (Benson & Voller, 1997). From this assertion springs the theory of multiple autonomies, or different legitimate types of autonomy for different cultures, groups and individuals. Positive psychology does not touch upon social autonomies and multiple autonomies; its discussions of autonomy center on the individual. However, positive psychologists, like all of us, need to learn or remember that the individual is always socially and culturally situated; it is impossible to think of an individual isolated from the context.

Dimension 4 has traversed a very large range of aspects of agency and autonomy. Dimension 5 deals with an aspect that has rarely, if ever, been discussed in the field of language learning: time.

7. Dimension 5: T = *T*ime

Hypothesis: Language learners with high well-being appraise themselves temporally in a positive way and have a time perspective that fits their needs for learning.

It's time to talk about time! Some positive psychologists focus on this topic (see Boniwell, 2011). This section is devoted to the non-linearity of time, temporal self-appraisal theory, the meaning of time perspective, the question of which time perspective is optimal and the applications of time to language learning.

7.1. Non-linearity of time

Consider the words of T.S. Eliot about the non-linearity of time, from Burnt Norton (1936):

> Time present and time past
> Are both perhaps present in time future,
> And time future contained in time past.
> ...
> What might have been and what has been
> Point to one end, which is always present.
> (Eliot, 1971: 13)

Ideas about language learners' possible selves suggest that time present and time past are indeed 'both perhaps present in time future'. Consider the ideal L2 self, a motivational self guide that is built on largely on images from the past (Dörnyei, 2009b) and that helps shape our present and future behavior. In this sense, 'all time is eternally present'. Possible selves exist not only in the future but also in the past and present. Ryan and Irie (2014) explained that our interpretations of past events, and therefore our possible past selves, continue to change. These interpretations help us form theories about our present selves, which then help shape what we hope and expect for ourselves in the future (see **motivation** and **self-concept**). The system is non-linear and multidirectional, with future images looping to affect present images, present images looping to influence past images, and past images looping to influence present and future ones.

7.2. Temporal appraisal theory

The perception people have about their past or future selves is related to the perception of their current selves. Many people have a tendency to perceive the past self less favorably and contend that they are better now than they used to be (Ross & Wilson, 2002; Wilson & Ross, 2001). They tend to view the future self more positively than the present self, and may state for example that they will be better later than they are now (Wilson *et al.*, 2012; see **self-concept**).

Boehm and Lyubomirsky (2011) argued that happy and unhappy people look differently on past life experiences (see **emotion**):

> Happy people are relatively more likely to report endowing (or savoring) past positive life experiences and contrasting negative life experiences (i.e., considering how much better off they are today), whereas unhappy people are relatively more likely to report endowing (or ruminating about) negative experiences and contrasting positive experiences (i.e., considering how much worse off they are today). (Boehm & Lyubomirsky, 2011: 672)

7.3. The meaning of time perspective

The important time construct known as time perspective has received much attention from positive psychologists and calls for attention from language learning researchers. Time perspective is defined as a preferential trajectory or direction of an individual's thought toward the past, present or future, which exerts a dynamic influence on his or her experience, motivation, thinking and behavior (Boniwell, 2011). Time perspective has cognitive and affective aspects; it is a mental process that implies an emotional response to imagined time zones (past, present or future) and a preference for locating action in them. The future and the past can influence present behavior to the degree that they are part of a person's everyday cognition. Most studies have focused on the future time perspective.

It is often argued that the future time perspective differentiates humans from animals, which always operate in the present and do not have the abstraction and conceptualization to perceive the future (Boniwell, 2011). People who live primarily in the present rather than thinking about the future are more prone to hedonistic and fatalistic behaviors that can become dangerous, such as smoking, sexual promiscuity and significant alcohol consumption (Boniwell, 2011). Negative rumination on the past relates to depression, low self-esteem, unhappiness and aggression (Lyubomirsky & Nolen-Hoeksema, 1995), but positive rumination about the past reflects an ability to enjoy life (Bryant *et al.*, 2005).

Positive psychologists generally view time perspectives as follows:

- past-positive (focusing on happy memories);
- past-negative;
- present-hedonistic (pleasure- and excitement-oriented, living for the moment);

- present-fatalistic (tending to be hopeless and attributing control to outside forces rather than the self);
- future (not yet broken down into positive and negative aspects, though Boniwell called for future-positive and future-anxious dimensions).

7.4. Which time perspective is optimal?

Across socioeconomic, cultural and gender boundaries, future time perspective is associated with a number of positive outcomes, such as self-efficacy, high motivation, strong responsibility, organizational and planning ability, academic performance, delayed gratification and even eating healthy foods and flossing teeth (Boniwell, 2011). Future time perspective is negatively correlated with depression and hopelessness (Breier-Williford & Bramlett, 1995). In fact, there are so many benefits to a future time perspective that 'a large number of theorists and researchers have claimed that a focus on the future is fundamental to well-being and positive functioning' (Boniwell, 2011: 299; for an example of such thinking, see Boyd-Wilson *et al.*, 2002). However, there is only a small positive association between present-hedonistic time perspective on the one hand and life satisfaction and recreation satisfaction on the other (Boniwell, 2011). Moreover, an extreme future perspective might lead a person to become a workaholic, having low regard for friendship needs, taking no time for an occasional necessary self-indulgence, and ignoring community and cultural traditions (Boniwell & Zimbardo, 2004).

Boniwell (2011) contended that the past-positive time perspective shows the strongest associations with well-being, as found with older adults and with various student samples. Past-positive time perspective also relates to positive affect, meaning in life and self-actualization. 'It may be that the positive past holds the keys to happiness' (Boniwell, 2011: 299). On the other hand, a past time perspective that is too strong can make individuals overly conservative, cautious, and averse to change and new experiences (Boniwell, 2011).

Although academic success is burnished by having a future time perspective and though a past-positive time perspective makes us feel happy, having a dominant time perspective such as that might not be all that it is cracked up to be. Instead, '[a] balanced TP [time perspective] has been proposed as a more positive alternative to living a life as a slave to any particular temporal bias' (Boniwell, 2011: 300). As Zimbardo stated, 'In an optimally balanced time perspective, the past, present and future components blend and flexibly engage, depending on a situation's demands and our needs and values' (Zimbardo, 2002: 62). Boniwell found that people with balanced time perspectives scored in the top half of all three positive time perspectives, and in the bottom half on the present-fatalistic and past-negative perspectives.

7.5. Time in language learning

There are many reasons why time is important to language learning. Learners' age is measured in years and months, and theorists believe there is a critical or sensitive period for most people to learn another language (Singleton & Lengyel, 1995). In educational institutions, the learner's progress toward proficiency is usually broken down into days, weeks, months, semesters and years. However, the 'same duration of events as measured by the clock may be experienced very differently' (Boniwell, 2011: 296) in the subjective time of the learner. 'Furthermore, in one's mind time can flow backward as well as forward' (Boniwell, 2011: 296).

Despite the importance of time in language learning, time perspective has rarely been directly discussed among language learning theorists and researchers. However, it is easy to see that the topic of goal setting, often mentioned in the language field, lends itself to the future time perspective, while monitoring goal attainment during a task involves the present time perspective, and looking back to evaluate goal attainment over a longer period of time requires at least some past time perspective. Thoughts about the possible self, both past and future, can certainly be associated with time perspective. Beliefs about how long it takes to learn a language, how much time needs to be dedicated daily or weekly to become proficient and, indeed, whether proficiency is even possible in one's lifetime are all connected with time perspective. It would be appropriate for the language learning field to explore time perspective in a direct way. In the meantime, I will move on to dimension 6, which deals with two important factors: hardiness and habits of mind.

8. Dimension 6: H= *H*ardiness and *H*abits of Mind

Hypothesis: Language learners with high well-being develop hardy attitudes and hardy action patterns and have useful habits of mind.

Hardiness and habits of mind are factors that are connected in various ways with virtues and strengths of character (see **character strengths**).

8.1. Hardiness

Results of research on hardiness have been available for decades (e.g. Kobasa, 1979; Maddi & Kobasa, 1984) and are present in the 21st century (e.g. Maddi, 2002, 2004, 2006). One of the founders of this area of study, Salvatore Maddi, contended in 2006 that hardiness legitimately belongs within the domain of positive psychology. His main purpose was

> to add hardiness ..., which reflects existential courage, to the [positive psychology] mix.... That this fits into positive psychology is clear in that hardiness is believed to facilitate turning stresses to advantage, growing in such enhanced performance considerations as creativity, wisdom, and fulfillment, and maintaining or enhancing physical and mental health in the process. (Maddi, 2006: 160–161)

Key attitudes and action patterns

Originally developed by Maddi and Suzanne Kobasa, the concept of hardiness is founded on existential personality theory (Kobasa & Maddi, 1977), but hardiness goes beyond innate personality alone; it is learned (Maddi, 2006).

> The observation that some corporate executives and managers remained healthy, while others got sick as a function of stressful work and life events, led Kobasa (1979) to formulate the concept of ... 'hardiness' as a possible explanation for individual differences in response to stress.... Theoretically, as a function of their psychosocial developmental history, hardy (authentic) persons possess a greater openness to experience on a variety of levels, a higher sense of control and mastery, and increased confidence and commitment to life, work, self and others. (Bartone, 1996: 3)

Hardiness is largely conceptualized as a combination of three attitudes, known as the three 'C's: commitment, control and challenge. These three attitudes have different benefits. Strength of *commitment* leads a person to remain involved no matter how difficult or stressful things get, instead of becoming isolated or alienated. A person who is strong in *control* wants to influence outcomes, rather than withdrawing into passivity. A person who is strong in the realm of *challenge* rejects easy comfort and accepts stresses as a normal part of life and an opportunity to learn. These three hardy attitudes offer the existential courage and motivation 'to do the hard work of turning stressful circumstances from potential disasters to growth opportunities instead' (Maddi, 2006: 160). These attitudes are a learned cognitive/emotional amalgam that serves as a personality buffer.

If hardy attitudes are present, the resulting courage and motivation facilitate functioning with hardy action patterns that (a) build social support, (b) foster transformational coping (involving perspective-taking and understanding), and (c) encourage effective self-care, such as physical exercise. These hardy action patterns are 'attitude-motivated mechanisms for dealing effectively with stressful circumstances in a manner that enhances health and performance' (Maddi, 2006: 165).

Where it all began

There have been hundreds of studies on hardiness around the world (Maddi, 2006). One of the early ones (Maddi & Kobasa, 1984) grew out of a corporate situation. Specifically, in a longitudinal research project, hardiness was investigated as a basis for resilience among Illinois Bell Telephone (ITB) workers who were dealing with major stressors. The study began when AT&T, the parent company for ITB, had a federally regulated monopoly over the telephone industry. However, deregulation occurred during the study, smashing the security of ITB workers. According to the study, approximately two-thirds of the workers in the sample struggled and suffered immensely under the weight of stress, while one-third showed remarkable vitality and energy. Hardiness was identified as the key difference between these subgroups. 'Specifically, the resilient employees were characterized by the cognitive/emotional amalgam of hardy attitudes of commitment, control, and challenge[, which] ... were positively intercorrelated' (Maddi, 2006: 163). Those with hardy attitudes had hardy action patterns. While facing the stressful circumstances, they built patterns of interaction that encouraged mutual assistance, developed coping mechanisms that transformed potential disasters into opportunities, and took care of themselves physically and mentally. Since that early study, hardiness has been researched in education and other fields.

Distinctions

Hardiness is not the same as optimism. Some studies have shown that, compared with optimism, (a) hardiness is a more powerful and pervasive influence on the active or problem-solving coping mode and (b) it protects against denial. Whereas hardiness reflects existential courage, optimism can, according to Maddi (2006), include a degree of naïve complacency. (For different views, see **optimism**.) Hardiness is not identical to spirituality or religiousness, though there are some modest correlations between hardy attitudes and religiousness (see **character strengths**) and negative correlations between each of them and measures of depression and anger (Maddi, 2006). Hardiness is not exactly resilience, either, but is a basis for resilience, as mentioned above (see **resilience**).

Hardiness and language learning

Hardy attitudes and hardy action patterns are relevant to language learning. Regarding hardy attitudes necessary to move toward proficiency, the learner: must be committed and must not swerve off the track into isolation and inactivity; must attempt to be in control, at least to some extent, rather than being passive; and must learn to accept challenges and stresses as a normal part of language learning, instead of being trapped in ongoing state of anxiety (see **emotion**). Hardy action patterns are also necessary for language learners. Specifically, learners require social support, need to cope effectively through perspective-taking and understanding, and must take care of themselves in order to learn effectively (see also Hiver, Chapter 7 of this volume). Looking at learner narratives (Oxford, 2011a), I can identify many language learners who have shown hardy attitudes and hardy action patterns. Hardiness training programs, which train college students and working adults in developing hardy attitudes and hardy action patterns, have shown promise (Maddi, 2004, 2006), and it is possible that such programs would benefit language learners in many age groups and settings.

8.2. Habits of mind

Based on extensive research on effective, successful, intelligent individuals across many fields of endeavor, Costa and Kallick (2008) identified the habits of mind that characterize such individuals. Some of the character strengths set out by the Values in Action (VIA) Institute (see section 10) are related to the habits of mind (see **character strengths**). The word 'habit' in the phrase 'habits of mind' is key, because effective individuals habitually use these behaviors to reach their best performance. Examples of habits of mind are thinking flexibly, striving for accuracy, thinking about thinking, persisting (see **perseverance**), listening with understanding and empathy, finding humor, and communicating with accuracy and precision.

Definition of a habit of mind

Costa and Kallick (2008) defined a habit of mind this way:

> A Habit of Mind is a composite of many skills, attitudes, cues, past experiences, and proclivities. It means that we value one pattern of intellectual behaviors over another; therefore, it implies making choices about which patterns we should use at a certain time. It includes sensitivity to the contextual cues that signal that a particular circumstance is a time when applying a certain pattern would be useful and appropriate. It requires a level of skillfulness to use, carry out, and sustain the behaviors effectively. It suggests that after each experience in which these behaviors are used, the effects of their use are reflected upon, evaluated, modified, and carried forth to future applications. (para. 7)

Master chart of habits of mind and applications to language learners

Table 2.1 is a master chart that lists the 16 habits of mind from Costa and Kallick (2008) and my proposed applications of each habit of mind to learners who have high well-being. I do not assert that habits of mind *cause* high well-being or vice versa, but I contend that there is a connection that

Table 2.1 Habits of mind as applied to language learners with high well-being

Habit of mind (Costa & Kallick, 2008)	*Language learners who have high well-being ...*
1. Persistence (see **perseverance** and **character strengths**)	stay with a task, use strategies to solve problems, and change strategies if some strategies do not work
2. Managing impulsivity (i.e. being reflective) (see **character strengths**)	are deliberate and reflective, considering multiple alternatives
3. Listening with understanding and empathy (see **empathy** and **character strengths**)	are empathetic and therefore are good listeners
4. Flexibility (see **character strengths**)	think flexibly, changing their approach and style as needed
5. Thinking about thinking (metacognition)	think about thinking and are conscious of their own ways of learning
6. Striving for accuracy	strive for accuracy in learning and using the target language
7. Questioning and posing problems	ask questions and pose problems concerning the target language, the target culture, and the language learning process
8. Applying past knowledge to new situations	learn from past experiences and apply their experiential knowledge to new situations as relevant
9. Thinking and communicating with clarity and precision	think and communicate with clarity and precision, thus avoiding vagueness and overgeneralizations about themselves, the target language, and the target culture
10. Gathering data through all the senses	learn languages and cultures through all the senses, thus taking advantage of multiple regions of the brain
11. Creating, imagining, innovating (see **motivation** and **character strengths**)	are creative, intrinsically motivated individuals who encourage feedback and strive for greater fluency and balance
12. Responding with wonderment and awe (see **meaning** and **motivation**)	are awed by the beauty of language, culture, and communication, and are open to inspired consciousness and peak experiences (see Oxford & Cuéllar, 2014)
13. Taking responsible risks (see **hardiness** and **character strengths**)	take responsible risks and accept the stress of uncertainty and challenge
14. Finding humor (see **character strengths**)	enjoy and share humor but not at the expense of others
15. Thinking interdependently (see **empathy** and **character strengths**)	are collaborative in their learning and bring a collaborative, open, compassionate, empathetic attitude to interactions in the target culture
16. Remaining open to continuous learning (see **meaning**)	view themselves as lifelong learners of the target language and culture and remain in a vigorous, questing mode

deserves research. I caution that a given language learner will probably not be equally skilled in all 16 habits of mind, and various learners will differ in their profiles of habits of mind; see Costa and Kallick (2008) for a full description of each.

Relationships between habits of mind and learning strategies

Learning strategies, such as reasoning, planning and managing emotions, overlap with habits of mind. Learning strategies are 'activities consciously chosen by learners for the purpose of regulating their own language learning' (Griffiths, 2013: 36). They are consciously employed, goal-directed operations that the learner uses to aid the acquisition, storage, retrieval and use of information, and they are often used in combination (strategy chains) (Oxford, 1990, 2011b). Learning strategies make learning more effective and more efficient (Oxford, 1990, 2011b) and are targeted to increase language proficiency and achievement (Gunning & Oxford, 2014; Oxford, 1990, 2011b). They are related to agency, autonomy and self-regulation (Griffiths, 2013; Oxford, 2011b; see **agency and autonomy**). Strategies are often used consciously and intentionally (for live examples of intentional self-teaching of strategies, see Kao & Oxford, 2014; Ma & Oxford, 2014). Learning strategies actively help to construct 'terms and conditions of learning' (cf. Lantolf & Pavlenko, 2001: 145) and can become habits through frequent use (Oxford, 1990). Patterns of strategy use often differ somewhat by gender, age, culture, academic major, motivation and classroom versus independent setting (Chamot, 2007; Griffiths & Oxford, 2014; Gunning & Oxford, 2014). Unsuccessful learners, compared with successful language learners, select and use strategies in a desperate, random way (Griffiths, 2013; Oxford, 1990, 2011b). Fortunately, strategies are teachable and learnable (Chamot, 2007; Cohen, 2011; Cohen & Weaver, 2006; Gunning & Oxford, 2014).

I have identified four strategy domains. Cognitive learning strategies, such as activating knowledge, reasoning, conceptualizing in detail (e.g. analyzing), conceptualizing broadly (e.g. synthesizing, summarizing, and combining), going beyond the data (e.g. predicting, inferring) are 'deep processing strategies, which facilitate understanding, increase meaningful mental associations, and … [encourage] long-term retention of information' (Oxford, 2011b: 29–30). Affective strategies help learners (a) activate supportive emotions, beliefs and attitudes, and (b) generate and maintain motivation. Sociocultural-interactive strategies enable learners to interact to learn and communicate, overcome knowledge gaps in communicating, and deal effectively with sociocultural contexts and identities. Metacognitive strategies or metastrategies, such as planning, monitoring and evaluating, help guide the use of all other strategies in the language learning process. Habits of mind, as portrayed by Costa and Kallick (2008), can be organized into these very strategy domains (see Table 2.2).

Table 2.2 Habits of mind and corresponding learning strategy domains

Habits of mind (Costa & Kallick, 2008)	*Corresponding learning strategy domains (Oxford, 2011b)*
Flexibility; striving for accuracy; questioning and posing problems; applying past knowledge to new situations; thinking with clarity and precision; gathering data through all the senses; and creating, imagining and innovating	Cognitive learning strategies
Thinking about thinking (metacognition); taking responsible risks; persistence; and remaining open to continuous learning	Metacognitive learning strategies (also known as metastrategies, Oxford, 2011b)[4]
Managing impulsivity; listening with understanding and empathy (also a social strategy); responding with wonderment and awe; and finding humor	Affective learning strategies
Communicating with clarity and precision; thinking interdependently; and listening with understanding and empathy (also an affective learning strategy)	Sociocultural-interactive learning strategies

In short, habits of mind are marks of effective, successful individuals, and these habits distinctly overlap with Oxford's (2011b) learning strategy domains. Both habits of mind and learning strategies are closely related to self-regulation, autonomy and agency (see **agency and autonomy**).

9. Dimension 7: I = *I*ntelligences

Hypothesis: Language learners with high well-being recognize their own intelligences and take advantage of those intelligences for learning and living.

Intelligences are the key focus of Howard Gardner and one of the main interests of Robert Sternberg, both of whom disputed the dominant model of standardized intelligence testing.

> Sternberg (1985) challenged mental abilities researchers to pay more attention to the creative and practical aspects of intelligence, and Gardner (1993) even defined an intrapersonal intelligence that concerns access to one's feeling life, the capacity to represent feelings, and the ability to draw upon them as a means for understanding and [a] guide for behavior. (Salovey *et al.*, 2011: 239)

These major contributions are explained in this section.

9.1. Howard Gardner's work on multiple intelligences

As noted by Peterson (2006) in his book *A Primer in Positive Psychology*, Gardner might or might not regard himself as a positive psychologist, 'but he certainly helped to set the stage for the field [of positive psychology] by his attention to excellence in a way that did not diminish anyone' (p. 213). Gardner produced 'the best-known contemporary statement about the plurality of abilities' (Peterson, 2006: 211).

Gardner's theory

In this theory, each person has a certain set of intelligences. In *Frames of Mind: The Theory of Multiple Intelligences*, Gardner (1983) asserted that an intelligence is a set of biopsychological potentials to process information that can be activated in a cultural context to solve problems or create valuable products. He argued that the intelligences explicated in his theory arose through evolution because they were important to the human species. He also contended that these intelligences were largely independent of each other, had distinct developmental progressions, and were marked by the existence of savants, prodigies and other exceptional individuals.

In various iterations of his theory, he identified the following intelligences: (a) musical, (b) logical-mathematical, (c) verbal-linguistic, (d) visual-spatial, (e) bodily-kinesthetic, (f) interpersonal (social), (g) intrapersonal (introspective), (h) existential (largely spiritual) and (i) naturalistic (ecological) (Gardner, 1983, 1993, 1999, 2004, 2011). His work was intended to empower individuals, not to restrict them to a specific domain of intelligence. His concepts have been both debated and attacked. The theory of multiple intelligences has captured the attention of many experts who believe that the use of standardized intelligence tests has been overly limiting.

Possible applications of these Gardner's intelligences to language learning

Most or perhaps even all of the intelligences proposed by Gardner have relevance to the learning of languages and cultures. For instance, verbal-linguistic intelligence, involving abilities in reading, writing, speaking, listening and vocabulary, is obviously relevant to language learning. Musical intelligence relates to sounds, rhythms, pitches and tones, all of which are pertinent to pronunciation in the target language. Visual-spatial intelligence is likely to be important in learning to write Chinese characters and the Russian Cyrillic alphabet, as well as appreciating works of art from the target culture and following maps while visiting cities where the target language is spoken. In learning the target language, bodily-kinesthetic intelligence assists with understanding and producing physical gestures and other forms of body language. Interpersonal intelligence is essential for interacting with others in the target language, for being sensitive to others' moods and needs, and for fitting into the culture effectively. Intrapersonal intelligence, which involves introspective and self-reflective capabilities, helps language learners understand their emotions and motivations and enables them to deal with the shifting identities that occur during language learning. Logical-mathematical intelligence is focused on logic, abstractions, reasoning, numbers, critical thinking and possibly learning the logic of grammar. Existential intelligence is similar to spiritual intelligence, and many individuals find that their learning path is made easier through spirituality; moreover, existential intelligence helps learners make sense of the spiritual beliefs of those in the target culture. Naturalistic intelligence involves nurturing one's natural surroundings and understanding the role of humanity within the ecosphere. Languages are inherently part of ecosystems and reflect those ecosystems. Moreover, the environment is an increasingly prevalent topic in language textbooks and in conversations among learners and native speakers of the target language.

Assessment in context

There is no simple, straightforward assessment of multiple intelligences. Instead of standardized tests, Gardner (1991) called for assessment in context, which would rely on information about an individual's abilities obtained in the course of everyday activities. Gardner linked assessment in context to ongoing, individualized strategies used by master craftspeople to train and evaluate their apprentices. He encouraged individuals to present portfolios of projects and accomplishments, not just standardized test scores and grade point averages, to admissions or hiring committees (Gardner, 1993). Because assessment in context is creative and individualistic, it does not lend itself to the type of evidence of psychometric validity available through standardized tests. This, of course, has been a source of criticism.

Debate

Other criticisms have arisen from the seemingly subjective selection of criteria for identifying the intelligences in Gardner's theory and from the fact that the intelligences might not be as independent of each other as Gardner thought. A few critics have also argued that certain of Gardner's intelligences, such as musical, are abilities or aptitude rather than intelligences and have complained that Gardner expanded the definition of intelligence beyond its ordinary scope (containing only the linguistic and logical-mathematical abilities measured by IQ tests). However, Gardner (1998) responded that it is unwarranted to assume that particular human abilities and not others can be arbitrarily viewed as intelligence. I think it is entirely justifiable to say that the traditional definition of intelligence as measured by IQ tests is far too narrow, particularly as that definition relates to language learning. Many dimensions of intelligence support language learning. Gardner's theory, despite any shortcomings, helps us honor multiple aspects of intelligence that might otherwise be ignored in the language learning field.

9.2. Robert Sternberg's triarchic theory of intelligence

Like Gardner, Sternberg (1985, 1997) disliked the narrowness of traditional IQ testing. He devised a triarchic theory of intelligence involving practical, creative and analytical intelligences.

Sternberg's model

Practical intelligence in Sternberg's model refers to 'street smarts' or real-world adaptability that fits the solution to the context. Creative intelligence means intuitively divergent responses to novel tasks or new ways of solving problems that the majority of people would not think of. Analytical intelligence refers to the types of information-processing and critical-thinking skills found on traditional intelligence tests. It is possible for a person to have more than one of these types of intelligence. For Sternberg, successful intelligence is what helps the individual succeed in life, according to the definition of success in that individual's own sociocultural context.

The triarchic theory of intelligence has critics who argue that the theory is not supported by psychometric (standardized IQ testing) research. That criticism seems strange, given that ordinary IQ tests were never designed to measure practical intelligence and creative intelligence. Sternberg's theory clearly goes beyond such tests.

Possible language learning applications

I believe his theory is applicable to language learners. For example, some language learners have street smarts, or the practical intelligence to deal with almost anything that comes up in encountering the target culture. Other language learners think divergently and creatively as they develop new strategies for language learning and deal with novel situations and tasks. Still others have analytical intelligence that helps them learn and apply grammar, make sense of the masses of vocabulary they encounter, and make their way through target language texts. Some learners have two of these intelligences, and the most fortunate ones are those with all three.

Intelligences as depicted by Gardner and Sternberg go a long way toward making a good life, yet they are often accompanied by particular strengths of character. Character strengths are the theme of dimension 8.

10. Dimension 8: C = *C*haracter Strengths

Hypothesis: Language learners with high well-being have a range of character strengths that help them in their learning and their lives.

Character strengths and virtues have been discussed since the days of ancient philosophers, but their meaning and importance are just as fresh in the 21st century. This section synthesizes efforts of the Values in Action (VIA) Institute to systematize universal character strengths and virtues and the resulting list, and it also applies this information to successful language learners.

10.1. Efforts of the VIA Institute to identify universal character strengths

The Mayerson Foundation created the VIA Institute in 2000 to explore positive youth development, but the focus later expanded to optimal human development in general. Despite arguments against considering character, value and virtue (some positivists had viewed such factors as philosophical and subjective rather than psychological and objective), the VIA Institute aimed to uncover and organize these individual-difference variables. Paul Peterson and Martin Seligman (2004) joined forces to produce the VIA Classification of Character Strengths and Virtues (see VIA Institute, 2014). In this system, 24 character strengths are subsumed by six virtues (see Table 2.3), and they are all morally valued by society.

The VIA researchers initially worried that character, value and virtue were culturally bound constructs (e.g. punctuality as a positive trait has little meaning in some cultures but is important in others, so it cannot be called universal). Through their own in-depth surveys of influential philosophical and religious traditions around the world and throughout history, the researchers came to realize that there are widely valued, universal or core virtues, which are shown through character strengths (Peterson, 2006). These virtues could be manifested somewhat differently across cultures but could nevertheless be considered universal, according to Peterson. The researchers decided not to ally their system with an a priori theory of virtue or good character, such as Aristotle's, and therefore opted to provide a descriptive classification rather than a theoretically based taxonomy (Peterson, 2006). They scoured research addressing good character 'from psychiatry, youth development, character education, religion, philosophy, organizational studies, and of course psychology' and even looked at character strengths in cultural products such as 'popular songs, greeting cards, bumper stickers, obituaries and testimonials, mottoes and credos, ... personal ads ... [,] graffiti, Tarot cards, the profiles of Pokémon characters, and the Hogwarts residence halls in the Harry Potter books' (Peterson, 2006: 141).

Table 2.3 Virtues and character strengths, and their applications to language learners with high well-being

Virtue	*Character strength*	*Language learners with high well-being ...*
Wisdom and knowledge (1–5)	1. *Creativity*	show creativity in coming up with relevant learning strategies to meet their needs, finding new opportunities to practice the language, and putting words and sentences together in novel ways for communication (see **habits of mind**)
	2. *Curiosity*	are curious about and even fascinated by the language, the culture, and everyday learning experiences (see **habits of mind**)
	3. *Love of learning*	love learning enough to be somewhat systematic about mastering new skills (see **habits of mind**)
	4. *Open-mindedness*	are open-minded, particularly when they encounter different practices and attitudes in the target culture and when they recognize that the syntax and pragmatics of the target language differ from their own (see **habits of mind**)
	5. *Perspective*	have perspective, i.e. understand the ways of the target language and culture and, when possible or necessary, help other learners understand as well (see **habits of mind**)
Courage (6–9)	6. *Authenticity*	are authentic, thus presenting themselves genuinely when dealing with educators, other learners and members of the target culture, and being aware of and responsible for their **emotions** and actions
	7. *Bravery*	bravely deal with threat, challenge, difficulty, or pain (see **hardiness**); face the personal, social, and physical rigors of language learning with equanimity; take relevant risks, such as participating in a study-abroad program that involves striking up conversations with native speakers of the target language
	8. *Persistence*	are persistent in that they complete tasks and persevere despite obstacles and difficulties (see **perseverance** and **habits of mind**); take pleasure in task completion
	9. *Zest*	display zest or a sense of adventurousness in learning the new language and culture
Humanity (10–12)	10. *Kindness*	are kind to educators, other learners, and members of the target culture and thereby establish the social foundation for learning and using the language
	11. *Love*	sometimes feel love for their teachers (Oxford & Cuéllar, 2014) and others involved in the language learning process and appreciate the process itself
	12. *Social intelligence*	display social and emotional intelligence in the language classroom and in the target culture (see **emotional intelligence**)

Justice (13–15)	13. *Fairness*	are fair and unbiased toward others, including people in the target culture
	14. *Leadership*	encourage their own group to get things done while maintaining positive relationships
	15. *Teamwork*	are effective members of a team in doing learning projects and preparing for language or cultural events; also join teams with target language speakers when appropriate
Temperance (16–19)	16. *Forgiveness/ mercy*	show forgiveness and mercy when they are wronged by an educator, a fellow language learner, or a member of the target culture
	17. *Modesty/ humility*	are modest and humble in not flaunting their linguistic or cultural abilities, which may be greater than those of other people around them, and not seeking the spotlight
	18. *Prudence*	are prudent, protecting themselves against undue risks – but still taking risks that are useful for learning the language (see character strength 7 in this table and **habits of mind**)
	19. *Self-regulation*	are self-regulated (exerting self-control) regarding actions, emotions, and cognitions through the use of language learning strategies (see Oxford, 2011b)
Transcend-ence (20–24)	20. *Appreciation of beauty and excellence*	appreciate their own skills, the skills of others, and the beauty and excellence of their own language and culture and the target language and culture
	21. *Gratitude*	are grateful to educators, other learners, and members of the target culture who help them learn the language and to supportive family members and friends; and remember to express their gratitude
	22. *Hope*	hope that they can become proficient in the language, can understand the culture, and can use their competence to make a better world (see **hope**)
	23. *Humor*	leaven their learning with humor, so that they and others can relax and learn more effectively (see Oxford, 1990, 2011b; see **optimism**)
	24. *Religiousness/ spirituality*	have coherent beliefs about the meaning of life and about appropriate conduct, although they might not subscribe to a particular religious dogma (see **meaning**)

10.2. List of character strengths

The resulting list of character strengths is based on the concept that each such strength meets the following criteria: it is cross-culturally recognized; it contributes to fulfillment, satisfaction and happiness; it is morally valued rather than just instrumental to an outcome; it produces admiration rather than jealousy; it has an obvious negative antonym; it is trait-like and measurable but neither 'fixed [n]or necessarily grounded in immutable biogenetic characteristics' (Peterson, 2006: 139); it is distinct from other character strengths; it is dramatically embodied in certain individual paragons and in some young prodigies; it can be absent in some people; and it is cultivated by some societal institutions and practices (Peterson, 2006; Peterson & Seligman, 2004).

Table 2.3 presents the names of the virtues and the character strengths from the VIA Classification of Character Strengths and Virtues, along with my applications to language learners with high well-being. Note that this table does not suggest that having high well-being *causes* particular virtues and character strengths, or that these virtues and character strengths *cause* high well-being; nevertheless, I argue that a relationship exists and is worth researching. Different learners will naturally have contrasting profiles of character strengths.

Many of the VIA character strengths (Peterson, 2006; Peterson & Park, 2011), such as creativity, curiosity and open-mindedness, overlap with **habits of mind**, described earlier. This stands to reason, because character strengths, like habits of mind, are habitual, deeply rooted and positive parts of the individual. Dimension 9, described next, continues the idea of key elements of the human being by focusing on self factors.

11. Dimension 9: S = *S*elf Factors (*S*elf-Efficacy, *S*elf-Concept, *S*elf-Esteem and *S*elf-Verification)

Hypothesis: Language learners with high well-being possess self-efficacy, positive self-concepts, and high self-esteem, and use self-verification positively.

In this section I discuss four self factors which are often explored in positive psychology: self-efficacy, self-concept, self-esteem and self-verification.

11.1. Self-efficacy

Research on self-efficacy comes from the social cognitive area (Bandura, 1997) but has been adopted by positive psychologists (Maddux, 2011; Peterson, 2006). Self-efficacy is the person's level of confidence (belief) that he or she can successfully carry out an action to achieve a specific goal in a particular setting under certain conditions (Bandura, 1997; Zimmerman, 2000).

> The basic premise of self-efficacy theory is that 'people's beliefs in their capabilities to produce desired effects by their own actions' (Bandura, 1997, p. vii) are the most important determinants of the behaviors people

choose to engage in and how much they persevere in their efforts in the face of obstacles and challenges. (Maddux, 2011: 335; see **perseverance**)

The theory comes from a long line of philosophical and psychological thinking about control and helplessness. Maddux distinguished self-efficacy from intentions, motivations and personality traits. He noted that measures of 'general self-efficacy' have not been as useful as more specific self-efficacy measures.

Social cognitive theory

Social cognitive theory, from which self-efficacy is drawn, assumes that people actively, agentically shape their environments and are not passive reactors (Bandura, 2006; see **agency**). It further assumes that we are capable of symbolic thought, including the ability to understand cause–effect relationships, to grasp that actions produce results, and to recognize that we can be the origin of actions that affect our environments. The development of personal agency begins in infancy. The responsiveness of environments to the infant's or young child's attempts at control and exploration help to develop efficacy beliefs. We continue to develop efficacy beliefs and a sense of agency throughout our lifespan.

Main sources of information for self-efficacy

There are five main sources of information for efficacy beliefs: (a) our own performance experiences, as long as we attribute the outcome to our own efforts; (b) vicarious experiences, or observing the consequences of others' behaviors, which have implications for what we think we can do ourselves; (c) imagined experiences, or seeing ourselves or others behaving effectively or ineffectively in imagined situations; (d) verbal persuasion, or what others tell us we can or cannot do; and (e) physiological and emotional states, with positive states becoming associated with success and negative states becoming linked with failure (Bandura, 1997; Maddux, 2011).

Relationships to psychological and physical well-being

Self-efficacy is important because it is related to psychological and physical well-being. Having a sense of control over our behavior and our environment is 'essential for happiness and a sense of psychological well-being' (Maddux, 2011: 338). In terms of mental health, low self-efficacy is related to depression, anxiety, avoidant behavior, substance abuse and eating disorders (Maddux, 2011). Regarding physical health, high self-efficacy is tied to adopting positive health behaviors and ceasing unhealthy ones. Efficacy beliefs influence many biological processes, such as the workings of the immune system, and these processes affect health and disease (Maddux, 2011).

Self-efficacy and self-regulation

Self-efficacy is related to self-regulation in the pursuit of desired goals. (Note that this formulation is not the same as Vygotsky's theory of self-regulation.) As Maddux stated, 'Self-regulation (simplified) depends on three interacting components …: goals or standards of performance; self-evaluative reactions to performance; and self-efficacy beliefs' (Maddux, 2011: 339). Self-efficacy beliefs influence the goals we set, our choices of goal-directed behavior, our degree of effort, our persistence (see **perseverance**), and the efficiency and effectiveness of our problem-solving (Maddux, 2011). If we have high self-efficacy in the face of problems, we are likely to focus on finding solutions to those problems, but if we have low self-efficacy, we are more likely to reflect on our inadequacies, thus detracting from problem-solving efforts (Bandura, 1997).

Maddux stated quite eloquently:

> The timeless message of research on self-efficacy is the simple, powerful truth that confidence, effort, and persistence are more potent than innate ability. In this sense, self-efficacy is concerned with human potential and possibilities, not limitations, thus making it a truly 'positive' psychology. (Maddux, 2011: 341)

Self-efficacy in language learning

Research shows that self-efficacy is correlated with the frequency of use of language learning strategies (Chamot, 2004; Chamot *et al.*, 1996). Learners with high self-efficacy tend to show agency and autonomy through using learning strategies, which also promote movement toward language proficiency. Efforts to teach language learners to employ optimal learning strategies for specific tasks could have excellent results in terms of self-efficacy.

11.2. Self-concept

According to Rubio (2014), 'self-concept is a complex construct consisting of different dimensions or selves, namely physical, social, familial, personal, academic, and many other situational ones' (p. 43). Self-concept is composed of a person's self-schemas or self-beliefs in particular dimensions. Self-evaluations, such as 'I am exciting', 'I am athletic', 'I am beautiful' or 'I am lazy', define the person's self-schemas, and a collection of self-schemas constitutes a person's overall self-concept. Rubio (2014) pointed out that a person does not have a high or low self-concept, though a person has high or low self-esteem (see below).

> Self-concept can be defined by a description of the different selves that the individual generates.… Consequently, self-concept is unique for each

> individual and developed newly in every evaluation, and it is formed dynamically throughout life. (Rubio, 2014: 47)

Thus, it is impossible to talk about a stable self-concept for a given individual.

Evaluation

Self-concept is the picture that is evaluated by the self (Rubio, 2014). Competence and worthiness 'form the two basic valuing dimensions of self-concept' (Rubio, 2014: 52; see also **self-esteem**). Self-concept includes among other things the past, present and future selves. As we know from the discussion of **motivation** above, future selves are individuals' ideas of what they might become, what they would like to become (the ideal self) or what they are afraid of becoming (the feared self). Possible selves may function as motivators for certain behavior (Markus & Nurius, 1986; Myers, 2009; see **motivation**).

Factors influencing self-concept

Rubio's neurogenerative perspective argues that self-concept is affected by past experiences and education, values, personality, and dispositional and situational states. New 'self-concept portraits' are created 'every time competence and worthiness are in play' (Rubio, 2014: 48). From a phenomenological viewpoint, 'it is the perception of performance and previous experiences that mainly influence the formation of the self-concept (Mruk, 2006)' (Rubio, 2014: 48).

Mercer's (2011b) book, *Towards an Understanding of Language Learner Self-Concept*, similarly identifies a range of influences on the self-concepts of individuals learning another language. Mercer asserted that internal and external factors play roles in helping shape the self-concept. Internal factors include internal comparisons across domains within the self-concept network, belief systems and affective reactions. External factors include: social comparisons with others, especially peers; feedback from significant others; perceived experiences of success and failure; previous experiences of language learning and use in formal or informal contexts; and critical experiences (summarized by Rubio, 2014). Language learners' self-concepts, in the eyes of Mercer, 'are part of a complicated network of self-beliefs and are formed through a myriad of interconnected factors, all of which may be processed differently depending on other psychological factors and motivations within the individual' (Mercer, 2011b: 167).

Further applications of self-concept to language learning

Regarding language learner's self-concept, Dörnyei (2009b) contended that future self-guides have a major function for motivating learners (see **motivation**). Language learners 'are motivated to reach a condition where their self-concept matches their personally relevant self-guides' (Dörnyei, 2009b: 18). As noted by Rubio (2014), studies by Lau *et al.* (1999) and Yeung and Wong (2004) validated the existence of a separate self-concept for languages and found that speakers of multiple languages have separate self-concepts in each language.

11.3. Self-esteem

Hewitt (2011: 219) noted that talking about self-esteem (and I would add talking about any self-related construct) contributes 'to what Michel Foucault called "technologies of the self", creating the very terms and instruments whereby the self is experienced'. In many cultures, widespread discussion has enhanced the importance of self-esteem until it is now seen as 'a fundamental human need … [with] profound consequences for every aspect of our existence' (Branden, 1994: 3; quoted in Rubio, 2014: 44).

Self-esteem is 'the [high–low] evaluative quality of the self-image or self-concept' (Dörnyei, 2005: 211; quoted in Rubio, 2014: 43). According to Rubio (2014), self-esteem is both 'a process of evaluation and the emergent evaluation' (p. 42). He commented that 'self-esteem processes of evaluation follow similar patterns of activation for all human beings, i.e., complex[,] intertwined connections of affect and thought which result from self-evaluations' (p. 47), while self-concept is more unique and individualized.

Social construction of self-esteem

In *The Oxford Handbook of Positive Psychology*, Hewitt (2011) revealed that self-esteem is related to four ideas, acceptance, evaluation, comparison and efficacy, which have great importance in certain cultures but not necessarily in all cultures. He drew his self-esteem ideas from US culture rather than from other cultures. Self-esteem in the US is founded on the concept of unconditional acceptance of the child within society, and later social evaluations of the individual will either enhance or damage the individual's self-esteem. The individual also makes comparisons of himself or herself with other people and with the ideal self, and favorable comparisons, particularly those based on competence in the physical and social environment, enhance self-esteem. As suggested by Hewitt, these ideas are drawn from basic American cultural values, such as individual responsibility to carve out a social space, to make friends, and to act independently and effectively.

However, even within a mostly individualist culture such as the US, contrasting values battle each other. For example, there is a culturally communitarian impulse toward (a) accepting everyone as a worthy human being, regardless of qualifications; (b) interpreting the pursuit of happiness as 'satisfaction with one's current place in life'; and (c) believing that 'self-esteem is an entitlement' without the necessity of any particular effort (Hewitt, 2011: 218). On the other hand, the same culture has an opposite value that

(a) forcefully demands individual competition and competence, (b) interprets the pursuit of happiness as 'a future state of enjoyment dependent upon successful individual effort' (Hewitt, 2011: 218), and (c) contends that 'self-esteem is not a right' but a privilege (Hewitt, 2011: 218). It is no wonder that '[l]ongstanding cultural disputes are thus encoded' (Hewitt, 2011: 218–219). Though many people agree on the importance of attaining self-esteem, they disagree on how to attain it, indicated Hewitt.

A developmental view of self-esteem

Harter (1999) (cited in Rubio, 2014) presented a developmental view of self-esteem. In early childhood, individuals are not aware of their sense of worthiness or competence. Worthiness becomes an issue when individuals feel accepted either conditionally or unconditionally by their parents (Rogers, 1961); self-esteem thus begins with external acceptance and is later reinforced through self-acceptance. Middle childhood is marked by the emergence of a sense of competence in multiple domains in school. Adolescence focuses largely on worthiness, for example body image in relation to social acceptance and success. In adulthood, experiences of success or failure in problem-solving and interpersonal relationships help shape self-esteem. Thus, different elements of self-esteem take precedence at different times in the lifespan.

Early research on self-esteem

Early research cited by Rubio (2014) portrays different views on self-esteem. For White (1963), self-esteem results from the relationship between the actual self and the ideal self (see **motivation**) and the individual's drive for effectance, that is, a sense of competence while mastering skills to adapt to the environment. Rosenberg (1965) argued that social contact strongly influences self-esteem and that higher self-esteem is related to propinquity between the ideal self and the real self. For Coopersmith (1967), antecedents of a person's self-esteem are parental warmth, clear limits and respectful treatment, and self-esteem predicts behaviors.

In self-esteem evaluations, the two components of competence and worthiness receive equal weight (Branden, 1969). According to Branden (1969), the individual feels a need to maintain at least moderate self-esteem, and when this does not happen, pseudo self-esteem may arise. Within a cognitive perspective, Epstein (1985) argued that self-esteem is a hierarchical structure that includes (a) basic, stable self-esteem; (b) intermediate self-esteem, related to general domains of experience; and (c) situation-specific self-esteem in particular domains (in Rubio, 2014).

Phenomenological perspective on self-esteem

Mruk's (2006) phenomenological perspective, as explained by Rubio, holds that self-esteem results from the evaluation of competence and worthiness in an elaborate interaction between the world and perceived experiences in it, with outcomes accounting for positive and negative behavior. Perceptions of *high competence and high worthiness* lead to high self-esteem. However, if these senses are too high, they can create anti-empathetic attitudes and classroom conflict. Perceptions of *low competence and low worthiness* lead to low self-esteem, which in turn leads to feelings of dependence and insecurity, negative attitudes toward learning, and possible depression. Perceptions of *high competence and low worthiness* result in a lack of balance, with the individual devoted largely to over-achieving in school or other domains but being defensive when success is challenged by others. Achieving a goal can be such a dominant drive that it separates the individual from peers, creating a low sense of belonging. Perceptions of *low competence and high worthiness* result in a defensively self-centered, pseudo self-esteem in which the individual, if his or her sense of worthiness is challenged, lashes out aggressively. Narcissistic behavior and bullying can emerge (Rubio, 2014).

Self-esteem and willingness to communicate

Self-esteem has been studied in relation to willingness to communicate. Individuals who have strong communicative apprehension (fear of communicating with another individual) tend to have lower self-esteem, because they assume that others will believe they have little to offer or will respond negatively (McCroskey & Richmond, 1990). In the language learning field, MacIntyre *et al.* (1998) developed a model of willingness to communicate that involved affiliation and confidence. See also the work of Fonseca Mora and Toscano Fuentes (2007) regarding willingness to communicate in a foreign language, mentioned by Rubio (2014). Gregersen and MacIntyre (2014) developed a series of language classroom activities meant to increase learners' willingness to enter into target language exchanges.

Heightening self-esteem

What if we want to help a language learner change his or her low self-esteem? It would help to consider the degree to which the learner actually values his or her combination of perceived low competence and perceived low worthiness. It is possible to heighten self-esteem only if the value of high self-esteem trumps what the individual is 'gaining' at present through perceptions of low competence and low worthiness.

It does not help to merely tell people that they are better than they think. 'Attempting to raise others' self-esteem by simply telling individuals with negative self-views that they are wrong about themselves is unlikely to bear fruit' (North & Swann, 2011: 470). Instead, fostering self-esteem involves taking the person's frame of reference and accepting and valuing the person for who he or she is (Rogers, 1961). Acceptance of the person's self-view is the first step to change. Positive comments have the potential to raise the person's self-esteem only if they accompany verification of the person's self-view (see **self-verification** below). For example, it is possible to offer confirmatory negative feedback in an emotionally positive way. '[T]his combination of accepting another's reality or truth while slowly and gently infusing positivity raises self-esteem' (North & Swann, 2011: 471).

Reasoner's (1982) model for building self-esteem has five dimensions: security, identity, belonging, purpose and competence. Rubio (2014) added his earlier ideas (Rubio, 2007) and those of Andres and Arnold (2009) to support and expand Reasoner's model in the direction of language learning and teaching. *Security* involves the feeling of emotional and physical safety, and this includes consistent teacher patterns, acceptance of learner errors as being normal, and positive feedback for learners. *Identity* in Reasoner's model refers to the perception people have about themselves. Teachers can aid identity by honoring learners' uniqueness, building positive self-images, encouraging self-awareness, and showing acceptance and care. A *sense of belonging* involves the feeling of acceptance within a group. Teachers can foster this sense by encouraging approval and support from peers, developing a class identity that values each member, and offering learners chances to serve others. A *sense of purpose* in Reasoner's model involves having objectives and direction in life. Teachers can encourage this sense by setting realistic expectations, by offering help as learners set and achieve goals, by giving adequate task time and by displaying confidence in students' progress. A *sense of competence* in this model encompasses the feeling of having the necessary aptitude and ability to accomplish tasks. Teachers can build this sense by having learners use self-evaluation checklists, using positive feedback, providing challenges that are appropriate to existing skills, and orienting work to individuals' multiple abilities (see **intelligences**).

11.4. Self-verification

It could be argued that not all language learners engage in self-verification, but it is an intriguing process that calls for attention even if it is not pervasive. Self-verification is personal confirmation of one's own views about oneself and is assumed to be a basically adaptive process, though it is not without paradox. '[O]nce people form their self-views, these self-views come to provide them with a powerful sense of coherence and a related capacity to predict and control their worlds' (North & Swann, 2011: 465). By promoting psychological coherence within the core self, self-verification fosters authenticity, that is, the unobstructed operation of the core self; it also reduces anxiety and improves health (North & Swann, 2011). Furthermore, self-verification is involved with interpersonal relationships. The yearning for self-verification encourages people to enter into trusting relationships with those whom they consider 'honest', that is, those who reflect back to them their own views about themselves. Such relationships lead to the sense of feeling understood, a key element in intimacy (North & Swann, 2011).

The process of self-verification seems readily understandable when a person's *positive* self-views are verified through exterior forces, such as good grades, positive feedback and personal relationships. Because people seek coherence, those with high self-esteem prefer positive feedback and gravitate toward those who see them in a positive light (North & Swann, 2011). However, there is an unexpectedly dark side to self-verification, in that people with low self-esteem are more comfortable with feedback and interpersonal relationships that verify their *negative* self-views (North & Swann, 2011). For instance,

> Swann and Pelham (2002) found that college students with negative self-views who had roommates who appraised them positively made plans to find a new roommate. In a similar way, married people with negative self-views became less intimate with partners who saw them in a more positive way than they saw themselves (e.g., Burke & Stets, 1999; De La Ronde & Swann, 1998…). (North & Swann, 2011: 466)

Moreover, low self-esteem students were anxious when receiving good grades that were inconsistent with their negative self-views, and they were more comfortable with failing grades (North & Swann, 2011). Thus, self-verification can be maladaptive for those with low self-esteem because it strengthens their already negative self-views. While North and Swann's ideas are very important, these researchers failed to remark that self-esteem and hence self-verification are domain specific. A person might have high self-esteem in one domain, such cooking, but low self-esteem in another domain, such as language learning. It would seem that for self-verification, self-esteem and self-concept, the salient feedback and relationships are the ones specifically associated with the domains of self that are of greatest importance to the individual at a given time.

12. Summary of Dimensional Hypotheses

In the sections above, I have presented a hypothesis for each of the dimensions of the EMPATHICS model. As shown in the Appendix, the EMPATHICS model is aimed at expanding prior positive psychology models, such as the PERMA model, so as to more realistically show the relationships among variables and to provide a fuller, richer picture. My hypotheses are summarized in Table 2.4 for quick reference.

The hypotheses are just that: hypotheses rather than definitive claims. For many dimensions there is research evidence showing a linkage with

Table 2.4 The hypotheses regarding the EMPATHICS dimensions

Dimension	*Hypotheses: Language learners with high well-being ...*
1	recognize their emotions, manage them effectively and show empathy for others
2	seek and create meaning, which helps them be motivated
3	persevere in their learning
4	embody agency and autonomy
5	appraise themselves temporally in a positive way and have a time perspective that fits their needs for learning
6	develop hardy attitudes and hardy action patterns and have useful habits of mind
7	recognize their own intelligences and take advantage of those intelligences for learning and living
8	have a range of character strengths that help them in their learning and their lives
9	possess self-efficacy, positive self-concepts and high self-esteem, and use self-verification positively

well-being, but more evidence and greater depth of explanation are needed. We must avoid inferring causality in the hypotheses. High well-being does not *cause* empathy to arise in a language learner, nor does empathy *cause* a language learner to experience high well-being. Nevertheless, the connections shown in the hypotheses are well worth studying.

We must be aware that positive psychology is not a panacea. In the next section I point out areas in which positive psychology appears to be lacking.

13. What Positive Psychology Might be Missing

Positive psychology offers a tremendous amount of value to the language learning field. Nevertheless, positive psychology seems to lack certain elements, possibly because it is such a young field. Below are some problems that I see in relation to building a psychology of well-being for language learners, in two key areas: first, there is often a lack of contextualization in positive psychology; and second, positive psychology frequently seems to avoid talking about cultures.

13.1. Lack of contextualization

- Many positive psychology investigations seem decontextualized, relying on questionnaires with insufficient background data reported on the participants or their environments. For example, although many studies involve college students, there is rarely any information about classroom contexts and the interactions between teachers and students in those contexts. Family influences and home contexts were not a serious aspect of the positive psychology studies I have encountered. Ushioda's (2009) person-in-context relational view, which was crafted for the language learning arena but has wider implications, is not present in positive psychology, nor is any other comparable approach.

- Not all positive psychologists have been thinking in terms of complex dynamic systems in which multicomponent factors change rapidly and interrelate intricately, non-linearly and organically within specific social contexts. Snyder's (2002) hope theory and Wehmeyer's model of functional self-determination (Wehmeyer *et al.*, 2011) have dynamic multicomponents but do not seem to include the context/environment as a key component of the system. In applying positive psychology to language learning, we would do well to 'adopt a dynamic perspective that allows us to consider simultaneously the ongoing multiple influences between environmental and learner factors in all their componential complexity, as well as the emerging changes in both the learner and the environment as a result of this development.... A truly dynamic systems approach will need to bridge [the] gap between the inner mental world of the individual *and the surrounding social environment*' (Dörnyei, 2009a: 244, emphasis added).
- Though positive psychology pays significant attention to self factors, such as self-concept and self-esteem, it pays little attention to identity in the post-structuralist sense of 'social, discursive, and narrative options offered by a particular society in a specific time and place to which individuals and groups of individuals appeal in an attempt to self-name, to self-characterize, and to claim social space and social prerogatives... . [In the post-structuralist framework], identity becomes interesting, relevant, and visible when it is contested or in crisis' (Pavlenko & Blackledge, 2004: 19). The deep contextualization of identity and the self (Norton, 2000, 2014; Pavlenko & Lantolf, 2000) is generally missing in positive psychology.

13.2. Avoidance of talking about cultures

- Positive psychologists often step gingerly around the topic of culture except in the broadest terms, such as collectivist (interdependent) and individualist (independent) (Markus & Kitayama, 1991; Triandis, 1995, 1996).
- Hewitt (2011) used a 'national culture' or 'country culture' approach as he discussed contradictory cultural values in the US that help shape ideas about self-esteem. The problem was that he focused strictly on

value contrasts within majority or mainstream US culture, without mentioning that some minority cultures in the same country might have drastically different values.

- Much discussion of character strengths presents those strengths as 'culture free' or universal (Pedrotti *et al.*, 2011: 50; Peterson, 2006). Character strengths studies sometimes involved participants from different contexts and cultures but focused on cultural commonalities without simultaneously considering cultural differences. In my experience, life and learning are not 'culture free' and cultural differences and similarities are both important to understand.
- The editors of *The Oxford Handbook of Positive Psychology* (Lopez & Snyder, 2011) included a separate chapter on culture (Pedrotti *et al.*, 2011), rather than ensuring that culture would be a natural, expected part of most or all of the chapters. The culture chapter noted some culture-related investigations of optimism, subjective well-being and self-construals, but I believe culture could be more routinely featured in positive psychology research and in any such handbook.
- Positive psychology does not appear to address the inextricable relationship between culture and language (see Kramsch, 1998).

14. Conclusion

The dimensions of EMPATHICS – (a) emotion and empathy, (b) meaning and motivation, (c) perseverance, (d) agency and autonomy, (e) time, (f) hardiness and habits of mind, (g) intelligences, (h) character strengths, and (i) the self factors of self-efficacy, self-concept, self-esteem and self-verification – interact in complex and dynamic ways, as shown by the many bold-print indications of interrelationships throughout the chapter. These relationships are non-linear, organic and holistic, and point to the probability of higher-level aggregations or constellations that deserve theorizing and research. Greater attention to context, culture and complex dynamic systems would make positive psychology a truly solid foundation for the development of a psychology of language learner well-being.

Even now, the research and theory reflected in the EMPATHICS dimensions comprise a beneficial heuristic to suggest the array of positive psychology factors involved in language learning. As noted above, EMPATHICS highlights many important elements, such as meaning, empathy, hope, optimism, time (in the sense of time perspective), hardiness, habits of mind, character strengths and self-verification, which have not been investigated in the language learning realm, along with resilience and intelligences, which have only lightly been touched. These factors urgently need the systematic attention of language learning theorists and researchers. EMPATHICS also reminds us that many factors, such as emotions, motivation, agency, autonomy, time (in the sense of past, present and future selves), self-efficacy, self-concept and self-esteem, are already well known in the language learning arena but deserve additional research, particularly regarding language learners of different age groups in a range of different settings.

Aspects of any program for theory development, research and practice related to language learner well-being would need to be prioritized, sequenced and coordinated among teams of language learning experts. To clarify some key theoretical linkages we would plan research studies investigating one or more amalgam(s)/constellation(s) of factors at the same time. For instance, we might explore this combination: (a) a perseverance component (probably hope or resilience); (b) hardiness, which is a cousin of perseverance; (c) future time perspective, which theoretically feeds into hope, resilience and hardiness; and, of course, (d) demographic and contextual factors. Measures are available for all of these, and in-depth narrative research is also possible on these themes. Depending on the breadth of the study, measures of agency and self-esteem might also be useful. Based on the subsequent research findings and the updated theory, we would then conduct teacher development sessions that would help teachers offer ongoing, well targeted language learner development on interrelated positive psychology topics. Specifically, the language learner sessions might cover how and why learners could improve their own perseverance, hardiness and time perspective (all of which would likely have a spill-over effect on agency and self-esteem, though those two dimensions might not be session topics for learners). We would, of course, evaluate the effectiveness of these sessions for teachers and learners. See Vaillant (2000) for adaptive mental mechanisms and Cohn and Fredrickson (2010) and Seligman (2011) for in-depth discussions of durable positive psychology interventions. My hope is that we would avoid the current shortcomings of positive psychology while taking advantage of the many magnificent ideas and opportunities that it affords.

Appendix: The Development of EMPATHICS to Reflect Well-Being in Language Learning

The acronym EMPATHICS is based partly on what I have learned in my quarter century of narrative research[5] on language learning (e.g. Kao & Oxford, 2014; Ma & Oxford, 2014; Oxford, 1996, 2011a, 2013, 2014; Oxford & Cuéllar, 2014; Oxford *et al.*, 1991, 1996, 1998, 2005, 2007, 2014), and it also reflects the work of many others. EMPATHICS was created after positive psychologist Martin Seligman's (2011) well-being theory, consisting of positive emotions, engagement, relationships, meaning and accomplishment (PERMA), did not fully satisfy my needs in analyzing language learner narratives.

Three of my 2014 studies (Oxford, 2014; Oxford & Cuéllar, 2014; Oxford *et al.*, 2014) used my adaptation of Seligman's (2011) PERMA model of well-being to help with the last stage of analysis of written learner narratives. In each study, the first few stages of analysis were guided by grounded theory to discern the basic explanatory themes or theories arising from the data (Corbin & Strauss, 2007; Strauss & Corbin, 1998). For all three studies, PERMA was used largely to determine the extent to which that acronym and the concepts embedded in it would help in analyzing well-being in language learners' lives. For these three studies, we found that it was necessary to modify PERMA to make it analytically useful.

Revisions of PERMA are as follows (see Oxford & Cuéllar, 2014, for further details). First, we identified a range of emotions, not just positive ones, in the narratives. Second, we linked the dimensions of engagement and meaning and reported instances of 'meaningful engagement', because it is clear that learners tend to become engaged with that which has meaning to them. Thus, it was unrealistic to view the PERMA dimensions as non-overlapping, despite Seligman's (2011) statements that the dimensions are independent. Third, we discussed human relationships in their sociocultural contexts, since no relationships occur in isolation. Finally, we did not analyze the learner narratives by means of the 24 character strengths (Peterson, 2006) that were mentioned by Seligman (2011) as underlying the PERMA model, because he did not explain or give empirical results showing how these strengths were related to each of the PERMA dimensions. With our revisions, PERMA became much more functional for analyzing well-being in learner narratives.

After using our revised PERMA model as an analytic tool in the three studies, I still had the nagging feeling that PERMA was missing some key elements, such as perseverance, agency and self-esteem. Based on my experience in analyzing learner narratives, and especially analyzing the recent ones, various explanatory dimensions of well-being in language learning arose in my mind. Ultimately nine dimensions, some with subdimensions, eventually organized themselves into EMPATHICS. My goal in creating EMPATHICS is to apply well-being theory to the complex dynamic system of language learning. EMPATHICS is intended as an honest, energetic first step for opening up discussion about a psychology of well-being for language learners. It was fortuitous that this particular set of dimensions – EMPATHICS – emerged, because empathy is an important aspect of dimension 1 of language learner well-being.

Notes

(1) Imagination is the theme connecting the concept of imagined or possible selves with the concept of imagined communities. When the latter concept came into the language learning field, imagined communities at first meant communities that immigrants hoped to enter but to which they did not have access (Norton, 2001), but it

later expanded to encompass a range of other envisioned language learning contexts beyond learners' immediate networks (Murray, 2011).

(2) Seemingly in the minority, Staats (1989) used the term 'wishes' in defining hope. For Staats, hope is 'the intersection between wishes and expectations' (p. 367). However, Vaillant (2008) argued that wishes are words and are therefore linked with the left brain hemisphere, while hope comprises images and is therefore associated with the right brain (p. 104).

(3) Contrast Vaillant (2008), who averred that hope involved mental images rather than words.

(4) I tend to call these 'metastrategies' rather than 'metacognitive strategies' because they guide the use of not only cognitive strategies but also affective and sociocultural-interactive strategies (Oxford, 2011b).

(5) The narrative turn in language learning research has picked up great momentum (see, e.g. Barkhuizen, 2011; Barkhuizen *et al.*, 2014; Kalaja *et al.*, 2008).

References

Andres, V.D. and Arnold, J. (2009) *Seeds of Confidence: Self-esteem Activities for the EFL Classroom.* Rum: Helbling Languages.

Arnold, J. (ed.) (1999) *Affect in Language Learning.* Cambridge: Cambridge University Press.

Arnold, J. and Murphey, T. (eds) (2013) *Meaningful Action: Earl Stevick's Influence on Language Teaching.* Cambridge: Cambridge University Press.

Averill, J.R., Catlin, G. and Chon, K. (1990) *Rules of Hope.* New York: Springer-Verlag.

Baltes, P.B. and Kunzmann, U. (2003) Wisdom: The peak of human excellence in the orchestration of mind and virtue. *The Psychologist* 16 (3), 131–133.

Bandura, A. (1997) *Self-efficacy: The Exercise of Control.* New York: Freeman.

Bandura, A. (2006) Toward a psychology of human agency. *Perspectives on Psychological Science* 1 (2), 164–180.

Barkhuizen , G. (2011) Narrative knowledging in TESOL. *TESOL Quarterly* 45 (3), 391–444.

Barkhuizen , G., Benson, P. and Chik, A. (2014) *Narrative Inquiry in Language Teaching and Learning.* New York: Routledge.

Bartone, P.T. (1996) Stress and hardiness in US peacekeeping soldiers. Paper presented at the Annual Convention of the American Psychological Association, Toronto, Canada, August.

Batson, C.D., Ahmad, N. and Lishner, D.A. (2011) Empathy and altruism. In S.J. Lopez and C.R. Snyder (eds) *The Oxford Handbook of Positive Psychology* (pp. 417–426). New York: Oxford University Press.

Benard, B. (1991) *Fostering Resiliency in Kids: Protective Factors in the Family, School, and Community.* San Francisco: Western Regional Center for Drug Free Schools and Communities, Far West Laboratory.

Benson, P. (2007) State-of-the-art article: Autonomy in language teaching and learning. *Language Teaching* 40, 21–40.

Benson, P. (2011) *Teaching and Researching Autonomy* (2nd edn). Harlow: Pearson Longman.

Benson, P. and Voller, P. (1997) *Autonomy and Independence in Language Learning.* London: Longman.

Berry, J.W., Poortinga, Y.H., Segall, M.H. and Dasen, P.R. (2002) *Cross-cultural Psychology: Research and Applications* (2nd edn). Cambridge: Cambridge University Press.

Boehm, J.K. and Lyubomirsky, S. (2011) The promise of sustainable happiness. In S.J. Lopez and C.R. Snyder (eds) *The Oxford Handbook of Positive Psychology* (pp. 667–677). New York: Oxford University Press.

Boniwell, I. (2011) Perspectives on time. In S.J. Lopez and C.R. Snyder (eds) *The Oxford Handbook of Positive Psychology* (pp. 295–302). New York: Oxford University Press.

Boniwell, I. and Zimbardo, P.G. (2004) Balancing time perspective in pursuit of optimal functioning. In P.A. Lindley and S. Joseph (eds) *Positive Psychology in Practice* (pp. 165–178). Hoboken, NJ: Wiley.

Boyd-Wilson, B.M., Walkey, F.H. and McClure, J. (2002) Present and correct: We kid ourselves less when we live in the moment. *Personality and Individual Differences* 33 (5), 691–702.

Branden, N. (1969) *The Psychology of Self-esteem.* New York: Bantam.

Branden, N. (1994) *The Six Pillars of Self-esteem.* New York: Bantam.

Breier-Williford, S. and Bramlett, R.D. (1995) Time perspective of substance abuse patients: Comparison of the scales in Stratford Time Perspective Inventory, Beck Depression Inventory and Beck Hopelessness Scale. *Psychological Reports* 77 (3), 899–905.

Breznitz, S. (1986) The effect of hope on coping with stress. In M.H. Appley and R. Trumbull (eds) *Dynamics of Stress: Physiological, Psychological, and Social Perspectives* (pp. 295–306). New York: Plenum.

Brown Kirschman, K.J., Johnson, R.J., Bender, J.A. and Roberts, M.C. (2011) Positive psychology for children and adolescents: Development, prevention, and promotion. In S.J. Lopez and C.R. Snyder (eds) *The Oxford Handbook of Positive Psychology* (pp. 133–148). New York: Oxford University Press.

Bruner, J. (1998) Narrative and metanarrative in the construction of self. In M.D. Ferrari and R.J. Sternberg (eds) *Self-awareness: Its Nature and Development* (pp. 308–331). New York: Guilford.

Bryant, F.B., Smart, C.M. and King, S.P. (2005) Using the past to enhance the present: Boosting happiness through positive reminiscence. *Journal of Happiness Studies* 6 (3), 227–260.

Burke, P.J. and Stets, J.E. (1999) Trust and commitment through self-verification. *Social Psychology Quarterly* 62 (4), 347–360.

Camus, A. (1983) *The Myth of Sisyphus and Other Essays.* New York: Knopf.

Carver, C.S. and Scheier, M.F. (1998) *On the Self-Regulation of Behavior*. New York: Cambridge University Press

Carver, C.S. and Scheier, M.F. (2003) Three human strengths. In L.G. Aspinwall and U.M. Staudinger (eds) *A Psychology of Human Strengths: Fundamental Questions and Future Directions for a Positive Psychology* (pp. 87–102). Washington, DC: American Psychological Association.

Carver, C.S. and Scheier, M.F. (2012) *Perspectives on Personality* (7th edn). Boston, MA: Pearson.

Carver, C.S., Scheier, M.F. and Segerstrom, S.C. (2010) Optimism. *Clinical Psychology Review* 30, 879–889.

Carver, C.S., Scheier, M.F., Miller, C.J. and Fulford, D. (2011) Optimism. In S.J. Lopez and C.R.Snyder (eds) *The Oxford Handbook of Positive Psychology* (pp. 303–311). New York: Oxford University Press.

Chamot, A.U. (2004) Issues in language learning research and teaching. *Electronic Journal of Foreign Language Teaching* 1 (1), 14–26.

Chamot, A.U. (2007) Accelerating academic achievement of English language learners: A synthesis of five evaluations of the CALLA model. In J. Cummins and C. Davidson (eds) *The International Handbook of English Language Learning, Part 1* (pp. 317–331). Norwell, MA: Springer.

Chamot, A.U., Barnhardt, S., El-Dinary, P. and Robbins, J. (1996) Methods for teaching learning strategies in the foreign language classroom. In R.L. Oxford (ed.) *Language Learning Strategies Around the World: Cross-cultural Perspectives* (pp. 175–188). Manoa, HI: University of Hawaii Press.

Chartrand, T.L. and Cheng, C.M. (2002) The role of nonconscious goal pursuit in hope. *Psychological Inquiry* 13 (4), 290–294.

Clarke, D. (2003) Faith and hope. *Australian Psychiatry* 11 (2), 164–168.

Cohen, A.D. (2011) *Strategies in Learning and Using a Second Language* (2nd edn). London: Longman.

Cohen, A.D. and Weaver, S. (2006) *Styles- and Strategies-Based Instruction: A Teachers' Guide.* Minneapolis, MN: Center for Advanced Research on Language Acquisition, University of Minnesota.

Cohn, M.A. and Fredrickson, B.L. (2010) In search of durable positive psychology interventions: Predictors and consequences of long-term positive behavior change. *Journal of Positive Psychology* 5 (5), 355–366.

Cohn, M.A. and Frederickson, B.L. (2011) Positive emotions. In S.J. Lopez and C.R. Snyder (eds) *The Oxford Handbook of Positive Psychology* (pp. 13–24). New York: Oxford University Press.

Collins, A. (1988) *Cognitive Apprenticeship and Instructional Technology.* Technical Report No. 6899. Cambridge, MA: BBN Laboratories.

Cooper, M. (2003) *Existential Therapies.* Thousand Oaks, CA: Sage.

Coopersmith, S. (1967) *The Antecedents of Self-esteem.* San Francisco: Freeman.

Corbin, J. and Strauss, A. (2007) *Basics of Qualitative Research* (3rd edn). Thousand Oaks, CA: Sage.

Costa, A.L. and Kallick, B. (2008) *Learning and Leading with Habits of Mind: 16 Essential Characteristics for Success.* Alexandria, VA: Association for Supervision and Curriculum Development.

Csikszentmihalyi, M. (2008) *Flow: The Psychology of Optimal Experience* (2nd edn). New York: Harper.

Damasio, A. (1994) *Descartes' Error: Emotion, Reason, and the Human Brain.* New York: Penguin Putnam.

Deci, E.L. and Ryan, R.M. (1985) *Intrinsic Motivation and Self-determination in Human Behavior.* New York: Plenum.

Deci, E.L. and Ryan, R.M. (1991) A motivational approach to self: Integration in personality. In R. Dienstbier (ed.) *Nebraska Symposium on Motivation*, Vol. 38 (pp. 237–288). Lincoln, NE: University of Nebraska Press.

Deci, E.L. and Ryan, R.M. (2000) The 'what' and 'why' of goal pursuits: Human needs and the self-determination of behavior. *Psychological Inquiry* 11 (4), 227–268.

De La Ronde, C. and Swann, W.B., Jr (1998) Partner verification: Restoring shattered images of our intimates. *Journal of Personality and Social Psychology* 75 (2), 374–382.

Dewaele, J-M. (2010) *Emotions in Multiple Languages.* Basingstoke: Palgrave Macmillan.

Dewaele, J-M. (2013) Emotions and language learning. In M. Byram and A. Hu (eds) *Routledge Encyclopedia of Language Teaching and Learning* (2nd edn) (pp. 217–220). London: Routledge.

Dewaele, J-M. and MacIntyre, P. (2014) Two faces of Janus? Anxiety and enjoyment in the foreign language classroom. In P. MacIntyre and T. Gregersen (eds) *Positive Psychology in SLA* (special issue, *Second Language Learning and Teaching*), 237–274.

Dewaele, J-M., Petrides, K.V. and Furnham, A. (2008) The effects of trait emotional intelligence and sociobiographical variables on communicative anxiety and foreign language anxiety among adult multilinguals: A review and empirical investigation. *Language Learning* 58 (4), 911–960.

Dickinson, L. (1987) *Self-instruction in Language Learning.* Cambridge: Cambridge University Press.

Diener, E. (2011) Positive psychology: Past, present, and future. In S.J. Lopez and C.R. Snyder (eds) *The Oxford Handbook of Positive Psychology* (pp. 7–11). New York: Oxford University Press.

Dörnyei, Z. (2005) *The Psychology of the Language Learner.* Hillsdale, NJ: Erlbaum.

Dörnyei, Z. (2009a) Individual differences: Interplay of learner characteristics and learning environment. *Language Learning* 59 (Suppl. 1), 230–248.
Dörnyei, Z. (2009b) The L2 motivational self system. In Z. Dörnyei and E. Ushioda (eds) *Motivation, Language Identity and the L2 Self* (pp. 9–42). Bristol: Multilingual Matters.
Dörnyei, Z. (2009c) *The Psychology of Second Language Acquisition.* New York: Oxford University Press.
Eliot, T.S. (1971) Burnt Norton. In T.S. Eliot, *Four Quartets* (pp. 13–22). Orlando: Harcourt.
Epstein, S. (1985) The implications of cognitive-experiential self-theory for research in social psychology and personality. *Journal for the Theory of Social Behavior* 15 (3), 283–309.
Erikson, M.G. (2007) The meaning of the future: Toward a more specific definition of possible selves. *Review of General Psychology* 11 (4), 348–358.
Esch, E. (2006) Clash or crash? Autonomy ten years on. In R. Pemberton, S. Toogood and A. Barfield (eds) *Maintaining Control: Autonomy and Language Learning.* Hong Kong: Hong Kong University Press.
Farmer, R. (1994) The limits of learner independence in Hong Kong. In D. Gardner and L. Miller (eds) *Directions in Self-access Language Learning* (pp. 13–28). Hong Kong: Hong Kong University Press.
Farmer, R. and Sweeney, E. (1994) Self-access in Hong Kong: A square peg in a round hole? *Occasional Papers in Language Teaching 4* (pp. 24–30). Hong Kong: ELT Unit, Chinese University of Hong Kong.
Feldman, D.B. and Snyder, C.R. (2000) The State Hope Scale. In J. Maltby, C.A. Lewis and A. Hill (eds) *A Handbook of Psychological Tests*, Vol. 1 (pp. 240–245). Lampeter: Edwin Mellen.
Fonseca Mora, M.C. and Toscano Fuentes, C. (2007) Fostering teenagers' willingness to learn a foreign language. In F.D. Rubio (ed.) *Self-esteem and Foreign Language Learning* (pp. 91–104). Newcastle: Cambridge Scholars Publishing.
Frankl, V.E. (1984) *Man's Search for Meaning: An Introduction to Logotherapy.* Trans. I. Lasch. Boston, MA: Beacon.
Frederickson, B.L. (2001) The role of positive emotions in positive psychology: The broaden-and-build theory of positive emotions. *American Psychologist* 56 (3), 218–226.
Frederickson, B.L. (2003) The value of positive emotions: The emerging science of positive psychology looks into why it's good to feel good. *American Scientist* 91 (4), 330–335.
Frederickson, B.L. (2004) The broaden-and-build theory of positive emotions. *Philosophical Transactions of the Royal Society of London (Biological Sciences)* 359, 1367–1377.
Frederickson, B.L. and Branigan, C. (2005) Positive emotions broaden the scope of attention and thought–action repertoires. *Cognition and Emotion* 19 (3), 313–332.
Frederickson, B.L. and Joiner, T. (2002) Positive emotions trigger upward spirals toward emotional well-being. *Psychological Science* 13 (2), 172–175.
Frederickson, B.L. and Levenson, R.W. (1998) Positive emotions speed recovery from the cardiovascular sequelae of negative emotions. *Cognition and Emotion* 12 (2), 191–220.
Frederickson, B.L., Tugade, M.M., Waugh, C.E. and Larkin, G. (2003) What good are positive emotions in crises? A prospective study of resilience and emotions following the terrorist attacks on the United States on September 11, 2001. *Journal of Personality and Social Psychology* 84 (2), 365–376.
Freire, P. (2000) *Pedagogy of the Oppressed.* Trans. M.B. Ramos. New York: Bloomsbury.
Gao, X. and Zhang, L.J. (2011) Joining forces for synergy: Agency and metacognition as interrelated theoretical perspectives on learner autonomy. In G. Murray, X. Gao and T. Lamb (eds) *Identity, Motivation and Autonomy in Language Learning* (pp. 25–41). Bristol: Multilingual Matters.
Gardner, H. (1983) *Frames of Mind: The Theory of Multiple Intelligences.* New York: Basic Books.
Gardner, H. (1991) Assessment in context: The alternative to standardized testing. In

B.R. Gifford and M.C. O'Connor (eds) *Changing Assessments: Alternative Views of Aptitude, Achievement, and Instruction* (pp. 77–120). Boston, MA: Kluwer.

Gardner, H. (1993) *Multiple Intelligences: The Theory in Practice.* New York: Basic Books.

Gardner, H. (1998) A reply to Perry D. Klein's 'Multiplying the problems of intelligence by eight'. *Canadian Journal of Education* 23 (1), 96–102.

Gardner, H. (1999) *Intelligence Reframed: Multiple Intelligences for the 21st Century*. New York: Basic Books.

Gardner, H. (2004) *Changing Minds: The Art and Science of Changing Our Own and Other People's Minds*. Cambridge, MA: Harvard Business School Press.

Gardner, H. (2011) The theory of multiple intelligences. In R.J. Sternberg and B. Kaufman (eds) *The Cambridge Handbook of Intelligence* (pp. 485–503). Cambridge: Cambridge University Press.

Gardner, R.C. (2001) Language learning motivation: The student, the teacher, and the researcher. *Texas Papers in Foreign Language Education* 6 (1), 1–18.

Goleman, D. (2005) *Emotional Intelligence: Why It Can Matter More Than IQ* (2nd edn). New York: Bantam.

Gregersen, T. and MacIntyre, P.D. (2014) *Capitalizing on Language Learners' Individuality*. Bristol: Multilingual Matters.

Griffiths, C. (2013) *The Strategy Factor in Successful Language Learning.* Bristol: Multilingual Matters.

Griffiths, C. and Oxford, R.L. (2014) The twenty-first century landscape of language learning strategies: Introduction to this special issue. In R.L. Oxford and C. Griffiths (eds) *Language Learning Strategy Research in the Twenty-First Century* (special issue, *System: International Journal of Educational Technology and Applied Linguistics*) 43, 1–10.

Guiora, A.Z. (1983) Introduction: An epistemology for the language sciences. *Language Learning* 33 (1), 6–11.

Gunning, P. and Oxford, R.L. (2014) Children's learning strategy use and the effects of strategy instruction on success in learning ESL in Canada. *System* 43, 82–100.

Harper, D. (2013) Inspire, inspiration. Retrieved from http://www.etymonline.com/index.php?allowed_in_frame=0&search=inspire&searchmode=none (accessed November 2015).

Harter, S. (1999) *The Construction of the Self: A Developmental Perspective.* New York: Guilford.

Heine, S.J., Proulx, T. and Vohs, K.D. (2006) The meaning maintenance model: On the coherence of social motivations. *Personality and Social Psychology Review* 10 (2), 88–110.

Herman D. (2009) *Basic Elements of Narrative.* New York: Blackwell.

Hewitt, J.P. (2011) The social construction of self-esteem. In S.J. Lopez and C.R. Snyder (eds) *The Oxford Handbook of Positive Psychology* (pp. 217–224). New York: Oxford University Press.

Higgins, E.T. (1987) Self-discrepancy: A theory relating self and affect. *Psychological Review* 94 (3), 319–340.

Holec, H. (1981) *Autonomy in Foreign Language Learning.* Strasbourg: Council of Europe.

Holliday, A. (2003) Social autonomy: Addressing the dangers of culturism in TESOL. In D. Palfreyman and R.C. Smith (eds) *Learner Autonomy Across Cultures: Language Education Perspectives* (pp. 110–128). London: Palgrave Macmillan.

Horwitz, E. (2001) Language anxiety and achievement. *Annual Review of Applied Linguistics* 21, 112–126.

Horwitz, E. (2007) Words fail me: Foreign language anxiety crippling for some students. E. Horwitz interviewed by K. Randall. University of Texas at Austin feature story. Retrieved from http://www.utexas.edu/features/2007/language (accessed November 2015).

Horwitz, E. and Young, D.J. (eds) (1991) *Language Anxiety: From Theory and Research to Classroom Implications.* Englewood Cliffs, NJ: Prentice Hall.

James, W. (1987) *Writings 1902–1910* (2nd edn). New York: Library of America.

Kalaja, P., Menenzes, V. and Barcelos, A. (eds) (2008) *Narratives of Learning and Teaching EFL*. Houndsmills: Palgrave Macmillan.

Kao, T-A. and Oxford, R.L. (2014) Learning language through music: A strategy for building inspiration and motivation. In R.L. Oxford and C. Griffiths (eds) *Language Learning Strategy Research in the Twenty-First Century* (special issue, *System: International Journal of Educational Technology and Applied Linguistics*, 43), 114–120.

Keltner, D. (2009) *Born to be Good: The Science of a Meaningful Life*. New York: Norton.

Keyes, C.L.M. (2011) Toward a science of mental health. In S.J. Lopez and C.R. Snyder (eds) *The Oxford Handbook of Positive Psychology* (pp. 89–95). New York: Oxford University Press.

Kobasa, S.C. (1979) Stressful life events, personality, and health: An inquiry into hardiness. *Journal of Personality and Social Psychology* 37 (1), 1–11.

Kobasa, S.C. and Maddi, S.R. (1977) Existential personality theory. In R. Corsini (ed.) *Existential Personality Theories* (pp. 243–276). Itasca, IL: Peacock.

Kramsch, C. (1998) *Culture and Language*. Oxford: Oxford University Press.

Kristjánsson, C. (2013) Epilogue: A way with words – perspectives on the contributions and influence of Earl W. Stevick. In J. Arnold and T. Murphey (eds) *Meaningful Action: Earl Stevick's Influence on Language Teaching* (pp. 304–311). Cambridge: Cambridge University Press.

Lantolf, J.P. and Pavlenko A. (2001) (S)econd (L)anguage (A)ctivity theory: Understanding second language learners as people. In M.P. Breen (ed.) *Learner Contributions to Language Learning* (pp. 141–158). London: Longman.

Lantolf, J.P. and Thorne, S.L. (2006) *Sociocultural Theory and the Genesis of Second Language Development*. Oxford: Oxford University Press.

Lau, I.C., Yeung, A.S., Jin, J. and Low, R. (1999) Toward a hierarchical, multidimensional English self-concept. *Journal of Educational Psychology* 91 (4), 747–755.

Lave, J. and Wenger, E. (1991) *Situated Learning: Legitimate Peripheral Participation*. Cambridge: Cambridge University Press.

Lazarus, R.S. (1999) Hope: An emotion and a vital coping resource against despair. *Social Research* 66, 653–678.

Le Doux, J. (1998) *The Emotional Brain: The Mysterious Underpinnings of Emotional Life*. New York: Simon & Schuster.

Lewis, M. (2005) Bridging emotion theory and neurobiology through dynamic systems modeling. *Behavior and Brain Science* 28 (2), 169–245.

Linley, P.A., Joseph, S., Maltby, J., Harrington, S. and Wood, A.M. (2011) Positive psychology applications. In S.J. Lopez and C.R. Snyder (eds) *The Oxford Handbook of Positive Psychology* (pp. 35–47). New York: Oxford University Press.

Little, D. (1999) Learner autonomy is more than a Western cultural construct. In S. Cotterall and D. Crabbe (eds) *Learner Autonomy in Language Learning: Defining the Field and Effecting Change* (pp. 11–18). Frankfurt am Main: Lang.

Little, D. (2000) Learner autonomy: Why foreign languages should occupy a central role in the curriculum. In S. Green (ed.) *New Perspectives on Teaching and Learning Modern Languages* (pp. 24–45). Clevedon: Multilingual Matters.

Little, D. (2007) Language learner autonomy: Some fundamental considerations revisited. *Innovation in Language Teaching and Learning* 1 (1), 14–29.

Little, T.D., Hawley, P.H., Henrich, C.C. and Marsland, K. (2002) Three views of the agentic self: A developmental synthesis. In E.L. Deci and R.M. Ryan (eds) *Handbook of Self-determination Research* (pp. 389–404). Rochester, NY: University of Rochester Press.

Lopez, S.J. and Gallagher, M.W. (2011) A case for positive psychology. In S.J. Lopez and C.R. Snyder (eds) *The Oxford Handbook of Positive Psychology* (pp. 3–6). New York: Oxford University Press.

Lopez, S.J. and Snyder, C.R. (eds) (2011) *The Oxford Handbook of Positive Psychology*. New York: Oxford University Press.

Luthar, S., Cicchetti, D. and Becker, B. (2000) The construct of resilience: A critical evaluation and guidelines for future research. *Child Development* 71 (3), 543–562.

Luthar, S., Sawyer, J.A. and Brown, P.J. (2006) Conceptual issues in studies of resilience: Past, present, and future research. In B.M. Lester, A.S. Masten and B. McEwen (eds) *Annals of the New York Academy of Sciences, Vol. 1094: Resilience in Children* (pp. 105–115). Malden, MA: Blackwell.

Lyubomirsky, S. and Nolen-Hoeksema, S. (1995) Effects of self-focused rumination on negative thinking and interpersonal problem solving. *Journal of Personality and Social Psychology* 69 (1), 176–190.

Ma, R. and Oxford, R.L. (2014) A diary study focusing on listening and speaking: The evolving interaction of learning styles and learning strategies in a motivated, advanced ESL learner. In R.L. Oxford and C. Griffiths (eds) *Language Learning Strategy Research in the Twenty-First Century* (special issue, *System: International Journal of Educational Technology and Applied Linguistics*, 43), 101–113.

MacIntyre, P.D. (2002) Motivation, anxiety, and emotion in second language acquisition. In P. Robinson (ed.) *Individual Differences and Instructed Language Learning* (pp. 45–68). Amsterdam: John Benjamins.

MacIntyre, P.D. and Mercer, S. (2014) Introducing positive psychology to SLA. *Studies in Second Language Learning and Teaching* 4, 153–172.

MacIntyre, P.D., Clément, R., Dörnyei, Z. and Noels, K. (1998) Conceptualizing willingness to communicate in an L2: A situational model of L2 confidence and affiliation. *Modern Language Journal* 84 (2), 545–562.

MacIntyre, P.D., Mackinnon, S.P. and Clément, R. (2009) The baby, the bathwater, and the future of language learning motivation research. In Z. Dörnyei and E. Ushioda (eds) *Motivation, Language Identity and the L2 Self* (pp. 43–65). Bristol: Multilingual Matters.

Maddi, S.R. (2002) The story of hardiness: Twenty years of theorizing, research, and practice. *Consulting Psychology Journal* 54 (3), 173–185.

Maddi, S.R. (2004) Hardiness: An operationalization of existential courage. *Journal of Humanistic Psychology* 44 (3), 279–298.

Maddi, S.R. (2006) Hardiness: The courage to grow from stresses. *Journal of Positive Psychology* 1 (3), 160–168.

Maddi, S.R. and Kobasa, S. (1984) *The Hardy Executive: Health Under Stress*. Homewood, IL: Dow Jones-Irwin.

Maddux, J.E. (2011) Self-efficacy: The power of believing you can. In S.J. Lopez and C.R. Snyder, *The Oxford Handbook of Positive Psychology* (pp. 335–343). New York: Oxford University Press.

Marcel, G. (1962) *Introduction to a Metaphysic of Hope*. Trans. E. Craufurd. New York: Harper & Row. Original work published in 1944.

Marcos-Llinas, M. and Juan Garau, M. (2009) Effects of language anxiety on three proficiency-level courses of Spanish as a foreign language. *Foreign Language Annals* 42 (1), 94–111.

Markus, H. and Kitayama, S. (1991) Culture and the self: Implications for cognition, emotion, and motivation. *Psychological Review* 98 (2), 224–253.

Markus, H. and Nurius, P. (1986) Possible selves. *American Psychologist* 41 (9), 954–969.

Martel, Y. (2011) *Beatrice and Virgil: A Novel*. New York: Spiegel & Grau.

Maslow, A.H. (1962) *Toward a Psychology of Being*. Princeton, NJ: Van Nostrand.

Maslow, A.H. (1968) *Toward a Psychology of Being* (2nd edn). New York: Van Nostrand.

Maslow, A.H. (1970) *Motivation and Personality* (revised edn). New York: Harper & Row.

Maslow, A.H. (1971) *The Farther Reaches of Human Nature*. New York: Penguin Compass.

Masten, A.S. and Obradovic, J. (2006) Competence and resilience in development. In B.M. Lester, A.S. Masten and B. McEwen (eds) *Annals of the New York Academy of Sciences, Vol. 1094: Resilience in Children* (pp. 1–12). Malden, MA: Blackwell.

Masten, A.S., Cutuli, J.J, Herbers, J.E. and Reed, M-G.J. (2011) Resilience in development. In S.J. Lopez and C.R. Snyder (eds) *The Oxford Handbook of Positive Psychology* (pp. 117–131). New York: Oxford University Press.

McAdams, D.P. (1993) *Stories We Live By*. New York: HarperCollins.

McAdams, D.P. (2005) Studying lives in time: A narrative approach. In R. Levy, P. Ghisletta, J. Le Goff, D. Spini and E. Widmer (eds) *Advances In Life Course Research, Vol. 10: Towards an Interdisciplinary Perspective on the Life Course* (pp. 237–258). Amsterdam: Elsevier.

McCroskey, J.C. and Richmond, V.P. (1990) Willingness to communicate: A cognitive view. *Journal of Social Behavior and Personality* 5 (2), 19–37.

McDermott, D. and Snyder, C.R. (2000) *The Great Big Book of Hope: Help Your Children Achieve Their Dreams*. Oakland, CA: New Harbinger.

McIntosh, C.N. and Noels, K.A. (2004) Self-determined motivation for language learning: The role of need for cognition and language learning strategies. *Zeitschrift für Interkulturellen Fremdsprachenunterricht* 9 (2), 1–28.

Menezes, V. (2008) Multimedia language learning histories. In P. Kalaja, V. Menezes and A.M.F. Barcelos (eds) *Narratives of Learning and Teaching EFL* (pp. 199–213). London: Palgrave Macmillan.

Menninger, K. (1959) The academic lecture: Hope. *American Journal of Psychiatry* 116, 481–491.

Mercer, S. (2011a) The self as a complex dynamic system. *Studies in Second Language Learning and Teaching* 1 (1), 57–82.

Mercer, S. (2011b) *Towards an Understanding of Language Learner Self-concept*. Dordtrecht: Springer.

Michael, S.T. (2000) Hope conquers fear: Overcoming anxiety and panic attacks. In C.R. Snyder (ed.) *Handbook of Hope: Theory, Measures, and Applications* (pp. 355–378). San Diego, CA: Academic.

Moskowitz, G. (1978) *Caring and Sharing in the Foreign Language Class: A Sourcebook on Humanistic Techniques*. Boston, MA: Heinle & Heinle.

Mruk, C.J. (2006) *Self-esteem Research, Theory, and Practice: Toward a Positive Psychology of Self-esteem* (3rd edn). New York: Springer.

Murray, G. (2011) Imagination, metacognition, and the L2 self in a self-access learning environment. In G. Murray, X. Gao and T. Lamb (eds) *Identity, Motivation and Autonomy in Language Learning* (pp. 75–106). Bristol: Multilingual Matters.

Murray, G. (ed.) (2014) *Social Dimensions of Autonomy in Language Learning*. London: Palgrave Macmillan.

Murray, G., Gao, X. and Lamb, T. (eds) (2011) *Identity, Motivation and Autonomy in Language Learning*. Bristol: Multilingual Matters.

Myers, D.G. (2009) *Social Psychology* (10th edn). New York: McGraw-Hill Higher Education.

Nakamura, J. and Csikszentmihalyi, M. (2011) Flow theory and research. In S.J. Lopez and C.R. Snyder (eds) *The Oxford Handbook of Positive Psychology* (pp. 195–206). New York: Oxford University Press.

Noels, K.A., Clément, R. and Pelletier, L.G. (1999) Perceptions of teacher communicative style and students' intrinsic and extrinsic motivation. *Modern Language Journal* 83 (1), 23–34.

North, R.J. and Swann, W.B., Jr (2011) What's positive about self-verification? In S.J. Lopez and C.R. Snyder (eds) *The Oxford Handbook of Positive Psychology* (pp. 465–474). New York: Oxford University Press.

Norton, B. (2000) *Identity and Language Learning: Gender, Ethnicity, and Educational Change* (1st edn). London: Pearson/Longman.

Norton, B. (2001) Non-participation, imagined communities and the language classroom. In M.P. Breen (ed.) *Learner Contributions to Language Learning: New Directions in Research* (pp. 159–171). Harlow: Longman.

Norton, B. (2014) Identity and poststructuralist theory in SLA. In S. Mercer and M. Williams (eds) *Multiple Perspectives on the Self in SLA* (pp. 59–74). Bristol: Multilingual Matters.

Nunan, D. (1997) Designing and adapting materials to encourage learner autonomy. In P. Benson and P. Voller (eds) *Autonomy and Independence in Language Learning* (pp. 192–203). London: Longman.

Oxford, R.L. (1990) *Language Learning Strategies: What Every Teacher Should Know.* Boston: Heinle.

Oxford, R.L. (1996) When emotion meets (meta)cognition in language learning histories. In A. Moeller (ed.) *The Teaching of Culture and Language in the Second Language Classroom: Focus on the Learner* (special issue, *International Journal of Educational Research*, 23 (7)), 581–594.

Oxford, R.L. (2003) Toward a more systematic model of second language learner autonomy. In D. Palfreyman and R. Smith (eds) *Learner Autonomy Across Cultures* (pp. 75–91). London: Palgrave Macmillan.

Oxford, R.L. (2008) Hero with a thousand faces: Learner autonomy, learning strategies, and learning tactics in independent language learning. In S. Hurd and T. Lewis (eds) *Language Learning Strategies in Independent Settings* (pp. 41–63). Bristol: Multilingual Matters.

Oxford, R.L. (2011a) Meaning-making, border crossings, complexity, and new interpretive techniques: Expanding our understanding of learner narratives. *Zeitschrift für Fremdsprachenforschung (Journal of Foreign Language Research)* 22 (2), 221–241.

Oxford, R.L. (2011b) *Teaching and Researching Language Learning Strategies*. Harlow: Pearson Longman.

Oxford, R.L. (2013) Understanding language learner narratives. In J. Arnold and T. Murphey (eds) *Meaningful Action: Earl Stevick's Influence on Language Teaching* (pp. 95–110). Cambridge: Cambridge University Press.

Oxford, R.L. (2014) What we can learn about strategies, language learning, and life from two extreme cases. *Studies in Second Language Learning and Teaching* 4 (4), 593–615.

Oxford, R.L. (2015a) Expanded perspectives on autonomous learners. *Innovations in Language Learning and Teaching* 9 (1), 58–71.

Oxford, R.L. (2015b) How language learners can improve their emotional functioning: Important psychological and psychospiritual theories. *Applied Language Learning* 25 (1/2), 1–15.

Oxford, R.L. and Cuéllar, L. (2014) Positive psychology in cross-cultural narratives: Mexican students discover themselves while learning Chinese. *Studies in Second Language Learning and Teaching* 4 (2), 173–203.

Oxford, R.L., Ehrman, M.E. and Lavine, R.Z. (1991) Style wars: Teacher–student style conflicts in the language classroom. In S.S. Magnan (ed.) *Challenges for the 1990s for College Language Programs* (pp. 1–25). Boston, MA: Heinle/Thomson Learning.

Oxford, R.L., Lavine, R.Z., Felkins, G., Hollaway, M.E. and Saleh, A. (1996) Telling their stories: Language students use diaries and recollection. In R.L. Oxford (ed.) *Language Learning Strategies Around the World: Cross-Cultural Perspectives* (pp. 19–34). Honolulu, HI: University of Hawaii, Second Language Teaching and Curriculum Center.

Oxford, R.L., Tomlinson, S., Barcelos, A., Harrington, C., Lavine, R., Saleh, A. and Longhini, A. (1998) Clashing metaphors about classroom teachers: Toward a systematic typology for the language teaching field. *System: An International Journal of Educational Technology and Applied Linguistics* 26 (1), 3–51.

Oxford, R.L., Massey, K.R. and Anand, S. (2005) Transforming teacher–student style relationships: Toward a more welcoming and diverse classroom discourse. In C.

Holten and J. Frodesen (eds) *The Power of Context in Language Teaching and Learning* (pp. 249–266). Boston: Heinle & Heinle.
Oxford, R.L., Meng, Y., Zhou, Y., Sung, J. and Jain, R. (2007) Uses of adversity: Moving beyond L2 learning crises. In A. Barfield and S. Brown (eds) *Reconstructing Autonomy in Language Education: Inquiry and Innovation* (pp. 131–142). London: Palgrave Macmillan.
Oxford, R.L., Pacheco Acuña, G., Solís Hernández, M. and Smith, A.L. (2014) Positive psychology in action: Social and psychological themes reflected in first-person learner histories of bilingual adults. Paper presented at the International Conference on Language and Social Psychology, Honolulu, Hawaii, 21 June.
Pavlenko, A. (2006) Bilingual selves. In A. Pavlenko (ed.) *Bilingual Minds: Emotional Experience, Expression and Representation* (pp. 1–33). Clevedon: Multilingual Matters.
Pavlenko, A. and Blackledge, A. (2004) Introduction: New theoretical approaches to the study of negotiation and identities in multilingual contexts. In A. Pavlenko and A. Blackledge (eds) *Negotiation of Identities in Multilingual Contexts* (pp. 1–33). Clevedon: Multilingual Matters.
Pavlenko, A. and Lantolf, J. (2000) Second language learning as participation and the (re) construction of selves. In J.P. Lantolf (ed.) *Sociocultural Theory and Second Language Learning* (pp. 155–177). New York: Oxford University Press.
Pedrotti, J.T., Lopez, S.J. and Krieshok, T. (2008) Making hope happen: A program for fostering strengths in adolescents. Unpublished manuscript.
Pedrotti, J.T., Edwards, L.M. and Lopez, S.J. (2011) Positive psychology within a cultural context. In S.J. Lopez and C.R. Snyder (eds) *Oxford Handbook of Positive Psychology* (pp. 49–57). New York: Oxford University Press.
Pennycook, A. (1997) Cultural alternatives and autonomy. In P. Benson and P. Voller (eds) *Autonomy and Independence in Language Learning* (pp. 35–53). London: Longman.
Pennycook, A. (2001) *Critical Applied Linguistics: A Critical Introduction.* Mahwah, NJ: Erlbaum.
Perseverance (2015) *Merriam-Webster Dictionary.* http://www.merriam-webster.com/dictionary/perseverance (accessed November 2015).
Peterson, C. (2006) *A Primer in Positive Psychology.* New York: Oxford University Press.
Peterson, C. and Park, N. (2011) Classifying and measuring strengths of character. In S.J. Lopez and C.R. Snyder (eds) *Oxford Handbook of Positive Psychology* (pp. 25–33). New York: Oxford University Press.
Peterson, C. and Seligman, M.E.P. (2004) *Character Strengths and Virtues: A Handbook and Classification.* New York: Oxford University Press.
Peterson, C. and Steen, T.A. (2011) Optimistic explanatory style. In S.J. Lopez and C.R. Snyder (eds) *The Oxford Handbook of Positive Psychology* (pp. 313–321). New York: Oxford University Press.
Peterson, C., Seligman, M.E.P. and Vaillant, G.E. (1988) Pessimistic explanatory style is a risk factor for physical illness: A thirty-five-year longitudinal study. *Journal of Personality and Social Psychology* 55 (1), 23–27.
Piaget, J. (1981) *Intelligence and Affectivity: Their Relationship During Child Development.* Palo Alto, CA: Annual Reviews.
Pierson, H.D. (1996) Learner culture and learner autonomy in the Hong Kong Chinese context. In R. Pemberton, E.L. Li, W.W.F. Or and H.D. Pierson (eds) *Taking Control: Autonomy in Language Learning* (pp. 49–58). Hong Kong, Special Administrative Region: Hong Kong University Press.
Piller, I. and Takahashi, K. (2006) A passion for English: Desire and the language market. In A. Pavlenko (ed.) *Bilingual Minds: Emotional Experience, Expression and Representation* (pp. 59–83). Clevedon: Multilingual Matters.
Pintrich, P.R., Marx, R.W. and Boyle, R.A. (1993) Beyond cold conceptual change: The role of motivational beliefs and contextual factors in the process of contextual change. *Review of Educational Research* 63 (2), 167–199.

Polkinghorne, D.E. (1988) *Narrative Knowing and the Human Sciences.* Albany, NY: SUNY Press.

Porter Abbott H. (2002) *The Cambridge Introduction to Narrative*. Cambridge: Cambridge University Press.

Rand, K.L. and Cheavens, J.S. (2011) Hope theory. In S.J. Lopez and C.R. Snyder (eds) *The Oxford Handbook of Positive Psychology* (pp. 323–333). New York: Oxford University Press.

Reasoner, R. (1982) *Building Self-esteem: A Comprehensive Program.* Palo Alto, CA: Consulting Psychologists Press.

Ricard, M. (2003) *Happiness: A Guide to Developing Life's Most Important Skill.* Trans. J. Browner. New York: Little, Brown.

Rogers, C. (1961) *On Becoming a Person: A Therapist's View of Psychotherapy.* New York: Houghton Mifflin.

Rosenberg, M. (1965) *Society and Adolescent Self-image.* Princeton, NJ: Princeton University Press.

Ross, M. and Wilson, A.E. (2002) It feels like yesterday: Self-esteem, valence of personal past experiences, and judgments of subjective distance. *Journal of Personality and Social Psychology* 82 (5), 792–803.

Rothbart, M. (2007) Temperament, development, and personality. *Current Directions in Psychological Science* 16 (4), 207–212.

Rubio, F.D. (2007) Self-esteem and foreign language learning: An introduction. In F.D. Rubio (ed.) *Self-esteem and Foreign Language Learning* (pp. 2–12). Newcastle: Cambridge Scholars Publishing.

Rubio, F.D. (2014) Self-esteem and self-concept in foreign language learning. In S. Mercer and M. Williams (eds) *Multiple Perspectives on the Self in SLA* (pp. 41–58). Bristol: Multilingual Matters.

Ryan, R.M. and Deci, E.L. (2001) Self-determination theory and the facilitation of intrinsic motivation, social development, and well-being. *American Psychologist* 55 (1), 68–78.

Ryan, S. and Irie, K. (2014) Imagined and possible selves: Stories we tell about ourselves. In S. Mercer and M. Williams (eds) *Multiple Perspectives on the Self in SLA* (pp. 109–126). Bristol: Multilingual Matters.

Salovey, P., Mayer, J.D., Caruso, D. and Yoo, S.H. (2011) The positive psychology of emotional intelligence. In S.J. Lopez and C.R. Snyder (eds) *The Oxford Handbook of Positive Psychology* (pp. 237–248). New York: Oxford University Press.

Sartre, J-P. (1984) *Being and Nothingness.* Trans. H.E. Barnes. London: Routledge.

Schrank, B., Stanghellini, G. and Stade, M. (2008) Hope in psychiatry: A review of the literature. *Acta Psychiatrica Scandinavica* 118 (6), 421–433.

Schrank, B., Hayward, M., Stanghellini, G. and Davidson, L. (2011) Hope in psychiatry. *Advances in Psychiatric Treatment* 17 (3), 227–235.

Schumann, J. (1997) *The Neurobiology of Affect in Language.* Oxford: Blackwell.

Schunk, D.H. and Ertmer, P.A. (2000) Self-regulation and academic learning: Self-efficacy enhancing interventions. In M. Boekaerts, P.R. Pintrich and M. Zeidner (eds) *Handbook of Self-regulation* (pp. 631–650). San Diego, CA: Academic Press.

Seligman, M.E.P. (1991) *Learned Optimism.* New York: Alfred A. Knopf.

Seligman, M.E.P. (2006) *Learned Optimism: How to Change Your Mind and Your Life.* New York: Vintage.

Seligman, M.E.P. (2011) *Flourish: A Visionary New Understanding of Happiness and Well-being.* New York: Atria/Simon & Schuster.

Seligman, M.E.P., Reivich, K., Jaycox, L. and Gillham, J. (1995) *The Optimistic Child.* Boston, MA: Houghton-Mifflin.

Shogren, K.A., Lopez, S.J., Wehmeyer, M.L., Little, T.D. and Pressgrove, C.L. (2006) The role of positive psychology constructs in predicting life satisfaction in adolescents with and without cognitive disabilities: An exploratory study. *Journal of Positive Psychology* 1 (1), 37–52.

Sigelman, C.K. and Rider, E.A. (2012) *Life-Span Human Development* (7th edn). Belmont, CA: Wadsworth.
Silo [Rodríguez Cobos, M.L.] (2006) *Apuntes de psicología [Psychology Notes]*. Mendoza, Argentina: Universal Humanism. Retrieved from http://www.silo.net/collected_works/psychology_notes; also http://www.silo.net/system/documents/89/original/Apuntes_en.pdf (accessed November 2015).
Singleton, D. and Lengyel, Z. (1995) *The Age Factor in Second Language Acquisition: A Critical Look at the Critical Period Hypothesis.* Clevedon: Multilingual Matters.
Snyder, C.R. (1994) *The Psychology of Hope: You Can Get There From Here.* New York: Free Press.
Snyder, C.R. (2000) Hypothesis: There is no hope. In C.R. Snyder (ed.) *Handbook of Hope: Theory, Measures, and Applications* (pp. 3–21). San Diego, CA: Academic.
Snyder, C.R. (2002) Hope theory: Rainbows in the mind. *Psychological Inquiry* 13 (4), 249–275.
Snyder, C.R., Harris, C., Anderson, J.R., Holleran, S.A., Irving, L.M., Sigmon, S.T. *et al.* (1991) The will and the ways: Development and evaluation of an individual-differences measure of hope. *Journal of Personality and Social Psychology* 60, 570–585.
Snyder, C.R., Hoza, B., Pelham, W.E., Rapoff, M., Ware, L., Danovsky, M. *et al.* (1997) The development and validation of the Children's Hope Scale. *Journal of Pediatric Psychology* 22 (3), 399–421.
Snyder, C.R., Lapointe, A.B., Crowson, J.J., Jr and Early, S. (1998) Preferences of high- and low-hope people for self-referential input. *Cognition and Emotion* 12 (16), 807–823.
Snyder, C.R., Sympson, S.C., Michael, S.T. and Cheavens, J. (2000) The optimism and hope constructs: Variants on a positive expectancy theme. In E.C. Chang (ed.) *Optimism and Pessimism* (pp. 103–124). Washington, DC: American Psychological Association.
Snyder, C.R., Rand, K.L. and Sigmon, D.R. (2002a) Hope theory: A member of the positive Psychology family. In C.R. Snyder and S.J. Lopez (eds) *Handbook of Positive Psychology* (pp. 231–243). New York: Oxford University Press.
Snyder, C.R., Sheorey, H.S., Cheavens, J., Pulvers, K.M., Adams, V.H., III and Wiklund, C. (2002b) Hope and academic success in college. *Journal of Educational Psychology* 94 (4), 820–826.
Snyder, C.R., Lopez, S.J. and Pedrotti, J.T. (2011) *Positive Psychology: The Scientific and Practical Exploration of Human Strengths.* Thousand Oaks, CA: Sage.
Staats, S. (1989) Hope: A comparison of two self-report measures for adults. *Journal of Personality Assessment* 53 (2), 366–375.
Steger, M.F. (2011) Meaning in life. In S.J. Lopez and C.R. Snyder (eds) *Oxford Handbook of Positive Psychology* (pp. 679–687). New York: Oxford University Press.
Sternberg, R.J. (1985) *Beyond IQ: A Triarchic Theory of Intelligence.* Cambridge: Cambridge University Press.
Sternberg, R.J. (1997) A triarchic view of giftedness: Theory and practice. In N. Coleangelo and G.A. Davis (eds) *Handbook of Gifted Education* (pp. 43–53). Boston, MA: Allyn & Bacon.
Stevick, E. (1976) *Memory, Meaning, and Method.* Rowley, MA: Newbury House.
Stevick, E. (1980) *Teaching Languages: A Way and Ways.* Rowley, MA: Newbury House.
Stevick, E. (1990) *Humanism in Language Teaching.* New York: Oxford University Press.
Strauss, A. and Corbin, J. (1998) *Basics of Qualitative Research: Techniques and Procedures for Developing Grounded Theory* (2nd edn). Thousand Oaks, CA: Sage.
Swann, W.B., Jr and Pelham, B. (2002) Who wants out when the going gets good? Psychological investment and preference for self-verifying college roommates. *Self and Identity* 1 (3), 219–233.
Tiger, L. (1979) *Optimism: The Biology of Hope.* New York: Simon & Schuster.
Triandis, H.C. (1995) *Individualism and Collectivism.* Boulder, CO: Westview Press.

Triandis, H.C. (1996) The psychological measurement of cultural syndromes. *American Psychologist* 51 (4), 407–415.

Truebridge, S. (2014) *Resilience Begins With Beliefs: Building on Student Strengths for Success in School.* New York: Teachers College Press.

University of Missouri at Kansas City (2013) Making hope happen: Shane Lopez says hope is key to realizing goals. *UMKC Today*, 21 March. Retrieved from http://info.umkc.edu/news/making-hope-happen (accessed November 2015).

Ushioda, E. (2008) Motivation and good language learners. In C. Griffiths (ed.) *Lessons From Good Language Learners* (pp. 19–34). Cambridge: Cambridge University Press.

Ushioda, E. (2009) A person-in-context relational view of emergent motivation and identity. In Z. Dörnyei and E. Ushioda (eds) *Motivation, Language Identity and the L2 Self* (pp. 215–228). Bristol: Multilingual Matters.

Vaid, J. (2006) Joking across languages: Perspectives on humor, emotion, and bilingualism. In A. Pavlenko (ed.) *Bilingual Minds: Emotional Experience, Expression and Representation* (pp. 152–182). Clevedon: Multilingual Matters.

Vaillant, G.E. (2000) Adaptive mental mechanisms: Their role in a positive psychology. *American Psychologist* 55 (1), 89–98.

Vaillant, G.E. (2008) *Spiritual Evolution: How We Are Wired for Faith, Hope, and Love.* New York: Broadway Books.

van Deurzen, E. (2012) *Existential Counselling and Psychotherapy in Practice* (3rd edn). London: Sage.

van Lier, L. (2004) *The Ecology and Semiotics of Language Learning: A Sociocultural Perspective.* Dortrecht: Kluwer.

VIA Institute (2014) VIA classification of character strengths. Retrieved from http://www.viacharacter.org/www/Character-Strengths/VIA-Classification (accessed 30 November 2015).

Vygotsky, L.V. (1978) *Mind in Society.* Cambridge, MA: Harvard University Press.

Vygotsky, L.V. (1981) The genesis of higher mental functions. In J. Wertsch (ed.) *The Concept of Activity in Soviet Psychology* (pp. 144–188). Armonk, NY: Sharpe.

Waugh, C.E., Tugade, M.M. and Fredrickson, B.L. (2008) Psychophysiology of stress and resilience. In B. Lukey and V. Tepe (eds) *Biobehavioral Resilience to Stress* (pp. 117–138). Boca Raton, FL: CRC Press.

Wehmeyer, M.L. (1996) Self-determination as an educational outcome: Why is it important to children, youth, and adults with disabilities? In D.J. Sands and M.L. Wehmeyer (eds) *Self-determination Across the Lifespan: Independence and Choice for People with Disabilities* (pp. 15–34). Baltimore, MD: Paul H. Brookes.

Wehmeyer, M.L. (2001) Self-determination and mental retardation. In L.M. Glidden (ed.) *International Review of Research in Mental Retardation*, Vol. 24 (pp. 1–48). San Diego, CA: Academic Press.

Wehmeyer, M.L. (2005) Self-determination and individuals with severe disabilities: Reexamining meanings and misinterpretations. *Research and Practice in Severe Disabilities* 30, 113–120.

Wehmeyer, M.L. and Mithaug, D. (2006) Self-determination, causal agency, and mental retardation. In H. Switsky (ed.) *International Review of Research in Mental Retardation*, Vol. 31 (pp. 31–71). San Diego, CA: Academic Press.

Wehmeyer, M.L., Little, T.D. and Sergeant, J. (2011) Self-determination. In S.J. Lopez and C.R. Snyder (eds) *The Oxford Handbook of Positive Psychology* (pp. 357–366). New York: Oxford University Press.

Wenger, E. (1998) *Communities of Practice: Learning, Meaning, and Identity.* Cambridge: Cambridge University Press.

Werner, E. and Smith, R. (1992) *Overcoming the Odds: High-risk Children from Birth to Adulthood.* Ithaca, NY: Cornell University Press.

White, R. (1963) Ego and reality in psychoanalytic theory: A proposal regarding independent ego energies. *Psychological Issues* 3, 125–150.

Williams, S.L. (1995) Self-efficacy, anxiety, and phobic disorders. In J.E. Maddux (ed.) *Self-efficacy, Adaptation, and Adjustment: Theory, Research, and Application* (pp. 69–107). New York: Plenum.

Wilson, A.E. and Ross, M. (2001) From chump to champ: People's appraisals of their earlier and present selves. *Journal of Personality and Social Psychology* 80 (4), 572–584.

Wilson, A.E., Buehler, R., Lawford, H., Schmidt, C. and Yong, A.G. (2012) Basking in projected glory: The role of subjective temporal distance in future self-appraisal. *European Journal of Social Psychology* 42 (3), 342–353.

Wrobleski, K.K. and Snyder, C.R. (2005) Hopeful thinking in older adults: Back to the future. *Experimental Aging Research* 31, 217–233.

Yalom, I. (1989) *Love's Executioner and Other Tales of Psychotherapy*. New York: Basic Books.

Yeung, A.S. and Wong, E.K. (2004) Domain specificity of trilingual teachers' verbal self-concepts. *Journal of Educational Psychology* 96 (2), 360–368.

Zimbardo, P.G. (2002) Just think about it: Time to take our time. *Psychology Today* 35, 62.

Zimmerman, B.J. (2000) Attaining self-regulation: A social cognitive perspective. In M. Boekaerts, P.R. Pintrich and M. Zeidner (eds) *Handbook of Self-regulation* (pp. 13–39). San Diego, CA: Academic Press.

Part 1
Theoretical

3 Seeing the World Through Your Eyes: Empathy in Language Learning and Teaching

Sarah Mercer

My third piece of advice is to cultivate a sense of empathy – to put yourself in other people's shoes – to see the world from their eyes. Empathy is a quality of character that can change the world.
Barack Obama

Introduction

One of the most notable features of the modern world is our interconnectedness as human beings. More than ever before, we are linked to others across the globe socially and professionally. For language learners and educators, this interconnected world has transformed the nature of our opportunities for connecting and learning with and from others. It has literally opened our eyes and minds to a whole new wider world. However, making the most of these possibilities depends crucially on our ability to form effective, positive, collaborative relationships with others in both the real and virtual worlds. The key to meaningful high-quality interpersonal relationships is our capacity to empathise with others.

In this chapter, I wish to explore the role of empathy for language teaching and learning, highlighting its significance for teachers, learners and researchers. I begin by explaining what empathy is and how it can be positioned in respect to the positive psychology literature. I then consider areas in education and SLA more specifically in which I propose empathy could play an especially vital role given the centrality of relationships, social interaction, communication and intercultural competence in language learning and use. The chapter concludes with suggestions of how we could enhance empathy in practice as well as possible future directions for research in this area within the field of SLA.

What is Empathy?

We are social, relational beings

At its core, empathy is about how humans relate to one another. It is about how we seek to understand the minds and emotions of others and how we develop our relationships with other people. It is a core skill, which we need 'to make sense of behaviour and relate to others effectively' (Howe, 2013: 9). In recent years, there has been a considerable growth of interest in looking at humans as situated social beings, with a focus on relationships to people and settings. Specifically in SLA, we have witnessed the 'social turn' (Block, 2003), which has drawn attention to the ways in which learning and teaching are inherently socially situated processes. Studies from such sociocultural perspectives have typically examined how individuals relate to both the contexts in which they learn as well as the people they learn and use the language with.

Fields beyond SLA have also begun to highlight the importance and significance of relationships, including the relatively new area of social neuroscience. Research in this field tends to explore neural and social processes together and is linked to established disciplines such as social psychology. In social neuroscience, scholars start out from the premise that humans are fundamentally social beings who succeed by forming relationships with others to create emergent social groups (Cacioppo *et al.*, 2010). The survival and success of these groups depends on their social and collaborative behaviours. Indeed, this unique capacity for social understanding and cooperation has been proposed as one of the key reasons for the success of humans as a species (Lieberman, 2013). The theory behind this is what is known as the 'social brain hypothesis', which proposes that human intelligence did not evolve just in order to cope with ecological demands but, given the complexity of the world, human cognition actually evolved in ways which promoted social interaction and the importance of cooperation (Dunbar, 1998). Fundamentally, the thinking is that, as humans, we are neurally 'wired to be social' (Lieberman, 2013: ix) and it is in our human nature to seek out connections and interactions with others. In particular, 'we are naturally curious about what is going on in the minds of other people' (Lieberman, 2013: ix).

The 'mentalizing system' in the brain (Lieberman, 2013: 120), also known in some cases as the 'theory-of-mind' network, suggests that our brain is pre-programmed to see the world in terms of others and their mental states. We are reported to 'mentalize' about others and make educated guesses about what someone else is thinking and feeling hundreds of times per day as a regular part of our social interactional behaviour (Lieberman, 2013: 120). Crucially, 'mentalizing' not only allows us to imagine what someone is thinking or feeling at the precise moment we engage with them, but it also enables us to make the imaginative leap and consider how they might react to an event in the future, even to reflect on how they might react if certain circumstances were to change (Lieberman, 2013: 130). This human capacity for 'mindreading' is impressive but also highly complex, requiring an array of mental processes and skills, which led Lieberman (2013: 160) to conclude that 'empathy is arguably the pinnacle of our social cognitive achievements – the peak of the social brain'.

A key role in our capacity for empathy in the brain has been assigned to mirror neurons, which help us to imitate others but also potentially help us to read other people's emotions and thoughts. For example, when we look at another person's facial expression, the muscles in our own face become activated too, through mirror neurons, so that our face imitates the perceived expression of the other. In turn, these muscles send signals to our internal organs which stimulate physical states similar to those being experienced by the person we are seeing (Cozolino, 2013: 147). In other words, what we recognise as the emotions felt by others resonates in our entire emotional network. While there remains debate about the nature of the automaticity of these processes, an important point is that although we may share emotions with somebody, this does not automatically make us empathic. 'Empathy is not merely the consequence of the passive observation of emotional cues but it is subject to contextual appraisal and modulation' (de Vignemont & Singer, 2006: 437). This suggests that although we may be able to feel with another, other components, including some conscious cognitive processing, are necessary for this to translate from shared emotions to actual empathy.

A definition of empathy

Empathy is a complex construct surrounded by a plethora of related terms employed differently across a wide range of disciplines. Exploring the etymology of the word and its link to the German term *Einfühlung*, Howe (2013: 9) offers a rich but compact definition that highlights some of the key characteristics. He explains it as follows:

> *em*pathy, meaning 'into feeling' or 'feeling into'. The idea of getting 'into' a feeling is particularly important, particularly when we see and *feel* the world from the other's point of view, attempt to understand it, and seek to convey that understanding as we relate with those around us. (Original emphasis)

As De Waal (2009: 65) points out, the original German term foregrounds the idea of movement – 'of one individual projecting him- or herself into another'.

In order to feel empathy for somebody else, it is necessary to appreciate the nature of their minds and emotions. To this end, scholars have proposed the 'theory of mind', which is concerned with our awareness that others have minds too. It represents the idea that we are able to recognise that others have minds full of thoughts, feelings, desires, goals and beliefs, just as we have (see, e.g. Frith & Frith, 2005; Mitchell, 2011). It is the understanding that other people are complex mental beings in the same way as we are and have their own set of mental experiences separate to our own (de Vignemont & Singer, 2006). Naturally, this capacity to attribute mental states to others and use them to make inferences and interpretations about their behaviours is a key ingredient in our capacity to empathise. However, although the two concepts of theory of mind and empathy have sometimes been used synonymously, they are in fact distinct processes, with the first contributing to the latter (Singer, 2006).

In recent years, definitions of empathy have become more nuanced and the general consensus appears to suggest that it has three main components: affective empathy, cognitive empathy and an element often referred to as empathetic concern, although this last component is sometimes also conceptualised in terms of compassion or sympathy. For example, the third element for Howe (2013: 14) involves communication, as he argues that empathy requires us to communicate with compassion the fact that we have recognised and understood the other person's emotional experience. Thus, based on Davis (1994), Howe (2013: 14) defines empathy 'as an affective reaction to the emotions of another; the cognitive act of adopting another's perspective; a cognitively based understanding of other people; and the communication of such an understanding'. Krznaric (2014: 9) also distinguishes between the cognitive component as 'perspective taking' and the affective component as the 'shared emotional response' and suggests that both must be combined to serve as a drive for action. As Krznaric (2014: x) defines it, 'empathy is the art of stepping imaginatively into the shoes of another person, understanding their feelings and perspectives, and using that understanding to guide your actions'. De Vignemont and Singer (2006: 435) also emphasise the multiple components of empathy by explaining that merely cognitively taking somebody else's perspective does not fulfil the affective dimension of empathy and both the affective and cognitive component are needed together to classify as empathy. In their work in neuroscience, they suggest specifically that empathy involves observation, reflection and then action in relation to the perceptions of another's emotions (de Vignemont & Singer, 2006). Crucially, their work emphasises that empathy is not merely an automatic response to emotional cues but rather emerges from appraisal processes that follow observation, and can include and be influenced by conscious reflection, then possibly leading to action.

A related and important distinction needs to be made between empathy and sympathy. Howe (2013: 12) captures the difference beautifully when he writes, 'empathy puts me in your emotional shoes, sympathy simply tells you that I've walked there too'. In other words, sympathy differs from empathy as it does not require you to share the same emotions. You can feel sorry for someone because they are sad but you do not feel sad yourself. Further, empathy and sympathy are not automatically connected to acts of kindness (de Waal, 2009: 45). Instead, Cooper (2013: 23) makes the point that empathy need not be used for positive purposes and who benefits from empathic behaviours is perhaps a vital criterion to understand. She uses the example of the car salesperson who may consciously use empathic skills to manipulate customers for their own selfish gain, as opposed to someone who employs their empathy to understand and be of benefit to another. This dimension of empathy has also led to discussions in the literature about how a lack of certain facets of empathy and ability to imagine another's emotions, feelings and pain can often be found as a characteristic of sociopaths and psychopaths (see, e.g. Blair, 2005; Cooper, 2013).

On the whole, empathy is accepted as being a fundamental human characteristic, although de Waal (2009) convincingly shows how animals can have this capacity too. Gordon (2009: 32) argues that 'nature is on our side in creating strong, empathic societies. We are born with the capacity for empathy. An ability to recognize emotions transcends race, culture, nationality, social class, and age'. However, there are also individual differences in our capacities to empathise. It would seem that some people are better empathisers than others and there is a suggestion that differences in mirror neuron activity could account for some of these differences (Howe, 2013: 53). As with most personality traits, there is believed to be a blend of context and biological predisposition in our empathic capabilities – a mixture of nature and nurture (Howe, 2013: 63). A controversial question in this respect concerns the popular belief that males are less empathic than females and, at present, research hosts a variety of opinions about this (see, e.g. Christov-Moore *et al.*, 2014). One suggestion from studies conducted by Baron-Cohen and his colleagues (e.g. Baron-Cohen *et al.*, 2005) is that males and females differ in what they focus their attention on, rather than their inherent capacity for empathy. Males are believed to generally be more curious and focused on systems, whereas women tend to show more interest in emotions and other people. In reality, empathy appears to develop from a blend of biological differences and our unique personal social experiences (Howe, 2013: 31). This contextual developmental perspective also implies that a person has to have experienced and received empathy before they themselves can empathise with another. In educational contexts, this requires us to understand that those who often require the most empathy are those who have perhaps experienced it the least in their own lives (Howe, 2013). Further, it suggests that such learners who have had little experience with empathy may themselves find it difficult to empathise with others (Cooper, 2013). As teachers, it implies that we need to foster empathy in our pupils by serving as a role model in our behaviours, allowing learners to feel the positive effects of empathy so that they in turn are enabled to empathise with others.

Empathy in Positive Psychology

In positive psychology, there is a strong emphasis on the value of positive relationships for our well-being. Indeed, Peterson's (2006: 249) three-word summary of positive psychology is: 'Other people matter'. Relationships serve some of our basic human needs, such as our need to belong, to feel loved and understood, and to be supported socially (see, e.g. Lyubomirsky, 2010; Seligman, 2011). Two of the core pillars of Seligman's PERMA acronym are 'positive emotion' and 'relationships' (see the Appendix to Chapter 2 of the present volume) and, indeed, he goes as far as to say that 'very little that is positive is solitary' (Seligman, 2011: 20), highlighting the relational nature of human experience. One of the leading psychologists in the positive psychology movement, Barbara Fredrickson, and her team have conducted research which shows that being able to interact with others through positive social connections can lead to improved emotions and ultimately better health (Kok *et al.*, 2013). Their research is based on the hypothesis that 'positive emotions in turn promote perceived positive social connections, which in turn promote improved physical health' (Kok *et al.*, 2013: 3), suggesting a broaden-and-build positive upward spiral and thus the beneficial nature of positive relationships. Naturally, the underlying foundation of the ability to support and nurture positive relationships and facilitate understanding between individuals is having empathy for others.

Within positive psychology, empathy could be seen as having an additional function alongside its core role in positive relationships. The concept of 'meaning' in the fourth pillar of the PERMA acronym refers to serving a cause greater than ourselves that in some way furthers humanity and for this, too, it could be argued that empathy is a key ingredient in our ability to imagine with compassion how others feel, potentially others who lead lives remote and very different to our own (Cohen, 2009). Through empathic concern for others, we may be more willing to engage in charitable, pro-social behaviours driven by our empathy (cognitive, affective and compassionate) for the difficulties and situations of others (Howe, 2013; Krznaric, 2014). Indeed, for Krznaric (2014: xxii), this is perhaps the key contribution of empathy to society, which he argues has the potential to serve 'as a powerful tool that can both create radical social change, and give greater depth and meaning to our lives'. However, as de Vignemont and Singer (2006: 440) argue, affective empathy alone will not suffice for charitable action: to motivate pro-social behaviour, empathy must also include a sympathy or empathic concern element.

Empathy in Education

In education, there has been a wide recognition of the central role to be played by empathy and the importance of positive relationships for successful learning (e.g. Cozolino, 2013). Gordon (2009: 194) succinctly captures the centrality of the relationships we form with our learners as individuals, when she writes, 'to teach children, we must first reach them'. In other words, we must relate with and connect to our learners as people before we can hope to teach them anything. However, a word of caution is perhaps necessary so as not to create the impression here of overstating the case for empathy. While empathy does indeed represent a key competence for building positive relationships in the classroom, it alone is not sufficient for effective teaching and, naturally, other didactic and pedagogical skills and expertise are also necessary (Arnold, 2005). Underhill (2013: 204) proposes that teacher expertise has three main components; 'knowledge of the topic, skill with classroom methods and competence with inter- and intrapersonal relationships and the psychological learning atmosphere of the group'. He highlights the importance of the socio-emotional skills of teachers and the importance of their sensitivities towards the relational aspects of classroom life. As many others do, he draws attention to the work of Carl Rogers (Rogers & Freiberg, 1994), who suggested that the core qualities of a facilitator to enable learning include genuineness, non-judgemental regard and empathy (Underhill, 2013: 205).

Perhaps one of the areas of education that has most obviously benefited from an increased research focus on empathy has been bullying. O'Grady (2013) argues that bullying and empathy exist as polar opposites. Being able to take another person's perspective and notice commonalities between us and another, no matter how different they may at first seem, is central to empathetic behaviours and a vital skill necessary to reduce bullying. One of the most notable school programmes working towards promoting empathy among school children has been Mary Gordon's 'Roots of Empathy' programme. In this educational intervention, a baby is introduced to the classroom and, through prompted guided reflections and interactions with the baby, the children are encouraged to think about the nature of humanity, people, their feelings and emotional development. 'The program puts relationships at the centre of what creates a civil society' (Gordon, 2009: 6). The programme, started in Canada, has shown significant effects in reducing levels of aggression among school children while raising social/emotional competence and increasing empathy. The empirical studies conducted on the programme specifically show a reduction in 'proactive aggression' (associated with overt bullying) as well as 'relational or social aggression' (associated with covert bullying and other exclusionary behaviours) (Gordon, 2009: 169; Schonert-Reichl & Scott, 2009). As Gordon

(2009: 7) explains, 'Teaching children emotional literacy and developing their capacity to take the perspective of others are key steps towards collaboration and civility; they are indispensable steps towards preventing aggressive and bullying behaviours'.

Another area in which empathy has been considered to have a lot of positive potential is intercultural communication. Nowadays, teachers increasingly find themselves working in multiethnic and multicultural classrooms. This means not only that teachers must be able to empathise and interact appropriately, with understanding and respect for diversity, but also that pupils have to develop this competence too. Once again, research has shown that empathy can play a key role in promoting intercultural competence. Rasoal *et al.* (2011: 2) claim that, 'empathy can reduce intolerance, conflicts and discrimination, and increase understanding, respect and tolerance between people with similar as well as different ethnic and cultural backgrounds'. Daniel Goleman also states that empathy

> leads to caring, altruism, and compassion. Seeing things from another's perspective breaks down biased stereotypes, and so breeds tolerance and an acceptance of differences. These capacities are ever more called on in our increasingly pluralistic society, allowing people to live together in mutual respect and creating the possibility of productive discourse. (Goleman, 1996: 285)

In all classrooms, positive relationships among learners and positive group dynamics have been shown to be vital for successful learning. However, these are perhaps particularly important in contemporary language classrooms, in which communicative language teaching and learner-centred approaches tend to involve an increased use of group and pair work. In this respect, Dörnyei and Murphey (2003: 1) argue that 'group dynamics is probably one of the most – if not *the* most – useful subdisciplines in the social sciences for language teachers' (original emphasis). There are many dimensions that can contribute to positive group dynamics and effective learning and one of the most significant is the rapport developed between students and teacher, as well as among students (Frisby & Martin, 2010). As Harmer (2007: 113–114) explains, 'we might be the most well-prepared and knowledgeable teachers in our school, but if that interaction [between teacher and students] isn't working well, our ability to help students will be seriously compromised'. Naturally, rapport requires people to build sensitive, thoughtful, positive personal relationships, for which empathy would be a key ingredient. In language classrooms, this rapport can be especially important, given the need for a safe and secure environment in which learners feel confident and comfortable to be willing to speak up and use the foreign language. A recent approach aiming to promote an understanding of other peers' perspectives and how to work well together has been proposed by Murphey *et al.* (2014), who recommend getting learners to reflect on their ideal classroom peers and then consider to what extent they themselves fulfil these criteria for others. They found that imagining their ideal selves in relation to others helped the learners to be more helpful and resourceful for each other, thereby generating better group dynamics and a more effective cooperative learning atmosphere.

Indeed, one particular classroom format, which depends on positive relationships and healthy group rapport, is cooperative and collaborative learning models. Research suggests these formats can enhance relationships, motivation, positive attitudes towards learning and learner self-esteem, and promote higher-order thinking (Ehrman & Dörnyei, 1998: 245). Interestingly, cooperative learning structures not only require empathy in order to function well, but they have also been shown to lead to improved and enhanced interpersonal and empathic skills, suggesting that empathy is both an important ingredient and a beneficial outcome of such working structures (Ehrman & Dörnyei, 1998).

Empathy in Language Learning and Teaching

Although empathy plays a central role in education generally, there are certain key characteristics of the domain of language learning which suggest a specific relevance of empathy for our field. Research into the role of empathy in language learning is not entirely new, although it remains scarce. More than 40 years ago, Guiora *et al.* (1975: 48) argued that 'to speak a second language authentically is to take on a new identity. As with empathy, it is to step into a new and perhaps unfamiliar pair of shoes'. Guiora and colleagues' research looked specifically at the relationship between empathy and pronunciation. They found that higher levels of empathy suggest a better ability to imitate a native speaker's pronunciation (Guiora *et al.*, 1972) and, indeed, there have been several other studies which have also examined the role of empathy in learners' L2 pronunciation aptitude (e.g. Dewaele & Wei, 2012; Ozanska-Ponikwia & Dewaele, 2012; Rota & Reiterer, 2009).

Fundamentally, to use a language or to learn one requires communication and interaction with others. It is through language that we are able to share our thoughts, feelings, hopes and desires with others. Language also helps us to create bonds and form meaningful relationships with other people. As Byrnes (2013: 225) says, 'meaning-making with language is inherently social and involves another'. A central goal of many contemporary language classrooms is communicative competence. The aim is to help our learners use the language to communicate effectively with others. In this process, seeking to understand the mind of the person you are communicating with can greatly assist communication, whether you are listening or reading, or actively seeking to communicate a message through speech or writing. Ultimately, communication is about understanding how another person might interpret or misinterpret an act of communication and requires you to put yourself into the mind of the other to some degree (see also Lieberman, 2013: 287).

A key facet of communicative competence is sociocultural competence (for instance according to the Common European Framework of Reference), and empathy has an important role to play in promoting this competence, given that it can facilitate 'the ability to view one's own culture from the viewpoint of outsiders' (McAlinden, 2014: 72). Indeed, Calloway-Thomas *et al.* (1996; cited in Samovar *et al.*, 2010: 341) go so far as to claim that 'empathy is the bedrock of intercultural communication'. McAlinden (2014: 74) argues that the prefix *inter* in 'intercultural communication' highlights the relational nature of communication *between* two people.

A form of empathy that is more specifically conceived is 'cultural empathy' or 'ethnocultural empathy' (Rasoal *et al.*, 2011; Wang *et al.*, 2003). While the focus remains on empathy and all its key characteristics, the use of these terms specifies the relationship of empathiser and other as being between people of different cultures (Rasoal *et al.*, 2011: 7). Rasoal *et al.* (2011: 8) define ethnocultural empathy as 'feeling, understanding, and caring about what someone from another culture feels, understands and cares about'. Often, intercultural work focuses on insights and empathy with a specific culture. Wang *et al.* (2003) argue that we cannot think of people as independent of their contexts but understanding another person necessitates an understanding of their contexts and worlds as well as an awareness of our own, given our socially embedded nature as humans. Here there is an expectation that cultural empathy requires and is facilitated by an understanding and possible practical experiences with or in a specific other culture. However, it is possible that teachers and learners may not have had much experience of being in other cultures than their own. Furthermore, in the case of English as a foreign language, it is increasingly likely that interlocutors will be using English internationally as a lingua franca and thus none of the people involved in the interaction may be from cultures the others know anything about. In this case, a more general approach to empathy across cultures is required, which explores general concepts of culture and cultural awareness, and which Moran (2001: 110) terms 'a cultural-general understanding'. The focus in such an approach on learning is not about a specific culture per se but rather about understanding generic dimensions and features of culture. Typically, individuals become aware of their own perspectives and through awareness-raising become sensitised to the cultural facets of their own behaviours and that of others. Both critical reflection and self-awareness can facilitate empathic relationships. In work on intercultural competence, there are often tasks that involve reflecting on one's self through writing one's cultural autobiography or reflecting on personal discussion questions or critical experiences, to come to an awareness of one's self as a 'cultural being' (Moran, 2001: 98). This self-awareness is believed to be a prerequisite for empathising more fully with another cultural perspective. Moran (2001: 118) argues that this personal competence of being self-aware and mindful transcends or informs all the other competences involved in language learning, such as linguistic, communicative, cultural and intercultural competences.

My own approach to intercultural competence has been strongly influenced by my belief in the importance of interpersonal relationships and our shared humanity. I am wary of approaches that appear to essentialise cultures and focus on difference, taking contrastive perspectives and concentrating on 'problems' of intercultural communication. Instead, there is research that suggests that it might be especially useful and helpful to focus on exploring similarities between cultures (see, e.g. Moran, 2001; Rasoal *et al.*, 2011). Hoffman (2000: 294–295) has argued that 'seeing that people in other cultures have similar worries and respond emotionally as we do to important life events [...] should contribute to a sense of oneness and empathy across cultures'. We might therefore build on empathy to explore cultural similarities and examine positive intercultural experiences in order to further enhance our own and our learners' intercultural competence.

Empathy in Practice

An important consideration for practice in discussions of empathy concerns the extent to which empathy is dynamic and can be deliberately improved. Firstly, empathy has been shown to be dynamic across time and place. Research has revealed that moods and tiredness can affect our ability to be empathic at particular moments in time, but also that teachers with profound empathic skills tend to have a dynamic mental model of others, which 'evolves and fluctuates on a momentary and daily basis, revising its understanding and responses alongside the student's experience and responses' (Cooper, 2013: 87). A second form of dynamism across time stems from the potential in every individual to expand their empathic skills. As Krznaric (2014: 34) explains, 'empathy is not a fixed personality trait: it can rise and fall depending on the situation, and we can train ourselves to get better at it'. This dynamism means that our empathic skills can in principle improve and change over time. Gordon (2009: 124–125) compares the development of the skills of empathy with learning a second language. She highlights how in both you increase your fluency and abilities by having opportunities to use the skill in meaningful contexts. In the following sections, I consider how we could explicitly develop empathy as a skill among teachers, learners and researchers. Although for readability it is divided into sections, there is much overlap between the teacher and learner sections and many suggested approaches can be used with both.

Teachers and teacher training

Although some textbooks for teacher training now also refer to interpersonal skills, group dynamics and the concept of rapport (see, e.g. Harmer, 2007), a widespread explicit discussion of emotional intelligence and related competences such as empathic skills remains relatively uncommon. While it is likely that teachers in some settings will receive explicit training to promote their emotional intelligence or empathy, I suspect this is not always the case. One reason that empathy may fall short in pre-service training is that, in reality, there are often simply too many students and too little time (cf. Cooper, 2013) to cover everything needed and many programmes will simply prioritise methods and materials design. However, as this chapter has shown, empathy is central to successful language learning and classroom life and, indeed, without the requisite empathic and interpersonal skills, even the best materials may founder.

At the very least, pre-service teachers need to have an awareness of the importance of interpersonal skills in their language classrooms and the potential effects they can have on classroom life, interaction and intercultural communication. A way to approach this might be through discussions of how we express our emotions and how we can recognise them in others. We know that people often convey their emotional states consciously and unconsciously through their facial expressions and non-verbal cues such as gesture, body language, posture, eye contact, as well as tone and prosody of voice. Therefore, an empathic individual needs to be able to read and decode such forms of communication. As Goleman (1996: 43) says, empathic people 'are more attuned to the subtle social signals that indicate what others need or want'. This means learning to understand and recognise such signals can help teachers to develop their emotional intelligence skills. A way to do this could be to explore pictures, videos or images of facial expressions. For example, Berkeley's Greater Good website offers a quiz of facial expressions for emotional intelligence with useful explanations that could be discussed in class (http://greatergood.berkeley.edu/ei_quiz/). Trainee teachers could also be encouraged to complete and discuss questionnaires such as Rosenthal *et al.*'s (1979) 'profile of nonverbal sensitivity' (PONS). Gregersen (2007) has also used videos of learners' facial expressions and body language with pre-service teachers, whom she encouraged to interpret the video extracts through explicit discussions and reflection tasks. However, some caution is needed in respect to how we read facial expressions. Gregersen and MacIntyre (in press) remind us that cultural and social conventions can also lead us to 'mask our emotions' and we learn to repress certain emotional expressions in favour of more 'acceptable' or more 'neutral' versions. Learners can also deliberately control and consciously enact different emotions to those they are actually experiencing. For teachers, this means we have to learn to be sensitive to a range of non-verbal cues beyond facial expressions. This work on non-verbal language also serves as a useful reminder to us as teachers to be mindful of our own facial expressions and body language, and the messages and signals we may unconsciously be sending to our learners.

In addition to reading our learners' non-verbal communication, we can also learn to develop our skills to really listen without judgement, which is a key characteristic of empathic behaviours. This can be especially important when working with challenging pupils, who may have behavioural issues or feel unconnected to the group. Good empathic listening skills include listening attentively, letting people talk without interrupting and without judgement, and paying attention to non-verbal communication. As Howe says (2013: 120), 'sometimes just listening well can be enough'. Empathy also calls for authentic interaction without judgement (Gordon, 2009). It requires us to be able to put ourselves in somebody else's shoes and imagine what it is like to be that person in a particular situation without judging or evaluating them. A popular saying neatly captures the concept of a non-judgemental empathic stance that we should try to enact in every aspect of professional and personal lives – 'Don't judge someone till you have walked a mile in their shoes'. It is important to respond in a way that shows you have listened and appreciated the point of view without necessarily offering your view or interpretation of the experience.

Although we can to a certain extent promote empathy through training, Howe (2013: 200) argues that it has to be lived and experienced and can only ever be a 'participant activity'. For example, consciously reflecting on other people's behaviour can be one way to develop empathy. We can perhaps better appreciate their perspective if we pause to reflect on why they might have behaved in a certain way, considering what factors might have influenced them and what their feelings and intentions might have been (Lyubomirsky, 2010: 181). This is especially useful when working with colleagues as well as pupils who may not always behave as we expect or would have anticipated. Another strategy for 'experiencing' empathy could be to discuss real-life scenarios and reflect upon possible reasons for learner behaviours, becoming sensitised to the diversity of possible reasons and avoiding jumping to hasty conclusions. As Howe (2013: 156) explains, we must engage in cognitive effort to truly imagine what it is like to be someone else, and this effortful perspective-taking can promote empathy in itself.

Another awareness-raising technique is to ask pre-service teachers to keep a reflective journal to record instances when they found themselves being empathic or observed someone else being empathic (cf. Krznaric, 2014: 33). A wonderful opportunity for such conscious reflection would be in respect to the practicum that many pre-service teachers have to undertake. This frequently presents valuable instances for empathising through reflection with both the learners in the classes they teach and observe as well as in respect of the teachers whom they might be working with or watching teach. Reflecting on a diversity of perspectives is important, as teachers need to be able to have empathy for all their learners, not just those with whom they find it perhaps easier to empathise (Cooper, 2013). An even more experiential technique for promoting empathy (cf. Krznaric, 2014: 'experiential adventures') would be to start learning a new foreign language – to remind oneself of the emotions that accompany the experience of learning to speak and present oneself in a foreign language. Again, keeping a reflective journal of this experience could provide a rich insight into what it feels like to begin learning a new language.

Another way of taking somebody else's perspective is to make the imaginative leap into the life of another through the use of literature, art or film. 'When we are moved by a play or a film or by a novel, we are moved because we begin imaginatively to live the lives of the characters we are watching or reading about' (Howe, 2013: 179). Indeed, this has been a key approach suggested with respect to empathy as well as intercultural competences (see, e.g. Schumm Fauster, 2011). For example, I have recently benefited enormously from reading about learner perspectives such as those of Martinez (2014) – a pupil with special needs who in her autobiography reported with humour and insight the passive bullying she was subjected to at school. Young adult literature in particular represents an especially rich resource for enhancing teachers' own empathy for pupils. It enables teachers to see the world again from the insider perspective of a young adult and helps them to empathise with the concerns and perspectives of learners (see, e.g. Palacio, 2013; Schmatz, 2013).

Generally, teachers have a responsibility to also serve as role models for empathic behaviours, modelling empathy through their own relationships with learners and also colleagues. In team teaching settings, in which the teachers' interpersonal relationships are especially salient to learners, it is particularly important to model positive interpersonal skills. We convey our empathy and respect for others through how we interact, the language we use and the tone in which we respond to learner questions and offer feedback. Indeed, our general interactional patterns with learners can send powerful messages about our attitudes and respect for our learners and can play a central role in the development of positive rapport (Cooper, 2013: 32).

Working with learners

For learners, it is important that their empathic skills are promoted not only to aid their in-class interactions with their peers but also to cultivate their intercultural competence, which we seek to develop as part of their overall linguistic communicative competence. As with teachers, it can be powerful for learners to actively imagine other lives through literature, films, role-plays, photos and art; to this end, learner should be encouraged not only to read, discuss and interpret it but also to write it or enact it themselves (e.g. Krznaric, 2014; Schumm Fauster, 2011). One especially effective method for fostering empathy among learners can be through the use of drama and role-play, by using their imagination (see, e.g. Cooper, 2013; Goldstein & Winner, 2012; Stern, 1980). Acting necessitates getting into the mind of the character being enacted and using the imagination to imagine what it is like to be that person. It requires the actor to feel and convey to others the feelings, thoughts and intentions of the characters portrayed. Goldstein and Winner (2012: 33) conclude that role-play and drama can help learners 'to develop enhanced empathy and gain greater insight into others' beliefs and emotions'. Given that role-play is a familiar type of activity in many communicative language teaching classrooms, it would be relatively easy to adapt tasks to focus on interpersonal and social elements using empathy to enact various experiences of language use, with learners adopting a variety of roles and identities.

With respect to developing learners' interactional and active listening skills, they can be asked to take part in 'conversation meals'. Instead of a food menu, they have a menu of conversation, with questions that are designed to encourage deeper, more meaningful conversations that move beyond more superficial interactions, and discuss instead 'the big issues of life that matter to individuals of every culture and generation' (Krznaric, 2014: 110). Having worked with these conversations with my own learners, I feel it is important to prepare the learners for them through explicit discussions and readings about empathy and listening skills. Following the conversational meals, it is also necessary to debrief in plenary, reflecting on how it felt and what the learners gained from the experience, in respect not only to how they interacted but how they felt about the way in which their partners responded to them. These listening skills can extremely valuable in all forms of interaction and communication, which lie at the heart of classroom life and language use in general.

With respect to language teaching, it is perhaps also important to reiterate that empathy does not mean perpetual harmony in class and, indeed, in a communicative classroom, some debate and critical disagreement are healthy. Being empathic does not mean giving up your perspective but it means being able to imagine and understand others without necessarily agreeing.

Researchers

Finally, another group of people in SLA who often depend on and in some cases would benefit from enhanced empathy are researchers. Firstly, given some of the discourse in the paradigm debates and research rhetoric generally, it would be helpful for researchers occasionally to seek to understand the world through somebody else's eyes and exert some empathy. Once again, an empathic perspective does not automatically imply agreement but it does imply respect, understanding and appreciating the perspective of others and it typically leads to more care in how we listen and respond to others. Secondly, instead of qualitative research specifically, Howe (2013) draws attention to the role of empathy in phenomenological, hermeneutic and, indeed, any interpretative research aimed at understanding subjective human experience. Referring to Spinelli (1989), Howe stresses the importance of empathy for data-collection approaches, such as interviewing, but also for the reading of and analysis of qualitative data, in which the researcher must learn to listen well to participant voices (in text and speech) and attempt truly to see the world through their eyes without judgement.

Future Directions

Currently, empathy appears to be a popular topic in a range of fields, such as politics, education, psychology, neuroscience and sociology – even Barack Obama has placed it in centre stage, as can be seen from the opening quote. Its broad appeal and relevance is a sign of both our interconnected world and our growing recognition of the fact that our world is composed of relationships that are to be valued and treasured as the basis of all successful interactions. In any educational setting, human and social interactions are at the centre of effective functioning and empathy is an invaluable skill in nurturing all types of positive relationships, whether they are with pupils, colleagues, parents or head teachers. However, it strikes me that empathy is especially relevant to language learning, with its focus on communication, cultural diversity and the centrality of social interactions.

The next step for SLA is to put empathy more solidly on the research agenda. There is much to be learned from work in other disciplines and work on related constructs such as emotional intelligence, emotional literacy, relational pedagogy, evidence-based programmes on social and emotional learning (SEL), such as 'Roots of Empathy' (Gordon, 2009), as well as from interventions to promote empathy among the medical professions (e.g. Shanafelt *et al.*, 2005; Shapiro, 2008; Stepien & Bearnstein, 2006). The first step will be for researchers to clarify their definitions and understandings of empathy as a complex, multicomponent construct. Naturally, in psychology, several well established measures of both cognitive and affective empathy exist, and these could also be used in SLA studies (e.g. Davis, 1983; Hogan, 1969; Lawrence *et al.*, 2004; Mehrabian & Epstein, 1972). However, work by Zaki *et al.* (2008) raises interesting questions about the contextuality of such studies. They examined affective empathy and found it can be used to predict empathic accuracy only when the other person's expressivity, which allows their thoughts and feelings to be read, is taken into account. In other words, their study considered empathy as an interpersonal process. Thus, given this relational nature, I would suggest that there might be reasons to focus on empathy as 'taking place between the empathizer and the other person' (Rasoal *et al.*, 2011: 8). This would suggest taking interpersonal relationships as the core unit of analysis for understanding the dynamic and situated nature of empathy (cf. Gergen, 2009). As Howe (2013: 187) argues, 'empathy has to be a property of the relationship, not just of the individual'. This means it is important to look not necessarily at the constituent components of empathic relationships (such as learner and teacher), but rather at the 'relationality' of the relationship' (Biesta, 2004: 13). Indeed, Guiora (1967; cited in Guiora *et al.*, 1972), as one of the earliest researchers examining empathy and foreign language learning, defined empathy as 'a process of comprehending in which a temporary fusion of self–object boundaries' exists. More recently, Cameron (2013: 3) has described empathy as 'one person connecting with another, reaching across gaps between Self and Other to understand how 'the Other' feels and thinks, lives their life, and sees their world'. The important elements to note are the relational nature of empathy as well as the use of the term 'process' to highlight its dynamic nature that a person actively engages in. Interestingly, Cameron (2013: 3) applied complex dynamic systems theory 'to understand discourse and empathy as systems in continuous flux' and there seems to be much potential in this line of thinking, given the multifaceted nature of empathy as a cognitive, affective, social and behavioural process and its dynamic character across different timescales and contexts. The model of empathy she proposes is a multi-level dynamic model that allows the multiple facets and dimensions of empathy to be brought together. In particular, she uses a complexity perspective to help view self and other as both individuals and collectives, and her work looks at the dialogic and interactional nature of empathy and how it can be co-constructed with real or imagined others (see Cameron, 2013: 8).

If empathy does indeed come naturally to us as humans (De Waal, 2009), then we have a good basis on which to further promote and enhance this capacity among language teachers and learners. In general, empathy presents us with a positive, optimistic view of the future of language teaching and intercultural encounters, and this makes it worthy of further empirical study to clarify in what ways we can best foster this among those involved in teaching and learning languages. As Cooper (2013: 3) explains, empathy is not some 'sentimental or woolly' construct or approach to teaching, but rather it represents a fundamental human social capacity that we need to succeed, given our relational nature and the centrality of communication. It is therefore time that empathy featured more prominently on the research agenda in SLA.

References

Arnold, R. (2005) *Empathic Intelligence: Teaching, Learning, Relating*. Sydney: University of New South Wales Press.

Baron-Cohen, S., Knickmeyer, R.C. and Belmonte, M.K. (2005) Sex differences in the brain: Implications for explaining autism. *Science* 310 (5749), 819–823.

Biesta, G.J.J. (2004) 'Mind the gap!' Communication and the educational relation. In C. Bingham and A.M. Sidorkin (eds) *No Education Without Relation* (pp. 11–22). New York: Peter Lang.

Blair, R.J.R. (2005) Responding to the emotions of others: Dissociating forms of empathy through the study of typical and psychiatric populations. *Consciousness and Cognition* 14 (4), 698–718.

Block, D. (2003) *The Social Turn in Second Language Acquisition*. Washington, DC: Georgetown University Press.

Byrnes, H. (2013) Renting language in the ownership society. Reflections on language use and language learning in a multilingual world. In J. Arnold and T. Murphey (eds) *Meaningful Action: Earl Stevick's Influence on Language Teaching* (pp. 222–240). Cambridge: Cambridge University Press.

Cacioppo, J.T., Berntson, G.G. and Decety, J. (2010) Social neuroscience and its relationship to social psychology. *Social Cognition* 28 (6), 675–685.

Calloway-Thomas, C., Cooper, P.J. and Blake, C. (1999) *Intercultural Communication: Roots and Routes*. Boston, MA: Allyn & Bacon.

Cameron, L. (2013) A dynamic model of empathy and dsypathy (Living with uncertainty, working paper 60). Retrieved from http://www.open.ac.uk/researchprojects/livingwithuncertainty (accessed November 2015).

Christov-Moore, L., Simpson, E.A., Coudé, G., Grigaityte, K., Iacoboni, M. and Ferrari, P.F. (2014) Empathy: Gender effects in brain and behavior. *Neuroscience and Biobehavioral Reviews* 46 (4), 604–627.

Cohen, A. (2009) Empathy and what it teaches us. At http://positivepsychologynews.com/news/aren-cohen/200912126410 (accessed November 2015).

Cooper, B. (2013) *Empathy in Education: Engagement, Values and Achievement* (reprint edition). New York: Bloomsbury 3PL.

Cozolino, L. (2013) *The Social Neuroscience of Education: Optimizing Attachment and Learning in the Classroom*. New York: Norton.

Davis, M.H. (1983) Measuring individual differences in empathy: Evidence for a multidimensional approach. *Journal of Personality and Social Psychology* 44, 113–126.

Davis, M.H. (1994) *Empathy: A Social Psychological Approach.* Madison, WI: Brown and Benchmark.

De Vignemont, F. and Singer, T. (2006) The empathic brain: How, when and why? *Trends in Cognitive Science* 10 (10), 435–441.

De Waal, F. (2009) *The Age of Empathy: Nature's Lessons for a Kinder Society*. London: Souvenir Press.

Dewaele, J.-M. and Wei, L. (2012) Multilingualism, empathy and multicompetence. *International Journal of Multilingualism* 9 (4), 352–366.

Dörnyei, Z. and Murphey, T. (2003) *Group Dynamics in the Language Classroom*. Cambridge: Cambridge University Press.

Dunbar, R.I.M. (1998) The social brain hypothesis. *Evolutionary Anthropology: Issues, News, and Reviews* 6 (5), 178–190.

Ehrman, M.E. and Dörnyei, Z. (1998) *Interpersonal Dynamics in Second Language Education: The Visible and Invisible Classroom*. Thousand Oaks, CA: Sage.

Frisby, B.N. and Martin, M.M. (2010) Instructor–student and student–student rapport in the classroom. *Communication Education* 59 (2), 146–164.

Frith, C. and Frith, U. (2005) Theory of mind. *Current Biology* 15 (17), R644–R645.

Gergen, K.J. (2009) *Relational Being: Beyond Self and Community*. Oxford: Oxford University Press.
Goldstein, T.R. and Winner, E. (2012) Enhancing empathy and theory of mind. *Journal of Cognition and Development* 13 (1), 19–37.
Goleman, D. (1996) *Emotional Intelligence: Why It Can Matter More Than IQ*. London: Bloomsbury.
Gordon, M. (2009) *Roots of Empathy: Changing the World Child by Child*. New York: The Experiment.
Gregersen, T. (2007) Breaking the code of silence: An exploratory study of teachers' nonverbal decoding accuracy of foreign language anxiety. *Language Teaching Research* 11 (2), 51–64.
Gregersen, T. and MacIntyre, P. (in press) *Optimizing Language Learners' Nonverbal Behavior in the Classroom: From Tenet to Technique*. Bristol: Multilingual Matters.
Guiora, A.Z. (1967) Toward a systematic study of empathy. *Comprehensive Psychiatry* 8, 375–383.
Guiora, A.Z., Brannon, R.C.L. and Dull, C.Y. (1972) Empathy and second language learning. *Language Learning* 22 (1), 111–130.
Guiora, A.Z., Paluszny, M., Beit-Hallahmi, B., Catford, J.C., Cooley, R.E. and Dull, C.Y. (1975) Language and person studies in language behaviour 1. *Language Learning* 25 (1), 43–61.
Harmer, J. (2007) *The Practice of English Language Teaching* (4th edition). Harlow: Pearson.
Hoffman, M.L. (2000) *Empathy and Moral Development*. Cambridge: Cambridge University Press.
Hogan, R. (1969) Development of an empathy scale. *Journal of Consulting and Clinical Psychology* 33, 307–316.
Howe, D. (2013) *Empathy: What It Is and Why It Matters*. Basingstoke: Palgrave Macmillan.
Kok, B.E., Coffey, K.A., Cohn, M.A., Catalino, L.I., Vacharkulksemsuk, T., Algoe, S.B., Brantley, M. and Fredrickson, B.L. (2013) How positive emotions build physical health: Perceived positive social connections account for the upward spiral between positive emotions and vagal tone. *Psychological Science* 24 (7), 1123–1132.
Krznaric, R. (2014) *Empathy: A Handbook for Revolution*. Croydon: Rider.
Lawrence, E.J., Shaw, P., Baker, D., Baron-Cohen, S. and David, A.S. (2004) Measuring empathy: Reliability and validity of the Empathy Quotient. *Psychological Medicine* 5, 911–920.
Lieberman, M.D. (2013) *Social: Why Our Brains Are Wired to Connect*. Oxford: Oxford University Press.
Lyubomirsky, S. (2010) *The How of Happiness: A Practical Approach to Getting the Life You Want*. London: Piatkus.
Martinez, F. (2014) *What the **** Is Normal¿!* London: Virgin Books.
McAlinden, M. (2014) Can teachers know learners' minds¿ Teacher empathy and learner body language in English language teaching. In K. Dunworth and G. Zhang (eds) *Critical Perspectives on Language Education* (pp. 71–100). Cham: Springer International. Retrieved from http://link.springer.com/chapter/10.1007/978-3-319-06185-6_5 (accessed November 2015).
Mehrabian, A. and Epstein, N. (1972) A measure of emotional empathy. *Journal of Personality* 40, 525–543.
Mitchell, P. (2011) Acquiring a theory of mind. In A. Slater and G. Bremner (eds) *An Introduction to Developmental Psychology* (2nd edition) (pp. 357–384). Chichester: BPS Blackwell.
Moran, P. (2001) *Teaching Culture: Perspectives in Practice*. Boston: Heinle.
Murphey, T., Falout, J., Fukuda, T. and Fukada, Y. (2014) Socio-dynamic motivating through idealizing classmates. *System* 45, 242–253.
O'Grady, P. (2013) The positive psychology of empathy. What is the opposite of

bullying? At https://www.psychologytoday.com/blog/positive-psychology-in-the-classroom/201303/the-positive-psychology-empathy (accessed November 2015).
Ozanska-Ponikwia, K. and Dewaele, J.-M. (2012) Personality and L2 use: Openminded and self-confident individuals are more likely to be active and proficient L2 users. *EUROSLA Yearbook* 12, 112–134.
Palacio, R.J. (2013) *Wonder*. London: Corgi Children's.
Peterson, C. (2006) *A Primer in Positive Psychology*. Oxford: Oxford University Press.
Rasoal, C., Eklund, J. and Hansen, E.M. (2011) Toward a conceptualization of ethno-cultural empathy. *Journal of Social, Evolutionary, and Cultural Psychology* 5 (1), 1–13.
Rogers, C.R. and Freiberg, H.J. (1994) *Freedom to Learn* (3rd revised edition). New York: Prentice Hall.
Rosenthal, R., Hall, J.A., DiMateo, M.R., Rogers, L.P. and Archer, D. (1979) *Sensitivity to Nonverbal Communication. The PONS Test.* Baltimore, MD: Johns Hopkins University Press.
Rota, G. and Reiterer, S. (2009) Cognitive aspects of pronunciation talent: How empathy, mental flexibility, working memory and intelligence interact with phonetic talent. In G. Dogil and S. Reiterer (eds) *Language Talent and Brain Activity* (Trends in Applied Linguistics 1) (pp. 67–96). Berlin: Mouton de Gruyter.
Samovar, L.A., Porter, R.E. and McDaniel, E.R. (2007) *Communication Between Cultures* (6th edition). Belmont, CA: Thomson Learning.
Schmatz, P. (2013) *Bluefish*. London: Walker.
Schonert-Reichl, K.A. and Scott, F. (2009) Effectiveness of 'The Roots of Empathy' program in promoting children's emotional and social competence: A summary of research findings. In M. Gordon *The Roots of Empathy: Changing the World Child by Child* (pp. 239–252). New York: The Experiment.
Schumm Fauster, J. (2011) The role of young-adult literature in developing socio-cultural competency. In T. Pattison (ed.) *IATEFL 2010 Harrogate Conference Selections* (pp. 226–228). Canterbury: IATEFL.
Seligman, M.E.P. (2011) *Flourish: A New Understanding of Happiness and Well-Being – And How To Achieve Them*. London: Nicholas Brealey.
Shanafelt, T.D., West, C., Zhao, X., Novotny, P., Kolars, J., Habermann, T. and Sloan, J. (2005) Relationship between increased personal well-being and enhanced empathy among internal medicine residents. *Journal of General Internal Medicine* 20 (7), 559–564.
Shapiro, J. (2008) Walking a mile in their patients' shoes: Empathy and othering in medical students' education. *Philosophy, Ethics, and Humanities in Medicine* 3 (1), 10.
Singer, T. (2006) The neuronal basis and ontogeny of empathy and mind reading: Review of literature and implications for future research. *Neuroscience and Biobehavioral Reviews* 30 (6), 855–863.
Spinelli, I. (1989) *The Interpreted World: Introduction to Phenomenological Psychology*. London: Sage.
Stepien, K.A. and Baernstein, A. (2006) Educating for empathy. *Journal of General Internal Medicine* 21 (5), 524–530.
Stern, S.L. (1980) Drama in second language learning from a psycholinguistic perspective. *Language Learning* 30 (1), 77–100.
Underhill, A. (2013) The inner workbench: Learning itself as a meaningful activity. In J. Arnold and T. Murphey (eds) *Meaningful Action: Earl Stevick's Influence on Language Teaching* (pp. 202–218). Cambridge: Cambridge University Press.
Wang, Y.-W., Davidson, M.M., Yakushko, O.F., Savoy, H.B., Tan, J.A. and Bleier, J.K. (2003) The Scale of Ethnocultural Empathy: Development, validation and reliability. *Journal of Counseling Psychology* 50 (2), 221–234.
Zaki, J., Bolger, N. and Ochsner, K. (2008) It takes two: The interpersonal nature of empathic accuracy. *Psychological Science* 19 (4), 399–404.

Websites

(All last accessed November 2015.)

Berkeley's Greater Good facial expression quiz: http://greatergood.berkeley.edu/ei_quiz/
SEL website: http://www.casel.org/social-and-emotional-learning

Useful websites for exploring empathy in educational contexts

http://startempathy.org
http://cultureofempathy.com
http://www.rootsofempathy.org

4 The Dynamics of Past Selves in Language Learning and Well-Being

Joseph Falout

In some educational systems, students get marched through successive years of compulsory language education. Some seem to run happily ahead of the bunch, while others are dragged along against their will. Research has shown that learners' past selves can determine which type of learning experience they will have (Falout, 2016). Past selves are images of who one has been, and what one has gone through and done, as constantly assembled and reassembled through the self-stories one tells to oneself, and hears about or co-constructs with others. Past selves extend into self-beliefs (e.g. Dweck, 2006; Weiner, 2000) and 'can be regarded to broadly overlap with nomenclature from differing disciplines and perspectives, such as self-narration, autobiographical memory, remembered self, remembering self, history-in-persons, habitus, attributions, retrospection and antecedent conditions' (Falout, 2016: 48).

Predictions based on past selves research in language learning (Falout & Maruyama, 2004; Falout *et al.*, 2009) posit that those who blame themselves during difficulties early in their learning will become more susceptible to helplessness when facing the learning challenges ahead. Meanwhile, those externalizing their blame when things go wrong will become more likely to develop adaptive coping strategies that bring them greater resilience under the stresses of learning, and they will more likely achieve higher language abilities during their formal education. Also, those with positive past language learning selves will more often receive the social support they need to stay motivated in learning, from teachers, friends and family, while learners with negative past language learning selves will likely believe that social support would have been the best thing to have helped them regain their lost motivation (Falout, 2012; Falout *et al.*, 2013a).

This chapter explains from a positive psychology perspective how past selves influence language learning and well-being, as constituted by adaptive coping, resilience to stresses, subjective control, hedonic decision-making, eudaemonic self-appraisals, and temporal self-comparison and self-regulation. Also discussed are implications for improving and enriching language learners' perspectives of themselves in their pasts, presents and futures.

Subjective Control

People get into habits of saying particulars about themselves that may not be true, but the telling and retelling of it eventually makes it so. Many language students might repeatedly play back images in their mind of themselves sitting in a classroom long ago, looking upon a marked-up test with a grade, or the faces of their classmates or teacher reacting to their utterances in the language. Students might often think to themselves or say to others, 'I'm no good at languages. I never was and I never will be', or 'I'm a language person. It has always come to me naturally'. Beliefs like these come from learners' past successes, failures, struggles, hopes, joys and more – experiences that in memory form a psychological construction of their past selves. These play dynamic and crucial guiding roles to students in determining resilience and persistence, assistance to peers, or helplessness, in the stresses of formal education and the demands of language learning (Falout, 2016).

Any small personal failure can cause temporary helplessness (Seligman, 2006). People can also become helpless by watching others become helpless (Peterson *et al.*, 1993), particularly if they see themselves and their situations as similar, through a process known as observational learning, also termed modeling (Bandura, 1997). Even groups of people can become convinced that they are ineffective at solving problems or completing tasks together (Peterson *et al.*, 1993). For example, some pairs from one study (Simkin *et al.*, 1983) were given solvable, collaborative problems, most of which they could complete, while other pairs were given unsolvable problems. After experiencing repeated failures, the pairs given unsolvable problems were then given solvable ones. However, they had already developed expectancies, from what they had perceived as failed collaborations, which made them believe solving the newer problems together was not likely, even though they had started to complete a small portion of them. Their prior failures on the unsolvable problems, though fresh, were but memories, and their present confidence and verve to attend to the solvable problems had been sufficiently diminished. Their nascent, temporally immediate past selves were falsely telling them that their efforts were futile in this situation. Believing this message prevented them from imagining that solving the problems together was possible, which diminished their sense of hope; their motivations and cognitions flagged.

Encouraging the growth of people's potentials for finding meaning in life, for building the reserves that help recovery from setbacks, and for helping people to flourish, 'positive psychology at the subjective level is about valued subjective experience: well-being, contentment, and satisfaction (in the past); hope and optimism (for the future); and flow and happiness (in the present)' (Seligman & Csikszentmihalyi, 2000: 5). This includes helping people gain subjective control by understanding their own habitual styles in explaining their experiences (Seligman, 2006), meaning the ways they shape their autobiographical memories. Seligman (2006) underscores that people who retain positive outlooks do not necessarily keep historically accurate self-knowledge, and that non-depressed people are more likely to distort their personal pasts, skewed toward brighter experiences, than those who suffer from depression. Depressed individuals may not necessarily experience a higher rate of misfortune or lower rate of fortune; it may be that they are less able to process their positive experiences, emotionally and cognitively, than those who do not suffer from depression (Werner-Seidler & Moulds, 2011).

What matters for subjective happiness and control in people's lives are the explanations they give themselves about whatever good or bad befalls them, or how people interpret their past selves, as expounded in the works of attribution theory (e.g. Weiner, 2000) and mindsets (e.g. Dweck, 2006). This does not mean lying to oneself about oneself; it means keeping one's self-perspective positive. Optimistic outlooks relate to tendencies to believe failures are temporary setbacks, happening only under certain conditions, and are not to be taken personally, and that successes come from one's own qualities. Pessimistic outlooks relate to the opposite: tendencies to believe failures reflect permanent traits, while successes result from temporary luck that has little to do with one's own qualities (Seligman, 2006). These outlooks in turn influence people's present emotions, such as hope, and future-directed actions, such as recovering from hardships and achieving goals (Seligman, 2006).

An implication for education is that outlooks can be changed through practice. Positive outlooks can be nourished, while negative outlooks can be improved by helping people to focus upon and habituate how they make, interpret and use memories of their past selves. In this vein, happiness interventions were undertaken by adult participants and tested in one study (Seligman *et al.*, 2005). All five interventions plus the placebo started with reflecting on one's past, with different exercises invoking memories from different temporal distances, some more distal, others more immediate.

The first intervention, *gratitude visit*, included thanking someone in person for a kindness they had done. *Three good things in life* involved writing up three positive experiences at the end of the day, each day for one week. *You at your best* began by identifying and writing about a time when one's best qualities brought out an optimal experience, and reading and reflecting upon this story each day for a week. *Identifying signature strengths* involved taking a survey that helped identify one's top five personal strengths, then consciously using these more frequently throughout the following week. *Using signature strengths in a new way* started just as the previous exercise did, but with individualized feedback added, then consciously using only one of these personal strengths but in a creatively different way each day for the following week. The placebo for the control group, *early memories*, involved writing about one's early memories each night for a week. All of the activities, including the placebo, yielded some increases in level of happiness and decreases in depressive symptoms, with the largest positive changes occurring from the *gratitude visit*, for up to one month. For up to six months, lasting positive changes came from *three good things in life* and *using signature strengths in a new way*.

Some of these interventions were used in classrooms in a positive psychology program for grade-school children, with resulting increases in engagement, enjoyment, achievement, empathy, cooperation, assertiveness and self-control in school (Seligman *et al.*, 2009). Also, versions of these exercises with follow-up therapy sessions comprised a major portion of a 14-part positive psychotherapy program that lowered remission rates of clients with depression (Seligman *et al.*, 2006). The program included identifying the signature strengths of a significant other, and identifying the signature strengths of family members. The extension from past selves to past others indicates the powerful influences others can have on us, even through our memories of how they were, or how we imagine them to have been. These activities helped to process autobiographical and significant-other biographical content, possibly changing personal meaning of past experiences (i.e. reframing) in a way more positive for present outlooks, and possibly changing the way or the habits (i.e. rehabituating) of explaining past experiences to oneself.

Given the long-term nature of language learning and the need for persistence, students with various psychological make-ups, language abilities and learning strengths and weaknesses, might benefit from similar interventions. For example, studies into language learning demotivation and remotivation (Falout, 2012; Falout *et al.*, 2013a) showed that students with positive past language learning selves, compared with those with negative selves, displayed more positive emotions regarding the learning in and out of class, perceived greater self-confidence, and were more likely to choose to study the language were it not compulsory. Moreover, they were more likely to react quickly and adaptively to learning stresses, and were thus better at attaining motivational recovery in the short term, and staying more resilient in the long term. Thus language classrooms with a diversity of learners have both reasons (i.e. struggling students) and resources (i.e. modeling opportunities from flourishing students) to habituate beneficial ways of constructing past selves, improving specific weaknesses or fortifying different strengths, with positive psychology interventions. The interventions themselves can also be designed as language learning activities and fit into syllabi or curricula. It is important to remember that students' self-appraisals relating to learning can change over time, so students might benefit from such interventions on different occasions over the years.

Hedonic Decision-Making and Eudaemonic Self-Appraisals

Judging one's well-being in the past can be called 'evaluated well-being', done by the remembering self, while sensing one's well-being in the present can be called 'experienced well-being', done by the experiencing self (Kahneman & Riis, 2005). People usually make decisions for their present and future based on what they believe is more suitable for them, the perceptions of which are formed primarily by the remembering self rather than the experiencing self. This is referred to as the dominance of the remembering self in hedonic decision-making, answerable to 'What do you want to do next?', and eudaemonic self-appraisals, answerable to 'What do you think of your life so far?' (Kahneman & Riis, 2005). Comparable questions for language learners would be 'How do you think you will do in your next experience with the language?' and 'How do you feel about your learning so far?' According to Kahneman's (2011) hypothesis of the dominance of past selves, students would tend to think and act based on expectations and self-appraisals made not by their experiencing self but by their remembering self, perhaps at the expense of their present and future learning and well-being.

To illustrate this dominance of past selves, Kahneman (2011) presents three experiments. The first compared patients under the same surgical procedures, who were awake and reporting their in-the-moment levels of pain. Despite similar high levels of pain reported throughout most of the operation, patients whose operations lasted longer, and thus who would have experienced a greater amount of pain all together, would later give overall evaluations of pain lower than those by patients whose operations were shorter. The second experiment involved participants keeping their hands in water cold enough to cause mild pain. One trial lasted 60 seconds, the other 90 seconds. The water conditions were exactly the same in both trials, except for the final 30 seconds of the longer trial, in which the water temperature was increased, but only very slightly, from 13 to 14 degrees Celsius. Upon finishing, participants were not informed about time durations or temperature conditions, but were asked that if one of trials were to be repeated, which they would choose. The majority preferred to repeat what in fact was the longer and thus more painful one. In the third experiment, students kept a daily diary of their spring vacations with a day-by-day evaluation. They gave an overall rating of their vacation when it was over, and were asked whether they would like to repeat the vacation or not.

The summation of this study indicates what also happened in the previous two studies: 'Statistical analysis established that the intentions for future vacations were entirely determined by the final evaluation – even when that score did not accurately represent the quality of the experience that was described in the diaries' (Kahneman, 2011: 398).

The salient factors across all three studies are that the durations of events were neglected, while last impressions of events became lasting. In other words, sensations perceived by the experiencing self eventually were superseded by evaluations made by the remembering self. In the first two experiments, with the operations and the hands in cold water, painful events that lasted longer but ended with gradual reductions of pain were perceived as less severe than shorter events that ended abruptly at moments of greater pain. In the third experiment, vacations that had more negative than positive days but ended positively were perceived as more satisfying than those that had more positive than negative days but ended negatively. Kahneman identifies these effects as errors in retrospection, or thinking back to the past, errors that could lead to decision-making that works against people's best interests. In sum, beginning, peak and end moments of experiences left greater impressions on people about the overall quality of their experiences than all the other moments combined (Kahneman, 2011).

Pivotal moments may thus influence language learners' perceptions of themselves and their learning more than a whole range of other learning experiences. This means unrepresentative moments in tasks, lessons, homework, units, semesters and so forth can contribute to false overall impressions. For example, a student may have enjoyed most of the semester and learned a lot, but due to a troubling performance in the last class, or on the final test, the student might devalue the whole year's experience and degrade self-image in relation to the learning. Or another student might decide to quit one language and begin studying a different one, whereas sticking with the original language would have paid off, with a stronger academic record, better linguistic abilities and more-rewarding language learning experiences overall.

Kahneman (2011) wonders why anyone would be inclined to choose paths that could cause extra, unnecessary pain, or why they would neglect taking substantive portions of their past experiences into consideration for making decisions that could critically influence their future experiences. He asserts that rational beings, knowing in advance the total amount and quality of pain they would undergo, would most certainly choose negative experiences that end more quickly and incur less overall pain. Additionally, knowing in advance the pleasures they would have, most people would more logically choose positive experiences that maximize their well-being. Kahneman (2011: 385) concludes, 'Tastes and decisions are shaped by memories, and the memories can be wrong.... An inconsistency is built into the design of our minds'.

Interpreted differently, these seemingly maladaptive functions of the remembering self might simultaneously represent human strengths (e.g. Schacter, 2012). The remembering self may not be able to calculate the aggregate of pleasure or pain increments during events as they unfold, as can be done when the sensations of the experiencing self are carefully recorded. But such memory focus or alteration might actually serve to protect the self. The duration or moment-by-moment details of past events might not be the important parts to consider for decision-making. The remembering self might follow rules of thumb that are proven over the course of evolution as beneficial for both basic survival and emotional well-being. Situations that ended well might be better to revisit than those that ended poorly (cf. experiment 3). In planning for survival, returning to a previously productive hunting ground makes more sense than returning to one that has not provided well in the past. Similarly, unpleasant situations that gradually improved may have offered a sense of hope or control, while those that ended abruptly at a time when hope was not present might be taken as ending only out of luck, rather than by one's control or when one had the self-regulation to cope with the situation (cf. experiments 1 and 2). In planning for basic survival and increased well-being, the dominance of the remembering self may arguably act as an adaptive trait.

Schacter (2012) reasons that an error-prone memory is integral to its creative strengths as part of its adaptive constructive processes. Humans are good at predicting the hedonic consequences of experiences they never had (Gilbert & Wilson, 2007). Imagining oneself in a future event is a mental simulation known as prospection. It induces foresight and planning, and requires complex cognitive assembling of relevant information, a salient source of which is often one's autobiographical past. Thus, a crucial role of retrospection is to help make accurate predictions, or at least predictions that inspire actions that benefit the person (Schacter *et al.*, 2007). Learning from our past selves, and from others' experiences, about how we might become in the future occurs through many of the same neural paths and processes. Retrospection, prospection and theory of mind (imagining others' thoughts and feelings) overlap in the interconnected regions across the brain, called the default mode network (Spreng & Grady, 2009). Memories are not direct recordings of events, but reconstructions that rely on flexible selections and combinations of information about one's past. Similarly, prospection constructs future simulations through creative combinations and manipulations of episodic memories of self and remembered autobiographical information about others. Retrospection and prospection interact and strengthen each other, and they build from and build into creativity, cognitive flexibility, associative and convergent thinking, generalization and abstraction, goal-directed cognition, and autobiographical planning (Schacter, 2012).

These very same desirable cognitive capacities, by their nature, may also lead to errors or otherwise undesired outcomes in retrospection and prospection. During retrospection, the memory of an original episode may become distorted by the erroneous incorporation of a similar something that was experienced before (gist-based error) or after (post-event misinformation) the original episode, or not even experienced but heard about or seen (associative error). Additionally, something simply thought about, or purely imagined information, can become incorporated into episodic memory (memory inflation), and it seems highly possible that this error can also result from imagining the future (Schacter, 2012).

Future predictions can lack accuracy or practicability when they: focus on peak or end moments, causing an overestimation or underestimation of the actual event (unrepresentative simulation); neglect seemingly inessential moments, causing mis-estimation of the total moments when added together, such as the time it will actually take to get something done (essentialized simulation); over-represent the beginning moments or fail to play out the full scenario, delaying preparatory measures or retarding growth of adaptive processes needed when the actual time comes (abbreviated simulation); and incorporate into the prediction present feelings or information from the present context that will unlikely be there when the time actually comes and, in doing so, fail to imagine a more likely context of the future event (decontextualized simulation) (Gilbert & Wilson, 2007). Another error is the belief that, while the self may have changed much in the past, the present self is stable in its personalities, values and preferences, and not likely to change much in the future (the end-of-history illusion) (Quoidback *et al.*, 2013).

Many errors in prospection are based, at least in part, on misrecognizing or misapplying what can be learned from the past self. These errors can act antithetically to well-being, and they can be mitigated or avoided by learning about potential future events from others, particularly those within one's social network, who have gone through similar experiences already (Gilbert *et al.*, 2009). Thus, theory of mind enriches the interconnected processes of retrospection and prospection, crucially applying past and future selves together as a way to boost each other's strengths. Prospection itself improves cognitive and emotional well-being, with multiple adaptive benefits, including increased coping under stress, hope and optimism, positive attitudes toward others, and social bonding (Schacter, 2012).

Teachers using motivational interventions based on retrospection and prospection need to be aware of their potential errors and provide an approach that attempts to avoid these errors (Falout, 2013a). For example, students experiencing helplessness in language learning may be unreceptive to encouragements of envisioning their future selves using the language because the dominance of their past selves prevents them from imagining this possibility. These students may first need to reframe their past experiences related to the language before they can envision their future with it (Falout, 2016). Such reappraisals may come naturally as students gain better learning experiences than they had before, or from doing activities that foster temporal self-comparisons and bring meaning, such as the previously mentioned positive psychology interventions. Exercises like these could help learners to process past negative learning experiences, and appreciate past positive learning experiences.

Temporal Self-Comparison

Research (Falout *et al.*, 2013b; Fukada *et al.*, in press; Murphey *et al.*, 2012) has shown that students can experience positive changes in their past selves related to language learning alongside self-reported increases in present effort to learn, and concomitant increased significant correlational values. These results indicate that past selves and present learning relate proportionally, meaning their valences (i.e. level of negativity or positivity) tend to go up or down together, as they also do with future selves. In short, past selves are improvable, and improved past selves can lead to improved learning.

Changeability and stability of the self-concept or self-image within any temporal time frame – past, present or future – can enable one to adapt to numerous challenges. According to possible selves theory (Markus & Nurius, 1986), past selves are malleable and can be carried with one throughout life, helping to define self-concept and to regulate action, such as memories of childhood prompting an adult to return home for the holidays. Self-perceived stable traits, what one thinks one always is, are based on past selves (Markus & Nurius, 1986). Imagining different types of selves that one might become, such as living in an ideal future situation or suffering from an unfavorable future situation, can powerfully compel action toward becoming something desired or away from something feared. Also termed 'future self guides' because of their motivational potential, future selves arise from past self-images and are informed by present comparisons with others (Markus & Nurius, 1986).

People also seem naturally inclined to make temporal comparisons of themselves to feel better and to promote a sense of present well-being (Strahan & Wilson, 2006). Research based on temporal self-appraisal theory (Wilson & Ross, 2001) has shown that people wish to feel they are on a trajectory of continual improvement, and therefore tend to derogate or downgrade their past selves, particularly more distal past selves, and praise their present and future selves. The more immediate the past and present selves, the more likely these will receive positive appraisals, as they are temporally close to the present self. Negative experiences of the past become psychologically distanced to protect present self-image, while gains in positive affect and motivation can be made when past accomplishments and future successes are psychologically drawn close to the temporal present (Grysman *et al.*, 2013; Kanten & Teigen, 2008; Keyes, 2000; Strahan & Wilson, 2006).

Self-comparisons are psychologically formed through creative processes. Past selves, subjectively constructed in the present, can be reinterpreted at any given moment. Such modifications are commonly made to improve or preserve one's present self-image. During temporal self-comparisons, past selves can therefore be psychologically manipulated to appear similar or dissimilar to present selves. Furthermore, temporal self-comparisons are domain-specific, such as abilities relating to a specific school subject, and they can depend upon mindsets of whether or not self-change is possible. Those believing in the self as a stable entity might be more apt to idealize their past selves, in order to cope with present distress and provoke positive moods, whereas those believing in one's improvable capacities may tend to cope by derogating these past selves (McFarland & Buehler, 2012). People even tend to expect greater improvements in themselves in the future than they do for most of their peers (Kanten & Teigen, 2008). These manipulations and exaggerations serve the self beneficially, by instilling an optimistic perspective.

Another function of temporal self-comparison is to maintain a sense of self-continuity. People of all ages share narratives of their own and of others' past selves to nourish social and familial bonds, and to clarify present self-concept. Both younger and older adults create self-continuity from remembering their autobiographical narratives. Younger adults are more likely to use past selves for directing future-oriented planning, problem solving and proactive step-taking, while older adults have a greater range of past selves to draw on, and they tend to regard them more positively than younger adults do of their own past selves (Bluck & Alea, 2009; Chessell *et al.*, 2014). Older adults have more temporally immediate future selves than younger adults, and temporal self-continuity appears to come naturally with aging (Chessell *et al.*, 2014; Frazier *et al.*, 2000). The greater their sense of self-continuity, it seems the more likely their hoped-for and feared selves balance each other. For example, the hope of maintaining one's present good health is offset by the fear of losing it. Temporal self-continuity, especially for older adults, can be linked with perceived physical good health, subjective control over one's health, and overall life satisfaction (Frazier *et al.*, 2000).

Shared autobiographical narratives can help people to take the perspectives of others and to regulate their own emotions. Children commonly grow up hearing stories of their parents' and relatives' childhoods, usually at family gatherings such as at the dinner table. Not only do the personal histories of family members, as told and retold, construct familial continuity and bonding, but they can also be informative in constructing one's own life story. When adolescents are familiar with stories of their parents' childhoods, with related consequences of their actions and feelings they had felt, and who incorporate these perspectives into their own value systems, they seem to be better adjusted in their world than those who do not know or do not take the perspectives from their parents' past selves. Adolescents with this perspective-taking, compared with those without, report lower levels of anxiety, depression, aggression and other antisocial behaviors (Fivush *et al.*, 2011). Well-being seems adaptable from shared constructions and reconstructions of autobiographical narratives, especially when done with significant others.

Sharing autobiographical narratives relating to language learning (i.e. language learning histories) would therefore seem helpful for learning and well-being. In the classroom, the teacher and students alike might recount their stories of language learning, and students can gain deeper perspectives and appreciation about language learning struggles, joys, purposes and paths to achievement. Chances to create classroom narratives themselves may also be important, as would fostering an environment conducive for building the close social bonds necessary for taking the perspectives of others. Finally, students may benefit from reflecting upon their own individual language learning selves in different temporal domains in order to deepen self-continuity and make meaning of their learning.

Temporal Self-Regulation

Language learning can be a highly fulfilling lifelong journey of personal and professional development, relationship building and social engagement, and positive emotional expansion and flourishing (Dewaele & MacIntyre, 2014; Oxford & Cuéllar, 2014). On the other hand, language learning can be perceived as an undesirable, inescapable and uncomfortable if not painful situation to be endured, as can occur in certain educational contexts, for instance in Iran (Sahragard & Alimorad, 2013), Japan (Falout, 2013b; Kikuchi, 2013), South Korea (Kim & Kim, 2013) and Vietnam (Trang & Baldauf, 2007). Particularly where language education is compulsory, students can often lose self-confidence, subjective control, motivation and meaning in their learning.

Especially for students who find themselves lost on the long path of language learning, with negative past selves holding them back from learning in the present, a good place to practice temporal self-regulation is in the classroom. Classrooms naturally afford a potentially intimate social realm, the medium in which self-images are socially exemplified and shared, psychologically and collectively constructed, physically enacted and explored, and interpersonally validated (e.g. Bandura, 1997; Chen *et al.*, 2006). Furthermore, when class members provide each other with mutual care, students can move beyond past self hang-ups related to the subject of study and get on with the learning (e.g. Boekaerts, 1993).

The following vignettes offer glimpses into temporal self-regulation via cherishing the good moments, reframing the bad moments and creating temporal self-continuity in language learning. For these kinds of pedagogical applications, it is important that students know beforehand the purposes and degrees of sharing that will be involved, as this allows them to adjust the amount of public disclosure they find comfortable, and that teachers remain sensitive to this and give students the option to keep their reflections private.

Cherishing the good moments

One way of improving the valence of past selves when negative, and fortifying it when positive, is to become more accustomed to recognizing and cherishing the good moments. Not just students but also teachers might try the following exercises, as investigated by Gregersen *et al.* (2014). *Three good things* (as described above in relation to the study by Seligman *et al.*, 2005) is an activity of reflecting back on the day and then writing up three positive experiences from that day, including one's own reasoning for why each experience happened; this is done each day for a week. The experiences might be related to language learning or teaching, but not necessarily. *Savoring* is an activity of looking out for and noticing in the present a positive moment as it is occurring, and paying conscious attention to it. The moment might relate to language learning or teaching. Then in reflection participants write about how it felt, why it happened, and how one might be able to have a similar experience in the future. Students and teachers can share these experiences with another person, document this person's reactions, and write how this sharing felt. In the Gregersen *et al.* (2014) study, these exercises of personal reflections of the immediate past may have influenced the overall gains in positivity of future self-images. Additionally, the activities seemed to help the participants make connections between personal goals of language learning and teaching with the continuity of their daily lives and their broader life circumstances.

Activities like these might be used as material for the language classroom. One rationale for sharing good moments, as opposed to keeping them private in journals, might be that when feelings about the self are shared publicly, they can become more deeply internalized and more easily accessible in memory (Tice, 1999). Therefore, students and even their teachers might share their happy moments from recent days, even with whole-class groups, in the supportive and caring environment possible within a classroom circle (Falout, 2014), or perhaps somewhat more intimately in small groups or pairs. The greater the sharing, the greater are the opportunities for social modeling (Bandura, 1997).

Classroom publications might also make appropriate forums for sharing positive feelings and immediate past experiences related to language learning. Murphey's (2014) students learn positive affirmation songs in class, and choose a song to teach to someone outside of class, which often is a family member or close friend. Afterwards, students write their own case studies about these experiences, and compile these into class booklets. They commonly report that these experiences bring greater bonding with significant others, increased meaning-making and connections from the lyrics to their lives, and higher levels of positive affect.

The publications are also distributed to the next year's students. Past year's students can act as coping models for next year's students when describing in their reports how they were initially distressed by but then prevailed in this challenging project. This can boost next year's students' resiliency (Bandura, 1997). Also, the descriptions of past year's students' successes may act as testimonials, the reading of which can impart even greater gains in next year's students' well-being, compared with having not been exposed to peer testimonials (Layous *et al.*, 2013). In sum, teaching others something positive and meaningful using the target language, reflecting on it and sharing the reflections can result in students becoming agents of change in promoting well-being for themselves and for others in their social networks.

Reframing the bad moments

Simply writing about one's negative emotional past experiences can help one to process these experiences cognitively, and to improve present mood and physical health (e.g. Smyth & Pennebaker, 1999). For students both floundering and flourishing, they can write their language learning histories, which usually contain mixtures of positive and negative experiences, in an inclusive recollection of distant through to immediate past learning experiences, or an abridged version thereof, to share in the classroom. Investigations have suggested that a link occurs between sharing language learning histories and a reframing effect of negative experiences (Falout *et al.*, 2013b; Fukada *et al.*, in press; Murphey *et al.*, 2012), as well as increases in pre-existing language learning strengths, such as self-beliefs and strategy use (Murphey *et al.*, 2005).

Sharing past negative learning experiences can help learners to process them emotionally and cognitively. In other words, it can help learners to accept their negative experiences, learn from and make meaning of them, and become emotionally and cognitively unburdened by them so that they can move forward in their learning. Students can become coping models for each other when they share stories of their learning struggles and eventual successes and facility in using the language. Similarly, hearing about others' joy in learning and self-regulation strategies can provide practical suggestions and hope for doing well in language learning (Falout *et al.*, 2013b; Fukada *et al.*, in press; Murphey *et al.*, 2012).

Learned optimism is an activity in which students and teachers write about three adverse experiences throughout the day, then include beliefs and interpretations about why the events happened, the potential future consequences of the events, predictions of how one's beliefs about the events might influence the self and others, and a list of counter-evidence of the interpreted causes and predicted consequences (Gregersen *et al.*, 2014). Gregersen *et al.* (2014) caution that the notion of adverse experiences is relative, and that learners with optimistic outlooks might have troubles identifying such moments in their day. Used as the third of three positive psychology interventions (the first two were *three good things* and *savoring*, described above), it was explicable that this reframing activity worked in concert with the other activities for increasing language learners' and teachers' sense that a positive future self was attainable.

Seligman (2006) delineates the steps with learned optimism activities. Explaining in external form (i.e. by writing) beliefs about why the negative event happened – putting one's inner voice outside the self – acts as a way to distance oneself from the self-beliefs. This can suspend self-judgments, based on habitual explanations of past negative experiences, which helps people to see that their self-beliefs following negative events are often distorted or inaccurate, and the imagined consequences are often catastrophizations, meaning worst-case scenarios that are out of proportion with what is likely to happen. The final step is to search for counter-evidence that the self-beliefs are indeed distortions and that the imagined consequences are only catastrophizations. Therefore, learned optimism is less about becoming positive and more about learning to avoid negativity (Seligman, 2006).

Creating temporal self-continuity

The interconnected nature of retrospective and prospective processes means that thinking of the self in one temporal domain simultaneously exercises thinking of the self in the other temporal domains (Schacter, 2012; Schacter *et al.*, 2007). This implies that any temporal-based self-image activity can have an influence on one's concept of self-continuity. Various interventions used to help learners visualize, script, plan actions toward and even mock perform positive future scenarios relating to second language abilities and uses have been shown to increase learners' present self-confidence and self-regulation in learning (Magid & Chan, 2012; Sampson, 2012). Other studies that included mixtures of past, present and future self-image reflection activities for the classroom indicated gains in language-use self-image not only within each of these three temporal domains, but in strengthened interrelationships between each domain, suggesting an increased sense of temporal self-continuity (Falout *et al.*, 2013b; Fukada *et al.*, in press; Murphey *et al.*, 2012).

Some interventions may capitalize on the complex interplay of temporal and social contexts of self and other images in more subtle ways, ways that can invoke the creative uses of students' past selves and past others. For example, in imagining the ideal classmates whom students would like to learn with, students probably form their idealized images based on past classmates (Murphey *et al.*, 2014). In a mental comparison of these idealized images of others with present self-image, learners may see a discrepancy between what the self desires to receive from ideal classmates and what the self does for actual classmates. Seeing this discrepancy may prompt students to help others more in the ways that they wish to be helped themselves. When descriptions of ideal classmates are shared among actual classmates, newer images of what is possible for self and others can emerge, leading to motivated behaviors of language learning assistance across the classroom. Investigations in classrooms have shown strong connections between self-perceived behaviors of classmates and of self in mutual language learning assistance, specifically in ways that the learners themselves had idealized. Idealizing classmates can therefore help students work more closely together toward their language learning goals for their futures (Murphey & Iswanti, 2014; Murphey *et al.*, 2014).

Conclusions

Past selves play a crucial role in the development of language learners' dispositions, attitudes, values and self-beliefs. Past selves can help shape the nature of learners' approaches to learning, their social interactions that influence their own and others' learning, and the eventual lifetime trajectories related to language use. Continued research into positive psychology interventions that specifically relate to language learners' experiences and self-images would assist teachers wishing to help learners who are struggling in their language educations, and to reinforce the strengths of learners who are thriving. One of the things becoming recognized through classroom-based research (e.g. Fukada *et al.*, in press; Murphey *et al.*, 2014) is that these distinctions may not always be so clear cut; some learners have strengths in some areas at certain times, and weaknesses in other areas at different times. Embracing these and other diversities among learners, and coming together to share their experiences, insights and hopes, generates opportunities for all to mutually adapt, find meaning and flourish.

Acknowledgments

My gratitude to Mika Falout for astute advice on previous drafts of this chapter.

References

Bandura, A. (1997) *Self-efficacy: The Exercise of Control*. New York: W.H. Freeman.

Bluck, S. and Alea, N. (2009) Thinking and talking about the past: Why remember? *Applied Cognitive Psychology* 23 (8), 1089–1104.

Boekaerts, M. (1993) Being concerned with well-being and with learning. *Educational Psychologist* 28 (2), 149–167.

Chen, S., Taylor, L.S. and Jeung, K. (2006) Collective self-verification among members of a naturally occurring group: Possible antecedents and long-term consequences. *Basic and Applied Social Psychology* 28 (2), 101–115.

Chessell, Z.J., Rathbone, C.J., Souchay, C., Charlesworth, L. and Moulin, C.J.A. (2014) Autobiographical memory, past and future events, and self-images in younger and older adults. *Self and Identity* 13 (4), 380–397.

Dewaele, J.-M. and MacIntyre, P.D. (2014) The two faces of Janus? Anxiety and enjoyment in the foreign language classroom. *Studies in Second Language Learning and Teaching* 4 (2), 237–274.

Dweck, C.S. (2006) *Mindset: The New Psychology of Success*. New York: Ballantine.

Falout, J. (2012) Coping with demotivation: EFL learners' remotivation processes. *TESL-EJ* 16 (3), 1–29.

Falout, J. (2013a) Prospecting possible EFL selves. *Language Teacher* 37 (5), 45–49.

Falout, J. (2013b) The social crux: Motivational transformations of EFL students in Japan. In T. Coverdale-Jones (ed.) *Transnational Higher Education in the Asian Context* (pp. 132–148). Basingstoke: Palgrave Macmillan.

Falout, J. (2014) Circular seating arrangements: Approaching the social crux in language classrooms. *Studies in Second Language Learning and Teaching* 4 (2), 275–300.

Falout, J. (2016) Past selves: Emerging motivational guides across temporal contexts. In J. King (ed.) *The Dynamic Interplay Between Context and the Language Learner* (pp. 47–65). Basingstoke: Palgrave Macmillan.

Falout, J. and Maruyama, M. (2004) A comparative study of proficiency and learner demotivation. *Language Teacher* 28 (8), 3–9.

Falout, J., Elwood, J. and Hood, M. (2009) Demotivation: Affective states and learning outcomes. *System* 37 (3), 403–417.

Falout, J., Murphey, T., Fukuda, T. and Trovela, M. (2013a) Japanese EFL learners' remotivation strategies. In M. Cortazzi and L. Jin (eds) *Researching Cultures of Learning: International Perspectives on Language Learning and Education* (pp. 328–349). Basingstoke: Palgrave Macmillan.

Falout, J., Fukada, Y., Murphey, T. and Fukuda, T. (2013b) What's working in Japan? Present communities of imagining. In M.T. Apple, D. Da Silva and T. Fellner (eds) *Language Learning Motivation in Japan* (pp. 245–267). Bristol: Multilingual Matters.

Fivush, R., Bohanek, J.G. and Zaman, W. (2011) Personal and intergenerational narratives in relation to adolescents' well-being. In T. Habermas (ed.) The development of autobiographical reasoning in adolescence and beyond. *New Directions for Child and Adolescent Development* 131, 45–57.

Frazier, L.D., Hooker, K., Johnson, P.M. and Kaus, C.R. (2000) Continuity and change in possible selves in later life: A 5-year longitude study. *Basic and Applied Social Psychology* 22 (3), 237–243.

Fukada, Y., Murphey, T., Falout, J. and Fukuda (in press) Essential motivational group dynamics: A three-year panel study. In R. Breeze and C.S. Guinda (eds) *Essential Competencies for English Medium University Teaching*. Dordrecht: Springer.

Gilbert, D.T. and Wilson, T.D. (2007) Prospection: Experiencing the future. *Science* 317 (5843), 1351–1354.

Gilbert, D.T., Killingsworth, M.A., Eyre, R.N. and Wilson, T.D. (2009) The surprising power of neighborly advice. *Science* 323 (5921), 1617–1619.

Gregersen, T., MacIntyre, P.D., Finegan, K.H., Talbot, K. and Claman, S. (2014) Examining emotional intelligence within the context of positive psychology interventions. *Studies in Second Language Learning and Teaching* 4 (2), 327–353.
Grysman, A., Prabhakar, J., Anglin, S.M. and Hudson, J.A. (2013) The time traveling self: Comparing self and other in narratives of past and future events. *Consciousness and Cognition* 22 (3), 742–755.
Kahneman, D. (2011) *Thinking, Fast and Slow.* London: Penguin Books.
Kahneman, D. and Riis, J. (2005) Living, and thinking about it: Two perspectives on life. In F.A. Huppert, N. Baylis and B. Kaverne (eds) *The Science of Well-Being* (pp. 285–304). Oxford: Oxford University Press.
Kanten, A.B. and Teigen, K.H. (2008) Better than average and better with time: Relative evaluations of the self and others in the past, present, and future. *European Journal of Social Psychology* 38 (2), 343–353.
Keyes, C.L.M. (2000) Subjective change and its consequences for emotional well-being. *Motivation and Emotion* 24 (2), 67–84.
Kikuchi, K. (2013) Demotivators in the Japanese EFL context. In M.T. Apple, D. Da Silva and T. Fellner (eds) *Language Learning Motivation in Japan* (pp. 206–224). Bristol: Multilingual Matters.
Kim, Y.-K. and Kim, T.-Y. (2013) English learning demotivation studies in the EFL contexts: State of the art. *Modern English Education* 14 (1), 77–102.
Layous, K., Nelson, S.K. and Lyubomirsky, S. (2013) What is the optimal way to deliver a positive activity intervention? The case of writing about one's best possible selves. *Journal of Happiness Studies* 14 (2), 635–654.
Magid, M. and Chan, L. (2012) Motivating English learners by helping them visualize their ideal L2 self: Lessons from two motivational programmes. *Innovation in Language Learning and Teaching* 6 (2), 113–125.
Markus, H. and Nurius, P. (1986) Possible selves. *American Psychologist* 41 (9), 954–969.
McFarland, C. and Buehler, R. (2012) Negative moods and the motivated remembering of past selves: The role of implicit theories of personal stability. *Journal of Personality and Social Psychology* 102 (2), 242–263.
Murphey, T. (2014) Singing well-becoming: Student musical therapy case studies. *Studies in Second Language Learning and Teaching* 4 (2), 205–235.
Murphey, T. and Iswanti, S. (2014) Surprising humanity! Comparing ideal classmates in two countries. *ETAS Journal* 31 (2), 33–35.
Murphey, T., Chen, J. and Chen, L-H. (2005) Learners' constructions of identities and imagined communities. In P. Benson and D. Nunan (eds) *Learners' Stories: Difference and Diversity in Language Learning* (pp. 83–100). Cambridge: Cambridge University Press.
Murphey, T., Falout, J., Fukada, Y. and Fukuda, T. (2012) Group dynamics: Collaborative agency in present communities of imagination. In S. Mercer, S. Ryan and M. Williams (eds) *Psychology for Language Learning: Insights from Research, Theory and Practice* (pp. 220–238). Basingstoke: Palgrave Macmillan.
Murphey, T., Falout, J., Fukuda, T. and Fukada, Y. (2014) Socio-dynamic motivating through idealizing classmates. *System* 45, 242–253.
Oxford, R.L. and Cuéllar, L. (2014) Positive psychology in cross-cultural narratives: Mexican students discover themselves while learning Chinese. *Studies in Second Language Learning and Teaching* 4 (2), 173–203.
Peterson, C., Maier, S.F. and Seligman, M.E.P. (1993) *Learned Helplessness: A Theory for the Age of Personal Control.* New York: Oxford University Press.
Quoidbach, J., Gilbert, D.T. and Wilson, T.D. (2013) The end of history illusion. *Science* 339 (6115), 96–98.
Sahragard, R. and Alimond, Z. (2013) Demotivating factors affecting Iranian high school students' English learning. In M. Cortazzi and L. Jin (eds) *Researching Cultures of*

Learning: International Perspectives on Language Learning and Education (pp. 308–327). Basingstoke: Palgrave Macmillan.

Sampson, R. (2012) The language-learning self, self-enhancement activities, and self perceptual change. *Language Teaching Research* 16 (3), 317–335.

Schacter, D.L. (2012) Adaptive constructive processes and the future of memory. *American Psychologist* 67 (8), 603–613.

Schacter, D.L., Addis, D.R. and Buckner, R.L. (2007) Remembering the past to imagine the future: The prospective brain. *Nature Reviews Neuroscience* 8 (9), 657–661.

Seligman, M.E.P. (2006) *Learned Optimism: How to Change Your Mind and Your Life*. New York: Vintage Books (original work published in 1990).

Seligman, M.E.P. and Csikszentmihalyi, M. (2000) Positive psychology: An introduction *American Psychologist* 55 (1), 5–14.

Seligman, M.E.P., Steen, T.A., Park, N. and Peterson, C. (2005) Positive psychology progress: Empirical validation of interventions. *American Psychologist* 60 (5), 410–421.

Seligman, M.E.P., Rashid, T. and Parks, A.C. (2006) Positive psychotherapy. *American Psychologist* 61 (8), 774–788.

Seligman, M.E.P., Ernst, R.M., Gillham, J., Reivich, K. and Linkins, M. (2009) Positive education: Positive psychology and classroom interventions. *Oxford Review of Education* 35 (3), 293–311.

Simkin, D.K., Lederer, J.P. and Seligman, M.E.P. (1983) Learned helplessness in groups. *Behaviour Research and Therapy* 21 (6), 613–622.

Smyth, J.M. and Pennebaker, J.W. (1999) Sharing one's story: Translating emotional experiences into words as a coping tool. In C.R. Snyder (ed.) *Coping: The Psychology of What Works* (pp. 70–89). New York: Oxford University Press.

Spreng, R.N. and Grady, C.L. (2009) Patterns of brain activity supporting autobiographical memory, prospection, and theory of mind, and their relationship to the default mode network. *Journal of Cognitive Neuroscience* 22 (6), 1112–1123.

Strahan, E.J. and Wilson, A.E. (2006) Temporal comparisons, identity, and motivation: The relation between past, present, and possible future selves. In C. Dunkel and J. Kerpelman (eds) *Possible Selves Theory, Research and Application* (pp. 1–15). New York: Nova Science.

Tice, D.M. (1999) Self-concept change and self-presentation: The looking glass self is also a magnifying glass. In R.F. Baumeister (ed.) *The Self in Social Psychology* (pp. 195–217). New York: Psychology Press.

Trang, T.T.T. and Bauldauf, R.B. (2007) Demotivation: Understanding resistance to English language learning. The case of Vietnamese students. *Journal of Asia TEFL* 4 (1), 79–105.

Weiner, B. (2000) Intrapersonal and interpersonal theories of motivation from an attributional perspective. *Educational Psychology Review* 12 (1), 1–14.

Werner-Seidler, A. and Moulds, M.L. (2011) Autobiographical memory characteristics in depression vulnerability: Formerly depressed individuals recall less vivid positive memories. *Cognition and Emotion* 25 (6), 1087–1103.

Wilson, A.E. and Ross, M. (2001) From chump to champ: People's appraisals of their earlier and present selves. *Journal of Personality and Social Psychology* 80 (4), 572–584.

5 Language Learning and Teaching: What's Love Got To Do With It?

Ana Maria F. Barcelos and Hilda Simone H. Coelho

People are what they love. Descartes stated: 'I think, therefore I am'. I invert Descartes and say: 'I love, therefore I am'.
Rubem Alves

The role of affective factors and emotions in the field of applied linguistics (AL) has been the focus of several studies (e.g. Aragão, 2007, 2011; Arnold, 1999; Imai, 2010; So, 2005), with an emphasis on motivation and anxiety for the most part. In education, some studies have pointed out how emotions may affect students' motivation and identities, as well as teacher practices (Zembylas, 2004). More recently, several studies have started investigating other kinds of emotions, such as enjoyment (Dewaele & MacIntyre, 2014) and hope (Ciarrochi *et al.*, 2007; Murphey & Carpenter, 2008). Yet, the emotion of *love*, despite being an emotion that all human beings feel, has not been investigated much in AL, apart from some studies on emotions and multilinguals looking at how love is expressed linguistically and in different cultures (Dewaele, 2008).

Love is part of our human essence and of our everyday life. Yet many would agree that people are afraid of love, especially when the issue is about love in education. Ana experienced an episode at first hand that demonstrated the fear of using the word *love* in education. While on sabbatical in Canada, she attended a class on effective language teaching. One day, while discussing a text by hooks[1] (2003), one professor asked how we can better love our students. One student, very shocked and angry about the use of the word 'love', said it was not necessary to love students: it was important to talk about respect, but love was not important. Can we not talk about love in education? What is wrong with talking about love in the classroom?

This episode does not seem to be an isolated incident. It appears that, as a society, in education and in language learning, we shy away from discussions concerning love. According to Steiner (2000), even in education, love is so feared that in some books on emotions, such as LeDoux (1996), this word in not mentioned even once, while fear is mentioned more than 70 times. Steiner adds that in the book *Emotional Intelligence* by Goleman (1995), there are only three mentions of love in one specific chapter and only nine throughout the rest of the book. It surprises us because medicine has shown how love is connected to recovering from illness and also to improving intelligence (Moraes, 2008). Not even in our syllabuses is love mentioned. We talk about specific competences, pedagogical knowledge and classroom management skills, but nobody expects teachers to love their pupils (Aiazzi, 2007). Coleman-Kiner (2011) also pointed out how absent the word 'love' is, especially in school leadership, and how it is sometimes substituted by 'ethics of care', 'caring adults' and 'emotional intelligence'. For her, 'it is almost as if we are afraid to say that our work is a purely human endeavour – that our jobs are to develop human beings' (Coleman-Kiner, 2011: para. 3). Paraphrasing Swain (2013) talking about emotions in AL, love is the elephant in the room in education and in AL. In other words, it seems that love is indeed a four-letter word! Yet, we argue that love is one of the most important emotions that effective teachers can cultivate and nurture.

Seligman (2009) states that 'Raising children, I realized, is more than fixing what is wrong with them. It is about identifying and nurturing their strongest qualities, what they own and are best at, and helping them find niches in which they can best live out these positive qualities' (p. 4). By the same token, understanding and focusing on love in language learning and teaching allows us to stop looking for and talking about what is wrong with our students and to look for and talk more about what is right with them; it is more about seeing what is best in our students and about us. Love allows us to do that. As Seligman (2009) states, 'we take for granted a certain amount of hope, *love*, enjoyment, and trust because these are the very conditions that allow us to go on living' (p. 8, emphasis added). According to MacIntyre and Mercer (2014), the goal of positive psychology is to 'help people lead better lives' by developing 'tools to build positive emotions, greater engagement, and an appreciation of meaning in life and its activities' (p. 154). Thus, we believe that understanding more about love as a positive emotion can contribute to a sense of well-being in teachers and learners. What we try to bring to this chapter is a view of love as already discussed by different authors in the field of education to expand our view of love in language learning and teaching.

This chapter looks at the role of this specific emotion in language teaching and learning. In the first part, we discuss some common myths and misrepresentations about love in education. In the second, we bring together the different definitions of love in education and social sciences in general and draw out the key components of a definition of love in AL. In the third section, we point out how love, language learning and teaching are related. We conclude by giving suggestions for research on love in AL.

Myths and Misrepresentations About Love in Teaching: What Love is Not

In this section, we briefly present some myths that may explain why some of us may feel scared of using the world *love* in education. The first myth posits that affect in education excludes academic knowledge, rigour and serious learning (Freire, 1996). Freire defends affect, arguing it should never disturb rigorous practice. On the contrary, he believes that affect and joy are necessary in a system where disrespect to students is so common. Education means being open and available to the joy of living; not too sweet, nor too bitter.

The second myth suggests that emotions will impair professionalism (Noddings, 1999). According to this common view, professionalism is equated with having a detached, cool and dispassionate relationship with students and that feeling too much for one's students may lead to burnout. Noddings (1999) argues that caring relations are the foundation for successful pedagogical activity. These caring and trusting relations help us to listen to our students and this will help them to accept what teachers try to teach and help them to see teachers' efforts as cooperative work. In addition, in getting to know their students through dialogue, teachers gain important information on how to base their lessons on students' needs (Noddings, 1999). Being attuned to the needs and wants of learners is one essential part of a teacher's role, as was emphasized in the humanistic movement some years ago.

These two myths illustrate why it is important to talk about love in education and in language learning and teaching. As we hope to show in this chapter, love is the foundation of our lives and the essence of what makes us human. Thus, learning cannot be separated from love. According to Maturana and Varela (1987), all learning is through love. They see life and love as two inseparable unities. They explain, 'we humans must live in love, trusting each other, to be physiologically and psychically healthy' (Maturana & Verden-Zoller, 2008: 226). We can conclude this section with an understanding of love which, unlike the myths above, views it as 'a combination of care, commitment, knowledge, responsibility, respect and trust. All these factors work interdependently' (hooks, 2003: 131).

The Meanings of Love in Education: What Love Is

In this section, we show how love is understood by key educators and researchers such as Day (2004), Liston (2000, 2008), Freire (2005), hooks (2003), Maturana and Verden-Zoller (1996) and Fredrickson (2013), in order to open a conversation about the role of love in education and to build a definition of love from which language educators can work. Some of these educators do not always use the word *love*, and instead may use words such as passion; however, we have chosen to include them in our discussion here because we believe they are talking about love in a broader sense and not in a limited, common-sense way as people think of love, as only romantically or sexually related. Drawing on the insights from all of these contributions, we offer our definition of love towards the end of this section.

Love as a passion for teaching

Love can come disguised under different names. One of these is the word *passion*, used by Christopher Day, a professor at the University of Nottingham and author of books on teachers' lives, emotions and change. Day (2004) uses the word *passion* instead of love, but we see it as similar to love and ideas of love shared by other authors.

Passion is seen as an essential element in teaching and at the heart of what teaching is or should be. Passion is the element that sustains teachers when they face difficult scenarios. When teachers' sense of self, efficacy and commitment are threatened, their personal lives and their lives in the workplace are destabilized. They may become increasingly vulnerable and this vulnerability can make them more passive and conservative in the classroom as their passion dies and their main goal becomes just to survive school (Day, 2004).

Teaching is more than the mastery of pedagogical content knowledge and skills. Good teaching requires 'both intellectual and emotional commitment' and this is a professional necessity, not a luxury (Day, 2004: 12). Day warns us that when teachers are not feeling passionate or do not have freedom to know who they are or to be themselves in the classroom, they 'explode', that is, they explode emotionally in inappropriate ways in the school or classroom, or they may even leave the profession.

Day (2004) describes and characterizes what being a passionate teacher is like. He explains that, first, being a passionate teacher involves self-knowledge. In order to care for someone, teachers need to know who they are, their strengths and limitations, how they can grow in order to respond to their learners' needs. Second, teachers who are passionate about their work know that who they are, as well as what they teach, must connect emotionally with each student. In the classroom, this passion translates into a strong desire for all students' success, which is communicated through humour, interpersonal warmth, patience, empathy and support of their pupils' self-esteem. Thus, passion can help teachers to be more committed, resilient and effective. Third, passionate teachers are more likely to work together with their colleagues in their schools. Such collaboration is a key ingredient of a loving school environment conducive to more effective teaching.

Attentive love

Daniel P. Liston (2000), Professor of Education at the University of Colorado, USA, explores the various ways reason and emotion interact to affect the practice of teaching and the education of teachers. He sees love in the context of love of inquiry, of discovery and of creation – a way to reach beyond ourselves. A teacher who loves teaching shares this love of learning with students and teaches students about it, trying to instil in them this love for the subject as well. To quote him: 'To love teaching is to give of yourself in a way that can be so tenderly vulnerable' (Liston, 2000: 92). Thus, for Liston, love in education means attending to the situation, to the students in the classes, finding ways to connect students, looking for the good in them and seeing them in ways that assume and build upon the good they bring with them. This is similar to what the positive psychology movement stresses, namely, to build on students' potential, to see the good in them and to develop their signature strengths (MacIntyre & Mercer, 2014).

According to Liston (2000), there are three kinds of love: romantic, transformative (engaged) and attentive love. Romantic love is as described above, when teachers try to infuse learners with their love for teaching and learning. It is vulnerable and subject to pain and rejection from students, which can fill the teacher's soul with despair (Liston, 2000: 82–83). Liston (2008) expands these notions and defines transformative love as to our capacity to overcome obstacles in teaching, a form of quiet heroism. Attentive love stems from the basic assumption that 'good exists within each student' and the willingness to 'see our students more clearly and justly' (Liston, 2008: 389). In other words, it is a desire to do good, to 'reach beyond ourselves', 'a yearning that defines in part, what it means to be human'; 'when we approach students with this understanding and pursue the good within each one, we honor them and their search for good' (Liston, 2008: 389). In order to do that, teachers need to temporarily suspend their own agendas and expectations to be able to see students' realities in their own terms. It demands seeing the 'genius' in each student, as Murphey (2012) worded it. It demands a sort of daily mindfulness to notice each student and their frustrations, interests and anxieties. However, this does not come easily. It demands effort, discipline and sacrifice on the teacher's part; given the myriad of other demands on teachers' time, energy and resources, this can be difficult to achieve in practice.

Love as amorous responsibility

Paulo Freire (1996), the Brazilian educator, sees love/affect as a specific practice of human beings. Thus, education is an act of love. There is no dialogue if there is not love. Freire talks about love as inherent to the activity of dealing with people, with human beings, to be open to other people's suffering or puzzles. According to Freire (1979: 92), 'there is no education without love; those who are not able to love incomplete human beings are not able to be educators. They are not able to become education professionals.'

We are human beings who learn how to be humans in interacting and dialoguing with others. Especially in language learning, interacting and dialoguing are essential to learning and to developing good relationships in the classroom, which foster the conditions for communication. To teach is to have affect for students and to be open to this affect as a form of interaction and communication. This does not mean that a teacher has to like everybody in the same way. It means that we are not afraid of affect or of expressing it. A distorted form of affectivity for Freire means disrespect towards students' curiosity and language; it means to not teach, not respect students' experiences, not give them limits and to deny their freedom and curiosity.

Freire (2005) uses the term *amorosidade* (amorosity), which includes the perspectives of intelligence, reason, embodiment, ethics and politics on our personal and collective experiences. *Amorosidade* also includes emotions, feelings, desires, decisions, curiosity, creativity, intuition and the beauty of life. Affectivity and *amorosidade* for him are basic factors of human life and education. This *amorosidade* is enacted when establishing teaching and learning relationships that are more dialogical and respectful. To Freire, teachers' amorous responsibility is formative. This amorous dimension of teaching and relating cannot be ignored for learning to happen. *Amorosidade* does not exclude developing the work with commitment, involvement, competence and seriousness. Much the opposite: *amorosidade* is an essential condition for all these things to happen.

Love as freedom and growth

hooks, an American author, feminist and social activist, sees love as a combination of care, commitment, knowledge, responsibility, respect and trust. Caring teachers must cultivate students' emotional growth, directly or indirectly. According to her, the act of knowing is an act of love, of entering and embracing the reality of the other, of allowing the other to enter and embrace our own; 'in such knowing, we know and are known as members of one community' (hooks, 2003: 132). hooks uses the word 'love' in the sense of daring and growth. It is worth citing her here at length:

> Love in the classroom prepares teachers and students to open our minds and hearts. It is the foundation on which every learning community can be created. Teachers need not fear that practicing love in the classroom will lead to favoritism. Love will always move us away from domination in all its forms. Love will always challenge and change us. This is the heart of the matter. (hooks, 2003: 137).

Education, then, is the practice of freedom that promotes growth. It is an act of love that promotes spiritual and mental growth in our learners and in ourselves as teachers.

The biology of love

Maturana and Verden-Zoller (1996) argue that love is the grounding emotion for our human existence. Love is to accept others legitimately, allowing the other to be what she or he is, without requirements. Human existence depends entirely on interactions grounded on love. They argue that love is not a special emotion; on the contrary, it is an everyday biological phenomenon and, therefore, an ordinary emotion that conserves our existence. Humans have the capacity to love, which 'needs not to be learned, it can be allowed to be or it can be denied' (Maturana & Verden-Zoller, 1996: para. 21). For Maturana and Verden-Zoller, all social interactions are grounded on love because love is the only emotion that allows the other to legitimately be – to exist – and thus to engage in society. Emotions such as rejection and indifference make interactions hierarchical and imbued with power struggle. The emotion of rejection denies the emotion of love, denies the other, causing an end to social interactions. The result of rejection is exclusion. When denying the other, we exclude the other from our environment, or they exclude themselves.

What we learn from Maturana's research (Maturana, 2005; Maturana & Verden-Zoller, 1996) is that we are 'loving animals and our intelligence and creativity in the domain of human well-being depends on our being loving animals' (Maturana & Verden-Zoller, 1996: para. 20). He is categorical in affirming that 'the only emotion that expands intelligence is love and this is so because intelligence has to do with the acceptance of the legitimacy of the other and the expansion of the possibility for consensuality that such acceptance entails' (para. 20). Under this concept of love as the grounding emotion for social interactions, Maturana questions the way we teach our children at school and what kind of education we really want. If we understand love as the acceptance of the other legitimately, our children should learn to accept and respect themselves so they will accept and respect the other. Accepting themselves means being able to see their mistakes and respect mistakes as opportunities for growth and change, not as the occasion for humiliation and punishment. By accepting themselves, children will not fear, envy or deprecate others. As recent literature on positive psychology in language learning suggests (MacIntyre & Mercer, 2014), catering for positive emotions in the classroom will contribute to language teachers and learners' well-being and, thus, more effective learning. In this way, the concept of love, as defined by Maturana, in language learning and teaching implies the creation of a classroom environment of acceptance of and respect for learners' learning processes and their mistakes as part of this process and their growth.

This growth happens when teachers stimulate social interaction and lower competition among students. For Maturana (2005), competition denies oneself and others, because, in a competitive situation, we are being judged in reference to someone else's view. In a socially interactive classroom, however, children are allowed to experience learning through love – that is, through acceptance. This is the stage where we see the importance of the teacher's role. Through interaction, teachers model respect for and acceptance of themselves and the group for their learners. Teachers will respect pupils as they are – not as they are expected to be. The biology of love makes this mutually respectful relationship possible as long as we are living in it, in the emotion of love (Maturana, 2005).

Love as positivity resonance

Fredrickson (2013), an American social psychologist who conducts research on emotions and positive psychology, defines love as positivity resonance, or a micro-moment of love, that is, the attunement to each other's emotions, resulting in mutual care and regard for each other. According to Fredrickson, 'Love is that micro-moment of warmth and connection that you share with another living being' (p. 10). Fredrickson believes that these micro-moments can increase our ability to understand and empathize with others, increasing our social connections and positive emotions. This micro-moment of love changes our minds and expands our awareness of our environment and of our own selves. For the author, 'Love draws you out of your cocoon of self-absorption to attune to others. Love allows you to really see another person, holistically, with care, concern, and compassion' (p. 10).

This is one of the most important aspects of the emotional climates of the classroom. According to Fredrickson, if we are not able to connect to others, we shut ourselves off from creating opportunities for positivity resonance and life-learning. Love, for Fredrickson, involves investing in the well-being of others.[2] Over time, positivity resonance may build embodied rapport, social bonds and commitment. Teachers can provide more caring classrooms with more positive emotions and connections for students, something that researchers in AL have begun to stress more recently (see MacIntyre & Gregersen, 2012; Murphey, 2014; Oxford, 2014). Thus, love is not confined to our minds and hearts, but is embedded and unfolds between and among people. In short, love unfolds and reveals itself in the space between teachers and learners in the language classroom. It resides within connections and relationships that are (or should be) at the basis of all the interaction that occurs in language learning environments, especially in the language classroom.

Love and Language Teaching and Learning

So far, we have summarized how love has been discussed in the field of education and (social) psychology. What about language teaching and learning? What do these all definitions of love have in common and how do they relate to language learning and teaching? First, love for all these researchers means ethics, growth, care, respect, freedom and dialogue. Love means seeing the potential in all learners and being open to feeling love to all human beings. Second, language and love are essential parts of being human and, thus, fundamental aspects of any kind of teaching and learning.

Although the word love has not been used much in the literature, at least explicitly, we can already see seeds of it in its aliases used in language learning and teaching. First, it was present in the humanistic movement that blossomed in the 1970s, with its emphasis on emotions and students' and teachers' well-being in the classroom. The classic book by Moskowitz (1978), *Caring and Sharing in the Foreign Language Class*, was one among many to propose activities to create a loving environment and to have love as a priority for language teaching practice. We could say that although the word *love* was not used at that time, what the humanistic movement did was to bring *love* into language learning and teaching, since this movement emphasized feelings, social relations, responsibility, intellect and self-actualization (Mehrgan, 2012). Various authors discussed in this chapter have also stressed these aspects of the humanistic movement in their definitions and visions of love. More recently, a lot of the ideas of the humanistic movement seem to have made a comeback, with plenty of studies which focus on students' signature strengths, well-being and positive emotions (MacIntyre & Gregersen, 2012; MacIntyre & Mercer, 2014; Murphey, 2014; Oxford, 2014).

Aiazzi (2007) defends the notion that love is essential to language teaching. She sees love and learning as two interrelated processes and states that a new humanism can be reached through love. The author also talks about the difficulty of bringing love into our teaching, and finds four reasons for this. First, it is difficult to dissimulate our feelings and emotions when we love someone, either positive or negative. Thus, to build trust, teachers and learners need to learn to accept themselves and their limitations and be vulnerable enough to disclose their vulnerability to each other. Second, teaching with love demands the difficult task of accepting our students as unique and trying to understand and love them with all their complex personalities, beliefs and selves. Third, supporting learners in their cognitive and emotional goals is very demanding for teachers if they do not love their students. Finally, although helping learners become more autonomous and self-reliant is the most sincere love a teacher can provide, Aiazzi (2007) claims that this, too, is often arduous.

Murphey *et al.* (2010) have also proposed 'emotional belonging' as preceding learning and as a condition for individuals and groups to thrive in learning, a similar perspective to that of other authors discussed here, such as Freire, Maturana and Verden-Zoller, and Fredrickson. In Brazil, we have also started talking about this (see Barcelos, 2010, 2012; Barcelos & Coelho, 2010), suggesting that love activities can be used in teacher professional development as well as in language learning and teaching to promote students' and teachers' well-being, better quality of life, positivity, and better learning and teaching. In practical terms, this has meant a change in attitude and a change in our postures as teacher educators. As discussed by the authors cited in this chapter, love means respect, ethics, care and an openness of heart that makes it possible for positivity resonance. Thus, in all our classes and courses, we practise love in at least (but not exclusively) three ways. First, we learn to listen to our students and create a nurturing space for their (language) learning histories. We listen to them in a caring way, valuing all the stories they tell, even (indeed, especially) the ones with emotions of despair and sorrow, and we try to encourage them to see themselves with more positive and loving eyes. Second, we open the space for students to talk about themselves and create a safe environment where everyone learns from each other and can grow. Third, our classes are very collaborative and involve students and teachers giving constructive feedback to each other (using action logs, language learning histories, visual narratives and reflective tasks). In short, the key element is *compassionate listening* and acceptance of each other as perfect imperfect human beings. Listening to students with compassion helps us build a loving environment in which they learn to trust themselves and each other more and recognize their own potential for growth.

In all these studies in language learning and teaching, although the word *love* is not necessarily used, they all emphasize respect, ethics and care in promoting well-being, which ties into what positive psychology in language learning and teaching is about. In other words, these studies can be thought of as revisiting some of the issues that the humanistic movement addressed some 40 years ago.

Final Thoughts: A Word of Love

'Love and belonging are irreducible needs of all men, women and children. We're hardwired for connection. It's what gives purpose and meaning to our lives. The absence of love, belonging and connection always leads to suffering'
Brené Brown

In this chapter, we have looked at different definitions of love in education and how it has been perceived by researchers within education, psychology and biology in order to better understand its meaning in the classroom and to encourage its research in AL. Looking at all these definitions of love, it is striking to see some similarities. Researchers (Fredrickson, 2013; hooks, 2003; Maturana & Verden-Zoller, 1996) agree that love is our basic human condition. It must be understood as an essential element in our lives. Love is the capacity to accept and respect oneself and is intrinsically related to the capacity to respect and accept others. Liston (2000) and Freire (1996) agree on the importance of awakening students' potential. Enhancing students' potential, believing in them and focusing on their signature strengths are focused on in positive psychology, as more recent articles in this field have shown, as well as other books on emotions in language learning (see Andreas & Arnold, 2009; Rubio, 2007). Promoting a safe environment in which teachers and learners can thrive and excel is done only through true affection, through love. hooks (2003) also affirms the importance of love as a combination of emotions that leads us to embrace each other's reality and thus display empathy, which is so important for meaningful relationships (see Chapter 3). Maturana and Verden-Zoller (1996) argue that love is the emotion that constitutes social life; denying it will bring suffering and illness. In order to prevent this, we must connect with each other and look for micro-moments of positivity resonance, as Fredrickson (2013) advises.

We believe that, in terms of research, in the field of education AL would benefit from further empirical exploration of love and its relationship with the process of teaching and learning a language. More specifically, we suggest that the following questions (it is not by any means an exhaustive list) may guide further studies and work on *love* in AL:

- What micro-moments of positivity resonance are there in the language classroom and in schools where language teachers teach?
- How can we support language student-teachers in becoming qualified practising teachers and investigate the role that love plays in this transition from student to teacher?
- What is the relationship between love and success in language learning and teaching?
- What is the relationship between love and other important concepts in AL, such as teacher and learner motivation, identity, agency and beliefs?
- What are the identities of teachers and learners who act with love?
- Does love play a role in the resilience exhibited by some learners and teachers in adverse conditions of language learning and teaching?

Having sought to understand how love can be defined, we now offer some suggestions on how love can contribute to more effective language learning and teaching as well as to a better quality of life. In teaching, we hope teachers feel more encouraged to understand what love in education means. It is not the sentimentalist notion of just 'loving students' and not really ethically and morally caring for them and their education. It means really seeing them for who they are. In this sense, a first practical suggestion would be for teachers to understand this, reflect about themselves, their emotions and the beliefs or myths they hold about love. We suggest reading about love and trying to live it in daily practice. Watch and listen to students. In small acts, in tiny gestures and actions in class, start to really get to know them. Notice their greatness. This means being in awe of students and seeing their wonder as human beings, full of potential and deserving love, respect and care. Help them notice this about themselves as well.[3] Furthermore, if things get difficult in the classroom, teachers can ask themselves these questions:

- What would love do now?
- How can I bring more love into what I do?
- How can I teach with more love?
- How can I see my students with more loving eyes?

Asking these questions will help teachers shift the focus to students' positive elements as well as their own. Lastly, love in the classroom is enacted and enhanced through humanizing practices, rapport, micro-moments of positivity resonance and emotional belonging (Murphey *et al.*, 2010). As suggested here and based on Fredrickson (2013), these moments of positivity resonance can be brought into loving classrooms if we seek to instil these daily practices:

- Create opportunities for students to share interests and positive memories, joys, dreams and hopes, and express and encourage optimism in each other. To this end, Murphey *et al.* (2014) used newsletters and action logs.
- Do physical activities together. Encourage students to talk while walking, taking hikes together, juggling, singing songs with gestures and other physical activities that encourage sharing (Murphey, 2014).
- Share jokes, humour and opportunities to laugh at the same time.
- Maintain rituals that bond the class as a group (Dornyei & Murphey, 2003).
- Watch movies and videos and then talk about experiences of shared admiration and elevation.

In conclusion, we hope this chapter helps teachers not to be ashamed of love and to bring it back where it belongs: in education, in the classroom and in our language learning conversations. We hope teachers, teacher educators and researchers continue to understand love as an essential part of teaching and learning languages. We hope that it becomes a common word and a more commonly researched emotion in AL in the coming years.

Notes

(1) Bell Hooks (stylized bell hooks) is Gloria Jean Watkins' pen name.
(2) See Oxford (2014) for an interesting perspective on the use of well-being theory in language learning and teaching.
(3) A great source of inspiration for teachers is Murphey's book *Teaching in Pursuit of Wow!* (2012).

References

Aiazzi, A.M. (2007) Teaching as a matter of love. *Humanizing Language Teaching*, 9 (3). Retrieved from http://www.hltmag.co.uk/may07/stud02.htm (accessed 22 June 2012).

Andreas, V. and Arnold, J. (2009) *Seeds of Confidence: Self-esteem Activities for the EFL Classroom*. London: Helbling Languages.

Aragão, R.C. (2007) São as histórias que nos dizem mais: emoção, reflexão e ação na sala de aula. Unpublished PhD dissertation, FALE/UFMG, Belo Horizonte.

Aragão, R.C. (2011) Beliefs and emotions in foreign language learning. *System* 39 (3), 302–313.

Arnold, J. (ed.) (1999) *Affect in Language Learning*. Cambridge: Cambridge University Press.

Barcelos, A.M.F. (2010) Building school–university partnership in a continuing language teacher education project: The role of emotions in creating learning communities. Paper presented at the 3rd Latin American Congress on Language Teaching Education (III Clafpl), Taubaté, SP, Brazil, November.

Barcelos, A.M.F. (2012) Developing emotional literacy in the language class. Workshop presented at VIII Seminário de Ensino de Língua Estrangeira e IV Seminário de Ensino de Língua Materna. Passo Fundo, RS, Brazil, October.

Barcelos, A.M.F. and Coelho, H.S.H. (eds) (2010) *Emoções, reflexões e (trans)form(Ações) de alunos, professores e formadores de professores de línguas*. Campinas: Pontes.

Brown, B. (2012) *Daring Greatly: How the Courage To Be Vulnerable Transforms the Way We Live, Love, Parent, and Lead*. New York: Gotham.

Ciarrochi, J., Heaven, P.C.L. and Davies, F. (2007) The impact of hope, self-esteem, and attributional style on adolescents' school grades and emotional well-being: A longitudinal study. *Journal of Research in Personality* 41 (6), 1161–1178.

Coleman-Kiner, A. (2011) Fearless talk about love in education. Blog entry, retrieved from https://oldsow.wordpress.com/2011/06/10/fearless-talk-about-love-in-education/ (accessed 24 January 2015).

Day, C. (2004) *A Passion for Teaching*. London: Routledge/Falmer.

Dewaele, J.M. (2008) The emotional weight of 'I love you' in multilinguals' languages. *Journal of Pragmatics* 40 (10), 1753–1780.

Dewaele, J.M. and MacIntyre, P.D. (2014) The two faces of Janus? Anxiety and enjoyment in the foreign language classroom. *Studies in Second Language Learning and Teaching* 4 (2), 237–274.

Dornyei, Z. and Murphey, T. (2003) *Group Dynamics in the Language Classroom*. Cambridge: Cambridge University press.

Fredrickson, B. (2013) *Love 2.0*. New York: Hudson Street Press.

Freire, P. (1979) *Educação e Mudança*. São Paulo: Paz e Terra.

Freire, P. (1996) *Pedagogia da Autonomia*. São Paulo: Paz e Terra.

Freire, P. (2005) *Teachers as Cultural Workers: Letters to Those Who Dare Teach*. Boulder, CO: Westview Press.

Goleman, D. (1995) *Emotional Intelligence*. New York: Bantam Books.

hooks, b. (2003) *Teaching Community: A Pedagogy of Hope*. New York: Routledge.

Imai, Y. (2010) Emotions in SLA: New insights from collaborative learning for an EFL classroom. *Modern Language Journal* 94 (2), 278–292.

Ledoux, J. (1996) *The Emotional Brain: The Mysterious Underpinnings of Emotional Life*. New York: Simon & Schuster.

Liston, D. (2000) Love and despair in teaching. *Educational Theory* 50 (1), 81–102.

Liston, D. (2008) Critical pedagogy and attentive love. *Studies in Philosophy and Education* 27 (5), 387–392.

MacIntyre, P.D. and Gregersen, T. (2012) Emotions that facilitate language learning: The positive-broadening power of the imagination. *Studies in Second Language Learning and Teaching* 2 (2), 193–213.

MacIntyre, P. and Mercer, S. (2014) Introducing positive psychology to SLA. *Studies in Second Language Learning and Teaching* 4 (2), 153–172.

Maturana, H. (2005) *Emoções e Linguagem na Educação e na Política*. Belo Horizonte: UFMG.

Maturana, H.R. and Varela, F.J. (1987) *The Tree of Knowledge: The Biological Roots of Human Understanding*. Boston, MA: Shambhala Publications.

Maturana, H.R. and Verden-Zoller, G. (1996) Biology of love. In G. Opp and F. Peterander (eds) *Focus Heilpadagogik*. Munchen/Basel: Ernst Reinhardt. Retrieved from http://www.lifesnaturalsolutions.com.au/documents/biology-of-love.pdf (accessed 25 June 2014).

Maturana, H.R. and Verden-Zoller, G. (2008) *Origins of Humanness in the Biology of Love*. (ed. P. Bunnell). Exeter: Imprint Academic.

Mehrgan, K. (2012) Humanistic language teaching: A critical look. *Advances in Digital Multimedia* 1 (4), 184–188.

Moraes, R.J. (2008) *Inconsciente sem Fronteiras*. São Paulo: Ed. Ideias e Letras.

Moskowitz, G. (1978) *Caring and Sharing in the Foreign Language Class: A Sourcebook on Humanistic Techniques*. Boston, MA: Newbury House.

Murphey, T. (2012) *In Pursuit of Wow!* Tokyo: ABAX.

Murphey, T. (2014) Singing well-becoming: Student musical therapy case studies. *Studies in Second Language Learning and Teaching* 4 (2), 215–235.

Murphey, T. and Carpenter, C. (2008) The seeds of agency in language learning histories. In P. Kalaja, V. Menezes and A.M.F. Barcelos (eds) *Narratives of Learning and Teaching EFL* (pp. 17–34). London: Palgrave Macmillan.

Murphey, T., Prober, J. and Gonzales, K. (2010) Emotional belonging precedes learning. In A.M.F. Barcelos and H.S.H. Coelho (eds) *Emoções, Reflexões e (trans)form(ações) de Alunos, Professores e Formadores de Professores de Línguas* (pp. 43–56). Campinas: Pontes.

Murphey, T., Barcelos, A.M.F. and Moraes, R.B. (2014) Narrativizing our learning lives through action logs and newsletters. *Revista Contexturas* 23, 99–111.

Noddings, N. (1999) 'Two concepts of caring'. *Philosophy of Education*. Retrieved from http://ojs.ed.uiuc.edu/index.php/pes/article/view/2024/719 (accessed November 2015).

Oxford, R. (2014) What we can learn about strategies, language learning, and life from two extreme cases: The role of well-being theory. *Studies in Second Language Learning and Teaching* 4 (4), 593–615.

Rubio, F.D. (2007) *Self-esteem and Foreign Language Learning*. Newcastle: Cambridge Scholars.

Seligman, M.E.P. (2009) Positive psychology, positive prevention and positive therapy. In S.J. Lope and C.R. Snyder (eds) *Oxford Handbook of Positive Psychology* (pp. 3–12). New York: Oxford.

So, D. (2005) Emotion processes in second language acquisition. In P. Benson and D. Nunan (eds) *Learners' Stories: Difference and Diversity in Language Learning* (pp. 42–55). Cambridge: Cambridge University Press.

Steiner, C. (2000) The meming of love: Invention of the human heart. Keynote lecture at the 3rd Adolescence Health Conference at the Royal College of Physicians in London.

Retrieved from http://www.emotional-literacy.com/meming.htm (accessed 20 June 2012).
Swain, M. (2013) The inseparability of cognition and emotion in second language learning. *Language Teaching* 46 (2), 1–13.
Zembylas, M. (2004) The emotional characteristics of teaching. *Teaching and Teacher Education* 20, 185–201.

Part 2
Empirical

6 Positive Psychology Exercises Build Social Capital for Language Learners: Preliminary Evidence

Tammy Gregersen, Peter D. MacIntyre and Margarita Meza

In the seminal article on positive psychology, Seligman and Csikszentmihalyi (2000) identify three pillars for the field: positive character traits, positive emotions and positive institutions. Each of these pillars can be central to the field of SLA, where there is strong potential to integrate previous lines of research with emerging positive psychology principles, concepts and actions (MacIntyre & Mercer, 2014). Positive psychology is 'not a spectator sport' (Peterson, 2006), meaning that there is a strong emphasis in the field on developing activities that produce positive outcomes, both inside and outside the classroom. In language pedagogy, there have been efforts to develop individualized activities that promote learning (e.g. Gregersen & MacIntyre, 2014). Within positive psychology, there have been a number of exercises that have been tested and shown to have positive effects on individuals, activities such as expressing gratitude, savoring prior experiences and performing altruistic acts, to name only three (Seligman *et al.*, 2005). The emphasis on empirical research means that positive psychology exercises (PPEs) must be shown to be effective (Mongrain & Anselmo-Matthews, 2012; Seligman *et al.*, 2009). Within psychology, the emphasis on evaluating PPEs has been on their effect on personal health and well-being. However, the social turn (Block, 2003) emphasizes that the social and historical context must be taken into account when examining what it means to be learning or acquiring a language. In this chapter, we use mixed methods to explore both the emotional and the social consequences of enriching an extracurricular language conversation program with PPEs. In particular, we argue that language learning can be facilitated by PPEs in the context of emerging friendships that provide learners with positive emotional experiences and intangible resources for language acquisition (i.e. building social capital).

Positive Emotions

One of the most influential theories in positive psychology is the broaden-and-build theory of positive emotion (Conway *et al.*, 2013; Fredrickson, 2001; Fredrickson & Branigan, 2005). The theory provides insight into how positive affective experiences not only broaden the way a person (the language learner in the present study) experiences the world, but also support well-being by building resources for the future (Fredrickson, 2001, 2003). The theory holds that, on the one hand, negative emotions such as language anxiety, anger or frustration tend to narrow learners' thought-action repertoires, so that learners are poised to act in self-protective ways, including limiting participation in class or avoiding eye contact when speaking to other people. Positive emotions, on the other hand, tend to broaden learners' dynamic moment-to-moment thought-action repertoires, leading them to acquire various types of personal resources that endure beyond the timescale of the positive emotion itself (see Fredrickson, 2001). Personal resources, such as techniques to increase coping and resiliency, increase the potential for learning progress through the formation of adaptive spirals of feeling, thinking and acting (MacIntyre & Gregersen, 2012). Fredrickson and Branigan (2005) demonstrated that positive emotion resulted in broader attention, greater working memory, enhanced verbal fluency and increased openness to information. Positive emotion can facilitate enduring success by opening avenues of constructive thoughts and actions, and should not be considered simply the absence or opposite of negative emotions; they are two different dimensions of experience with different roles to play in learning (MacIntyre & Gregersen, 2012; Dewaele & MacIntyre, this volume).

There are two key implications of the broaden-and-build theory that are especially applicable to language learning. On the 'broaden' side of the theory, the factors that promote personal development are best conceptualized as uniquely personal. It is nearly impossible to identify generic techniques that teachers can use to promote growth for all students and

> intervention efforts will likely need to take individual differences in personality, abilities, and interests into account to maximize the goodness of fit between school experiences and students' emotions. For example, what is a positive extracurricular activity for one student may not be for another. Such consideration should thus include attention to students' unique personal strengths and environmental assets. (Reschly *et al.*, 2008: 429)

The process of designing activities that promote the personal growth of an individual must take into account the context in which the learner operates as well as his or her unique configuration of thoughts, feelings, experiences, preferences, strengths, hopes and anxieties (among other things).

The PPEs evaluated by Seligman *et al.* (2005) were adapted to individual circumstances, including expressing gratitude to specific other persons and using an individual's strengths in a new way. Evaluation of the effects of the PPEs showed that they produced gains in happiness and a reduction in depressive symptoms, some over a short term (days) and others over the longer term (months). We suggest that an applied approach to PPEs is best undertaken at the individual level, wherein a project can be tailored to the unique person who is the learner-in-context.

On the 'build' side of Fredrickson's theory is the notion of accumulating resources that will aid in overcoming future adversity and undoing the effects of negative emotion. Character traits such as hardiness, resilience and autonomy can be seen as attributes that develop over time (Peterson, 2006). But these attributes function in an interpersonal, social context that typically has not been considered in positive psychology (see Oxford, Chapter 2 of the present volume; see also Waterman, 2013). Within the SLA context, how might we characterize the nature of the resources that are being built along with positive emotions? We suggest that the concept of social capital can be applied in this context.

Building social capital

Social capital is a well known concept in several areas of the social sciences. Pierre Bourdieu defines social capital as 'the aggregate of the actual or potential resources which are linked to possession of a durable network of more or less institutionalized relationships of mutual acquaintance or recognition' (Bourdieu, 1985: 248). Social capital describes ways in which a person might access resources or benefits because of the people they know and groups to which they belong (Sobel, 2002). The term 'social capital' often is used to reflect the accumulation of potential resources, accessed via other people, upon which a person might draw in times of need. Our use of 'social capital' is most consistent with Nawyn *et al.*, who define it as 'networks that have the potential to provide either material or nonmaterial resources (including achieving physical and mental health, a sense of personal safety, and feeling integrated into a community and valued by others in that community)' (Nawyn *et al.*, 2012: 257).

Robert Putnam's book *Bowling Alone* (2000) argued that there has been a precipitous decline in social capital in the United States over the past few decades, which has diminished civic participation and the connections between individuals and their communities. The title of his work suggests that individuals now prefer to bowl alone instead of within an organized league with their peers. Although Putnam has been accused of romanticizing the idea of social capital (Portes, 1998), it is not difficult to imagine the role that interpersonal connections within a community might play in acquiring a language. In a study of immigrants to an economically disadvantaged and socially isolated community, Nawyn *et al.* highlight the non-economic value of the social capital provided by knowing the dominant language. They conclude, 'By viewing language as a form of community-level social capital beyond what can be exchanged for economic benefits, we can see the connections between linguistic isolation and migrants' social citizenship' (Nawyn *et al.*, 2012: 276).

Although scholars such as Bourdieu and others consider the ways in which social capital can turn into economic benefits (e.g. referral for a job), our focus here is on the interpersonal side of learning and developing social capital based on relationships formed by language learners. Luthans *et al.* (2004) suggest that material resources, combined with human capital (*what you know*) and social capital (*who you know*), lead to a desirable state they called positive psychological capital, which is associated with confidence, hope, optimism and resilience. Two key ingredients of the Luthans model, developing one's self and getting to know other people, can be facilitated through participation in PPEs.

The major goal of the present study is to examine closely a set of six PPEs that were employed to facilitate language learning within a 12-week extracurricular conversational English program. The exercises themselves tend to be novel experiences for learners, with a goal of relationship-building and interpersonal engagement, helping to set a positive context in which language learning can occur. These exercises, however, do not directly teach language skills as might be done in a classroom but instead are designed to help build positive emotion and interpersonal resources. Part of the rationale for the study was to examine how the exercises might be perceived within the overall language learning process. Empirically testing PPEs has been a key concern of research (MacIntyre & Mercer, 2014; Peterson, 2006); testing the efficacy of PPEs presents an opportunity for teachers and course designers to gather systematic data on issues of concern for learning. This chapter can be seen as both a preliminary examination of specific PPEs and an example of applied research undertaken on emotions in SLA. This study takes a small-scale, mixed methods, individual-oriented approach.

To capitalize on the individuality of each learner in the study (see Gregersen & MacIntyre, 2014), we personalized the techniques within the framework of a peer-mentoring group activity called 'Conversation Partners'. Both quantitative and qualitative data were gathered from the learners and their conversation partners to triangulate our understanding of what is happening during the PPEs. The six PPEs that were used involved: laughter, exercise, pets, music, gratitude and altruism. The specific activities were not chosen to be language learning exercises per se but rather exercises that set a positive psychological and social context in which language learning can take place. The reasons for choosing each type of PPE are summarized below.

The Six PPEs

Technique 1: Laughter

Humor is a reaction that improves our ability to cope and to savor the positive in our lives. As a coping mechanism, humor tends to alleviate tension and anxiety (Kuiper & Martin, 1993; Moran & Massam, 1999; Yovetich *et al.*, 1990), helping to shield individuals from the physical repercussions of stress (Lefcourt & Martin, 1986; Martin & Dobbin, 1988; Martin & Lefcourt, 1983). Introducing humor into the classroom can make learning more pleasurable (Bryant & Zillmann, 1988; LoShiavo & Shatz, 2005). Laughter helps to preserve a healthy perspective during difficult times and increases the visible expression of happiness, improving a person's capacity to cope with negative, narrowing experiences (Bryant & Veroff, 2007).

Technique 2: Exercise

In the short term, physical activity stimulates positive, broadening emotional states and in the long term regular exercise is associated with deeper happiness (Argyle, 2001; Sarafino, 2002). The short-term effects of exercise arise in part because it causes the release of endorphins, which are morphine-like substances produced in the brain. Frequent and stable exercise routines have been shown to diminish depression and anxiety, increase the rate and accuracy of work, nurture self-esteem, promote fitness and improve cardiovascular function. Habitual physical activity also reduces or averts the weight gain associated with aging. Routine physical activity lowers the perils of heart disease and cancer and is linked to living longer. Moreover, individuals who make it a habit are often accompanied by other people while exercising and so reap the benefits of extra social networking on their global subjective well-being (Carr, 2004).

Technique 3: Interact with animals (pets)

Interactions with pets increase neurochemicals that are connected to bonding and relaxation and also improve immune system functioning (Charnetsky *et al.*, 2004). The use of pets in a therapeutic setting has been shown to reduce physical pain in patients with chronic disorders. Kaminski *et al.* (2002) found that heart rates, parents' ratings of their child's emotion, and display of positive affect could be enhanced through the presence of pets. The physiological and emotional components of pet-assisted therapy result in positive affect and emotion enhancement. Play is essential to children and pets are a distraction from emotional and physiological stress. Researchers found that children report less pain, want more interaction and want a pet at home when, after pet-assisted therapy, they are asked what three wishes they would make (Kaminski *et al.*, 2002). The interaction between humans and pets assists in developing social skills that can be applied to interactions with people (Wisdom *et al.*, 2009). Odendaal (2000) attributes the bonding effects of pet-assisted therapy to the interaction of humans and dogs as they fulfill their reciprocal need for attention. Physiological measures also demonstrated that the dogs benefit from the exchange.

Technique 4: Listening to music

Music therapy has incorporated a variety of different elements, such as making music, composing songs, or passively listening. Whereas music as therapy is often aimed at encouraging emotional expression, there can be many other goals, including stress or anxiety relief, emotion improvement and enhancement of quality of life for people who are ill. Compared with a control group, the 116 participants in one study who received music therapy showed significantly greater reductions in stress, anxiety and depression. The music therapy involved listening to a half-hour of soothing music twice daily for two weeks (Chang *et al.*, 2008). In the arena of language learning, Murphey (2010) used music and song to provide cultural and linguistic elements with respect to English language learning and to help motivate his Japanese students. In another study, Murphey (2014) demonstrated that singing and teaching with movement produced positive emotions and had an effect on learners' and teachers' well-being. Furthermore, using music provided value-added linguistic outcomes, like rhyming, blending, vowel changes, assonance, alliteration and rhythm.

Technique 5: Express gratitude

Gratitude surfaces in relationships when we acknowledge that we are the beneficiaries of the behavior of others; expressing gratitude is good for our health (Peterson, 2006). A series of studies has shown that individuals who maintain diaries of events for which they are grateful benefit from improved health and higher subjective well-being compared with those who keep diaries of daily stresses and similar events (Emmons & Shelton, 2002). Counting one's blessing is a manifestation of gratitude, in which individuals identify what they are grateful for, identify the source of the blessings and then link their gratitude to the perceived sources (Emmons & Shelton, 2002). Expressing gratitude to a specific person in a letter has been shown to have an enduring positive effect on the letter writer.

Technique 6: Engage altruism

Our actions are driven by altruism if our most salient goal is to improve the well-being of another individual, with ulterior egocentric motives in the distant background. Instances of empathic emotion often evoke altruistic motivation, in part because of the emotional reaction we have upon observing another person in need of help that we can provide. This emotional response is likened to sympathy, compassion and tenderness. Batson and his team (Batson, 1991; Batson *et al.*, 2002) have demonstrated that altruistic helping behavior is a response prompted by empathic emotion instead of egoistic triggers. One of the reasons why altruistic acts make us happier is that being generous leads us to view others with greater compassion, because we usually discover positive qualities in those we care about. Furthermore, altruistic behaviors promote a feeling of connectedness and community, which has been shown to be one of the robust elements to enriching our happiness. As a conduit to gratitude, altruism also helps us value and feel appreciative of our own good fortune. Moreover, acting upon our altruistic tendencies enhances our self-esteem and makes us feel useful, offering a means to exercise our strengths and talents in meaningful ways. Finally, exemplifying kindness can ignite a chain reaction of positivity – being generous to others may incentivize them to be grateful and generous to others, who in turn pay it forward to others (Lyubomirsky, 2008).

The Present Study

The present study examines learners participating in the Conversation Partners program. We believe that the active ingredient in the PPEs as employed in our context is the opportunity for novel and enjoyable social interaction with a native speaker. Our goal is to describe the participants' experience, with a focus on whether shared novel activities tend to increase positive affect and enhance social capital. Our focus is based on research that suggests positive emotions such as enjoyment are an important precursor to broader thought-action repertoires and are thus a significant contributor to increased learning (Fredrickson, 2003; MacIntyre & Gregersen, 2012). Our assumption is that the relationships developing within the Conversation Partners program will enable the building of resources among the learners.

Method

Participants

Three Brazilian learners (we will use the pseudonyms 'Anna', 'Tina' and 'Bea') and two Japanese learners ('Nashi' and 'Miki') of a second language who were enrolled in levels seven and eight (of eight) in an Intensive Academic English program at a US university consented to participate in this research. All five were women between the ages of 20 and 23 and had spent only a few months in the US before the study began. The university has a formal Conversation Partner program which pairs American or highly proficient English-speaking students with language learners who are in the Intensive Academic English program. According to the university catalogue:

> Partners meet a minimum of one hour each week throughout the academic year. It is required that students speak English for one hour during the time they are together. This provides a cultural exchange for both partners, while one is learning English in a conversational setting. Students have the opportunity to improve English skills, experience American culture, and share their own culture with others.

All five language learners had registered for the Conversation Partners program and had been recommended by the director of the program as viable candidates for this research project. By the end of the semester in which the study was carried out, all of the participants had passed the linguistic exit requirements for the Intensive Academic English program.

Procedures

All participants volunteered to participate in the study and gave their informed consent; the project and procedures were approved by the university's research ethics board. After accepting our invitation to participate, each language learner was paired with a research assistant, who was well versed in second-language teaching methodology and was also a female student at the same university. Three of the assistants were studying TESOL (Teaching English to Speakers of Other Languages) and two were psychology majors with particular interest and experience in second-language learning. The efforts of the assistants were coordinated through weekly meetings and emails and the procedures were executed across participants as consistently as possible in both form and content.

During the first meeting between individual research assistants and their conversation partners, participants responded to a series of open-ended interview questions aimed at discovering each language learner's particular attraction to music genres, exercise preferences, favorite pets, sources of laughter, things for which gratitude was felt, and altruistic actions that incite interest. Information from the interview was used to individually tailor the six PPEs that were completed in the next 12 weeks. Table 6.1 reflects how each of the PPEs accommodated each participant.

During the next 12 weeks, the research assistants and their conversation partners met once a week, alternating between a regular week and a week featuring a PPE activity (six in total). The partners met at different locations depending on the type of PPE that was scheduled. During each session, the research assistant asked her partner immediately upon meeting to self-rate

Table 6.1 Description of PPEs tailored to the proclivities of each participant

	Music	*Exercise*	*Pets*	*Laughter*	*Gratitude topics*	*Altruism*
Anna	Alternative rock	Hot yoga	Cuddled cat (has one at home in Brazil)	Online videos of babies laughing	Physical, emotional, spiritual	Placed anonymous 'thank you' notes on janitors' unattended carts
Nashi	Classic pop (e.g. Beatles)	Hot yoga	Played with cat	Laughter yoga – oral instructions	Friends	Volunteered at the local food bank for the needy
Miki	Japanese pop	Climbing on 'rock wall' at university gym	'Hung out' with military service dog	'Chicken dance' video	Travel opportunities	Wrote 'pick-me-up' notes to friends for exam week
Tina	Reggae	Walk on indoor track	Played with researcher's dog	Laughter yoga video	Family, opportunity, education	Wrote cards to sick children
Bea	Brazilian pop	Halloween Zumba	Played with military service dog	Laughter yoga video	Christmas-related topics	Gave sweets to random strangers

her emotion[1] on a thermometer diagram, on a scale from 1 (negative emotion) to 10 (positive emotion); the diagram was based on MacIntyre and Gardner's (1991) 'anxometer'. All of the measures were taken on separate slips of paper so that participants did not have access to their previous responses. Once the baseline rating of emotion was completed, partners together carried out their weekly activities. In weeks featuring a PPE, participants were asked to self-rate their emotion following the exercise. As the session progressed, partners engaged in a mixture of tutorial, conversation and explicit instruction, where linguistic and/or cultural issues were taken up. At the end of the weekly session, participants self-rated their emotion and then wrote a short narrative about their reactions to the PPE (if applicable in a given week). The English-speaking partners also wrote their immediate reactions as research notes in order to share in the moment and record important anecdotes. One final interview was carried out at the end of the 12-week period, where language learning participants were asked to provide a commentary on the process as a whole.

The data analysis includes both quantitative and qualitative components. The ratings of emotion provide some indication of how participants reacted to the PPEs. Ratings will be presented for each individual, as well as aggregated for each of the PPE activities and compared with the ratings of 'regular' weeks. The qualitative data were analyzed using a variation on a grounded theory approach (Strauss & Corbin, 1990). First, the comments of the participants and their conversation partners for each activity were read repeatedly to generate a short list of recurring themes that were reflected in the journals, research notes and final interview data. Grouping similar themes into broader categories (i.e. axial coding) ascertained that all the participants had commented on two categories of experience: relationship/rapport-building and the reaction to the personalized PPEs. This process was completed by an independent rater who had no other role in the study. After identifying the two major themes in the data, two raters who were familiar with positive psychology independently coded the data for those two themes. Each rater repeatedly read the text of the qualitative data, highlighting segments that described either the process of relationship/rapport-building or specific reactions to PPEs. Only excerpts that were coded consistently by both raters as instances of one of the themes are reported below. To maintain the language learners' voices, we use their words precisely as they had been shared.

Results and Discussion

The results will be presented in two sections. First, the ratings of emotions made by each participant will be examined. The sample size is too small for a statistical comparison, so only descriptive statistics and raw data will be presented. Second, we will examine the comments made by the participants to better understand the ways in which they engaged with their conversation partners using PPEs and their reactions to the activities.

Quantitative results

Table 6.2 shows the average change in self-ratings of positive emotion during both the regular sessions and the PPEs for each of the participants. All of the participants experienced an increase from pre- to post-ratings during the regular weeks, but all participants showed even greater gains during the weeks with a PPE. The difference between gains during regular weeks versus PPE weeks ranged from 0.2 to 1.0 points. Although we cannot test the statistical significance of the comparison due to the small sample size, the consistency of the gains is noteworthy (complete data for all participants are presented in the Appendix to this chapter).

Table 6.3 presents data showing the change in emotion during the sessions for each PPE for each individual. We can observe that, on average, altruism (1.2) produced the smallest change and both exercise and laughter (2.2) showed the greatest gains. However, these results must be interpreted with caution because the sequence of PPEs was the same for all participants and both exercise and laughter were the last sessions of the Conversation Partners program. Had the order of the PPEs been randomized, we would be better able to comment on the effects attributable to each specific PPE.

Table 6.2 Mean gain in positive emotion from beginning to end of session

	Nashi	*Miki*	*Tina*	*Anna*	*Bea*
Regular sessions	1.8	2.95	0.5	1.0	0.7
PPE sessions	2.0	3.3	1.0	2.0	0.9

Table 6.3 Increases in self-ratings for each participant per PPE

Learner	*Music*	*Gratitude*	*Altruism*	*Pet*	*Exercise*	*Laughter*
Nashi	2.0	2.0	1.0	2.0	3.0	2.0
Miki	4.0	3.0	2.5	3.0	3.3	4.0
Tina	1.0	1.0	0	0	2.0	2.0
Anna	2.0	1.0	2.0	3.0	2.0	2.0
Bea	0.5	1.0	0.5	1.0	1.0	1.0
Mean	*1.9*	*1.6*	*1.2*	*1.8*	*2.3*	*2.2*

The music, exercise, laughter, pet, gratitude and altruism PPEs all produced gains in positive emotion. Every PPE increased participants' pre- and post-PPE self-rankings from an average of 1.2 to 2.3 points on a scale of 10. Not only did all participants report an increase in their positive emotion immediately after the PPE, but the positive emotion was carried through and increased again after the instructional portion of the sessions. The qualitative data address the role that the PPEs may play in the learning process.

Qualitative results

Excerpts from both the learners and their partners include descriptions of positive emotion and elements of social capital – trust, relationship-building and friendship – interwoven in the responses. As the developing relationships took the foreground within the encounter, the PPEs served as a specific context in which that relationship could develop in novel ways that were tailored to the preferences of the individual learner. With this approach to building the resources of the relationship, the details of language seemed to take a background position. Although this approach seems to have facilitated a positive emotional tone, it left some learners questioning the connection between the PPEs and their language learning, as we report in the final few excerpts below.

Positive emotional tone

The emerging relationships had the quality of being between peers rather than teacher–student or tutor–tutee. Both Anna and Tina suggested that the PPEs helped to facilitate the process by which conversation partners 'become friends'.

> **Excerpt 1**: I think [the PPEs] helped to build our conversations together in the beginning. I felt more comfortable and encouraged to do more 'American things' in public places when I was with you. You helped my confidence when I was in the new places. (Excerpt from Anna's final interview)

> **Excerpt 2**: During our meeting I feel comfortable to not be discouraged by my mistakes and difficulties, because I know this is the only way to learn. The fact that my partner is very patient help me a lot. She usually ask me interesting questions, which is motivating.... After our meeting I felt better than before because I felt like I have done something good to try to improve my speaking, which is a big goal. I think this is satisfaction. (Excerpt from Tina's narrative after music PPE)

> **Excerpt 3**: After our meeting, as usual, I was feeling better and less stressed than before. While walking, I felt relaxed. As usual, when we

> are talking I feel good for being practicing my English with an 'American' friend. This takes me away from my routine along with other Brazilians, which is good. In addition, in the course of time, our conversations start to require from me different vocabulary. Sometimes it is hard, but it is also challenging. (Excerpt from Tina's narrative after exercise PPE)

Excerpts 1 and 3 suggest that the PPEs allowed learners to interact with Americans and American things in ways that they had not previously done, which is part of building social capital. The positive emotions that are facilitated within these relationships would be expected to lead to successful learning outcomes, such as the vocabulary development described in excerpt 3. Rather than experiencing discouragement when making mistakes (which Tina acknowledges are necessary for learning), the positive context is found to be motivational (excerpt 2), allowing for greater comfort and confidence (excerpt 1). This is the essence of Fredrickson's broaden-and-build theory of positive emotion: setting a positive emotional context allows learning to happen efficiently with low levels of stress.

Evoking positive emotion as a way to reduce the impact of negative emotion and to buttress resiliency has been at the foundation of the broaden-and-build theory (Fredrickson, 2001). In terms of language learning, acquiring the vocabulary to describe emotional experience can enhance the sharing of that experience (Dewaele, 2010). The following excerpt from Miki's partner's research notes demonstrates the connection between music and emotion, which helped with understanding a difficult vocabulary item (the word 'bittersweet').

> **Excerpt 4**: We listened to music. Miki showed me a song by her favorite singer and explained that the song helped her feel better when she was unhappy. I showed her a song that had a similar effect on me and we discussed the word 'bittersweet'. (Excerpt from Miki's partner's research notes after music PPE)

As Murphey's (2010, 2014) research suggested, music can activate learners' emotions very quickly, providing an opportunity for learning to take place at a deep level. Excerpt 4 shows how learning a difficult linguistic item can be facilitated by partners introducing each other to their preferred music.

Tailoring the activities to the personal preferences of the learner allowed for both positive emotions and interpersonal connections. Sharing music was one form of connection but the partners also found common ground in their core values. In reflecting on the gratitude activity during her final interview, Anna commented that 'It feels good to do nice things for other people'. Further, Tina describes how the gratitude exercise offered a meaningful opportunity to reflect upon her own values and connect with her conversation partner:

> **Excerpt 5**: It was good to list some of the things for which I'm grateful. I focused on the aspects that are related to my experience living in a different country and learning a second language. This activity generated interesting subjects that allowed us to know a little bit more about things we value in life and that motivate us to pursue our goals. Although we have absolutely different histories of life, we could realize that we have similar values, for example, we both agree that our greatest gratitude is by our families. (Excerpt from Tina's journal after gratitude PPE)

The building of relationships within the program was facilitated by shared values. Meaningful opportunities to express shared values and to connect with other people also were facilitated by the altruism exercise. Tina chose to write a letter to a sick child as her altruistic act. In her description of the activity, she alludes to its positive effects, including an improvement in mood, with the added benefit of finding common ground with people across linguistic and national boundaries.

> **Excerpt 6**: Making the card to a girl who has been battling a serious illness was very nice. I felt good because I think when she receives it, for her probably does not matter if I am American or not, if I speak English fluently or not. It is good to know that I can help putting a smile in her face. Particularly I believe that acts of benevolence are beneficial for those who practice and for those who receive exactly the same way. Among other positive effects, my mood also got better while doing it. (Excerpt from Tina's narrative after altruism PPE)

Making a contribution to the community by (presumably) putting a smile on the face of a sick child reinforces the value of actively participating in the community despite linguistic limitations; altruism is connected to a higher purpose that Tina herself suggests brings beneficial results to both the giver and receiver. This example demonstrates that, with altruism, positive emotional effects and a connection with others can be generated even if the target recipient is unknown and the activity is done anonymously. With altruism, a learner can engage positively with her community and express unselfish values that transcend particular languages and cultures (Haski-Leventhal, 2009). By writing to a sick child in hospital, Tina has found a way to connect to the local community and she has done it in English (with the help of her conversation partner). Perhaps it is unusual to think of altruism as a language learning strategy or resource, but its effect on social capital is easy to envision.

If altruism can be considered an unusual language learning resource, then interaction with animals is even more unconventional. Yet, the activity involving pets also produced positive emotions and interpersonal connections among the participants.

> **Excerpt 7**: We got a dog to play together this time. I was so excited! I love dogs, and the dog was very cute, calm, smart. I really enjoyed meeting [my partner] and talking to her too! After the dog went back, we talked many things. I had a lot of fun. I'm looking forward to meet her next time! (Excerpt from Bea's narrative after pet PPE)

Although the interaction with an animal was described as 'a lot of fun' for Bea, another participant had a more meaningful encounter. In the case of Anna, interacting with her conversation partner's cat provided much-needed emotional comfort:

> **Excerpt 8**: The animals were the best because I love cats so much, and I miss my own cat in Brazil, so it made me feel more at home. (Excerpt from Anna's narrative after pet PPE)

Although her response to the PPE is written in just a few words, Anna's reaction occurred in the context of a difficult breakup of a romantic relationship. Her conversation partner elaborated:

> **Excerpt 9**: This exercise could not have come at a better time. Anna had just broken up with a guy that she had been dating for a couple months and it wasn't the greatest breakup scenario that could have happened. I brought her to my house and while she told me about everything that had happened with this boy, she was cuddling and playing with my cat. Anna loves cats and has expressed how much she misses her cat at home in Brazil. Her mood was very low on this day because of everything that had happened with the boy, but she said that the conversation with me and the time spent with my cat was very helpful. (Excerpt from Anna's partner's research notes after animal PPE)

Both the animal and the conversation partner in excerpts 8 and 9 served as indirect language learning resources for Anna. The encounters helped to bolster emotional resilience in dealing with a romantic breakup and moving on to focus on other activities, including learning English. In terms of building social capital, both the partner and the animal provide connections to 'others' in the community that help the learner feel less alone. Anna is not going to learn English from the cat, but Anna is going to learn English if it helps in mending her broken heart.

It would appear that the conversation partners and the PPEs helped to create positive emotional tone and opportunities for building the relationships that provide social capital, even if the participants tended not to think of these things as 'learning English'.

Questioning the role of PPEs in learning

One of the learners, Anna, suggested that the PPEs did serve a purpose but she discounted the effect on learning the language, although she recognized the effect on the relationship.

> **Excerpt 10**: I think [the PPEs] helped to build our conversations together in the beginning. I felt more comfortable and encouraged to do more 'American things' in public places when I was with you. You helped my confidence when I was in the new places. But I think that they were not so helpful in learning English but just to help us become friends. It did not seem different to me when we would hang out without activities and when we hang out with activities because we just have fun together and that is what made me happy to be talking in English. (Excerpt from Anna's final interview)

In a similar way, Tina questioned the role of the music exercise and later the exercise activity:

> **Excerpt 11**: I'm not sure about the effect of the music, but I can say that being a closet place made me feel less shy, thus more comfortable because there was no people listening to our conversation. (Excerpt from Tina's narrative after music PPE)

> **Excerpt 12**: I could not identify how exactly exercising influenced my mood. After our meeting, as usual, I was feeling better and less stressed than before. While walking, I felt relaxed. As usual, when we are talking I feel good for being practicing my English with an 'American' friend. This takes me away from my routine along with other Brazilians, which is good. In addition, in the course of time, our conversations start to require from me different vocabulary. Sometimes it is hard, but it is also challenging. (Excerpt from Tina's narrative after exercise PPE)

In the following excerpt from Anna's final interview, she indicates that her oral communication might not have improved very much, in spite of the positive outcomes we have been discussing thus far.

> **Excerpt 13**: I don't think my 'talking' has improved so much but I am more comfortable using English more often than I was before. Because we were friends it made me more comfortable to use English and not worry about being incorrect. I also was challenged when I would hang out with you and your friends because you all talk so fast and I had to concentrate to follow the things you were saying. It was scary at first but then I like it so much because it was very good practice. You and your friends are so kind too because you help me understand if I am

confused and also it is fun to watch how American girls talk to each other. (Excerpt from Anna's final interview)

Feeling comfortable enough to talk with a specific person is a defining feature of willingness to communicate (MacIntyre *et al.*, 1998), one of the strongest predictors of L2 communication. With repeated, enjoyable episodes of authentic communication, we suggest that the Conversation Partners program does indeed set the groundwork for language learning, and it does so in part through development of positive emotion and social capital. The excerpts from the learners have conveyed feelings of comfort and confidence, and increased levels of motivation, all of which have been shown in the research literature to facilitate language learning (MacIntyre & Gregersen, 2012). Although the learners themselves might not always see the connections between language learning and the social capital built within interpersonal relationships, as teachers and researchers we can take comfort from watching the process play out, as described in the following excerpts:

> **Excerpt 14**: We met at one of our usual meeting spots for coffee and chatted about life. We have truly become more like friends than 'research participants'. Our conversations are very 'free-flowing' and we cover a multitude of topics. Anna is really thankful for these casual conversational settings because she has commented about how in her language classrooms, it is very formal and academic language and she wants to know more slang and have more casual exchanges with people. Outside of our research meetings, I have also introduced her to my friends and exposed her to group settings with very casual, but fast paced exchanges with a multitude of people. She has commented that it is definitely more challenging but loves the energy and learning new 'words and phrases in American English'. (Excerpt from Anna's conversation partner's notes after regular week 7)

> **Excerpt 15**: Because it was our last time meeting, we both had gotten each other a gift and exchanged them. We talked about the semester and about all things that had happened and it was literally just a moment of friendship – laughing, talking, drinking hot chocolate and reminiscing. It was the perfect way to end our time together. (Excerpt from Anna's partner's research notes after regular week 11)

Free-flowing conversation between friends who value each other, face challenges together, and are talking, laughing and learning is consistent with both the principles of positive psychology and effective language teaching.

Conclusion

The Conversation Partners program is part of an institutional response to the need to build interpersonal connections between learners and others in the community. This study provides both quantitative and qualitative evidence that positive emotional engagement and social connections were developed through personalized encounters. There is evidence in both the quantitative emotion ratings and the narrative excerpts above of the positive psychological capital that Luthans *et al.* (2004) associate with confidence, hope, optimism and resilience. The PPEs that were introduced to the program because of this research project appeared to have a small incremental effect over and above the effect of the regular weekly program; future research would be required to confirm this result. As Reschly *et al.* (2008: 429) found, '[t]he identification and inclusion of personal and environmental assets in educational planning may increase the likelihood of students experiencing positive emotions in school, encouraging an "upward spiral" of success'. Although the present data-set is small, we see preliminary evidence of all three pillars of positive psychology supporting positive outcomes. The positive institutional programming (Conversation Partners combined with PPEs) capitalizes on individual character traits with an explicit goal of increasing positive emotions and building relationships as a context to facilitate language learning. A broader outcome of the approach taken in this study is social capital that provides access to non-material resources such as 'a sense of personal safety, and feeling integrated into a community and valued by others in that community' (Nawyn *et al.*, 2012: 257). Social capital provides a novel way to conceptualize some of the resources that learners are building as they interact with members of the host community, resources that are alluded to in Fredrickson's (2001) broaden-and-build theory. These results encourage potential future development of language learning interventions that are inspired by positive psychology.

Note

(1) We are using the term 'emotion' throughout this chapter, although the more cumbersome term 'emotion-moods' might be used instead. Emotions are short-lived reactions to events. In some cases, however, the term 'mood', which reflects more diffuse affective experiences that can be difficult to attribute to a specific cause or event (Reeve, 2015), might also apply.

Appendix: Raw Data

Table 6.4 Participants' self-ranking of emotion before, during and after control and experimental tutorials with their conversation partners

	Nashi	*Miki*	*Tina*	*Anna*	*Bea*
Regular (week 1)					
Pre-tutorial	7	8	8	6	8
Post-tutorial	9	9.7	9	8	8.5
Music PPE (week 2)					
Pre-PPE/tutorial	6	5	7	8	8
Post-PPE/pre-tutorial	9	8	8	9	8.5
Post-tutorial	8	9	8	10	8.5
Regular (week 3)					
Pre-tutorial	7	3	8	8	5
Post-tutorial	8	8.5	8	9	6
Gratitude PPE (week 4)					
Pre-PPE/tutorial	6	7	8	8	8
Post-PPE/pre-tutorial	8	10	9	8	8.5
Post-Tutorial	8	10	9	9	9
Regular (week 5)					
Pre-tutorial	8	6	9	8	8
Post-tutorial	10	9	9	9	9.5
Altruism PPE (week 6)					
Pre-PPE/tutorial	8	7.5	8	8	8
Post-PPE/pre-tutorial	9	9	8	10	8.5
Post-tutorial	9	10	8	10	8.5
Regular (week 7)					
Pre-tutorial	7	7	8	7	8
Post-tutorial	9	10	9	8	9
Pet PPE (week 8)					
Pre-PPE/tutorial	7	7	8	3	7
Post-PPE/pre-tutorial	9	10	8	4	8
Post-tutorial	9	10	8	6	8
Regular (week 9)					
Pre-tutorial	6	5	7	8	7
Post-tutorial	8	9	8	9	7
Exercise PPE (week 10)					
Pre-PPE/tutorial	7	6.7	6	7	7
Post-PPE/pre-tutorial	9	10	8	8.5	8
Post-tutorial	10	10	8	9	8
Regular (week 11)					
Pre-tutorial	6	8	8	8	8
Post-tutorial	6	10	8	8	8
Laughter PPE (week 12)					
Pre-PPE/tutorial	8	6	7	8	6
Post-PPE/pre-tutorial	9	9	9	10	6.3
Post-tutorial	10	10	9	10	7

References

Argyle, M. (2001) *The Psychology of Happiness* (2nd edition). London: Routledge.

Batson, C. (1991) *The Altruism Question: Towards a Social Psychological Answer*. Hillsdale, NJ: Erlbaum.

Batson, C., Ahmad, N., Lishner, D. and Tsang, J. (2002) Empathy and altruism. In C.R. Snyder and S. Lopez (eds) *Handbook of Positive Psychology* (pp. 485–498). New York: Oxford University Press.

Block, D. (2003) *The Social Turn in Second Language Acquisition*. Washington, DC: Georgetown University Press.

Bourdieu, P. (1985) The forms of capital. In J. Richardson (ed.) *Handbook of Theory and Research for the Sociology of Education* (pp. 241–258). New York: Greenwood.

Bryant, F.B. and Veroff, J. (2007) *Savoring: A New Model of Positive Experience*. Mahwah, NJ: Lawrence Erlbaum Associates.

Bryant, J. and Zillmann, D. (1988) Using humor to promote learning in the classroom. *Journal of Children in Contemporary Society* 20, 49–78.

Carr, A. (2004) *Positive Psychology: The Science of Happiness and Human Strengths*. New York: Routledge.

Chang, M.Y., Chen, C.H. and Huang, K.F. (2008) Effects of music therapy on psychological health of women during pregnancy. *Journal of Clinical Nursing* 17, 2580–2587.

Charnetsky, C.J., Riggers, S. and Brennan, F. (2004) Effect of petting a dog on immune system functioning. *Psychological Reports* 3, 1087–1091.

Conway, A.M., Tugade, M.M., Catalino, L.I. and Fredrickson, B.L. (2013) The broaden-and-build theory of positive emotions: Form, function, and mechanisms. In S.A. David, I. Boniwell and A. Conley Ayers (eds) *The Oxford Handbook of Happiness* (pp. 17–34). New York: Oxford University Press.

Dewaele, J.M. (2010) *Emotions in Multiple Languages*. Basingstoke: Palgrave Macmillan.

Emmons, R. and Shelton, C. (2002) Gratitude and the science of positive psychology. In C.R. Snyder and S. Lopez (eds) *Handbook of Positive Psychology* (pp. 459–484). New York: Oxford University Press.

Fredrickson, B.L. (2001) The role of positive emotions in positive psychology: The broaden-and-build theory of positive emotions. *American Psychologist* 56, 218–226.

Fredrickson, B.L. (2003) The value of positive emotions. *American Scientist* 91, 330–335.

Fredrickson, B.L. and Branigan, C. (2005) Positive emotions broaden the scope of attention and thought–action repertoires. *Cognition and Emotion* 19 (3), 313–332.

Gregersen, T. and MacIntyre, P.D. (2014) *Capitalizing on Language Learners' Individuality: From Premise to Practice*. Bristol: Multilingual Matters.

Haski-Leventhal, D. (2009) Altruism and volunteerism: The perceptions of altruism in four disciplines and their impact on the study of volunteerism. *Journal for the Theory of Social Behaviour* 39 (3), 271–299.

Kaminski, M., Pellino, T. and Wish, J. (2002) Play and pets: The physical and emotional impact of child-life and pet therapy on hospitalized children. *Children's Health Care* 31, 321–335.

Kuiper, N.A. and Martin, R.A. (1993) Humor and self-concept. *Humor* 6, 231–270.

Lefcourt, H.M. and Martin, R.A. (1986) *Humor and Life Stress: Antidote to Adversity*. New York: Springer-Verlag.

LoSchiavo, F.M. and Shatz, M.A. (2005) Enhancing online instruction with humor. *Teaching of Psychology* 32 (4), 247–250.

Luthans, F., Luthans, K.W. and Luthans, B.C. (2004) Positive psychological capital: Beyond human and social capital. *Business Horizons* 47, 45–50.

Lyubomirsky, S. (2008) *The How of Happiness: A Scientific Approach to Getting the Life You Want*. New York: Penguin.

MacIntyre, P.D. and Gardner, R.C. (1991) Investigating language class anxiety using the focused essay technique. *Modern Language Journal* 75, 296–304.

MacIntyre, P.D. and Gregersen, T. (2012) Emotions that facilitate language learning: The positive-broadening power of the imagination. *Studies in Second Language Learning and Teaching* 2 (2), 193–213.
MacIntyre, P.D. and Mercer, S. (2014) Introducing positive psychology to SLA. *Studies in Second Language Learning and Teaching* 4 (2), 153–172.
MacIntyre, P.D., Clement, R., Dornyei, Z. and Noels, K.A. (1998) Conceptualizing willingness to communicate in a L2: A situational model of L2 confidence and affiliation. *Modern Language Journal* 82, 545–562.
Martin, R.A. and Dobbin, J.P. (1988) Sense of humor, hassles, and immunoglobulin A: Evidence for a stress-moderating effect of humor. *International Journal of Psychiatry in Medicine* 18, 93–105.
Martin, R.A. and Lefcourt, H.M. (1983) Sense of humor as a moderator of the relation between stressors and moods. *Journal of Personality and Social Psychology* 45, 1313–1324.
Mongrain, M. and Anselmo-Mathews, T. (2012) Do positive psychology exercises work? *Journal of Clinical Psychology* 68, 382–389.
Moran, C. and Massan, M. (1999) Differential influences of coping humor and humor bias on mood. *Behavioral Medicine* 25, 36–42.
Murphey, T. (2010) Gracias a la vida – musica que me ha dado tanto: Songs as scaffolded-languaging for SLA. In A. Hermont, R. Esprito Santo and S. Cavalcante (eds) *Linguagem E Cognição* (pp. 241–255). Belo Horizonte: PUC Minas.
Murphey, T. (2014) Singing well-becoming: Student musical therapy case studies. *Studies in Second Language Learning and Teaching* 2 (2), 205–235.
Nawyn, S.J., Gjokaj, L., Agbenyiga, D.L. and Grace, B. (2012) Linguistic isolation, social capital, and immigrant belonging. *Journal of Contemporary Ethnography* 41 (3), 255–282.
Odendaal, J.S. (2000) Animal assisted therapy – magic or medicine? *Journal of Psychosomatic Research* 49 (4), 275–280.
Peterson, C. (2006) *A Primer in Positive Psychology*. Oxford: New York.
Portes, A. (1998) Social capital: Its origins and applications in modern sociology, *Annual Review of Sociology* 24, 1–24.
Putnam, R.D. (2000) *Bowling Alone: The Collapse and Revival of American Community*. New York: Simon & Schuster.
Reschly, A.L., Huebner, E.S., Appleton, J.J. and Antaramian, S. (2008) Engagement as flourishing: The contribution of positive emotions and coping to adolescents' engagement at school and with learning. *Psychology in the Schools* 45 (5), 419–431.
Reeve, J. (2005) *Understanding Motivation and Emotion* (5th edition). Toronto: Wiley.
Sarafino, E. (2002) *Health Psychology* (4th edition). New York: Wiley.
Seligman, M.E.P. and Csikszentmihalyi, M. (2000) Positive psychology: An introduction. *American Psychologist* 55 (1), 5–14.
Seligman, M.E.P., Steen, T.A., Park, N. and Peterson, C. (2005) Positive psychology progress: Empirical validation of interventions. *American Psychologist* 60, 410–421.
Seligman, M.E.P., Ernst, R.M., Gillham, J., Reivich, K. and Linkins, M. (2009) Positive education: Positive psychology and classroom interventions. *Oxford Review of Education* 35 (3), 293–311.
Sobel, J. (2002) Can we trust social capital? *Journal of Economic Literature* 40 (1), 139–154.
Strauss, A. and Corbin, J. (1990) *Basics of Qualitative Research: Grounded Theory Procedures and Techniques*. Newbury Park, CA: Sage.
Waterman, A.S. (2013) The humanistic psychology–positive psychology divide: Contrasts in philosophical foundations. *American Psychologist* 68 (3), 124–133.
Wisdom, J.P., Saedi, G.A. and Green, C.A. (2009) Another breed of 'service' animals: STARS study findings about pet ownership and recovery from serious mental illness. *American Journal of Orthopsychiatry* 79, 430–436.
Yovetich, N.A., Dale, J.A. and Hudak, M.A. (1990) Benefits of humor in reduction of threat-induced anxiety. *Psychological Reports* 66, 51–58.

7 The Triumph Over Experience: Hope and Hardiness in Novice L2 Teachers

Phil Hiver

Introduction

It is no secret that the immense rewards experienced by teachers in their practice come at a heavy price. Teaching, Palmer once wrote, is a 'daily exercise in vulnerability' (1998: 17) and more than a century ago the metaphor of 'war' was used to describe what goes on inside the classroom (see Alexander, 2008). Observers have deplored the general tendency to socialize new teachers into this profession by throwing them into the deep end and abandoning them to sink or swim (Farrell, 2009; Worthy, 2005). This 'Robinson Crusoe' approach (Lortie, 1966) ultimately increases the risk of novice teachers becoming casualties of the profession, a tremendously wasteful proposition given the financial and human costs to state-sector primary and secondary schools, many of which are already under-supported yet held to increasingly stringent measures of accountability (Fantilli & McDougall, 2009). It is also a cause for alarm given evidence that the effectiveness of their teaching may be the most powerful school-based factor in student achievement (Hanushek & Rivkin, 2006); however, what is also understood is that teachers generally attain a high level of expertise only after three to five years in the profession (Harris & Sass, 2011).

While it is clear the experience of some novice teachers is one of uncertainty and even hardship, this is not the case for all novice teachers. Educational research has undergone a shift from examining primarily deficit models and negative states to a consideration of models of success and perseverance, in order to promote quality retention of young teachers in the profession (Day *et al.*, 2007; Richardson *et al.*, 2014); however, this growth-oriented approach to research has made only modest headway in studies of L2 educators in second and foreign language contexts (see e.g. Dörnyei & Kubanyiova, 2014; Farrell, 2012; Hiver, 2015; Kiely & Askham, 2012). Recent initiatives to address new teacher retention and to maximize the effectiveness of early-service language teachers have focused primarily on professional issues: collaboration, collegiality, mentoring and supportive leadership (Brannan & Bleistein, 2012; Faez & Valeo, 2012; Shin, 2012). What remains poorly understood, however, are novice L2 teachers' personal needs – those in the psychological domain that contribute to teachers' sense of self and professional well-being – such as building confidence, developing feelings of effectiveness, encouraging positive self-esteem and enhancing self-reliance (Chubbuck *et al.*, 2001; Farrell, 2008). The current chapter reports on a study designed, in part, to address the omission of a more positively oriented approach from much of the recent teacher research literature.

In this study, I recount the experiences of a cohort of 19 novice language teachers over their first year teaching in the state sector. Situated within a conceptual framework of hope building, I investigate why some L2 teachers appear to be more successful than others in meeting the rigorous demands of their first year of teaching, explore the processes through which hope emerged, and examine the role this played in helping them overcome the demands of their novice year. This investigation highlights the potential of a positive psychological approach to engage with the professional lives of teachers, continue to help them grow, and enhance their professional well-being as they tackle the definitional tasks of early-stage practitioners.

Literature Review

Hope

For as long as humankind has existed, individuals have aspired to lofty ideals and ambitions, and pursued the unattained. We are, at our core, goal-oriented beings (Peterson & Seligman, 2004) and this assumption has been, and remains, the nucleus of hope research (Lazarus, 1999). Hope is a trilogy of concepts – goals, pathways to problem solution, and agency – that combine to influence the way individuals interact with their environment and with life events. This conceptualization of hope is what has come to be broadly termed *hope theory* (Snyder, 2000, 2002).

Goals are the cognitive anchors of hopeful thinking and provide a mental target with a temporal reference that can galvanize a sequence of actions (Snyder, 1994). High-hope individuals also need *pathways* – the ability to generate successful plans to meet those goals (Snyder *et al.*, 2002). The pathways component highlights the phenomenological nature of hope: if goals are not accompanied by plans for attainment, they will not be achieved (Snyder *et al.*, 1991). High-hopers also have the flexibility to produce alternative pathway workarounds when goal achievement is impeded by a barrier of some kind (Lopez *et al.*, 2000). Finally, without the perceived capacity or the determination to actually use the pathways to approach a goal, nothing would be accomplished. *Agency* is the self-referential thought regarding the appraisal of one's ability to reach a goal that propels movement along a pathway towards that goal (Bandura, 2001). Agentic thinking is essential to all goal-directed pursuits, but may be especially so when circumstances in life throw up barriers to goals (Snyder *et al.*, 1996). Given that agentic thought in the face of barriers will assist in motivating the individual to tailor a pathway of action to reach a goal, the agency and pathways components enhance each other throughout the process of goal pursuit (Lopez *et al.*, 2004). Empirical findings show that individuals who are generally hopeful can, at times, exhibit symptoms of hopelessness and vice versa (Lopez *et al.*, 2000). This suggests that hope comprises both patterned stabilities as well as situation-specific dynamicity.

Hope differs from optimism mainly with regard to the mechanisms for regulating goal-oriented behavior (Bruininks & Malle, 2005). Hope theory emphasizes how agency and pathways thoughts propel a protagonist toward goals, and views affect only as the by-product of goal-directed cognition (Shorey *et al.*, 2002). Optimism, on the other hand, is an attributional style (Seligman, 1998) that relates to how an individual explains the causes of life events and how they structure expectancies toward future events. Optimists are people who generally expect good things to happen to them; thus, optimism also comprises an affective disposition (Scheier & Carver, 1987). With optimism, the focal point is on the expectancy of positive outcomes, and this cognitive/affective attribution process is what is thought to drive behavior (Peterson, 2000).

Hardiness

A complementary strand of research has identified a psychosocial construct that includes cognitive, emotional and behavioral qualities thought to moderate the impact of hardship and anxiety on mental and physical health (Kobasa *et al.*, 1981). This is the personality disposition of hardiness. *Hardiness* is operationalized as a constellation of three Cs – subdimensions that function as a positive resistance mechanism to demanding life events and failures (Maddi, 1999). These are commitment, control and challenge (Kobasa, 1979). Hardy people have a general purpose and sense of meaning in life which allow them to approach potentially stressful situations with the belief that they are meaningful and interesting, thus exhibiting *commitment*. Individuals who have developed hardiness also feel and act as if they can *control* demanding life events, reflecting their feelings of agency. Finally, they see change as a *challenge* that presents opportunities for growth and development rather than as a threat. These three beliefs are thought to make hardy individuals less likely to quit when they encounter failures and setbacks (Kobasa *et al.*, 1982). The much wider-ranging literature on *perseverance*, voluntary continuation of a goal-directed task in spite of difficulties or discouragement, has not led to the development of an individual-difference construct that would account for a sustained and intentional pursuit of goals (Peterson & Seligman, 2004). Instead, information about perseverance has been inferred from the *commitment* dimension of hardiness, or measured using the construct of *grit*, which foregrounds long-term determination to achieve higher-order goals (Duckworth *et al.*, 2007).

A number of studies suggest that hardiness moderates the detrimental effects of failure on health and performance primarily through cognitive appraisal (Maddi, 2004). This refers to when people reframe their perceptions of events, thereby making high-hardiness individuals more likely to view life events as positive and controllable, and to see a sense of challenge in them rather than an imminent threat (Maddi, 1999). Research indicates that individuals high in hardiness become invested in events they encounter, believe they can transform or influence their outcome, and expect that change will be accompanied by growth or development (Allred & Smith, 1988). Thus, unlike their low-hardiness counterparts, they modify the way they think about upsetting events in order to explore, learn from and influence these. High-hardiness subjects have also been shown to exhibit increased frustration-tolerance in tasks that demand concentration and persistence because their mental outlook tends to reduce the intensity of events or experiences (Wiebe, 1991). This style of appraisal has also been linked with problem-focused and support-seeking coping (Vogt *et al.*, 2008), suggesting that high-hardiness individuals engage in adaptive coping strategies involving the transformation of difficult situations into more positive experiences, which in turn reduces the long-term negative health consequences of stress and anxiety (Williams *et al.*, 1992).

Why hardiness and hope pertain to L2 teachers

Having introduced these two positive psychology constructs, let me now address the question of their contribution to redressing the precarious existence of novice L2 teachers. In the study of how individuals manage to continue functioning despite being confronted with discouraging failure, hardiness has generated considerable interest and gained prominence within the literature on applied health sciences (Funk, 1992). Decades of empirical evidence demonstrate that the cognitive, emotional and behavioral qualities of hardiness can help us unravel why certain individuals are less likely to quit when they encounter setbacks (Maddi, 2013). It may come as somewhat of a surprise, therefore, that hardiness has received virtually no attention in research about teaching and learning (for a notable exception see Chan, 2003), and it has yet to feature in studies of L2 learning or teaching. While hardiness may appear to be a subsidiary focus of this study, the data I report below indicate that hope is contingent on mechanisms of hardiness, suggesting that these are intertwined within the L2 teachers' sense of self.

Fulfillment and thriving involve more than just the absence of negative affectivity; thus, the significance of hope is in its potential to add something positive to human existence. Interest in how hope can transform the lives of those in the teaching profession goes back to the writings of Michael Fullan (1997) and Herbert Kohl (1998) and extends more recently to the work of Robert Bullough and his colleagues (Bullough, 2011; Bullough & Hall-Kenyon, 2011, 2012). These authors agree that because hope and happiness are essential conditions for learning and professional well-being, hope clearly is of consequence for how teachers channel their professional efforts and for how we study teachers and their work. They and others (Birmingham, 2009; Duncan-Andrade, 2009; Edgoose, 2010) caution that taking teachers' hopefulness for granted or neglecting it altogether leads to declining aspirations, lower professional investment and diminished performance on the part of teachers. Thus, this study was designed to explore the hypothesis that constructing a sense of hope may lead novice L2 teachers to remain committed to the profession and outperform others.

Method

The research questions addressed in this study are:

(1) To what extent do novice L2 teachers construct a sense of hope over their first year of teaching?
(2) What are the mechanisms through which novice L2 teachers' hope develops?
(3) What role does the teachers' emergent hope play in helping them survive the demands of their novice year?

Participants

The 19 participants in this study were all first-year, secondary-school English teachers in the South Korean K-12 sector (ages 6–18 in this context). Using typical case sampling, I selected these 19 teachers from a cohort of teacher-inductees from the largest provincial office of education. As the researcher, I was interested in these participants because they were fairly typical of novice L2 teachers in this context. Participation in the study was voluntary and the teachers were free to opt out of the study at any time. The 19 participants ranged in age from 27 to 35, and more than four-fifths were female (89%), which roughly reflects the overall gender distribution in K-12 English classrooms. Growing competitiveness in the pool of prospective English teachers has allowed the Korean state sector to be more stringent in overall requirements, and many taking the qualifying exam already hold graduate degrees – often from US and UK universities. The English proficiency of newly certified teachers is typically above the C1 level of the Common European Framework of Reference for Languages (CEFR), roughly corresponding to the Superior level of the American Council on the Teaching of Foreign Languages (ACTFL), with some Koreans raised and educated abroad even returning to enter the English teaching profession (the case for 3 of these 19 teachers). Only one of the teachers in this group of 19 had passed the teachers' qualifying exam on the first try. As novices, these 19 teachers were assigned to schools on a needs-based system, rather than according to individual choice. Responsibilities in their first year included: taking on a full teaching load of 20 hours or more; overseeing a homeroom class, a time-consuming yet critical responsibility for beginning teachers in Korea; advising students on their academic performance; and developing extra-curricular projects.

Data collection

Data collection took place over the course of 12 months (2013–14) beginning in March – the start of the school year in South Korea. All data were collected with the signed consent of the teachers, who indicated their preference for using English as the medium of communication. Three primary sources of data were collected. Following others (Bruininks & Malle, 2005), I chose to explore the participants' layperson definitions of hope without first explicitly invoking a theoretical definition (i.e. one incorporating notions of agency and pathways thinking). First, using a scale that ranged from –5 at the low end to +5 at the top end, the teachers were asked to log onto an online portal and rate how hopeful they had felt once every month. These monthly ratings resulted in a graph of longitudinal time-series measurements over the course of 12 months. Secondly, introspective journals were written once every two months (for a total of six journal entries) and submitted through the same online portal. In these introspective journals, the participants were given prompts to respond to (e.g. *What has been your best in-class moment so far?*; *What do you now know about yourself as a teacher that you didn't previously realize?*; *How has your experience in the classroom so far matched your expectations?*). They were also given the alternative of writing freely about their experiences. No minimum or maximum word limits were imposed, and most introspective journal entries ended up as a mixture of a response to the topical prompt and a first-person diary entry, ranging from 300 to 700 words in length.

The final source of data, a stimulated-recall interview with each participant, was collected at the end of the school year. These interviews lasted 90–120 minutes. They each began with the participant being asked to look at their time-series graph and clarify what was happening at each of the 12 points along the time-series graph. On the second run-through, participants were asked to offer further explanation and rationale for particularly high and low points they had marked on the graph (i.e. *What had made these points such a hopeful/hopeless time¿*). On the final run-through, each teacher was asked to consider the entire graph and make several general statements about themselves in connection with the concept of hope (e.g. *Over the past year I have felt most/least hopeful when…*). These three complementary data sources were intended to provide a rich and contextually compelling representation of these teachers' hope trajectories during their first year on the job.

Data analysis

Graph data from the rating scales were analyzed using change-point analysis, while the qualitative data coding followed an iterative analysis that alternated between emergent themes from the data and existing explanations from theory.

Change-point analysis (CPA) is a robust statistical method used for analyzing time-ordered data when no parametric assumptions can be made with regard to random sampling, homogeneity of variance and normal distribution (Taylor, 2000). CPA generates cumulative sum (CUSUM) charts to detect whether and where a significant change has occurred in time-ordered data, and uses bootstrapping to provide both confidence levels (typically set at the 95% level) and confidence intervals for each change. CPA has advantages over other time-series data analytical methods, such as control charting or autoregressive integrated moving average (ARIMA) models, because: it frequently identifies changes missed by other analyses; it is capable of precision in determining multiple changes; and it can expose false detections (Box *et al.*, 2008). Data from each of the 19 time-series graphs were inputted into the Change-Point Analyzer software package and the plots and CUSUM charts were generated for each participant, along with tables of significant changes that included confidence levels and confidence intervals. From these, the resulting data with all the significant change incidents detected were outputted as more reader-friendly tables.

The data from the participants' introspective journals and interviews were analyzed using an iterative approach (Tracy, 2013) that entailed moving back and forth from emergent themes in the data to existing theories and models in the literature in order to connect and progressively refine these (Creswell, 2007). The first cycle involved coding all the data included for each participant descriptively and analytically in NVivo 10 software (e.g. *teaching as a flat-line career*; *feelings of powerlessness*). I then categorized and synthesized these descriptive and analytic codes into interpretive concepts that were informed by my reading of the background literature. In this second cycle, I also began looking for deviant data that did not appear to support the emerging themes, and revised conceptual categories (e.g. *perceptions of being denied agency*). Finally, I returned to the time-series graphs in order to triangulate and solidify the thematic ideas from the qualitative data. Here I employed a technique taken from the method of discourse tracing (LeGreco & Tracy, 2009): I identified turning points (i.e. moments at which *X* occurs) in the quantitative graph data and juxtaposed them with the journal and stimulated recall data to establish why and how the event was significant for the participant.

In reporting this study, I faced the challenge often encountered in qualitative research: providing a coherent research narrative to a reader with only limited access to the data. I have tried to overcome this by building a case from the bottom up (i.e. going from negative to positive) and, in the interests of principled extract selection, I have included stretches that best typified conceptual links in the data while still being representative of the respective participants' whole data-sets. While it may not be possible to avoid issues of subjectivity or researcher bias entirely in reporting data of this sort, transparency is essential. In all data reporting below, participant-chosen pseudonyms are used.

Trajectories of Hope

Sisyphean teaching

It was immediately apparent from the data just how spiritless an experience the initial months on their own were for many of these novice L2 teachers. Seventeen of the 19 teachers reported how they rapidly realized that what they initially thought would be a wholesome environment with conditions that were well within their control was instead a disorienting and overwhelming one. Teachers' comments reveal how this intensified their initial painful experiences of adjusting to classroom realities and only highlighted their powerlessness and disaffection.

> As a new teacher who had just passed the teacher's exam, I was completely devastated. I had absolutely no clue what real school was like, and I just didn't know what to do in that setting. (Jenny, interview)

Maria was one teacher in particular who began the year with a meager level of hope that was further reduced after just a single month of teaching (see Figure 7.1), in this case by perceptions that what the future held in store for her as a L2 teacher was not only objectionable to her but also felt entirely out of her control.

> I began to understand here that teaching is a flat-line career. I suddenly thought, 'Wait I've just started and I still have 30 years of this ahead of me?' I mean [...] there is a difference between having a real purpose and

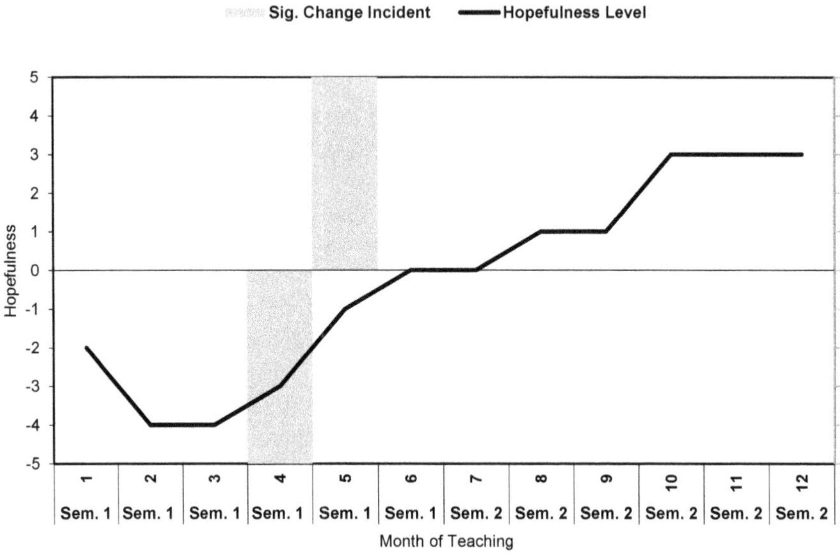

Figure 7.1 Change-point analysis: Maria

just spinning my wheels going nowhere. [...] I was so over teaching at the time. (Maria, interview)

Maria's early teaching experience reinforced the belief that her career choice held only the promise of a bleak, Sisyphean existence. Her choice of words in the extract above is suggestive when considering that the phrase 'flat-line' is commonly used to describe how one's vital signs cease functioning upon death. The perception of having very little influence over the direction of her career highlighted the relative meaninglessness of that path. Ironically, Maria's descriptions of goallessness alluded to the preoccupation of L2 teachers, particularly those in the public sector, with targets and objectives, albeit externally determined ones that pertain to student achievement on standardized tests.

Grace, on the other hand, had a particularly rare encounter with a hostile head of department in the second month of her teaching career that left her feeling disenchanted and cold (see Figure 7.2). This encounter suggests that there may be instances when hopelessness is contagious.

My mentor said to me one day mockingly 'You know what you've been doing so far, right? Well, I hope you enjoy it because that's what I've been doing for 21 years.' And I was disgusted by her comment because she was the one person who was supposed to have my back, you know. (Grace, interview)

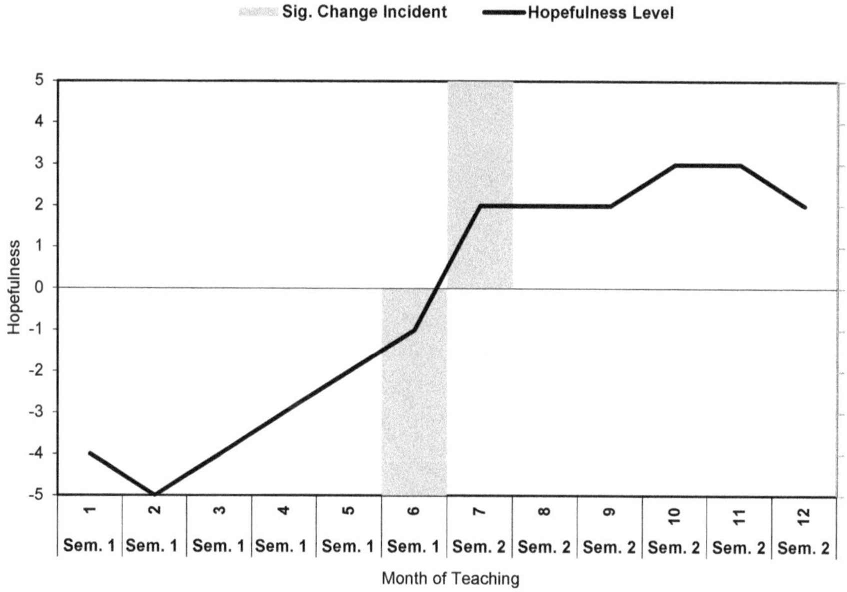

Figure 7.2 Change-point analysis: Grace

What rendered this incident even more crushing was Grace's expectation that her mentor, someone whose years of experience made her a potential role model and source of support, spoke and acted in a way that rejected her responsibility as a mentor and provided further reinforcement for the already elevated levels of helplessness and alienation that Grace was experiencing.

Whereas the dominant pattern of hope in this group of novice L2 teachers seems to parallel the trajectory of Maria and Grace (the case for 12 of the 19 teachers), other teachers in fact reported beginning with a reasonable measure of hope and positive expectations for success before losing it in the first few months of the year. The reasons cited by many teachers for this dip in hope involved a combination of fear and self-doubt.

> I have struggled and felt out of my league since the beginning of the semester. I was frightened and I felt left behind. [...] There was so much self-doubt in these past months. (Yuna, journal 2)

What surfaces from the data is that a lack of agency may be linked to the feelings of anxiety and fear these teachers reference. The teacher most characteristic of this pattern was Tony, whose trajectory of hope (see Figure 7.3) saw its first significant incident when it plummeted around month 4.

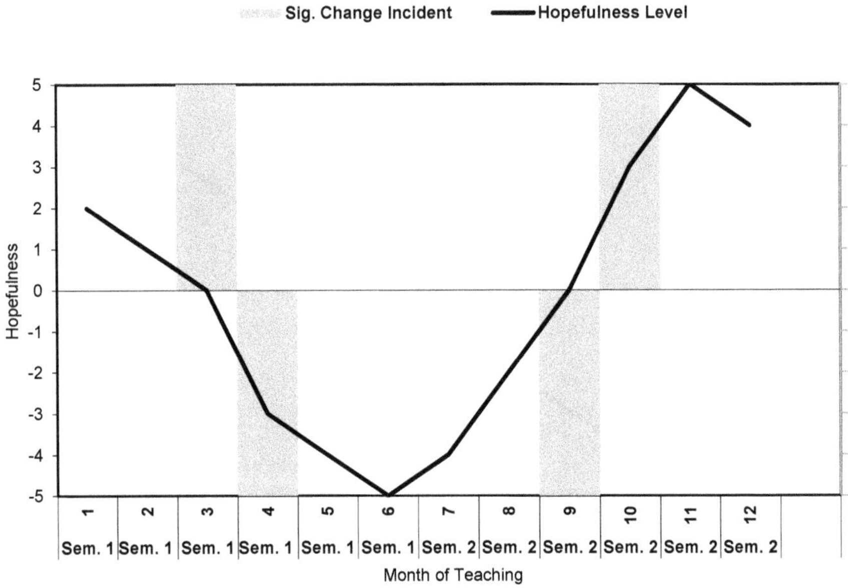

Figure 7.3 Change-point analysis: Tony

> Teachers are also just ordinary human beings like other people. We are not God. So, it was the constant threat of things that I couldn't control [...] that left me feeling very small. [...] Things got worse and worse, and so just the thought of entering school every morning built up my state of fear. (Tony, interview)

Understanding how individuals plunge to the depths of hopelessness can shed light on the process by which they then build their hopes anew. Generally, however, hopeful individuals should be capable of maintaining their pathways and agency despite being confronted with obstacles (Lopez *et al.*, 2000). In light of how easily and rapidly the drop-off was, what was reported by these L2 teachers as a high level of hope at the beginning of their first year may in fact have been closer to positive expectancies for the future that those striking out on a new experience often report – more sentiment than concrete hope (Rodriguez-Hanley & Snyder, 2000).

A renaissance of hope

While it would be very tempting to slip into a narrative about the distasteful experiences that eroded the hope of these L2 teachers' in their novice year, the data point in an entirely different direction – that these teachers were able to turn things around and build hope from despair. These teachers experienced a spark of hope that involved aspects of acclimation to their relentless struggle, and while there is no supporting evidence that this struggle abated, there was a gradual increase in purposeful behavior and consciousness that pathways to a solution did exist. The following comment reflecting on significant incidents from the participant's CPA chart shows this:

> I think the bad news is that it's easy to get me down in the short term. [...] But, the good news is that if you want to keep me down you have to kill me. (Young, interview)

What marks this transition as distinct from the earlier points in time is that many of these L2 teachers began to feel, speak and act as if demanding life events were under their control. In this respect, developing hardiness mechanisms of control can be thought of as a course correction of sorts for these teachers' plummeting hope.

One potent way some teachers found of rebounding from a low or coming to terms with their hope bottoming out was through constructively reframing their perception of events as fundamentally within their power to regulate or alter – something with clear parallels in the hardiness literature (Funk, 1992). Dana's account of her significant incident of change (see Figure 7.4) illustrates this.

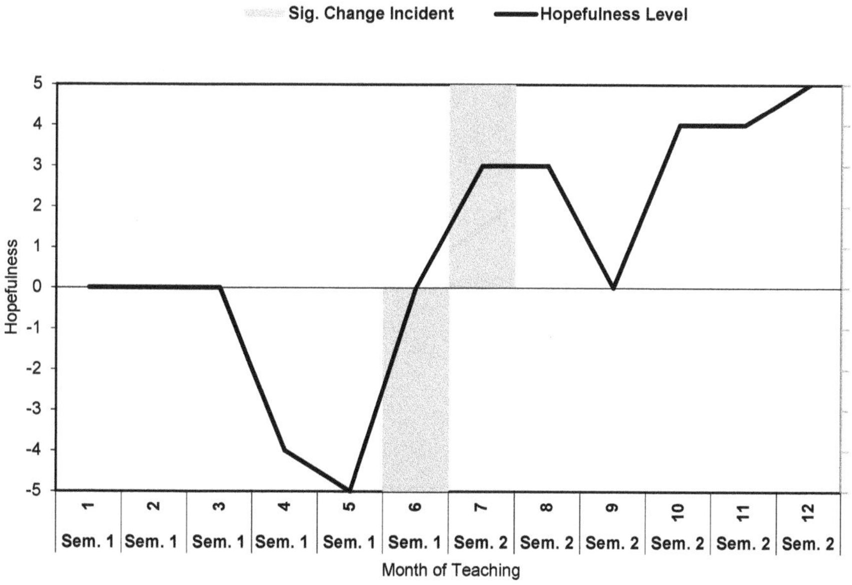

Figure 7.4 Change-point analysis: Dana

> We all want to believe in ideal cases [...]. But life is tough, and so you have to have guts. That's the only way to snap out of it and do something. If you are not in control, you have to take control. Because you only get one life, right¿ (Dana, interview)

Interestingly, Dana's hope trajectory data reveal that even with the overall trend upwards, her hope continued to dip and peak dynamically. In her comment below she indicates that hope emerged for her through iterative transformations as the elements drew on particular contextual demands in an adaptive path that continued into the present.

> I basically had to soldier up, you know. I think experiences are a way to generate learning, so [...] at least through that process I gained power and strategies to overcome other obstacles I will face in the future. (Dana, interview)

Jenny was another L2 teacher who alluded to the notion of a fluid, open-ended characterization of progress and success over obstacles. She experienced a significant incident in months 4 and 5 of her first year with a rapid upsurge in her levels of hope (see Figure 7.5), but what surfaced about Jenny's process of reframing challenges was that a non-linear, adaptive view was a more useful characterization.

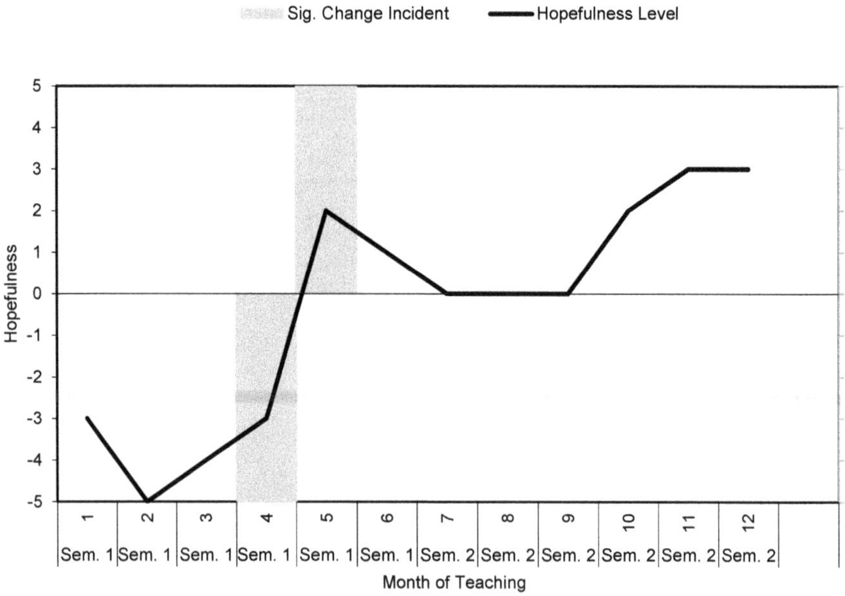

Figure 7.5 Change-point analysis: Jenny

> Because I am still a young teacher, I often miss out on seeing a big picture. But, I know that if I'm determined then things can sometimes solve themselves. Also, no quitter makes a good teacher. Whoever keeps moving forwards without quitting will succeed. [...] Rome wasn't built in a day. So, that's what I am trying even though it is hard right now. (Jenny, journal 4)

These increasingly purposeful attributions, of the type evidenced by Jenny and Dana, were accompanied by newly developed agentic feelings that led to increased awareness of how these teachers could transform their experience using oblique workarounds to overcome perceived barriers, where brute-force or head-on approaches did not work.

One unanticipated finding reported above was how goalless most L2 teachers were at the outset of their careers, and were simply going through the motions. However, a commonality in the journal data in the latter half of the year was that as teachers began to report having developed both goal- and pathway-generating capacities, these capacities appeared to mitigate the teachers' feelings of alienation and powerlessness, and allow them to regain control and begin to establish meaning and value previously lacking from their experience.

> So what if I am laughed at for expecting something constructive in my life and career? I am willing to be thought of as weird, crazy and notorious because I'm the only one who has goals for their life. (Maria, journal 3)

Young was one teacher for whom this was the case. She experienced a significant change in month 7 (see Figure 7.6), when her hopefulness rating became positive and began to climb in rapid increments. When asked to comment on what had happened differently from month 6 onwards, she recounted discovering how goals could neutralize her feelings of being directionless and function to keep her on the right track in her professional life.

> I realized early that the outcome of my teaching might not show immediately or explicitly, and I felt discouraged. [...] But I also thought that if I have a strong enough goal for what I am doing, then I know my efforts will pay off in the long run, and that will [...] help me endure the bad times without giving up hope. (Young, interview)

In month 8, an even more profound understanding grew from her first discovery when she started to consider the broader notion of purpose as a contributing force to her sense of career direction:

> Teachers need a concrete notion about why they teach. Recalling my first year of experience, it's hard to find a teacher who has clear goals

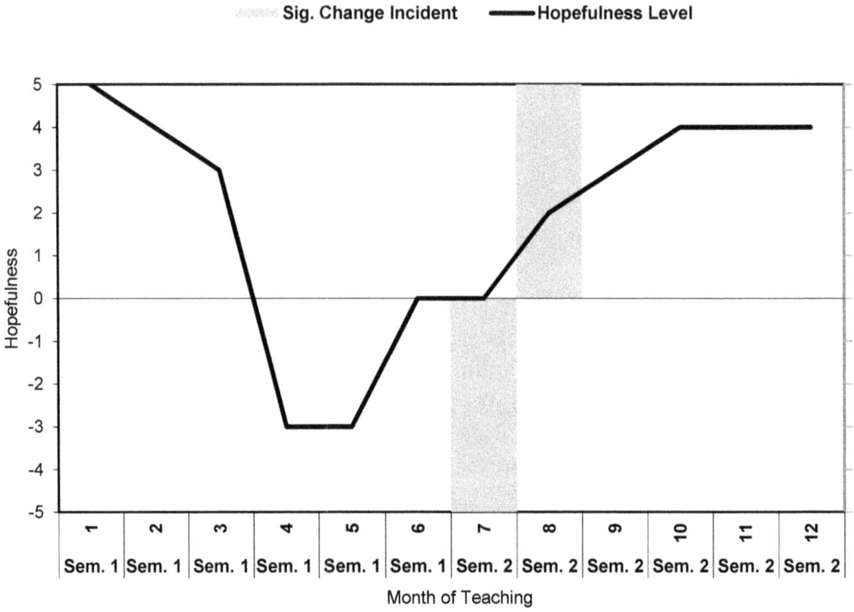

Figure 7.6 Change-point analysis: Young

> in their career. [...] But, when you have a clear idea of why you are a teacher, then it will be far more meaningful. (Young, interview)

Three exceptions to this general redemptive pattern were teachers who instead displayed attributions and behaviors typically found in low-hardiness individuals (Wiebe, 1991). They became overtly hostile, could think only of escape and withdrew from challenging circumstances in order to orient away from perceived threats to their self-efficacy and control.

> It's ridiculous that everything that goes on at school is my responsibility, so I don't know why I should be blamed for all those things. (Leah, journal 4)

> I really wanted to get out of that situation because I can't stand it anymore. So, I just spend a miserable time by myself. (Shinbi, interview)

Apart from these three exceptions, however, all the participants began to construct a sense that events were within their sphere of influence – a transition which generally took place between months 4 and 8 of the first year. Gaining feelings of control over powerlessness in turn led to increased agency and goal-directed energy in response to the challenging and upsetting environment that enveloped them. Thus, these agentic feelings now begin to anchor the teachers' hopeful behavior.

In pursuit of meaning and purpose

Against the backdrop of these L2 teachers' early experiences, it is apparent that meaningful hope for one's professional life is not an all-or-nothing proposition, nor is its development guaranteed to be a completely straightforward process. The data suggest that for many of the teachers in this study, the hope mechanisms of generating goals and finding successful pathways to meet those goals sparked a virtuous cycle within their self-concept by allowing them to reframe the perceived threats under which they worked as surmountable challenges, helping them to navigate past these punishing conditions. This began to animate their lives again with meaning and purpose, which, as an added consequence, accelerated the process of hope-building. The following data extract illustrates this fittingly.

> Being a teacher means dealing with trouble. And [...] you can't acknowledge defeat because that will be the end. So, the most important one is to keep your composure and just think about a solution and act promptly. [...] And if you can do that, you can stay on the right track and find a source of your own energy. (Yuna, journal 6)

As with Yuna's response above, what emerged from the majority of teachers' accounts was how they prioritized the alternative pathways component of hope. However, a number of teachers, such as Ally and Park quoted below, also commented that building hope was less an issue of 'finding their thing' and more one of letting purpose and meaning find them. In a sense, this formula combines the adaptive goal-pursuit of high-hope individuals with two of the qualities, namely, commitment and challenge, which characterize hardy individuals' typical approach to upsetting or uncertain circumstances.

> Teachers cannot live untruthfully. And, it makes no sense to teach without having thought about what is your cause. [...] You have to be honest and genuine to yourself because your students can easily spot a fake. But if you dedicate yourself to something bigger you can change your life and others' too. (Ally, journal 5)

This combination is peculiar because, first, goals typically must contain a degree of uncertainty – they are neither absolutely certain nor truly untenable – and so they require a degree of commitment. Secondly, their pursuit is often complicated by barriers, which must be interpreted as a challenge an individual can rise above.

> I feel most hopeful when I expect and see specific outcomes in my life and career. But, at the same time, if you pre-determine everything that is going to happen in life before it has taken place, you might be in danger of missing what is right and closing off opportunities which you could have benefited from. (Park, interview)

What can be observed is that beginning to generate goals and derive pathways to those goals allowed these teachers to gain feelings of control, which then cascade into the belief that difficulties in life are meaningful and interesting (demanding commitment), and the view that adversity is an opportunity for growth and development (representing challenge).

Thus, for these teachers, hope-building appears to involve adaptive processes that play out between coordinated components embedded within the self. Feelings of powerlessness evolve into increased agency; this control is then up-cycled (i.e. positively fed back) into goal-directed thought, which in turn feeds off the mechanisms of commitment and challenge to tap into pathways thinking that again enhances agency. Through repeated cycles, an outcome of sustained hopefulness emerges. Evidence can be seen in the data for this emergent outcome through the teachers' adaptive positive emotional responses to obstacles and barriers.

> Trusting in yourself to know what is right is essential to stay on the right track for continuing, and to minimize your confusion. (Cathy, journal 6)

> You have to let problems roll off you. [...] Even if I have to deviate from my original plans, I feel I'm most alive when I am taking the most appropriate road based on my own belief. (Maria, interview)

What this indicates is that hope can be conceptualized as an emergent, contextually constrained outcome pattern. The coordination of the sub-mechanisms for hope is revised through feedback loops, but there is no global control over this emergent outcome. It is developed by these teachers as a self-organized adaptation to the problems posed by their surroundings.

This adaptive outcome of renewed hope gave teachers a positive sense of meaning in life and allowed them to anticipate future ebbs and flows in their careers. For instance, returning to Tony's trajectory of hope (Figure 7.3) shows that he experienced a second significant incident in month 10, after which he describes himself as an almost entirely new person relative to the account of his earlier incident, in month 4:

> I don't really know how to explain it. But [...] it became common to feel inspired and to have impressive and exhilarating moments. And, that empowered me [...]. (Tony, interview)

Seen from a broad perspective, Tony could now be said to have reached a powerful, multidimensional state of hope which was rooted in past conflicts, foregrounded in his present well-being, yet still oriented toward his future fulfillment.

There were, however, three teachers who did not appear to develop the hope or hardiness mechanisms that the other 16 teachers did; in fact, just the opposite occurred. It seems that, presented with the initial challenges of their novice year, these three were unable to reframe their perceptions of events as positive and controllable, and thus they did not develop a sense of commitment to or challenge in their circumstances. Leah was one of these:

> Some days it feels like I don't want to be here anymore. I think a lot of unfair things happened to me this year, [...] and the more time goes on, the more I feel that people are working against me. So, some days I just don't see the point anymore. (Leah, interview)

Contrasting with this, however, the remaining 16 teachers began to adopt an entirely new lexicon with which to represent themselves and express their hope in journal entries and stimulated-recall interviews, employing terms such as *trust*, *brave*, *enthusiasm*, *inspired*, *empowered*, *persistence*, *belief*, *exhilarating*, *guidance*, *empathy* and *courage*. The comment by Dana below exemplifies this change of trajectory.

> I'm not a teacher with charisma, but rediscovering my courage has helped me to become a better person.[...] Occasionally I even have some magic moments when the world is a brighter place and everything seems to be turning out okay. (Dana, interview)

The teachers would not likely have chosen to narrate their perceptions of reality in this way unless they had recaptured meaning and purpose in their sense of self. Thus, the results reported here indicate that newfound direction and value came about through the joint emergence of hardiness and hope-building.

Discussion

The emergence of a hopescape

In exploring how L2 teachers come to construct a sense of hope in their novice year of teaching, the data suggest that hope can be construed as an outcome that emerges in response to the environmental demands experienced by these L2 teachers (see e.g. Kloos & Van Orden, 2009). Snyder has claimed that far from being a hardwired, rule-driven apparatus, 'hope is learned' (2002: 263) and this may indeed have been the case for many of these novice L2 teachers. Hope, for these teachers, was not an asset that existed 'offline' in some form of inactive, absolute state. Instead, sustained hope emerged as a dimension of teachers' self through adaptive restructuring within an immediate context. The teachers' feelings of powerlessness were to an extent provoked by the perceived lack of control over demanding contextual conditions. However, what was unforeseen was that this powerlessness would act as a catalyst for increased intentionality – itself one precursor to agentic thought and behavior – as if a conscious choice were made by these L2 teachers to assert control where they previously had none. The goal-directed thought and pathways thinking that developed concurrent to this served as reinforcing feedback for feelings of power and control. These then transformed into a commitment to a particular sense of meaning and purpose, and an openness to the challenges occasioned by change and uncertainty that again looped back into enhanced agency. Even the developmental trajectories of participants who began their first year with compositional elements of hope featured continuous interaction with these salient contextual factors.

One unanticipated finding from the data-set was the teacher participants' varying levels of goal expression. This was surprising given that they were all driven individuals who, in many cases, had expended several years of effort to enter the L2 teaching profession in the first place. Notions from social cognitive theory (Bandura, 1997) may shed light on the seeming impasse between agency and goal pursuit. The cognitive, motivational and affective processes through which self-efficacy is thought to affect human functioning enable people to exercise some control (i.e. agency) over environmental conditions they encounter (Bandura, 1994). There is robust evidence that individuals' self-efficacy beliefs play a mediating role in how goals, tasks and challenges are approached (Bandura, 1989, 2006). Depending on how well an individual believes they can do something, that individual's choices to act to reach a goal (i.e. their agentive stance) will be affected. Contextual experience strengthens self-efficacy, among other ways, through direct mastery experiences (i.e. dealing with a task successfully oneself) and vicarious social models (i.e. seeing other similar people succeed at a task through sustained effort) (Bandura, 1982). This also clearly extends to teachers' efficacy and their classroom behavior (Tschannen-Moran & Woolfolk Hoy, 2001). Self-efficacy expands as teachers gain experience, to include more complex self-beliefs and a richer understanding of a particular domain – as these novice teachers are likely to do. Nonetheless, many of these novice L2 teachers may not have had the first-hand mastery experiences or witnessed adequate social models capable of feeding back into their sense of self-efficacy and bolstering it. In extreme cases, such as with Grace or Tony, when circumstances or significant others actively instill anxiety and self-doubt that they do not have what it takes to be a teacher, this may even undermine the core self-efficacy beliefs necessary to instill agentic thought in the teachers' working self-concept. A modicum of individual agency is essential to spark alternative pathways to goal pursuit (Tennen *et al.*, 2002), and these findings suggest that perceptions of adequate self-efficacy must first be satisfied for any agency to take root in these L2 teachers. However, these conditions may materialize only after teachers have developed the beginnings of hardiness mechanisms (i.e. commitment and challenge) that buffer their self-concept from anxiety and self-doubt. Thus, for these participants hope as an emergent outcome was constructed in part through hardiness mechanisms.

Why go on?

Among the cohort of 19 L2 teachers, there were three 'leavers' who decided to leave the profession altogether following their novice year. This may further shed light on how the remaining 16 'hopers' adapted to and survived the demands of their novice year. Psychologists have long acknowledged that individual constructions of reality function as mental filters which an individual uses to make sense of the world, and may influence individuals' behavior (Hallion & Ruscio, 2011). When based on inaccurate mental assemblages, such as cognitive biases, these perceptual distortions can result in irrational actions and attributions. Instead of reframing their perceptions of events as positive and controllable, the three leavers developed attributions that manifested through their reliance on negative self-statements in nearly all their data. Going one step further, they also reported the sort of avoidance-oriented activity known to decrease sympathetic arousal to stressful stimuli, particularly when an individual encounters external forces that threaten their perceptions of control and raise overall anxiety (Williams *et al.*, 1992). Thus, by relying on a range of regressive coping responses that include denying that stressful events occurred, blaming oneself for the threat of events, and self-isolation to avoid change or taking responsibility, these three were unable to develop a sense of commitment to or challenge in their circumstances. In brief, they found it easier to give up or give in.

While virtually all the participants were able to identify things they would like to change or difficulties they would have liked to address, the three leavers reported goals framed only in the categories of mastery and achievement. They did not frame goals in genre categories related to meaningfulness, purpose or service; goals of belonging and immediacy; or other attitudinal goals. Thus, when the mechanisms of hardiness and hope did not take root and these goals no longer assumed prominence in their experience, the resulting sense of confusion reinforced their feelings of failure. On the other hand, teachers who developed the self-efficacy and agency necessary for goal pursuit found themselves able to reframe goal-directed thought from the typical 'mastery and achievement' goals to expanded categories that included aspects of meaningfulness and belonging. With hope-building, it pays to remember, goals are not an individual's *raison d'être*. They are simply tools that enable the pathways to outcomes of action, which themselves stimulate the appraisals of agency that propel action (Locke & Latham, 2006; Payne *et al*., 2007). However, the way goals are characterized, as either unidimensional or thick with layers and orientations, may play a significant role in contributing the necessary positive forces for L2 teachers to pull through their novice year in the profession and begin to flourish.

Conclusion

Although all situations may be construed hopefully, to the casual observer novice L2 teachers in many compulsory education settings must battle through conditions that make for a disproportionately demanding first year in the profession (Farrell, 2008). This study is among the first to examine the complexities of novice K-12 language teachers' professional experiences from a perspective of hope-building. The data indicate that these 19 teachers began their careers in a slump which left them feeling powerless, alienated and under constant threat. Making sense of hope does require the converse of despair, and the trajectory followed by the three leavers over their first – and ultimately only – year in the profession was an experience of compounding futility and hopelessness that failed to reverse itself. Yet, while teachers' hope may be shaken, it can also be regained. For the remaining teachers, developing the capacity to generate goals and produce pathways to those goals mitigated feelings of alienation and powerlessness, and allowed them to establish a sense of control over life events. These agentic feelings in turn enabled the hopers to reframe their appraisals of threat as obstacles that could be overcome, rather than immutable impediments. The evidence suggests that through open interaction among situational factors, the mechanisms of hope and hardiness feed off of each other adaptively and lead to emergent outcomes that provide these novice teachers with a positive sense of meaning in life and allow them to anticipate future ebbs and flows in their careers.

Conducting this study was immensely satisfying, not least because I have always felt myself to be firmly in the corner of novice L2 teachers and devoted to supporting them in their early-service years. At a time when the expectations for beginning teachers have never been higher or the challenges of teaching more daunting, there are undoubtedly a number of novice L2 teachers who may be generally disaffected, bewildered, angry and demoralized by the conditions of their first years on the job. However, the results of this study suggest that there is hope. For countless teachers, teaching gives meaning to life, and they could not imagine doing anything else. Here, then, is an intimate link between the sense of purpose these teachers possess and the process of developing hope within one's teaching persona. These individuals acknowledge their limitations, yet approach their daily practice with feelings of competence and self-esteem. They are selfless and committed, hopeful and happy. Developing and sustaining hope may be an uphill process. However, these findings hold promise that – consistent with positive psychology (Seligman & Csikszentmihalyi, 2000) – substantial numbers of early-career teachers can cultivate the qualities needed to feel more alive, more hopeful and happier.

References

Alexander, P. (2008) Charting the course for the teaching profession: The energizing and sustaining role of motivational forces. *Learning and Instruction* 18, 483–491.

Allred, K. and Smith, T. (1988) The hardy personality: Cognitive and physiological responses to evaluative threat. *Journal of Personality and Social Psychology* 56 (2), 257–266.

Bandura, A. (1982) Self-efficacy mechanism in human agency. *American Psychologist* 37, 122–147.

Bandura, A. (1989) Human agency in social cognitive action. *American Psychologist* 44, 1175–1184.

Bandura, A. (1994) Self-efficacy. In V.S. Ramachaudran (ed.) *Encyclopedia of Human Behavior* (vol. 4, pp. 71–81). New York: Academic Press.

Bandura, A. (1997) *Self-efficacy: The Exercise of Control*. New York: W.H. Freeman.

Bandura, A. (2001) Social cognitive theory: An agentic perspective. *Annual Review of Psychology* 52, 1–26.

Bandura, A. (2006) Toward a psychology of human agency. *Perspectives on Psychological Science* 1 (2), 164–180.

Birmingham, C. (2009) The disposition of hope in teaching. *Teacher Education Quarterly* 36 (4), 27–39.

Box, G., Jenkins, G. and Reinsel, G. (2008) *Time Series Analysis: Forecasting and Control* (4th edition). Hoboken, NJ: Wiley.

Brannan, D. and Bleistein, T. (2012) Novice ESOL teachers' perceptions of social support networks. *TESOL Quarterly* 46 (3), 519–541.

Bruininks, P. and Malle, B. (2005) Distinguishing hope from optimism and related affective states. *Motivation and Emotion* 29, 327–355.

Bullough, R.V. (2011) Hope, happiness, teaching and learning. In C. Day and J. Lee (eds) *New Understandings of Teacher Effectiveness: Emotions and Educational Change* (pp. 15–30). New York: Springer.

Bullough, R.V. and Hall-Kenyon, K. (2011) The call to teach and teacher hopefulness. *Teacher Development* 15 (2), 127–140.

Bullough, R.V. and Hall-Kenyon, K. (2012) On teacher hope, sense of calling, and commitment to teaching. *Teacher Education Quarterly* 39 (2), 7–27.

Chan, D. (2003) Hardiness and its role in the stress–burnout relationship among prospective Chinese teachers in Hong Kong. *Teaching and Teacher Education* 19, 381–395.

Chubbuck, S., Clift, R., Allard, J. and Quinlan, J. (2001) Playing it safe as a novice teacher: Implications for programs for new teachers. *Journal of Teacher Education* 52 (5), 365–376.

Creswell, J. (2007) *Qualitative Inquiry and Research Design: Choosing Among Five Traditions* (2nd edition). Thousand Oaks, CA: Sage.

Day, C., Sammons, P., Stobart, G., Kington, A. and Gu, Q. (2007) *Teachers Matter: Connecting Lives, Work and Effectiveness*. New York: McGraw-Hill.

Dörnyei, Z. and Kubanyiova, M. (2014) *Motivating Learners, Motivating Teachers: Building Vision in the Language Classroom*. Cambridge: Cambridge University Press.

Duckworth, A., Peterson, C., Matthews, M. and Kelly, D. (2007) Grit: Perseverance and passion for long-term goals. *Journal of Personality and Social Psychology* 92, 1087–1101.

Duncan-Andrade, J.M. (2009) Note to educators: Hope required when growing roses in concrete. *Harvard Educational Review* 79 (2), 181–194.

Edgoose, J. (2010) Hope in the unexpected: How can teachers still make a difference in the world? *Teachers College Record* 112 (2), 2–3.

Faez, F. and Valeo, A. (2012) ESOL teacher education: Novice teachers' perceptions of their preparedness and efficacy in the classroom. *TESOL Quarterly* 46 (3), 450–471.

Fantilli, R. and McDougall, D. (2009) A study of novice teachers: Challenges and supports in the first years. *Teaching and Teacher Education* 25, 814–825.

Farrell, T. (ed.) (2008) *Novice Language Teachers: Insights and Perspectives for the First Year*. London: Equinox.

Farrell, T. (2009) The novice teacher experience. In A. Burns and J.C. Richards (eds) *The Cambridge Guide to Second Language Teacher Education* (pp. 182–189). New York: Cambridge University Press.

Farrell, T. (2012) Novice-service language teacher development: Bridging the gap between preservice and in-service education and development. *TESOL Quarterly* 46 (3), 435–449.

Fullan, M. (1997) *What's Worth Fighting For in the Principalship?* (2nd edition). New York: Teachers College Press.

Funk, S. (1992) Hardiness: A review of theory and research. *Health Psychology* 11 (5), 335–345.

Hallion, L. and Ruscio, A. (2011) A meta-analysis of the effect of cognitive bias modification on anxiety and depression. *Psychological Bulletin* 137(6), 940–958.

Hanushek, E. and Rivkin, S. (2006) Teacher quality. In E. Hanushek and F. Welch (eds) *Handbook of the Economics of Education* (pp. 1051–1078). San Diego, CA: Elsevier.

Harris, D. and Sass, T. (2011) Teacher training, teacher quality and student achievement. *Journal of Public Economics* 95 (7–8), 798–812.

Hiver, P. (2015) Once burned, twice shy: The dynamic development of system immunity in language teachers. In Z. Dörnyei, P.D. MacIntyre and A. Henry (eds) *Motivational Dynamics in Language Learning* (pp. 214–237). Bristol: Multilingual Matters.

Kiely, R. and Askham, J. (2012) Furnished imagination: The impact of preservice teacher training on early career work in TESOL. *TESOL Quarterly* 46 (3), 496–518.

Kloos, H. and Van Orden, G. (2009) Soft-assembled mechanisms for the grand theory. In J.P. Spencer, M. Thomas and J. McClelland (eds) *Toward a New Grand Theory of Development? Connectionism and Dynamics Systems Theory Reconsidered* (pp. 253–267). Oxford: Oxford University Press.

Kobasa, S. (1979) Stressful life events, personality, and health: An inquiry into hardiness. *Journal of Personality and Social Psychology* 37 (1), 1–11.

Kobasa, S., Maddi, S. and Courington, S. (1981) Personality and constitution as mediators in the stress–illness relationship. *Journal of Health and Social Behavior* 22 (4), 368–378.

Kobasa, S., Maddi, S. and Kahn, S. (1982) Hardiness and health: A prospective study. *Journal of Personality and Social Psychology* 42 (1), 168–177.

Kohl, H. (1998) *The Discipline of Hope: Learning from a Lifetime of Teaching*. New York: Simon & Schuster.

Lazarus, R.S. (1999) Hope: An emotion and a vital coping resource against despair. *Social Research* 66 (2), 653–678.

LeGreco, M. and Tracy, S. (2009) Discourse tracing as qualitative practice. *Qualitative Inquiry* 15, 1516–1543.

Locke, E. and Latham, G. (2006) New directions in goal-setting theory. *Current Directions in Psychological Science* 15 (5), 65–68.

Lopez, S., Ciarlelli, R., Coffman, L., Stone, M. and Wyatt, L. (2000) Diagnosing for strengths: On measuring hope building blocks. In C.R. Snyder (ed.) *The Handbook of Hope: Theory, Measures, and Applications* (pp. 57–85). San Diego, CA: Academic Press.

Lopez, S., Snyder, C.R., Magyar-Moe, J., Edwards, L., Pedrotti, J., Janowski, K., Turner, J. and Pressgrove, C. (2004) Strategies for accentuating hope. In P. Linley and S. Joseph (eds) *Positive Psychology in Practice* (pp. 388–404). Hoboken, NJ: Wiley.

Lortie, D.C. (1966) Teacher socialization: The Robinson Crusoe model. In *The Real World of the Beginning Teacher* (ERIC Document Reproduction Service No. ED 030 616). Washington, DC. National Commission on Teacher Education and Professional Standards.

Maddi, S. (1999) Comments on trends in hardiness research and theorizing. *Consulting Psychology Journal* 51 (2), 67–71.

Maddi, S. (2004) Hardiness: An operationalization of existential courage. *Journal of Humanistic Psychology* 44 (3), 279–298.

Maddi, S. (2013) *Hardiness: Turning Stressful Circumstances into Resilient Growth*. Dordrecht: Springer.

Palmer, P. (1998) *The Courage to Teach*. San Francisco, CA: Jossey-Bass.

Payne, S., Youngcourt, S. and Beaubien, J.M. (2007) A meta-analytic examination of the goal orientation nomological net. *Journal of Applied Psychology* 92 (1), 128–150.

Peterson, C. (2000) The future of optimism. *American Psychologist* 55, 44–55.

Peterson, C. and Seligman, M. (2004) *Character Strengths and Virtues: A Handbook and Classification*. Oxford: Oxford University Press.

Richardson, P., Karabenick, S. and Watt, H. (eds) (2014) *Teacher Motivation: Theory and Practice*. New York: Routledge.

Rodriguez-Hanley, A. and Snyder, C.R. (2000) The demise of hope: On losing positive thinking. In C.R. Snyder (ed.) *The Handbook of Hope: Theory, Measures, and Applications* (pp. 39–54). San Diego, CA: Academic Press.

Scheier, M. and Carver, C. (1987) Dispositional optimism and physical well-being: The influence of generalized outcome expectancies on health. *Journal of Personality* 55, 169–210.

Seligman, M. (1998) *Learned Optimism*. New York: Pocket Books.

Seligman, M. and Csikszentmihalyi, M. (2000) Positive psychology: An introduction. *American Psychologist* 55 (1), 5–14.

Shin, S.-K. (2012) 'It cannot be done alone': The socialization of novice English teachers in South Korea. *TESOL Quarterly* 46 (3), 542–567.

Shorey, H.S., Snyder, C.R., Rand, K.L., Hockemeyer, J.R. and Feldman, D.B. (2002) Somewhere over the rainbow: Hope theory weathers its first decade. *Psychological Inquiry* 13 (4), 322–331.

Snyder, C.R. (1994) *The Psychology of Hope: You Can Get There From Here*. New York: Free Press.

Snyder, C.R. (2000) Hypothesis: There is hope. In C.R. Snyder (ed.) *The Handbook of Hope: Theory, Measures, and Applications* (pp. 3–21). San Diego, CA: Academic Press.

Snyder, C.R. (2002) Hope theory: Rainbows in the mind. *Psychological Inquiry* 13 (4), 249–275.

Snyder, C.R., Harris, C., Anderson, J., Holleran, S., Irving, L., Sigmon, S., Yoshinobu, L., Gibb, J., Langelle, C. and Harney, P. (1991) The will and the ways: Development and validation of an individual-differences measure of hope. *Journal of Personality and Social Psychology* 60 (4), 570–585.

Snyder, C.R., Sympson, S., Ybasco, F., Borders, T., Babyak, M. and Higgins, R. (1996) Development and validation of the state hope scale. *Journal of Personality and Social Psychology* 70 (2), 321–335.

Snyder, C.R., Rand, K. and Sigmon, D. (2002) Hope theory: A member of the positive psychology family. In C.R. Snyder and S.J. Lopez (eds) *Handbook of Positive Psychology* (pp. 257–275). Oxford: Oxford University Press.

Taylor, W. (2000) A pattern test for distinguishing between autoregressive and mean-shift data. Taylor Enterprises, Libertyville, Illinois. Retrieved from http://www.variation.com/cpa/tech/changepoint.html (accessed November 2015).

Tennen, H., Affleck, G. and Tennen, R. (2002) Clipped feathers: The theory and measurement of hope. *Psychological Inquiry* 13, 311–317.

Tracy, S. (2013) *Qualitative Research Methods: Collecting Evidence, Crafting Analysis, Communicating Impact*. Chichester: Wiley-Blackwell.

Tschannen-Moran, M. and Woolfolk Hoy, A. (2001) Teacher efficacy: Capturing an elusive construct. *Teaching and Teacher Education* 17, 783–805.

Vogt, D., Rizvi, S., Shipherd, J. and Resick, P. (2008) Longitudinal investigation of reciprocal relationship between stress reactions and hardiness. *Personality and Social Psychology Bulletin* 34 (1), 61–73.

Wiebe, D. (1991) Hardiness and stress moderation: A test of proposed mechanisms. *Journal of Personality and Social Psychology* 60 (1), 89–99.

Williams, P., Wiebe, D. and Smith, T. (1992) Coping processes as mediators of the relationship between hardiness and health. *Journal of Behavioral Medicine* 15 (3), 237–255.

Worthy, J. (2005) 'It didn't have to be so hard': The first years of teaching in an urban school. *International Journal of Qualitative Studies in Education* 18 (3), 379–398.

8 Advanced Language Learners' Experiences of Flow in the Hungarian EFL Classroom

Éva Czimmermann and Katalin Piniel

Introduction

In founding the field of positive psychology, Seligman and Csikszentmihalyi (2000) drew inspiration from positive emotion in general and the phenomenon of flow (Csikszentmihalyi, 1997) in particular. Both have been acknowledged to play an important role in the language classroom (Egbert, 2003; Gregersen & MacIntyre, 2014) but they are still not widely researched within applied linguistics. Csikszentmihalyi (1989, 1996) defines 'flow' as an experiential state characterized by intense focus and involvement that leads to improved performance on a task. Flow experiences are said to be characterized by optimal levels of task difficulty and intense involvement in a particular activity that is motivating, and offers manageable challenges with a perceived opportunity of control. In language classrooms, generally, advanced learners have been shown to be highly motivated (more so than their secondary-school peers) and, as they have achieved higher levels of proficiency, their level of self-efficacy (Mills, 2014) is thought to be high, and they are further believed to be less likely to experience language anxiety (Horwitz & Young, 1991), also thought of as an anti-flow experience (Csikszentmihalyi, 2003). Nevertheless, it is unclear whether these learners' classroom experiences, both on a general and on a task-specific level, can be characterized by peak moments of flow and to what extent. On a task-specific level, the study described in this chapter aimed to test what characteristics of tasks are linked to the positive experience of flow. As a result, we hope to gain a clearer view as to what can contribute to flow in the advanced-level foreign language classroom.

Background

Linley *et al.* (2006: 8) define positive psychology as 'the scientific study of optimal human functioning'. On the meta-psychological level, its aim is to synthesize 'both the positive and the negative aspects of human experience' (Linley *et al.*, 2006: 7); thus, it is interested in all subjective experience of individuals in different contexts throughout their lives. From a pragmatic perspective, Linley *et al.* suggest four levels of analysis: investigating the precursors or wellsprings of well-being; looking at the processes of optimal functioning; investigating the social mechanisms that enhance the well-being of individuals; and considering the outcomes or states that constitute a happy life.

The appearance of positive psychology has implications in education, educational psychology as well as educational research (Kristjansson, 2012). Within the educational context, we will restrict our study to the well-being of learners in the foreign language classroom; more specifically, we will focus on learners' optimal functioning (i.e. flow) and the factors that seem to support it, as well as those that seem to prevent it and lead to negative (anti-flow) experiences.

Flow

The models of flow are primarily based on the core concept of balancing challenges and skills in an ideal way. Through the years, these models have been extended in terms of the number of components and the dynamic relationships between these components (Csikszentmihalyi, 1988, 1996, 2003). In the present chapter, we rely on the so-called Four Channel Flow Model (Csikszentmihalyi, 2003), which (alongside flow) includes apathy, anxiety and boredom as anti-flow experiences. Apathy is said to stem from tasks requiring low challenges and low skills. In the L2 classroom, this can mean that learners with low-level skills do not have the opportunity to face real challenges or use their more developed skills and, as a result, they may lose interest in learning. Anxiety, on the other hand, can arise from tasks that present a high-level challenge for learners with low-level abilities; thus, upon attempting the difficult task, appraisal processes trigger high levels of state anxiety (Lazarus & Folkman, 1984) as the learners feel they are not equipped with the tools to solve that task. On the other hand, learners with a high level of abilities facing low-level tasks can easily experience boredom and lose interest in the task due to the lack of challenge.

Csikszentmihalyi (2003) also outlined a learning spiral within the framework of flow theory called the Growth of Complexity Through Flow. He claims that flow experiences stimulate learning, and during activities challenges are continually revised while new challenges also appear. In order to sustain the state of flow, the skills of the learner must be continuously improved to meet the higher levels of challenge; in this way, flow enhances development. By way of experiencing flow during learning activities, people can realize their potential at a maximum level since they are required to mobilize their skills in order to meet the challenging goals (Csikszentmihalyi, 1997).

Although few studies have focused on flow and language learning, some have investigated flow in connection with different language skills: for example, McQuillan and Conde (1996) looked at flow and reading skills and Abbott (2000) investigated flow related to writing skills. Others have studied flow experiences in the general L2 classroom context (e.g. Egbert, 2003). Overall, findings show that factors like interest, background knowledge, perceived benefit and the possibility of choices play a key role in prompting flow experiences, alongside a supportive classroom climate and the encouragement of creative thinking.

Task-specific flow

According to Csikszentmihalyi (1997), besides the random instances of experiencing flow in our everyday life in general situations, flow is most likely to appear when individuals are involved in well-structured, meaningful activities that offer a high level of challenge for which learners have just the adequate skills to meet by making an effort. Flow activities, or tasks, require focused attention, involvement and a certain level of expertise. Egbert in her study defined *task* on the basis of previous literature (e.g. Brown, 2000; Bygate *et al.*, 2001) as 'a stand-alone endeavor that has specific goals and a clear purpose and during the performance of which attention is paid to meaning rather than language' (Egbert, 2003: 501). She claims that a task stands alone in the sense that it contains all the necessary information and action to reach the goal in itself. A task is a more complex construct than an activity, as it can 'consist of many activities that lead to the goals' (p. 501). Dörnyei claims that a task-based framework is especially useful in L2 research because tasks provide 'researchable behavioral units' (Dörnyei, 2005: 80) and enable the application of specific and process-oriented approaches. Consequently, it can be fruitful to assess flow experiences not only at a classroom level but also at a task-specific level in order to improve the understanding of the complexity of flow phenomenon.

Egbert (2003) describes task-specific flow along four basic dimensions derived from the flow theory of Csikszentmihalyi (1975) and Csikszentmihalyi and LeFevre (1989). The four components of task-specific flow are as follows:

(1) The challenge–skills balance refers to the optimal balance between the challenges of the task and the individual's skills, which arouses the participant's will to explore and gradually successfully complete the task.

(2) Focused attention with a lack of interruptions and distractions is a prerequisite for flow. In flow theory (Csikszentmihalyi, 1997), focus is characterized by intense concentration and automaticity. Constant feedback may be a key to maintaining attention in language acquisition in a way such that learners are still able to focus on form and incorporate grammatical forms or new elements of the language. Egbert (2003) hypothesizes that both unintentional focus (which is closely related to flow) and noticing (a more conscious form of attention) may contribute to language learning, where flow supports greater fluency and noticing supports greater accuracy.
(3) Interest is important for the language learner to find the task intrinsically interesting or authentic in order to experience flow. Egbert (2003) lists characteristics of tasks that prompt learners' interest, for example the meaningful communication of an idea or the perceived authentic nature of language use. Creative and open-ended tasks may also raise the interest of students and require them to contribute actively to the task. Similarly, personalizing the learning process and making language classes more interesting by providing a great variety of tasks, including ones with unexpected elements, are recommended by Dörnyei and Csizér (1998) as a means of motivating language learners.
(4) A perceived sense of control is also important for flow. The sense of being able to control the learning situation (Egbert, 2003), where the learning situation is characterized by well articulated rules and mutual responsibilities, offers participants opportunities to exercise autonomy and self-expression.

Egbert hypothesizes a strong relationship between flow and language learning. She suggests a model of flow and language acquisition where the interplay among individual learner characteristics and classroom environment variables, such as task features, can lead to flow. Flow, in turn, leads to focused time on task and motivation for a person to engage in productive behaviors during the task; this combination of time and motivation leads to change in the learner's language skills (learning). This is parallel to Dörnyei's (2005) concept of the motivational L2 self, where experience is one of the main constructs that determine motivated learning behavior. In instructed language learning, teachers have the opportunity to influence the learning experience and, as such, they also have the ability to enhance flow in the classroom by planning the tasks carefully and laying an emphasis on the content of the task (Grabe & Stoller, 1997), providing interesting tasks for the learners and giving learners meaningful choices in connection with the tasks. In this way, a language learning environment featuring tasks especially designed to elicit and maintain flow is likely to lead to more positive classroom experiences and ultimately to enhance learning and language development (MacIntyre & Gregersen, 2012).

In spite of a few existing studies on flow in the language classroom, we know even less about the link between general and task-specific flow and the related anti-flow experiences of advanced learners studying a foreign language in higher education. Thus, the research questions that guided the present study were the following:

(1) Does flow occur in the Hungarian EFL classroom at university level?
(2) How is task-specific flow related to classroom flow?
(3) Do task variations (individual, pair or group work) contribute to students' task-specific flow experiences?
(4) How are anti-flow experiences (apathy, boredom and anxiety) related to task-specific flow?
(5) How are the perceived characteristics of the task (level of required abilities, difficulty, creativity) related to task-specific flow and anti-flow experiences?

Method

Participants

In order to investigate the research questions, a quantitative study was designed. The participants of the study were chosen based on convenience sampling (Dörnyei, 2007) and were composed of six groups of first-year BA English major students studying at a Hungarian university. The six groups attended language practice seminars led by three different teachers. The sample comprised 85 students (60 females and 25 males). The mean age of the participants was 19.8 years (SD 1.9). On average, the students had studied English for 9.2 years (SD 3.4). Of the 85 participants, 44 (51.8%) had an intermediate-level (B2) complex (written and oral) language certificate in English, according to the Common European Framework of Reference for Languages (2001), 36 (42.4%) had an advanced-level (C1) complex language certificate in English, four (4.7%) did not have a language certificate in English, and one (1.2%) had an advanced-level (C1) oral language certificate in English. Alongside these certificates, all participants presumably had passed the advanced-level (B2) school exit exam in English, as it is a requirement when applying for the English major.

Instruments

Previous studies have shown that the research of flow as a quantifiable dimension is possible as its components can be measured with the help of Likert scales (Egbert, 2003; Oláh, 2005). In order to collect data of students' experiences of flow, both classroom flow and task-specific flow (as well

Table 8.1 Descriptive statistics for each scale and their corresponding reliability coefficients

Scales	*Mean*	*Standard deviation*	*Cronbach's alpha*	*No. of items*
Classroom flow	3.53	0.69	0.70	11
Classroom challenge–skills balance	3.61	0.69	0.75	4
Classroom interest	3.48	0.79	0.88	7
Task-specific flow	3.56	0.64	0.86	15
Task-specific challenge–skills balance	3.56	0.72	0.65	4
Task-specific interest	3.18	0.99	0.85	4
Task-specific attention	3.86	0.92	0.72	3
Task-specific control	2.78	0.67	0.64	4
Task-specific boredom	1.78	0.70	0.73	4
Task-specific apathy	1.48	0.65	0.71	4
State anxiety	1.62	0.37	0.80	20

as anti-flow experiences of boredom, apathy and anxiety) were assessed with five-point Likert-type self-report items compiled in a questionnaire (Appendix A) and administered alongside a language production task. For each item, each point on the Likert scale was assigned a numerical value (e.g. Not at all = 1, Very much = 5; Never = 1, Almost always = 5). Reliability analysis was conducted using Cronbach's alpha values (see Table 8.1). A brief description of the scales follows.

Classroom flow was defined as the experience of flow as it appears in the context of the EFL classroom. Students' classroom flow experiences were measured with the help of Oláh's (2005) scale of flow, which has 11 items (e.g. When I am at a language practice class and I work on the tasks I get there, in general, I can say that I know exactly what I am supposed to do) (alpha = 0.70). The adapted scale, based on Egbert's (2003) enumeration of task-specific flow components and using principal components analysis, was shown to be a composite of two related constructs: classroom challenge–skills balance (explaining 50% of the total variance) and classroom interest (explaining 12% of the total variance).

Similarly to classroom flow, task-specific flow and anti-flow experiences were also assessed using five-point Likert-type scales. Based on Egbert's (2003) Perceptions Survey, task-specific flow was operationalized through four distinct constructs: interest (4 items), control (4 items), attention (3 items) and challenge–skills balance (4 items). Anti-flow experiences, in terms of task-specific boredom (4 items) and task-specific apathy (4 items), were also measured with the scales adapted from Egbert (2003). Besides these, state anxiety was assessed with the validated Hungarian version of the State Anxiety scale of Spielberger's (1970) State–Trait Anxiety Inventory (Sipos *et al.*, 1998). This instrument purports to measure state anxiety at a given moment in a specific context with the help of four-point Likert-scale items (e.g. I feel nervous) and is widely used for this purpose (Groth-Marnat, 2003). The scale proved to be a reliable measure for state anxiety (Sipos *et al.*, 1998). In the present study, Cronbach's alpha for the scale was 0.80.

The instruments were supplemented with items directed at demographic information concerning the participants' age, gender, the number of years of English language learning and the students' level of knowledge of English. Data concerning participants' level of language proficiency was gathered through self-reports of possessing a foreign language proficiency certificate and its level. Finally, Likert-type items assessing the perceived level of abilities required by the task, the perceived difficulty of the task and the perceived level of creativity required by the task were placed after the task-specific scales on the questionnaire.

A task the learners were asked to complete was designed based on the domino story task used by Wright *et al.* (1983). This is a creative writing and speaking task where students have to construct a narrative based on four 'picture dominos' placed in a meaningful order by the participants themselves. The main goals of the task were to create a story and share it with a peer learner. The task is formed in a way that it is equally suitable for

Table 8.2 The characteristics of the picture domino story task tasks and the criteria for task-specific flow (Egbert, 2003)

Conditions of flow (Egbert, 2003)	*Characteristics of the picture domino story task*
Clear goals	Create a story Share the story with another learner
Appropriate challenges	The task is suitable for all levels of proficiency The task is challenging but not too difficult
Sense of control	Students are able to adjust the level of the narration, the vocabulary and the complexity of grammar to their skills Manipulation of the storyline
Interest	Picture input Creating a meaningful story
Feedback	Teacher: questions, commentary, appraisal, smile Students: questions, smile and laughing, applause
Chance to focus	Good atmosphere, discipline, no distractions Clear instructions Interesting task

individual, pair and group work, with only minor variations in the instructions (see Appendix B).

The criteria for choosing the task were based on the conditions of flow described by Egbert (2003). In order to facilitate the occurrence of flow, the task was to be designed in a way that the basic conditions for flow were controlled for. According to Egbert (2003) these conditions are the perception of appropriate challenges, clear goals, an interesting task, sufficient time, immediate feedback, a sense of control and a chance to focus. The extent to which the task met these criteria was found to be appropriate by an experienced English language teacher and an expert researcher of flow participating in the flow research project of the Psychology Department of Eötvös Loránd University. Additionally, the task was also piloted with the participation of three students from the target population and an EFL teacher. The results of the pilot indicated that the task met all the requirements of task-specific flow (see Table 8.2).

Procedures

The research was conducted in a cross-sectional manner (Dörnyei, 2007). Instruments were drawn up, adapted, translated to learners' L1 (Hungarian), back-translated and piloted (using think-aloud protocols) with the help of potential participants. Data were collected during language practice classes for first-year English major students pursuing a BA degree. Teachers were presented with the aim of the study and the instruments and were asked for their cooperation in the study. All the teachers agreed to be involved in the research and to work with the researcher by delivering 'instructional treatment' (Dörnyei, 2007: 189) in their classes.

Data were collected during one session. First, the participants were asked to fill in the questionnaire, focusing on general experiences of classroom flow and anti-flow. Then the participants were randomly assigned to complete the picture domino task in individual, pair or group mode. It was important to control for the effect that certain groups had the same instructor, so the three activity modes were assigned to groups of different teachers. Consequently, differences among merged samples of groups working in the same task modes were not accounted for by teacher differences but rather by differences between task modes. Afterwards, the students filled in the task-specific scales with reference to their experiences during the task. In the present study, all the items referring to a present feeling were changed by referring to the past, and more specifically to the feelings the respondents experienced during the task they had just completed. This modification made it possible to assess task-specific (state) flow and anti-flow experiences without causing a distraction during task completion, which could have hindered the flow experience by disrupting students' attention. Participants were asked to provide a 'password' (a neutral word or a combination of numbers and letters) and to note this on each sheet of paper in order to make it possible to collate all the instruments belonging to the same respondent. All the questionnaires and task materials were collected at the end of the session by the researcher.

The data collected were recorded and analyzed using the statistical analysis software SPSS version 16.0. First, descriptive statistics were calculated. Based on Egbert's (2003) criterion, participants who averaged above 3.0 on the five-point classroom flow or the task-specific flow scale were viewed as having experienced flow. As the next step, inferential statistical procedures were used in order to seek answers to the research questions. Different flow-level groups were identified by way of cluster analysis, and correlation analysis was carried out on the data in order to test whether task-specific flow was linked to classroom flow and state anxiety. The relationship between task characteristics, task-specific flow elements and anti-flow states were also determined with the help of correlation analysis. Finally, analysis of variance (ANOVA) was used to test whether the task mode (individual work, pair work or group work) had any influence on the occurrence of task-specific flow.

Results and Discussion

The first research question focused on the experience of flow occurring in the Hungarian EFL classroom at university level. Data suggest that 74% of the participants experienced classroom flow and 71% experienced task-specific flow. As a next step, by way of exploring natural groupings of participants' data along the classroom flow and task-specific flow dimensions, two-step cluster analysis was carried out. First, three initial cluster centers were defined by hierarchical clustering, then non-hierarchical clustering was applied to define three final cluster centers around which sample members were grouped. The three emerging clusters represent groups of students experiencing flow at different levels of intensity. The largest number of students appeared in the group experiencing above-average classroom flow, indicating that, overall, most English major students experience flow in the language classroom. It seems that for a great number of students, English language classes at university level provide an optimal environment for experiencing flow frequently, probably by maintaining a satisfactory challenge–skills balance and catering for the interests of the learners. The domino task itself, however, generated average levels of flow experience, with most students (45 of the 85 participants) falling into the average task-specific flow cluster (see Table 8.3).

Focusing on the second research question, the Pearson correlation statistic was calculated to determine the relationship of task-specific flow

Table 8.3 Distribution of students in classroom (CL) flow and task-specific (TS) flow clusters

	Mean	*SD*	*Number of cluster members*
Below-average CL flow	2.16	0.38	9
Average CL flow	3.13	0.22	29
Above-average CL flow	4.04	0.31	47
Below-average TS flow	2.35	0.26	18
Average TS flow	3.30	0.23	45
Above-average TS flow	4.11	0.21	22

NB: The scale means are based on participants' responses on five-point Likert scales.

to classroom flow. There was a significant positive correlation between task-specific flow and classroom flow at the $p < 0.01$ level; however, its magnitude was rather modest ($r = 0.34$), which means that the two types of flow experience are somewhat related, but the measured constructs do not seem to be identical. Regarding the presence of flow in the language classroom, it is also informative to compare the mean values of classroom flow with anti-flow experiences and the respective mean values of the task-specific measures. As can be seen from Table 8.4, on a scale of 1–5, the mean values of both classroom flow and task-specific flow are above the theoretical average of 3.0, while mean values of all anti-flow states are below 2.0.

The statistically significant link between task-specific and classroom flow is also underpinned by Ryan *et al.* (1997), who state that repeated experience of enjoyment and competence at a task level can contribute to long-term development and adherence. Thus, it can be assumed that long-term adherence to learning (including lifelong learning) can also be facilitated by participating in intrinsically rewarding activities, such as flow-inducing activities (Csikszentmihalyi, 1997).

Table 8.4 Mean values of classroom (CL) flow, task-specific (TS) flow and anti-flow experiences

	Mean
CL flow	3.53
TS flow	3.31
TS boredom	1.77
TS apathy	1.47
State anxiety	1.61

Comparing our results with those from previous Hungarian school-based research, which measured classroom flow with the same instrument, it seems that university EFL students have higher levels of classroom flow than secondary school students in the general school context as investigated by Oláh (2005); or in music, mathematics and literature classes as studied by Jarunik (2007). Although the significance of this difference was not tested directly, we suggest that the conditions for flow, such as engaging the attention of students, raising their interest and adjusting the challenges of the class to the skills of the learners (Oláh, 2005), are more likely to be fulfilled at the university level than at the secondary school level. This may be attributed to the fact that in higher education, students mainly study subjects related to their interests and personal goals, which is less characteristic of secondary school contexts.

Although the mean values for task-specific flow were somewhat lower than those for the respective classroom indicator, it seems that the picture domino story task and the learning situation had appropriate characteristics for enhancing flow for most students. Similarly, although on a smaller sample, Egbert (2003) found that all but one of the 13 students participating in computer-based learning experienced flow in one or more of the tasks.

Finally, the relationship of classroom flow and task-specific flow was further analyzed by exploring the relationships between their components. According to Egbert (2003), there are four task-specific flow components (challenge–skills balance; interest; control; and attention), which were measured by subscales of the task-specific flow scale. The relationship of the components of classroom flow and task-specific flow were calculated by Pearson correlation analysis. The results (see Table 8.5) show that there is not only significant positive relationship between certain task-specific and classroom flow components of the same nature (e.g. classroom interest and task-specific interest; $r = 0.32$, $p < 0.01$), but certain components are also related to the main flow types (e.g. task-specific challenge–skills balance correlates positively with classroom flow; $r = 0.34$, $p < 0.01$). The magnitude of these relationships indicates that task-specific flow and classroom flow are related but different constructs and the same is true for their components.

Analyzing the relationships between the different flow components can provide further insight into the interrelatedness of the two types of flow (see Table 8.5). First of all, overall challenge–skills balance in the language classroom and task-specific challenge–skills balance were found to be positively correlated; moreover, classroom interest was found to be positively correlated with task-specific interest. Therefore, if learners feel that the EFL class is interesting and provides them with appropriate challenges on the task level, it is more likely that they will generally perceive learning in this classroom to be meaningful and interesting. A learning environment which promotes flow both at a classroom level and at a task-specific level is likely to foster further language development. Using well structured and engaging

Table 8.5 Correlations between classroom flow, task-specific flow and their components

	Classroom flow	*Classroom flow components*	
		Classroom interest	*Classroom challenge–skills balance*
Task-specific flow	0.34**	0.33**	0.28**
Task-specific challenge–skills balance	0.34**	0.28**	0.36**
Task-specific interest	0.30**	0.32**	
Task-specific control	0.26*	0.23*	
Task-specific attention			

*$p < 0.05$; **$p < 0.01$

activities in language teaching, as is also suggested by task-based instruction (Skehan, 2003), may play a crucial role in designing a flow-inducing learning environment that provides a certain degree flexibility, whereby activities can be tailored to the needs of the individuals.

The relationship between task-specific flow, its components (challenge–skills balance, interest, attention and control), and anti-flow experiences (boredom, apathy and anxiety) was also investigated with the help of correlation analysis (see Table 8.6).

All three anti-flow experiences were found to be negatively correlated with task-specific flow ($r = -0.59$; $r = -0.53$; $r = -0.36$; $p < 0.01$). Regarding the components of task-specific flow, interest and challenge–skills balance appear to have a firm negative relationship with all the three anti-flow experiences, while task-specific control is related only to task-specific boredom and the magnitude of this link is quite modest. Anti-flow experiences depict major connections with different components of task-specific flow. Both task-specific boredom and apathy have their strongest negative relationships

Table 8.6 Correlations between task-specific flow and its components, and anti-flow experiences

	Task-specific boredom	*Task-specific apathy*	*State anxiety*
Task-specific flow	−0.59**	−0.53**	−0.36**
Task-specific Challenge–skills balance	−0.28*	−0.45**	−0.54**
Task-specific interest	−0.61**	−0.49**	−0.28**
Task-specific attention	−0.70**	−0.54**	
Task-specific control	−0.23*		

*$p < 0.05$; **$p < 0.01$

with attention, while state anxiety is (negatively) related to challenge–skills balance the most.

Interestingly, the strongest inverse relationship was identified between task-specific flow and boredom. Although boredom has a negative relationship with all four task-specific flow components, it seems to be connected to task-specific flow primarily through task-specific interest and attention. Apathy also has a moderate negative correlation with interest and attention. Therefore, in order to prevent apathy and boredom, it is crucial to keep students interested and to facilitate their focusing on the ongoing activity. The findings of the present research suggest that in the presence of anti-flow experiences of boredom and apathy, the presence of interest and attention are also less likely, and vice versa.

Hidi suggests that interest plays a central role in the selection and processing of information, and that it facilitates 'cognitive functioning and learning' (Hidi, 1990: 549). Similarly, interest is in a complex relationship with attention. Hidi *et al.* (2004) argue that situational interest, which is part of interest-based motivation, is generated by certain characteristics of the environment, for example by its potential to facilitate focused attention and trigger positive affective reactions in the language learning situation. Egbert (2003) also reported that students were more focused during activities which excited their curiosity, in other words aroused their attention. This is especially important in light of the claim that attention is a prerequisite to learning a second language (Schmidt, 2001).

Furthermore, according to the present results, challenge–skills balance is not only negatively correlated with state anxiety but also with apathy and boredom. In the educational context of EFL learning, it means that challenges should be carefully adjusted to the actual level of the skills of language learners, as they may become bored, anxious or apathetic due to an imbalance caused by tasks being either too easy, too difficult, or unengaging.

Finally, control seems to be associated with boredom and shows no connection with anxiety or apathy. This suggests that students' feelings of a lack of control is closely associated with being bored rather than by being anxious or apathetic. Thus, providing learners with the opportunity to control certain aspects of their own learning or enhancing their sense of control over the outcome of a task is highly advisable if instructors want to keep learners involved and interested and avoid learners falling into apathy or a state of boredom.

With regard to the next research question, the level of task-specific flow was also compared among task modes – individual, pair or group work – with the help of ANOVA. It was hypothesized that the level of task-specific flow would be significantly higher in pair and group settings than in the individual setting. However, the one-way ANOVA showed that there was no significant difference in task-specific flow between groups assigned different task modes [$F(2, 82) = 1.01$, $p = 0.371$]. Thus, the results of the present study did not confirm the hypothesis that task mode contributes to differences in the level of task-specific flow experiences. Egbert (2003) also found that flow can be obtained by a great variety of task types, from group work to individual work. Nonetheless, we must keep in mind that a flow-inducing task design and classroom management require the teacher to be familiar with the needs and dynamics of the learner group. As Egbert (2003) points out, there are individual differences in the perception of the tasks; therefore, the subjective experiences of the students may show great variation. The greatest congruency of the task or classroom management method and the needs and abilities of the student may provide the most opportunities for effective and enjoyable (flow-like) learning (Oláh, 2005).

Concerning the task modes, our results echoed those of Shernoff *et al.* (2003), who found that learner engagement, relevant content, the possibility of learner control of the environment, and high challenge posed for the highly skilled learners are likely to lead to flow irrespective of whether the task requires individual or group work. In our sample, the ANOVA showed that there were no significant differences between groups in the perception of task difficulty [$F(2, 82) = 1.2$, $p = 2.54$], creativity [$F(2, 82) = 0.18$, $p = 0.98$] or level of required abilities [$F(2, 82) = 0.05$, $p = 0.95$] either. On a scale of 1–5, the level of required abilities was slightly above the average, the difficulty of the task was at a low level, and the level of creativity required by the task was high in all three modes for the task.

Pearson correlation analysis showed a moderate positive relationship between creativity and task-specific flow (see Table 8.7). Creativity is positively correlated with all the components of task-specific flow, but especially with attention and interest. With respect to the anti-flow experiences,

Table 8.7 Correlations between task characteristics, task-specific flow and anti-flow experiences

	Creativity	*Required level of abilities*	*Difficulty*
Task-specific flow	0.51**	0.26*	−0.09
Task-specific interest	0.44**	0.14	0.03
Task-specific control	0.36**	0.19	−0.07
Task-specific attention	0.45**	0.13	0.07
Task-specific challenge–skills balance	0.34**	0.40**	−0.25*
State anxiety	−0.11	−0.27*	0.35**
Task-specific boredom	−0.28**	−0.03	−0.09
Task-specific apathy	−0.27*	−0.12	0.16

*$p < 0.05$; **$p < 0.01$

creativity was found to be negatively correlated with task-specific boredom and apathy, although the relationship is not strong. Thus, it seems that language learners tend to find creative tasks interesting, and they also tend to focus their attention on such activities more than on activities which do not require creativity.

Interestingly, the required level of abilities has a low correlation with task-specific flow ($r = 0.26$; $p < 0.05$), and it has a moderate relationship with task-specific challenge–skills balance. Therefore, we can say that task-specific flow is slightly linked to the higher level of required abilities, provided that the challenges and the skills are well balanced. Finally, the results also indicate that state anxiety is positively related to difficulty but negatively related to the required level of abilities. This suggests that people tend to experience anxiety not because of the challenging nature of a task, but rather because of the perception of the task as being unmanageable at their level of skill. This is closely tied to findings of self-efficacy research in applied linguistics (Mills, 2014), according to which language anxiety is closely linked to the self-appraisal of abilities. In other words, learners may find that a task requires moderate-level abilities, but if they feel they do not possess this level of skill then this is likely to evoke the feeling of anxiety (Bandura, 1988).

Conclusion

In our study, using a pragmatic view of positive psychology as a framework (Linley *et al.*, 2006), we have focused on the factors that might play a role in language learners' processes of optimal functioning, as well as factors that can prevent flow experiences. By including both flow and anti-flow experiences in our research, we also believe that, on a meta-psychological level (see Linely *et al.*, 2006), we have taken a step, although perhaps not a major one, towards 'introduc[ing] the positive and integrating the negative' (Linely *et al.*, 2006: 7).

This study investigated advanced language learners' classroom flow as well as task-specific flow and anti-flow (boredom, apathy, and anxiety) experiences. Our findings indicate that the majority of our sample, who are studying in higher education on a program specific to foreign languages, tended to experience moderate to high levels of flow in the classroom. It seems that university students are more likely to experience flow in the classroom than are secondary school students. Our results also show that there appears to be a connection between flow experienced at the task level and that at the classroom level. Our data also suggest that the different anti-flow experiences are in varied relationships with particular aspects of flow: for instance, those learners whose attention is not captured by the language task are more likely to feel bored or apathetic, while those who find tasks too challenging are likely to experience higher levels of anxiety. Finally, our results suggest that the different modes of a task are not linked to the magnitude of the flow experience. Nonetheless, it seems that the more creativity is involved, the more likely it will be that learners find themselves in the flow channel. We can say that, overall, it is key to find the appropriate balance between the task challenge and the learners' skills. Language teachers should plan for different ways to engage learners' attention by using a variety of relevant and (most importantly) interesting activities to enhance the positive language learning experience. Nonetheless, in order to understand the underlying processes at play associated with the state of flow and to see how momentary experiences influence general dispositions, further in-depth longitudinal research is warranted.

Appendix A

Classroom flow questionnaire (English version)

Please choose a password (a neutral word or a combination of numbers and letters):

Please think about an average language practice class and share your experiences in the following way: Please put a cross (X) in the box to indicate how much the statement is true in your case. There are no right or wrong answers; we are interested in your experiences.

When I am at a language practice class and I work on the tasks I get there, IN GENERAL I can say that...

[Not at all; Not really; Neutral; Somewhat; Very much]

- I like these occasions
- I am absorbed in what I do
- I get bored
- I enjoy the experience of putting my abilities to use
- I get nervous

[Never; Rarely; Every once in a while; Sometimes; Almost always]

- I continuously feel that things are going smoothly
- I would do the tasks even if it was not required
- The tasks are uninteresting for me
- I'm generally engaged in the tasks we do
- I need to make an effort to concentrate on what is going on
- I am immersed in the tasks
- The tasks pose an exciting challenge for me, and I enjoy that I am able to do the tasks

- Generally, what I have to do is beyond me
- The requirements are high, which makes me nervous
- I get distracted
- As I can do things very easily, I am bored
- I know exactly what I am supposed to do
- The tasks are tiresome for me
- I feel that I can meet the requirements

[Very slowly; Rather slowly; Neither slowly or quickly; Rather quickly; Very quickly]
- Time passes...

[Strongly disagree; Disagree; Neither agree or disagree; Agree; Absolutely agree]
- Most of the time what I have to do is an exciting challenge for me

[At a low level; At a rather low level; At neither a high or low level; At a rather high level; At a high level]
- The abilities required by the situation are...

Now please provide the following biographical information:
Gender: female ( ) male ( )
Your age: ___ years
How long have you been learning English? For ___ years.
Do you have an English language exam? yes (   ) no (   )
If *yes*: what kind of exam is it? Put a cross (X) in the box:

	written part	oral part	complex (written and spoken part)
basic level			
intermediate level			
advanced level			

Please keep your password in mind.
Thank you for your participation!

Task-specific flow questionnaire (English version)

Password (neutral word or a combination of numbers and letter): ___

Please think about the task you have just done. How did you feel during the task? Please put a cross (X) in the box to indicate how much the statement is true in your case. There are no right or wrong answers; we are interested in your experiences.

[Strongly disagree; Disagree; Neither agree or disagree; Agree; Strongly agree]

- This task made me curious
- During this task I could make my own decisions about how to proceed
- This task was too easy
- When doing this task, I was completely absorbed in what I was doing
- This task was uninteresting for me
- I knew exactly what I had to do
- This task was fun
- During this task I was in control of what I was doing
- I got bored during the task
- While doing this task, I was thinking about other things
- What I had to do was beyond me
- I continuously felt that things were going smoothly
- I would do this task even if it were not required
- I felt that I had no control over what was happening during the task
- The task could not engage me
- When doing this task, I noticed that I was distracted
- This task was tiring
- This task was an exciting challenge for me, and I enjoyed that I could do what I had to do
- This task was interesting in itself
- During the task I could make decisions about how to proceed
- My attention wandered
- While doing the task, I was concentrating on what was going on at the given moment
- I did not have anything to do during the task
- I felt that I could meet the requirements

Please answer the following questions by circling the answer which best describes your opinion.

The abilities required by the task were …

- At a low level
- At a rather low level
- At neither a high nor a low level
- At a rather high level
- At a high level

Was the task difficult?

- Not at all
- To a certain extent
- At an average level
- Rather
- Absolutely

Did this task make you think in a creative way?

- Not at all
- To a certain extent
- At an average level
- Rather
- Absolutely

Please make sure that your password is included in all the papers that you hand in. Thank you for your participation!

Appendix B

The picture domino story task materials are shown in Figure 8.1. The instructions differed slightly for individual, pair and group work.

Figure 8.1 The picture domino story task materials

Individual work

You are going to complete a story-writing task. It is a writing and speaking task. First you will write a story, then you are going to tell your story to someone. Each of you will get four picture dominos. *[Teacher shows a domino]* These dominos have a picture at each end. Your task is to connect the dominos in such a way that the pictures make up a storyline. The dominos can be used in any order you like. You have to use all four dominos. You should put the dominos next to each other to make up a storyline and you should write down your story. You will get a separate paper for this. You have six minutes to write your story. Your story shouldn't be too long; you can write a very short story, as long as it makes sense. You can write down your full story or you can make notes that make you able to tell your story to someone. Consider that you have six minutes to write your story. [...] Now please tell your story to the person sitting next to you.

Pair work

You are going to complete a story-writing task in pairs. It is a writing and speaking task. You will write a story and you are also going to tell your story to someone. Each of you will get two dominos – so each pair has four picture dominos altogether. *[Teacher shows a domino]* These dominos have a picture at each end. Your task is to connect the dominos in such a way that the pictures make up a storyline. One of you lays down one domino and starts making up the story. The other person may lay a domino down next to another domino if he/she can continue the story. The dominos can be used in any order you like. You have to use all four dominos. You should put the dominos next to each other to make up a storyline and you should write down your story. Both of you should write down the story. You will get a separate paper for this. You have eight minutes to write your story. Your story shouldn't be too long; you can write a very short story, as long as it makes sense. You can write down your full story or you can make notes that make you able to tell your story to someone. Consider that you have eight minutes to write your story, so it is best to start writing the story while you discuss it, not just after the story is 'ready'. [...] Now please tell your story to the pair sitting the closest to you.

Group work

You are going to complete a story-writing task, working in groups of four. It is a writing and speaking task. You will write a story and you are also going to tell your story to someone. Each of you will get one domino – so each group has four picture dominos altogether. [*Teacher shows a domino*] These dominos have a picture at each end. Your task is to connect the dominos in such a way that the pictures make up a storyline. One of you lays down one domino and starts making up the story. Another person may lay a domino down next to another domino if he/she can continue the story. The dominos can be used in any order you like. You have to use all four dominos. You should put the dominos next to each other to make up a storyline and you should write down your story. All of you should write down the story. You will get a separate paper for this. You have eight minutes to write your story. Your story shouldn't be too long; you can write a very short story, as long as it makes sense. You can write down your full story or you can make notes that make you able to tell your story to someone. Consider that you have eight minutes to write your story, so it is best to start writing the story while you discuss it, not just after the story is 'ready'. [...] Now you please share your story with the group sitting the closest to yours.

References

Abbott, J.A. (2000) 'Blinking out' and 'having the touch': Two fifth-grade boys talk about flow experiences in writing. *Written Communication* 17, 53–92.

Bandura, A. (1988) Self-efficacy conception of anxiety. *Anxiety Research* 1, 77–98.

Brown, S. (2000) Tasks and the scholarship of teaching: A view from applied linguistics. *The Art and Science of Teaching* 6, 5–6.

Bygate, M., Skehan, P. and Swain, M. (eds) (2001) *Researching Pedagogic Tasks: Second Language Learning, Teaching and Assessment*. New York: Pearson.

Csikszentmihalyi, M. (1975) *Beyond Boredom and Anxiety*. San Francisco, CA: Jossey-Bass.

Csikszentmihalyi, M. (1988) Introduction. In M. Csikszentmihalyi and I.S. Csikszentmihalyi (eds) *Optimal Experience – Psychological Studies of Flow in Consciousness* (pp. 3–14). Cambridge: Cambridge University Press.

Csikszentmihalyi, M. (1989) The dynamics of intrinsic motivation. In R. Ames and C. Ames (eds) *Handbook of Motivation Theory and Research* (vol. 3, pp. 45–71). New York: Academic Press.

Csikszentmihalyi, M. (1996) *Creativity: Flow and the Psychology of Discovery and Invention*. New York: HarperCollins.

Csikszentmihalyi, M. (1997) *Flow – Az Áramlat*. Budapest: Akadémiai Kiadó.

Csikszentmihalyi, M. (2003) *Good Business: Leadership, Flow and the Making of Meaning*. London: Hodder and Stoughton.

Csikszentmihalyi, M. and LeFevre, J. (1989) Optimal experience in work and leisure. *Journal of Personality and Social Psychology* 56, 815–822.

Dörnyei, Z. (2005) *The Psychology of the Language Learner: Individual Differences in Second Language Acquisition*. Mahwah, NJ: Lawrence Erlbaum Associates.

Dörnyei, Z. (2007) *Research Methods in Applied Linguistics*. Oxford: Oxford University Press.

Dörnyei, Z. and Csizér, K. (1998) Ten commandments for motivating language learners: Results of an empirical study. *Language Teaching Research* 2, 203–229.

Egbert, J. (2003) The study of flow theory in the foreign language classroom. *Modern Language Journal* 87 (4), 499–518.

Grabe, W. and Stoller, F.L. (1997) Content-based instruction: Research foundations. In M.A. Snow and D.M. Brinton (eds) *The Content-Based Classroom: Perspectives on Integrating Language and Content* (pp. 5–21). White Plains, NY: Longman.

Gregersen, T. and MacIntyre, P.D. (2014) *Capitalizing on Language Learners' Individuality: From Premise to Practice.* Bristol: Multilingual Matters.
Groth-Marnat, G. (2003) *Handbook of Psychological Assessment* (4th edn). New York: Wiley.
Hidi, S. (1990) Interest and its contribution as a mental resource for learning. *Review of Educational Research* 60 (4), 549–571.
Hidi, S., Renninger, K.A. and Krapp, A. (2004) Interest, a motivational variable that combines affective and cognitive functioning. In D. Yun Dai and R.J. Sternberg (eds) *Motivation, Emotion, and Cognition* (pp. 89–114). Mahwah, NJ: Lawrence Erlbaum Associates.
Horwitz, E.K. and Young, D.J. (eds) (1991) *Language Anxiety: From Theory and Research to Classroom Implications.* Englewood Cliffs, NJ: Prentice Hall.
Janurik, M. (2007) Áramlatélmény az iskolai ének-zene órákon. *Magyar Pedagógia* 107 (4), 295–320.
Kristjansson, K. (2012) Positive psychology and positive education: Old wine in new bottles? *Educational psychologist* 47 (2), 86–105.
Lazarus, R.S. and Folkman, S. (1984) *Stress, Appraisal and Coping.* New York: Springer.
Linely, P.A., Joseph, S., Harrington, S. and Wood, A.M. (2006) Positive psychology: Past, present, and (possible) future. *Journal of Positive Psychology* 1 (1), 3–16.
MacIntyre, P. and Gregersen, T. (2012) Emotions that facilitate language learning: The positive-broadening power of the imagination. *Studies in Second Language Learning and Teaching* 2, 193–213.
McQuillan, J. and Conde, G. (1996) The conditions of flow in reading: Two studies of optimal experience. *Reading Psychology: An International Quarterly* 17, 109–135.
Mills, N. (2014) Self-efficacy in second language acquisition. In S. Mercer and M. Williams (eds) *Multiple Perspectives on the Self in SLA* (pp. 6–22). Bristol: Multilingual Matters.
Oláh, A. (2005) *Érzelmek, Megküzdés, Tökéletes Élmény.* Budapest: Trefort.
Ryan, R.M., Frederick, C.M., Lepes, D., Rubio, N. and Sheldon, K.M. (1997) Intrinsic motivation and exercise adherence. *International Journal of Sport Psychology* 28, 335–354.
Schmidt, R. (2001) Attention. In P. Robinson (ed.) *Cognition and Second Language Instruction* (pp. 3–32). Cambridge: Cambridge University Press.
Seligman, M.E.P. and Csikszentmihalyi, M. (2000) Positive psychology: An introduction. *American Psychologist* 55 (1), 5–14.
Shernoff, D.J., Csikszentmihalyi, M., Schneider, B. and Shernoff, E.S. (2003) Student engagement in high school classrooms from the perspective of flow theory. *School Psychology Quarterly* 18 (2), 158–176.
Sipos, K., Sipos, M. and Spielberger, C. (1998) A State–Trait Inventory (STAI) magyar változata. In F. Mérei and F. Szakács (eds) *Pszichodiagnosztikai vadenecum* (vol. 1, pp. 123–136). Budapest: Nemzeti Tankönyvkiadó.
Skehan, P. (2003) Task-based instruction. *Language Teaching* 36, 1–14.
Spielberger, C. (1970) *Manual for the State–Trait Anxiety Inventory.* Palo Alto, CA: Consulting Psychologists Press.
Wright, A., Betteridge, D. and Buckby, M. (1983) *Games for Language Learning.* Cambridge: Cambridge University Press.

9 Foreign Language Enjoyment and Foreign Language Classroom Anxiety: The Right and Left Feet of the Language Learner

Jean-Marc Dewaele and Peter D. MacIntyre

Introduction

Sometimes it can be difficult to see what has been right in front of us all along, but after it has been pointed out, suddenly it seems obvious. That observation describes how we felt in approaching the topic of language learning enjoyment. It is curious that it has not been named as a prominent concept in the literature on individual differences in SLA. Enjoyment is mentioned frequently by teachers and students alike; as a concept it certainly seems to be relevant to language learning and we suggest that it might just be an important part of the learning and communication process. However, a search across multiple electronic databases for scholarly works with language 'enjoyment' in their title yielded a total of only nine hits, including a mere two research articles in the SLA field. In one of those papers, Green reported that:

> No previous studies known to me have investigated possible relationships between the reported enjoyableness and the perceived effectiveness of different kinds of activities and techniques in order to discover whether students agree with those of us who believe that positive affect and effective teaching do indeed go hand in hand. (Green, 1993: 3)

Green's own results were encouraging – enjoyment and perceived learning effectiveness of the tasks did indeed go hand in hand across 17 activities tested, producing correlations between 0.46 and 0.78, with an impressive average (median) correlation of 0.68. The other research article found also reported little prior work on enjoyment but nonetheless noted that there 'are conflicting reports concerning the effects of enjoyment on the L2 process' (Brantmeier, 2005: 496). Indeed, Brantmeier's (2005) own data showed that enjoyment correlated positively with self-assessed ability as measured by a written recall task, but did not correlate significantly with scores on a multiple-choice test.

This state of affairs is reminiscent of the early 1980s, when the topic of language anxiety was not well understood. Teachers, learners and scattered research reports hinted at a potentially important role for anxiety in both language learning and communication, but the research results were mixed and confusing (Scovel, 1978). Development of both the conceptualization of language anxiety and its measurement has produced a much clearer picture of how it affects SLA (Horwitz *et al.*, 1986; MacIntyre & Gardner, 1989). Language anxiety has been linked to a range of sociobiographical and psychological variables (Dewaele, 2002, 2007a, 2007b, 2010, 2013a, 2013b, in press; Dewaele *et al.*, 2008; Dewaele & Shan Ip, 2013; Gregersen, & Horwitz, 2002) and has been described as a strong predictor of success (MacIntyre, 1999). A selective review of the literature (Horwitz, 2010) provides a timeline of 44 papers that consistently show the ways in which language anxiety, identified as a unique form of anxiety that is associated with second-language and foreign-language situations, reliably affects learning and communication. Sorting out conceptual and measurement issues led to productive work on language anxiety, and the same can be done for language enjoyment.

Interest in language enjoyment is part of an emerging trend in the SLA literature to shift focus toward positive emotions and their role as driving forces. MacIntyre and Gregersen (2012: 193), for example, argued that 'positive emotion has a different function from negative emotion; they are not opposite ends of the same spectrum'. Drawing on the broaden-and-build theory of emotion (Fredrickson, 2001, 2013), MacIntyre and Gregersen (2012) argue that a learner's imagination has a positive broadening power, leading to better learning outcomes and the building of resources (e.g. social support, personal confidence). Although there has been considerable prior interest in related issues, such as motivation, learner autonomy and humanistic teaching techniques, the conceptualization of positive emotion in SLA has lagged behind theoretical developments in other areas (see MacIntyre & Mercer, 2014).

With the emergence of positive psychology as a defined specialization, and with the broaden-and-build theory as a framework for understanding positive emotion, we propose that the time is right to closely examine enjoyment in foreign-language learning contexts. Perhaps the best way to explain the concept is to contrast it with a similar experience: pleasure. Csikszentmihalyi (2004) considers enjoyment to be separate from pleasure. Whereas enjoyment can be defined as a complex emotion, capturing interacting dimensions of challenge and perceived ability that reflect the human drive for success in the face of difficult tasks, pleasure is considered simply an agreeable feeling. On the one hand, enjoyments occur when people not only meet their needs, but exceed them to accomplish something new or even unexpected; on the other hand, pleasure is a simpler feeling that something likable is happening. To use an analogy from sports, it might be *pleasurable* to win a game by a wide margin but it is not necessarily a game anyone enjoys; alternatively, it is *enjoyable* to play well in a closely contested match where success might mean playing well and either winning or losing the game. Losing a game is not pleasurable but can be enjoyable if one has performed better than expected against a superior opponent. Enjoyment follows personal investment and requires having a stake in an outcome that matters to the person, something that is a self-relevant outcome. Because the stakes can be high, tasks that present an opportunity for enjoyment may also bring risk or anxiety. Csikszentmihalyi (1997, 2004, 2008) describes enjoyment as a key component of flow experiences. Flow is characterized as a 'sweet-spot' in optimally challenging activities, where one is neither feeling overwhelmed nor under-challenged. When completely absorbed in tasks set at optimal levels of challenge – not too easy and not too difficult – one can lose track of time and even lose the sense of self. Flow experiences have not been widely studied in foreign language (FL) education (see Egbert, 2004; see also Chapter 8 of the present volume).

The present chapter provides an in-depth analysis of research initially reported by Dewaele and MacIntyre (2014), who found that learners appear to experience more foreign language enjoyment (FLE) than foreign language classroom anxiety (FLCA), and there is a modest, negative correlation between the two concepts. Further, Dewaele and MacIntyre found that:

> participants who [had] already mastered several languages, who had reached a higher level in the FL, who felt more proficient than their peers, who had reached [a] higher level of education and who were older reported significantly more FLE and significantly lower levels of FLCA. In addition, those studying more FLs also scored significantly higher on FLE, where[as] FLCA was not associated with studying more FLs. (Dewaele & MacIntyre, 2014: 262)

Women experienced both higher FLE and higher FLCA. In addition, broad regional differences also were reported, with North Americans showing the highest scores on FLE accompanied by the lowest scores on FLCA; data from Asian respondents showed the opposite pattern. The large data-set, with over 1700 learners from around the world sampled by internet survey, will be examined in greater detail in the present chapter, which examines the relationship between enjoyment and anxiety, with a focus on the factorial structure of FLE and its conceptual development. Using qualitative data we will support the emerging concept of FLE with excerpts from respondents' accounts of their most enjoyable language learning experiences.

Research Questions

(1) What are the dimensions underlying FLCA and FLE, and specifically do anxiety and enjoyment items form two separate dimensions?
(2) How do learners describe the elements that are conducive to episodes of enjoyment of the FL?

Method

Participants

A total of 1742 multilinguals (1287 females, 449 males[1]) filled out the study questionnaire, described in the next section. While participants were, overall, relatively young (mean age 24 years, SD 8.5 years), their age range was wide, spanning 11 to 75 years. The sample had attained various levels of education, but overall was a well educated group (83% had a bachelor's or master's degree). A majority (76%) of the sample was studying one FL. Asked about how they would describe their mastery of the FL in general, a substantial proportion self-reported as high intermediate (41.7%) or advanced (28.2%), 0.5% reported to be beginners, 23.3% low intermediate and 6.4% intermediate.[2] Asked about their relative standing in the FL class, most considered themselves as average (44.2%) or above average (36.5%) learners, relative to their classmates; smaller proportions reported being at the extreme ends of the scale, with 2.4% reporting to be far below average and 6.7% to be far above average, with the remaining 9.8% reporting to be below average.

Close to half of the participants reported that they studied English as a FL ($n = 855$; 49%), followed by French ($n = 276$; 15.8%), Spanish ($n = 218$; 12.5%), Dutch ($n = 157$; 9.0%) and German ($n = 139$; 8.0%).

The participants reported 90 different nationalities, including many participants with double nationalities. The largest groups were Belgians ($n = 365$), followed by British ($n = 244$), Chinese ($n = 174$) and Americans ($n = 118$), along with many smaller groups ($n < 80$). Broad regional groups were created: the largest group consisted of Europeans ($n = 1171$; 67.1%), followed by Asians ($n = 229$; 13.1%), North Americans ($n = 149$; 8.5%), South Americans ($n = 92$; 5.3%) and Arabs ($n = 87$; 5.0%). The sample consisted of 456 bilinguals (26.1%), 555 trilinguals (31.8%), 415 quadrilinguals (23.8%), 202 pentalinguals (11.6%) and 70 sextalinguals (4%). The 44 remaining participants (2.5%) reported knowledge of 7 to 10 languages. A single category was created that included all participants with six or more languages. More details on the sample can be found in Dewaele and MacIntyre (2014).

The instrument

The questionnaire started with a sociodemographic section that generated the data reported immediately above. Next, participants were asked to indicate to what extent they agreed with 29 items describing the FL class, of which 8 were extracted from the FLCA scale devised by Horwitz *et al.* (1986) and the rest were FLE items (see the Appendix to this chapter). Responses were recorded on a standard 5-point Likert scale (strongly disagree = 1, disagree = 2, neither agree nor disagree = 3, agree = 4, strongly agree = 5). All items referring to FLE were positively phrased. Six of the eight FLCA items were phrased to indicate anxiety, while the other two items were phrased to indicate comfort (these items were recoded when computing total scores for the scale).

The final (open) item was: 'Describe one specific event or episode in your FL class that you really enjoyed, and describe your feeling in as much detail as possible'.

The questionnaire was pilot-tested with 15 participants. This led to the deletion of some items and the reformulation of others. The research design and questionnaire obtained approval from the Ethics Committee of the School of Social Sciences, History and Philosophy at Birkbeck College, University of London. The final version of the questionnaire was put online using Googleforms and an open call was addressed to multilinguals, including those who had participated in previous studies, asking them to forward the call to friends, teachers or students.

Data analysis

Our approach to data analysis can be described as the data-validation variant of a convergent parallel design (Cresswell & Plano Clark, 2011). In this design, both quantitative and qualitative data are collected at the same time, making it an efficient research design, especially for large samples. The purpose of the quantitative data in this approach is to identify the major dimensions underlying the items that measure FLCA and FLE. The purpose of the qualitative data is to provide examples of the statistical dimensions, written by learners themselves. Results provided by the two types of data are mixed and combined in the Discussion section below. One concern about this type of analytic approach is that

> [b]ecause the qualitative items are an add-on to a quantitative instrument, the items generally do not result in a complete context-based qualitative data set. However, they provide the researcher with emergent themes and interesting quotes that can be used to validate and embellish the quantitative survey findings. (Cresswell & Plano Clark, 2011: 81)

The analysis proceeded in two stages. In the first, an exploratory factor analysis, using a principal components analysis (PCA) with Varimax rotation, was used to determine which of the 29 items clustered together to form general factors. In the second stage, we examined the responses to the open-ended item that asked for examples of an enjoyable episode. The choice of data extracts reported below was guided by the principle that they had to be representative of the category, poignant, concise and interesting. In this way, we give a voice to participants, allowing us to add an emic dimension to the abstract, etic statistical dimensions.

Results

Assessing factor structure

The first step in the analysis examined whether the data met the assumptions underlying factor analysis. Cases with missing values were excluded list-wise. Bartlett's test of sphericity ($\chi^2 = 18{,}829$, d.f. $= 406$, $p < 0.0001$) and the Kaiser–Meyer–Olkin measure of sampling adequacy (KMO $= 0.91$) exceeded the recommended value of 0.6 (Kaiser, 1970). Thus, both suggested that factor analysis of the data was possible.

The second step involved examining the factor structure and naming the factors. Factors will be named by considering items that load above ± 0.50 on each of the factors. The number of factors to retain was determined by examining the scree plot of eigenvalues, testing various solutions, and choosing the most theoretically meaningful set of factors. The scree plot suggested four factors but the fourth factor received high loadings (a loading > 0.50) from only three items and generated cross-loadings with other factors – both are signs of over-factoring. Therefore, a three-factor solution was retained and rotated with both Varimax and Direct Oblimin criteria. The Varimax rotation sets the correlation between factors at zero (0) and produces results that reflect a simple structure in which items tend to load on only one factor. The Direct Oblimin rotation allows for correlations among the factors and it produces somewhat more complex solutions, including the need to interpret the correlations among factors and a stronger tendency for items to load on more than one factor. Although we present both solutions below, our emphasis will be on the simpler structure of the Varimax rotation.

The three-factor solution was tested using a principal components analysis of the covariance matrix. After rotation, the extracted factors accounted for 44.8% of the variance in the covariance matrix (see Table 9.1). The first factor explains 25.9% of the variance. After rescaling, Factor I obtained high positive loadings (> 0.50) from the eight items taken from the FLCA scale; all of the items worded to reflect high anxiety showed positive

Table 9.1 Result of the principal components analysis

Item	*Factor I*	*Factor II*	*Factor III*
Heart pounding	0.76	−0.13	0.09
Start to panic	0.76	−0.02	−0.07
Nervous and confused	0.74	−0.02	−0.19
Feel anxious	0.71	−0.02	−0.14
Other students speak better	0.70	0.02	−0.18
Confident speaker	−0.65	0.05	0.33
Embarrassed to volunteer	0.62	−0.10	−0.16
Don't worry about mistakes	−0.61	0.24	−0.03
Laugh off embarrassing mistakes	−0.30	0.29	−0.06
Laugh a lot	−0.06	0.77	0.19
Tight group	−0.04	0.76	0.06
Common 'legends'	0.00	0.73	0.01
Good atmosphere	−0.12	0.64	0.37
Teacher is supportive	−0.04	0.57	0.43
Teacher is friendly	−0.05	0.56	0.39
Teacher is encouraging	−0.05	0.56	0.43
Peers are nice	−0.14	0.54	0.18
Positive environment	−0.18	0.50	0.43
Enjoy it	−0.16	0.21	0.70
It's fun	−0.18	0.26	0.62
Don't get bored	−0.02	0.21	0.61
Learnt interesting things	−0.03	0.22	0.58
Feel proud	−0.14	0.17	0.52
Express myself better	−0.15	0.02	0.49
Cool to know a FL	−0.06	0.10	0.42
Worthy member of the class	−0.34	0.10	0.41
Different person during class	0.19	−0.03	0.37
Can be creative	−0.24	0.07	0.31
Making errors is part of learning	−0.19	0.25	0.29

factor loadings with Factor I and both of the reverse-coded items showed negative factor loadings (see Table 9.1). This factor clearly reflects *Foreign Language Classroom Anxiety*.

The second factor accounts for 13.0% of the variance and received loadings > 0.50 from eight items – those with keywords *laugh a lot, form a tight group, have common 'legends' (such as running jokes), a good atmosphere, teacher is supportive, friendly* and *encouraging, peers are nice* and *there is a positive environment.* All of the items on Factor II appear to reflect characteristics of

Table 9.2 The oblique rotation from the three-factor solution

Item	*Factor I*	*Factor II*	*Factor III*
Nervous and confused	**-0.76**	-0.15	-0.24
Start to panic	**-0.76**	-0.13	-0.12
Heart pounding	**-0.75**	-0.20	0.02
Feel anxious	**-0.72**	-0.13	-0.18
Other students speak better	**-0.72**	-0.10	-0.23
Confident speaker	**0.69**	0.20	**0.38**
Embarrassed to volunteer	**-0.65**	-0.20	-0.22
Don't worry about mistakes	**0.62**	**0.30**	0.04
Laugh off embarrassing mistakes	**0.32**	**0.30**	-0.00
Laugh a lot	0.17	**0.80**	0.30
Tight group	0.13	**0.75**	0.16
Common 'legends'	0.08	**0.71**	0.11
Good atmosphere	0.23	**0.71**	**0.46**
Teacher is supportive	0.16	**0.64**	**0.50**
Teacher is encouraging	0.16	**0.63**	**0.51**
Teacher is friendly	0.16	**0.63**	**0.47**
Positive environment	0.29	**0.59**	**0.50**
Peers nice	0.22	**0.58**	0.26
Enjoy it	0.27	**0.36**	**0.73**
It's fun	0.28	**0.40**	**0.66**
Don't get bored	0.12	**0.33**	**0.63**
Learnt interesting things	0.12	**0.33**	**0.61**
Feel proud	0.22	0.28	**0.54**
Express myself better	0.21	0.14	**0.50**
Worthy member of the class	**0.39**	0.22	**0.44**
Cool to know a FL	0.13	0.19	**0.43**
Different person during class	-0.15	0.02	**0.35**
Making errors is part of learning	0.25	0.33	**0.34**
Can be creative	0.28	0.16	0.34

Table 9.3 Correlation of Factors I–III

	I	*II*	*III*
I	1.00	0.25	0.20
II	0.25	1.00	0.34
III	0.20	0.34	1.00

Extraction method: principal component analysis.
Rotation method: Oblimin with Kaiser normalization.

the social setting or the presence of other people; therefore, the factor will be named *Foreign Language Enjoyment–Social.*

The third factor explained an additional 5.9% of the variance. It obtained high positive loadings from five items (*I enjoy it, it's fun, don't get bored, learnt interesting things* and *feel proud*). All of the items on Factor III appear to capture the personal reactions to learning that reflect relatively inner thoughts and feelings and therefore the factor will be named *Foreign Language Enjoyment–Private.* Factor III also produced smaller, noteworthy loadings (> 0.30) from nine other enjoyment items, suggesting a considerable degree of overlap between Factors II and III.

In Table 9.2, we present the oblique solution produced by Direct Oblimin rotation. The interpretation of the three factors is much the same and we would not choose to relabel them based on this alternative rotated factor solution. If anything, the oblique rotation emphasizes that the two enjoyment factors overlap to a greater extent than the Varimax rotation shows. For example, Table 9.3 shows that Factors II and III correlate at a modest $r = 0.34$. Furthermore, if we use the loading > 0.30 criterion, the number of cross-loadings increases dramatically. It should be noted also that both FLE–Social and FLE–Private correlate significantly with FCLA ($r = -0.25$ and $r = -0.20$ respectively). The oblique rotation does not separate the factors as cleanly as the Varimax rotation did; taken together, the results emphasize that these three factors are related to each other.

Selection of participants' views on enjoyable episodes in the FL class

One of the advantages of a mixed methods study such as this one is that the quantitative results can be reflected in learners' descriptions of experience, each enriching the interpretation of the other. In the present case, we focus on the two FLE factors (Social and Private) that emerged from the quantitative analyses. These factors show connections to the categories 'Peer recognition' and 'Teacher recognition' (146 and 116 comments respectively) for FLE–Social and to the categories 'Individual realization of progress' as well as 'Authentic use of the FL' for FLE–Private (108 and 26 comments respectively), as reported by Dewaele and MacIntyre (2014). The excerpts taken from the learners' responses are used below to help clarify the nature of the factors and to begin to link enjoyment to other aspects of the learners' experiences. If the factor analysis works to pull apart the concept of enjoyment by isolating principal components of the experience, the qualitative analysis below helps to put those components back together, as learners experience them *in situ*.

Close to two-thirds of participants ($n = 1076$) answered the open question, producing a total of 52,471 words. The average length of the feedback was only 48.8 words; that is, participants gave brief descriptions of enjoyable events. Even though the descriptions are brief, it was at times difficult to identify excerpts as indicative of only one of the factors, and we recognize that other interpretations can be made. In the following qualitative analysis, we will identify what we see as the most salient features of the excerpts as a way to further develop the conceptualization of FLE and its components. A fuller contextualization of FLE would require additional data collection.

FLCA

The first factor reported above is defined by the combination of social apprehension, worry and physical manifestations of anxiety in the language classroom. The open-ended question did not enquire about this dimension directly, and only 37 participants alluded to it. Participants (who are here and below denoted by two-letter codes, and are quoted verbatim and uncorrected) in the following three excerpts linked their FLCA to the obligation of using the FL with their usual teacher, their anxiety about fear of ridicule in front of peers, and the experience of using of the FL in real-life communication, which helped them overcome their anxiety.

> **ST** (female, 15): We had a cover teacher so I knew we would not have to speak French, relieved and no longer anxious, I could relax.

> **CC** (female, 21): [With this specific activity] not only [you] have more communication with your classmates, and you can say what you think. Don't have to worry about you will laugh at me, when I couldn't express yourself in English, the students will help me.

> **LA** (female, 20): I have been abroad for one year (to England and Spain). There I've spoken very little French (my L1). I was speaking in English or in Spanish whenever I had the opportunity to. It made myself much more confident (worrying less about people's reaction, putting things into perspective, accepting not to be always as accurate as I wish in what I am saying…) as far as now I am much more talkative when I speak English.

Some people are worriers by nature. MI reports in the following extract how she experienced FLCA both before and immediately after an oral presentation in the FL, and how happy she felt with the praise from the teacher.

> **MI** (female, 19): I had to prepare an oral group presentation, which lasted 10 minutes. The topic we were going to talk about wasn't very complicated. Still I got nervous before doing it. When we finished our presentation, I realized I'd forgotten something to say, but I didn't think it could affect [the] presentation. The teacher said to me that my

pronunciation and delivery of the work was very satisfactory. At that moment, I felt quite proud of myself. I'm usually told that my English is quite good, however, I'm not a very confident person.

These comments reflect the moderate negative relationship between FLCA and FLE (Dewaele & MacIntyre, 2014). Indeed, some participants linked the absence of FLCA to an increased enjoyment of the class ('I can relax', 'nobody will laugh at me'). Participant LA took a long-term perspective, explaining how the experience of being a FL user rather than just a FL learner had reconciled her with the fact that FL users do not need to be perfect in order to function effectively in the target language (cf. Dewaele, in press; Gregersen & Horwitz, 2002), which had lowered her FLCA and boosted her self-confidence and willingness to communicate in the FL. The above excerpt showed that FLCA did not stop MI from feeling proud of her performance.

FLE–Social

The second factor, FLE–Social, is defined by positive feelings, encouraging peers, nice teachers, and a supportive environment. A good atmosphere among teacher and peers seems to be a crucial element in producing enjoyment. The following three excerpts highlight the social dimensions of FLE–Social.

XZ (female, 42): The atmosphere is great and all members feel comfortable speaking Italian. What's more, we laugh a lot which is in my opinion very important when learning a language!

TX (female, 45): If everyone is happy in class it gives the extra boost to learn better and improve even though I make many mistakes both in spoken and written language. I also learned from my classmates a lot because since the beginning of the FL classes there [*sic*] were there with me and it is encouraging to see the familiar people you have studied with again. That gave me a sigh of relief and we are together again in the third year with different teachers of course!

DX (male, 20): I was telling my fellow students about my 3 month stay in Cuba and I noticed that they really enjoyed listening to what I have experienced, so I kept talking and I felt quite proud of how fluent I can tell a story. I felt confident and enjoyed 'showing off' my own skills.

In all three excerpts above, the social life of the classroom clearly comes into focus as learners engage in meaningful ways with their peers and teachers – people are laughing and enjoying each other's contributions to the group. In these excerpts, we see a cascading process of enjoyment, and evidence for the long-term relationship development referenced in the broaden-and-build theory (Fredrickson, 2001, 2013). Enjoyment ripples outward from the speaker and returns back to her or him in a self-reinforcing cycle that is a mirror image of the self-exacerbating nature of anxiety. Using Fredrickson's terminology, the sense of being familiar and comfortable in the language group is a part of the process of building resources for the future, a form of social capital upon which students can draw when times are tough (see Chapter 6 of this volume).

> **XL** (male, 18): During the Dutch lesson, a few weeks ago, we had to make groups and talk about photos, describe them as much as possible. I really enjoyed it because the atmosphere was great and we all felt like a group of friends working in a pleasant way on our photos. It helped everyone being confident about the FL, even though some people needed more time to talk (they were helped by everybody then).

Social support among peers, as mentioned at the end of XL's excerpt above, seems to be quite natural when a group has shared enjoyment. Given that language learners often must step outside their comfort zone, the facilitating effects of enjoyment can be powerful, as DD explains:

> **DD** (female, 19): When we had to perform something in my English FL class to practise our intonation and such, I chose a piece from my favourite show. It was a speech that has to be performed with a lot of energy and in a loud voice (which is something completely different than my usual self). But when I had said the first sentence, I felt relaxed and at ease. I enjoyed it so much that I wished the speech was longer so that I would be able to continue talking. I felt almost euphoric. That was the moment in which I realized how much my class had helped me to advance in talking English in front of an audience.

At the heart of the issue seemed to be a sense of the teacher as a participant in the learning situation. Some participants, such as XF, noticed and appreciated the skills of their teacher in creating a 'buzzing' atmosphere where everybody feels they have learnt something by the end of class:

> **XF** (female, 24): I love having a teacher who knows how to read the room and communicate with the class. Having a skilled teacher makes a huge difference to the answers to these questions, naturally. If I had been answering this a few months ago, with a different teacher, my answers would have been very different. I love it when the teacher can deliver appropriate content to everyone in the class without losing people's attention. I feel like it's been a great class when everyone has been learning, brains have been buzzing, energy is high and you go away feeling like you're further on than you were when you entered the room.

AY (male, 16): I enjoyed my MFL [modern foreign language] class when the teacher was ill and we had another teacher covering. She was a native speaker and added in to fill our wide gaps in colloquial and slightly less formal, more natural German. I really enjoyed that class because everyone was included and she treated us like equals although our grasp of the language was far from perfect.

In both excerpts above, the students are comparing teachers who create enjoyable classes with unnamed teachers who do not. However, the dividing line between teacher behaviour that is enjoyed versus anxiety-arousing can be razor thin (MacIntyre *et al.*, 2011). A classroom atmosphere that can accommodate teasing and other forms of humour must be handled adeptly, as in the three following instances:

MH (male, 21): When I was preparing an extra oral exercise for my Japanese class, I had to sing a song and the teacher have to evaluate my pronunciation ... and when I finished singing the teacher said joking: please take my seat and tell me how to sing in Japanese so well.

SM (female, 36): I was surprised when she thanked me so graciously, with the sensei honorific, and the low bow she gave. I appreciated that it was largely for everyone's amusement, but I enjoyed the gesture, even though I recall wringing my hands nervously, bowing and shaking my head. It was a fun moment for the whole class.

MW (female, 20): I remember a time when the teacher scolded me for helping my class mates and ended up been ordered to go in front of the class to correct the exercise knowing fully that I don't like attention which made me very nervous and saying things as jokes which made the class and teacher laugh and forget about me :)

There are many classroom activities that will be enjoyable for some, but likely not for all learners. Although some teacher-trainers might cringe at the techniques described in the responses of MH, SM and MW above, the learners themselves offered them as their example of enjoyment in the language classroom.

Enjoyment for one might not be enjoyment for all. For example, competition in the form of games or a public debate can place the focus on developing skills in a challenging atmosphere. For some students, this is arousing, motivating and enjoyable.

XX (female, 19): A very positive episode was my freshman year of high school, before the teacher drama, when we played a partner game where one person sat down away from a screen and the other person faced the screen and described the word on it in Spanish. The seated partner had to guess the word. I LOVE competition and games really enhance my memory, so I'd like to do things like that again.

RL (female, 23): During one of my speaking classes we were divided into 2 opposite groups. One group was for, the other was against. I can't really remember the topic of the discussion, but it was really challenging. We were supposed to prepare before the class and collect some arguments, data and research. As I remember this class was very fascinating, not only because it was a heated discussion, but also we were very involved in it and very productive; I forgot about the time. And I have an impression that this lesson had a great contribution into my speaking skills.

Teachers would do well to keep in mind one of the key lessons from positive psychology – the individual's unique configuration of traits, strengths and emotions makes it difficult to predict the reaction of individual students to specific exercises (Reschly *et al.*, 2008; Seligman *et al.*, 2005).

Overall, this limited collection of excerpts helps to demonstrate that a positive emotion such as enjoyment can have a significant social component that works both to broaden one's openness to new experiences as well as to build social relationships that serve as resources for the future. The second major dimension might be the one that comes to mind more easily in thinking about enjoyment, that is, the private feeling that accompanies success in the face of difficult tasks.

FLE-Private

The third dimension emerging from the principal components analysis was named the FLE–Private factor. Participants who mentioned experiences of private enjoyment in answer to the open question described the feelings and cognition that accompany enjoyment. Consistent with the definition of enjoyment, thoughts and feelings coalesce around a sense of accomplishment.

NN (male, 22): But I can remember when I was 14 and had French as FL we had to learn poems and be able to recite them to the class and the teacher would score how good we were at it. I can still remember 2 poems of Jacques Prévert even if it's been almost ten years. I remember the feeling of being able to speak full sentences with perfect accents and knowing the meaning of every single word and the sense of the whole thing together would just start to make sense and so would other sentences. I remember after doing my presentation feeling like a native French speaker, like nobody could say I was not able to speak French! I remember feeling happy and excited about it! I was not afraid of speaking or making mistakes.

> **MX** (female, 21): The exploration of lexical terms and being really engaged in the studying of the origins of words. We were looking at where certain words came from based on their Latin and Greek origins. I was excited to study something different and I was extremely intrigued with the history of words. I wanted to learn more, I craved the knowledge and I didn't ever want to leave the class.

> **XY** (male, 25): The teacher always begins the class with a discussion on a random topic, usually initiated by a story told by one of the students about his/her weekend etc. This spring I had been travelling in Japan with my family and I was telling about the trip and my emotions for around 15–20 minutes. I felt very free and almost forgot I was speaking a foreign language because the topic was very personal and I was so engaged.

Most episodes of enjoyment described by participants related to instances of personal triumph within the group, moments of private pleasure at the realization that they had progressed in the FL. This sense of accomplishment is not divorced from the social dimensions of learning in a group, but the emphasis is on personal success and pride.

> **EX** (female, 20): Being able to answer the really hard questions, gives me a great sense of satisfaction and gratification for the work I've put in. This way you know you are not doing all the exercise for naught.

> **CL** (female, 24): When I nailed the pronunciation on a sentence I read out loud in my seminar group.

Each of these examples presents positive affective states, but the term 'pleasure' does not seem to be strong enough to capture the essence of the experience. Feeling that one is happy and proud, gratified and satisfied, and that one has 'nailed' a difficult task are all consistent with the definition of enjoyment. At times, this feeling can be enhanced by social comparison.

> **TH** (female, 45): When I answered a question no one else in class understood or knew the answer to but I did. I felt happy and proud to know the answer.

The teacher can play a central role in stimulating FLE, but not always in a straightforward way. At times, students seemed to form a group that operated somewhat independently of the teacher.

> **IP** (female, 16): This was not a set exercise by my teacher. Two people next to me decided to not do the set work, choosing instead to speak to

> each other about anything they wanted but it had to be in French. They did very well and whenever they found they were stuck, they picked up a dictionary and solved their problem. As I listened I could tell they became more and more confident and excited about the language and eventually [I] joined in. By the end, they both said they had learnt more in those twenty minutes than they normally would in a week and really enjoyed the feeling of accomplishment, rather than the relief of finishing a boring workbook exercise and knowing you had no homework. It made me wish lessons were more like that all the time.

Discussion

The concept of FLE is proving to be rich and multifaceted. We have reported data analysis elsewhere showing that the FLE and FLCA scales are significantly negatively correlated ($r = -0.36$) and associated with a number of sociobiographical variables (Dewaele & MacIntyre, 2014). In this chapter, we have looked more deeply into the conceptualization and measurement of FLE. Not only did the Varimax rotation of the factor analysis above show that FLCA and FLE could be defined as separate dimensions, we also discovered an interesting, unanticipated differentiation of the social and the private components of the FLE scale. It must be emphasized, however, that although these three factors can be separated, the oblique rotation serves to remind us that there is a noticeable degree of overlap among them.

The qualitative section of the questionnaire invited participants to share a positive experience in their FL class and that provided a treasure trove of information. Excerpts from these open-ended responses allowed us to better understand the texture of enjoyable language learning experiences, but we consciously refrain from drawing firm conclusions from them.

The factor analysis confirms that anxiety forms a factor that is distinct from enjoyment. The concepts do not necessarily operate in a seesaw relationship, where one goes up and the other goes down, but rather they function somewhat independently. One participant, LA, mentioned that after having spent a year abroad, she had finally understood that nobody outside the classroom expects FL users to be perfect. This revelation allowed her to become more confident and more talkative in her FLs. There were interesting examples of FLE and FLCA going hand in hand in the qualitative data, as in MW's excerpt, where she says she said managed to overcome her anxiety and make jokes at the front of the class, relieving her own tension and making her peers and teacher laugh. Being filmed and made to analyse many errors may seem to be a form of cruel punishment to some students, but another of the respondents drew satisfaction from the fact that it allowed her to know that the numbers of errors she made decreased over time. Other learners described activities, including those with a competitive edge such as games and debates, that some teachers and students might prefer to avoid for fear of anxiety arousal. Yet, in these cases, positive emotion emerged from a potentially negative situation.

From a pedagogical perspective, these findings reflect many of the observations made by Gregersen and MacIntyre (2014) on ways for FL teachers to reduce FLCA and to boost enjoyment in the FL, or more generally to empower the students by giving them choice in the selection of classroom activities. From a theoretical perspective, these results confirm the importance of Csikszentmihalyi's (2004) distinction between pleasure and enjoyment, highlighting the potential risk inherent in instances of enjoyment. When the focus is on evidence of skill development in the face of challenge, the emotionally ambivalent tone of a classroom can resolve toward the positive and result in the shared experience of enjoyment (see MacIntyre, 2007).

The factor analysis also produced a factor labelled FLE–Social. This factor was composed of items with key words such as *laugh, common 'legends'*, a *tight group* with teachers and peers who are *nice, encouraging* and *supportive, positive environment* and a *good atmosphere*. In the qualitative data, the social side of FLE concept comes into clearer focus. Many students underlined the importance of doing well in front of their peers, and remembered instances where they 'nailed' it, as CL pointed out. Very often these positive events marked a new period in the student's learning curve: there seems to be a 'before' that is left behind as the new skills or mastery has been recognized in front of peers and teacher. Of course, teachers play a crucial part in nurturing the FLE of their students; how they relate with their students is extremely important. Teachers showing respect for the needs and limitations of students was cited many times in the data (not reported here). A teacher's judicious praise on a particular aspect of FL production can do wonders for a learner's feeling of achievement. Teachers being humorous and able to read the atmosphere in the classroom also were mentioned as facilitating enjoyment. It is perhaps the ability of the teacher to read the emotional atmosphere of the classroom, coupled with the characteristics and experiences of the students, that allows potentially risky teaching behaviours to produce enjoyment rather than anxiety in these cases.

Although there is a shared component of enjoyment, results also point to a private side of the concept. Private feelings are captured in phrases associated with Factor III such as *enjoy it, learnt interesting things, don't get bored, feel proud* and *it's fun*. We interpret this factor as indicating an internal sense of enjoyment in the face of challenges. The qualitative data point to instances of an inward pride, as in discussing something deeply personal or meaningful. There can be a sense of enjoying one's success in spite of obstacles presented by teachers or peers, a feeling of success that nobody can take away, as in the case of NN. The qualitative data also provide evidence of enjoyment of some teaching techniques that generally would be considered risky, even if done with benevolent intent (as in excerpts from MH, SM and MW). These private states suggest a contrast between past and present that is recognized by the learner as evidence of language development, especially in difficult areas. Future research might investigate whether FLE–Private has significant elements of pride associated with it. As it was defined in Factor III, however, the emphasis would be on the private feeling of enjoyment from accomplishing something that was difficult and in spite of obstacles.

Before concluding, we must note some of the limitations of the present study. Although we have a large sample, there is a tendency for the respondents to be female, well educated, and experienced learners. This may reflect a positive bias, in the sense that participants who are willing to complete an anonymous, voluntary, online survey about language learning may be the ones who especially enjoy language learning. Although we were hoping to gain insight into positive experiences, we cannot claim to have a random or representative sample. The bulk of the respondents came from Europe and the results may not generalize equally well to all areas of the world. In addition, all of the respondents had to have access to a computer in order to complete the web-based survey, and they had to be invited by someone who had heard about the research project. Although the size of the sample allows for advanced multivariate statistics, a large sample also can lead to small relationships being declared statistically significant.

The qualitative analysis also produced its challenges for interpretation. The extracts give only a brief sketch of FLE arising from a unique confluence of internal and contextual factors. Participants referred to their unique context at one specific point in time. They varied in their choice of temporal focus: many described an episode that ranged from a minute to an hour, while some described episodes spread over the academic year. We have pointed out elsewhere that 'longer timescales could be linked to qualitatively different interpretations of enjoyment' (Dewaele & MacIntyre, 2014: 255; see also Chapter 11 of the present volume). The categorization of episodes was also complicated by the fact that some respondents described specific events but others described a pattern of events or their perceptions of their classroom experience rather than the experience itself. Some participants spontaneously mentioned other positive emotions, such as pride and satisfaction, and others referred to negative emotions such as FLCA.

Thematic categorization of verbal data is a messy affair, as many observations touched upon multiple themes and could therefore have been categorized differently. Even brief entries, such as the comment reported above by SM who was thanked by her Japanese teacher with an amusing and exaggerated honorific, can produce multiple themes. Although the dominant theme in her response was identified as teacher skills, there are also elements of teacher and peer recognition, and even a hint of anxiety. The development of the concept of FLE would be facilitated by qualitative methods such as in-depth interviewing or focus groups that could provide richer, contextualized detail about enjoyable language learning episodes.

Yet, in spite of (or perhaps because of) the challenges encountered in this project, we are hopeful that future research will further clarify the conceptualization and measurement of FLE. Further quantitative research can explore the correlates, predictors and consequences of the dimensions of FLE. Detailed qualitative analysis is needed to further contextualize enjoyment within learners' experiences. With additional research and the insights it brings, we anticipate that the FLE concept will take its rightful place among variables relating to individual differences known to affect the language learning process.

Conclusion

Foreign Language Enjoyment can be defined as a separate dimension from Foreign Language Classroom Anxiety. Although a modest negative correlation exists between them, they certainly do not overlap completely. We have evidence to support our previous claim that absence of FLCA does not automatically mean that FLE is present (Dewaele & MacIntyre, 2014), although it is possible for FLE to be accompanied by FLCA. The present study also highlighted the fact that there are shades of meaning within FLE. One important dimension is social, in other words, the satisfaction that a learner can draw from a buzzing, positive FL classroom. A second dimension reflects private thoughts and feelings, including the internal pride and satisfaction a learner can experience when something difficult has been achieved. Finally, the positive atmosphere can be created by teachers but also by students, or by a combination of them as the comments revealed: many positive experiences reported by participants involved activities organized by the teacher that gave students a degree of freedom and latitude. These results help to reinforce the understanding that learners are not to be considered as passive recipients of knowledge but as active pursuers of linguistic know-how, authentic communicators in the FL, and valued members of the classroom's speech community.

The learning of a FL takes years and it is hard work. It is not surprising, then, that beginners do not enjoy the FL as much as advanced learners (Dewaele & MacIntyre, 2014). But learners at any level can have a breakthrough moment – it could involve correct pronunciation, a perfect accent in one sentence, making people laugh, or the ability to keep the floor for a long time because of an authentic interest of peers and teachers. As self-confidence grows, FLCA can be controlled as FLE is boosted. Given that the nature of FLE implies risk to the sense of self, the goal is not to eliminate FLCA any more than a runner would wish to eliminate one of her feet (even the sore, aching one). Learners will find their balance when both feet, enjoyment and anxiety, are brought into equilibrium. This is not meant to imply equal amounts or a linear process, but a sense of coordination between anxiety and enjoyment.

Appendix. The Questionnaire Items

The FLE scale

To what extent do you agree with the following statements?
[Strongly disagree; Disagree; Undecided; Agree; Strongly agree]

- I can be creative
- I can laugh off embarrassing mistakes in the FL
- I don't get bored
- I enjoy it
- I feel as though I'm a different person during the FL class
- I learnt to express myself better in the FL
- I'm a worthy member of the FL class
- I've learnt interesting things
- In class, I feel proud of my accomplishments
- It's a positive environment
- It's cool to know a FL
- It's fun
- Making errors is part of the learning process
- The peers are nice
- The teacher is encouraging
- The teacher is friendly
- The teacher is supportive
- There is a good atmosphere
- We form a tight group
- We have common 'legends', such as running jokes
- We laugh a lot

The FLCA scale

- Even if I am well prepared for FL class, I feel anxious about it
- I always feel that the other students speak the FL better than I do
- I can feel my heart pounding when I'm going to be called on in FL class
- I don't worry about making mistakes in FL class (reverse-coded)
- I feel confident when I speak in FL class (reverse-coded)
- I get nervous and confused when I am speaking in my FL class
- I start to panic when I have to speak without preparation in FL class
- It embarrasses me to volunteer answers in my FL class

Notes

(1) Six did not indicate their sex.
(2) The proportions were calculated for the 1044 participants who responded to this question.

References

Brantmeier, C. (2005) Nonlinguistic variables in advanced second language reading: Learners' self-assessment and enjoyment. *Foreign Language Annals* 38 (4), 494–504.

Cresswell, J.W. and Plano Clark, V.L. (2011) *Designing and Conducting Mixed Methods Research* (2nd edition). London: Sage.

Csikszentmihalyi, M. (1997) Happiness and creativity: Going with the flow. *Futurist* 31(5), 8.

Csikszentmihalyi, M. (2004) Pleasure vs. enjoyment. *Across the Board* 41 (2), 9.

Csikszentmihalyi, M. (2008) *Flow: The Psychology of Optimal Experience*. New York: Harper Perennial.

Dewaele, J.-M. (2002) Psychological and sociodemographic correlates of communicative anxiety in L2 and L3 production. *International Journal of Bilingualism* 6, 23–39.

Dewaele, J.-M. (2007a) Predicting language learners' grades in the L1, L2, L3 and L4: The effect of some psychological and sociocognitive variables. *International Journal of Multilingualism* 4, 169–197.

Dewaele, J.-M. (2007b) The effect of multilingualism, sociobiographical, and situational factors on communicative anxiety and foreign language anxiety of mature language learners. *International Journal of Bilingualism* 11, 391–409.

Dewaele, J.-M. (2010) Multilingualism and affordances: Variation in self-perceived communicative competence and communicative anxiety in French L1, L2, L3 and L4. *International Review of Applied Linguistics* 48, 105–129.

Dewaele, J.-M. (2013a) *Emotions in Multiple Languages* (2nd edn). Basingstoke: Palgrave Macmillan.

Dewaele, J.-M. (2013b) The link between foreign language classroom anxiety and psychoticism: Extraversion and neuroticism among adult bi- and multilinguals. *Modern Language Journal* 97, 670–684.

Dewaele, J.-M. (in press) Are perfectionists more anxious foreign language learners and users? In C. Gkonou, M. Daubney and J.-M. Dewaele (eds) *New Insights into Language Anxiety: Theory, Research and Educational Implications*. Bristol: Multilingual Matters.

Dewaele, J.M. and MacIntyre, P.D. (2014) The two faces of Janus? Anxiety and enjoyment in the foreign language classroom. *Studies in Second Language Learning and Teaching* 4, 237–274.

Dewaele, J.-M. and Shan Ip, T. (2013) The link between foreign language classroom anxiety, second language tolerance of ambiguity and self-rated English proficiency among Chinese learners. *Studies in Second Language Learning and Teaching* 3 (1), 47–66.

Dewaele, J.-M., Petrides, K.V. and Furnham, A. (2008) The effects of trait emotional intelligence and sociobiographical variables on communicative anxiety and foreign language anxiety among adult multilinguals: A review and empirical investigation. *Language Learning* 58, 911–960.

Egbert, J. (2004) A study of flow theory in the foreign language classroom. *Canadian Modern Language Review* 87, 499–515.

Fredrickson, B.L. (2001) The role of positive emotions in positive psychology: The broaden-and-build theory of positive emotions. *American Psychologist* 56, 218–226.

Fredrickson, B.L. (2013) Updated thinking on positivity ratios. *American Psychologist* 68 (9), 814–822.

Green, J.M. (1993) Student attitudes toward communicative and non-communicative activities: Do enjoyment and effectiveness go together? *Modern Language Journal* 77 (1), 1–10.

Gregersen, T. and Horwitz, E.K. (2002) Language learning and perfectionism: Anxious and non-anxious language learners' reactions to their own oral performance. *Modern Language Journal* 86, 562–570.

Gregersen, T. and MacIntyre, P.D. (2014) *Capitalizing on Language Learners' Individuality: From Premise to Practice*. Bristol: Multilingual Matters.

Horwitz, E.K. (2010) Foreign and second language anxiety. *Language Teaching* 43, 154–167.

Horwitz, E.K., Horwitz, M.B. and Cope, J. (1986) Foreign language classroom anxiety. *Modern Language Journal* 70, 125–132.

Kaiser, H.F. (1970) A second-generation little jiffy. *Psychometrika* 35, 401–415.

MacIntyre, P.D. (1999) Language anxiety: A review of the research for language teachers. In D.J. Young (ed.) *Affect in Foreign Language and Second Language Teaching: A Practical Guide to Creating a Low-Anxiety Classroom Atmosphere* (pp. 24–45). Boston: McGraw-Hill.

MacIntyre, P.D. (2007) Willingness to communicate in the second language: Understanding the decision to speak as a volitional process. *Modern Language Journal* 91, 564–576.

MacIntyre, P.D., Burns, C. and Jessome, A. (2011) Ambivalence about communicating in a second language: A qualitative study of French immersion students' willingness to communicate. *Modern Language Journal* 95, 81–96.

MacIntyre, P.D. and Gardner, R.C. (1989) Anxiety and second language learning: Towards a theoretical clarification. *Language Learning* 39, 251–275.

MacIntyre, P.D. and Gregersen, T. (2012) Emotions that facilitate language learning: The positive-broadening power of the imagination. *Studies in Second Language Learning and Teaching* 2 (2), 193–213.

MacIntyre, P.D. and Mercer, S. (2014) Introducing positive psychology to SLA. *Studies in Second Language Learning and Teaching* 4, 153–172.

Reschly, A.L., Huebner, E.S., Appleton, J.J. and Antaramian, S. (2008) Engagement as flourishing: The contribution of positive emotions and coping to adolescents' engagement at school and with learning. *Psychology in the Schools* 45 (5), 419–431.

Scovel, T. (1978) The effect of affect on foreign language learning: A review of the anxiety research. *Language Learning* 28 (1), 129–142.

Seligman, M.E.P., Steen, T.A., Park, N. and Peterson, C. (2005) Positive psychology progress: Empirical validation of interventions. *Tidsskrift for Norsk Psykologforening* 42 (10), 874–884.

10 Accentuate the Positive: Conceptual and Empirical Development of the Positive L2 Self and Its Relationship to L2 Proficiency

J. Lake

Positive psychology is based on empirical data and scientific methods that aim to make research results more replicable and cumulative. It 'does not rely on wishful thinking, faith, self-deception, fads, or hand waving' (Seligman & Csikszentmihalyi, 2000: 7). Perhaps because of this empirical emphasis, the field has incorporated numerous scales to measure new positive psychological constructs (e.g. Lopez & Snyder, 2003; Ong & Van Dulmen, 2007), along with bringing older concepts under the positive psychology umbrella. A similar process is taking place within the SLA domain as new ideas from positive psychology are combined with previous concepts to create a vibrant subfield with deep roots and a bright future (MacIntyre & Mercer, 2014).

There has been a growing amount of research on the concept of self in second language (L2) motivation studies (e.g. Csizér & Magid, 2014; Mercer & Williams, 2014). Much of the research has been inspired by Dörnyei and colleagues (Dörnyei, 2005, 2009; Dörnyei & Ushioda, 2009, 2011), who have developed a framework called the L2 motivational self-system. When looking at research outside of SLA in the literature about the self, the multitude of types of self-related theories and studies can be confusing (MacIntyre *et al.*, 2009; Mercer, 2011). One way that self-concept theory and research has been organized is through the generality or specificity of the self-constructs. Shavelson *et al.* (1976) wrote an important review of self-concept studies and measures used in educational contexts and created a hierarchical and developmental model. In their hierarchy, there is a unitary, stable, general self-concept that is composed of multidimensional lower-order facets that are less stable and more situation-specific. Marsh and colleagues have expanded and developed Shavelson *et al.*'s model (Marsh, 2007; Marsh &

Craven, 2006; Marsh & Shavelson, 1985), mostly by focusing on academic self-concept and elaborating the differing domain self-concepts that relate to it (e.g. Marsh *et al.*, 2000, 2005, 2008).

My approach to the present research is based on the idea that a hierarchical model could be used to organize various constructs that relate to positive self-constructs and motivation for the L2 field. The present study uses constructs that are all positively oriented. Three main levels of hierarchy are presented: a global level, an L2 domain level, and a more dynamic state-like level. This study is not arguing that 'negative' constructs, such as Dörnyei's (2005) concept of the ought-to L2 self or L2 anxiety (MacIntyre, 1999) should be avoided. Rather, the focus of the present study is on defining a concept of 'positive self' at a general level and 'positive L2 self' at a domain-specific level. The model under development here is not derived from previous models of the L2 self but reflects an attempt to organize concepts from positive psychology that might be relevant to self-concept and related to proficiency. This chapter builds on work reported by Lake (2013).

Attention to levels of specificity is common to hierarchical and multidimensional models of self. There is a general or global level and highly specific levels such as self-efficacy to do specific tasks, with differing domain 'middle' levels between (Swann & Bosson, 2010). At the global level, the self has no referent except the overall, whole, subjective sense of self; at the highly specific level, the referent is in relation to a specific situation or task; while at the mid-levels, the referent is to a particular domain. These levels form part of the self-system, that is, a motivated self-relevant meaning system that informs, constrains and guides interpretations of experience, goals, self-regulation and interpersonal relationships.

For example, take the psychology of interest (Silvia, 2006). As an emotional state, interest is always in relation to some object. For instance, an object of interest to a student might be the connection between the words 'helicopter' and 'pterosaur' – they share the Greek root 'pter', meaning 'wing'. Repeated experiences of similar objects of interest might lead the student to become interested in the domain of etymology or the history of the English language. In other words, states of interest may form into one of a person's enduring interests (Silvia, 2001; Silvia & Kashdan, 2009). Being interested in many domains or having many interests in turn may lead the student to trait-level interest, or what in the current study is called curiosity. At the trait level, there is no referent to objects (unlike at the state level) and no domain (unlike at the middle level): only the person as a whole.

After careful reading of the positive psychology literature and reflection on how various concepts might apply in an L2 learning context, specifically in Japan, a set of concepts were selected for the present study. These are not derived from a specific existing model but reflect an initial attempt to develop a model fitting together a structure that might be called 'the positive

L2-self' as a way to get the research ball rolling. All the concepts selected for the present study, including curiosity, interest, passion and mastery goal orientation, have a thread of learning or acquiring novelty/complexity running through them. Learning might be considered Janus-faced, with constructs such as curiosity, interest, passion and mastery goal orientation looking forward in time, and constructs like satisfaction and enjoyment have a quality of looking backward in time. As described by Seligman (2011), the notion of flourishing captures a bit of both forward- and backward-looking faces, while the other constructs included in the present model face forward, toward learning. The model is not meant to be exclusive of other concepts and future research hopefully will develop and elaborate the model proposed here.

The purpose of the present study is to empirically test a hierarchical, positive-oriented model of the self and its relationship to L2 proficiency. In the present study, a structural model was created with constructs at three levels of specificity: global positive self-concept, positive L2 domain-specific self, and positive L2 self-efficacy. L2 proficiency, the achievement measure, is at a similar specificity level to L2 self-efficacy. The global level employs strengths of flourishing, curiosity and hope. The positive L2 self employs concepts of interest, passion and mastery goal orientation applied to L2 learning. Finally, the positive L2 self-efficacy construct includes L2 speaking, listening and reading self-efficacy (L2 writing was not part of the curriculum at the participants' school).

The Global Positive Self

Global positive self: Flourishing

Flourishing is a multidimensional psychological construct meaning that one is mentally healthy over a period of time. Flourishing individuals have shown high levels of psychosocial functioning in a number of studies (Keyes, 2007; Reschly *et al.*, 2008; Ryff & Singer, 1998). Seligman (2002) originally promoted a version of flourishing to which happiness was central, but his 2011 reworking advocated a model called PERMA, composed of five elements: Positive emotion (of which happiness and life satisfaction are aspects), Engagement, Relationships, Meaning and Achievement. Positive emotion consists of emotions such as happiness, joy, amusement, interest and gratitude. Engagement refers to being absorbed, and finding flow, that is, using strengths to meet challenges in life. Relationships reflects having and maintaining positive personal relationships in life. Meaning refers to having purpose in life, that is, meaning that serves something greater and beyond oneself. For Seligman (2011), the target of positive psychology is flourishing, that is, well-being through having high levels of PERMA in life.

Other theories of psychological flourishing (e.g. Ryff & Singer, 1998, 2008; Keyes, 2007) overlap considerably with Seligman's PERMA model. Diener *et al.* (2010: 144) created the flourishing scale used in this study, which captures the 'major aspects' of flourishing.

Global positive self: Curiosity

Curiosity is a trait-like strength and refers to 'recognizing, embracing, and seeking out knowledge and new experiences' (Kashdan *et al.*, 2009: 988). In their study on the development of a curiosity measure, Kashdan *et al.* found that curiosity correlated positively with various other positive measures, such as openness to experience, happiness, personal growth, autonomy, positive relations with others and purpose in life. Curious people tend to look for opportunities to acquire knowledge and pursue new experiences. Curiosity works forward, then, by promoting the filling in of knowledge gaps, the recognition of potential learning material and the seeking out of new learning situations, thus leading to increased achievement and competence (Kashdan, 2004, 2009).

Global positive self: Hope

The hope construct is composed of elements such as clearly defining goals, thinking about ways to achieve those goals and motivating oneself to act toward goals. Hope is composed of two subcomponents that act toward goals: agency (agentic thinking) and pathways (pathway thinking). Hope–agency refers to the belief that one has the ability to initiate, act, persist and exert effort toward valued goals. It is the belief that one has volition and is in control of making progress toward goals; colloquially, it might be called 'willpower'. The hope–pathways concept refers to the belief that one can find a way or multiple ways to move toward a goal, even in the face of obstacles. Snyder *et al.* (2002) found that hope predicted academic achievement in college, and it has been shown to have effects on academic achievement in a number of other studies (Lopez, 2013; Snyder, 1994, 2000). Although hope can be characterized and measured as a trait or state, it is measured here at the trait level.

Positive L2 Self

Many researchers have pointed out the importance of middle-level concepts for organizing psychological processes (Mischel & Morf, 2003; Swann & Bosson, 2010; Swann *et al.*, 2007). Lake (2013) used mid-level L2 domain constructs to link general positive psychology constructs with more specific L2 motivation constructs. In Lake (2013), this middle level was given the label 'positive L2 self'. Although Dörnyei's L2 self-system uses discrepancy as an important part of the ideal and ought-to selves, in positive psychology, as with humanistic psychology, the emphasis is on being authentic and true to oneself (Ryff & Singer, 2008; Schlegel & Hicks, 2011; Seligman, 2002; Sheldon, 2002), rather than on reducing the discrepancy between a present and a future ideal. The positive L2 self can be defined by interest, passion and mastery goals.

Positive L2 self: Interest

The importance of interest in positive psychology (e.g. Fredrickson, 2001, 2009; Kashdan & Silvia, 2009) and learning theories (e.g. Dewey, 1913; Hidi & Renninger, 2006; Silvia, 2006) suggests that it be included in the construct of the positive L2 self. In addition, interest is a component of many theories of motivation, such as demotivation (e.g. Kikuchi, 2013), contemporary expectancy-value theories of motivation (e.g. Eccles & Wigfield, 2002; Wigfield & Eccles, 2002), self-efficacy theory (e.g. Bandura, 1997, 2008), flow theory and autotelic activities (e.g. Csikszentmihalyi, 1990; Egbert, 2003), learning environments and engagement (e.g. Hunter & Csikszentmihalyi, 2003; Shernoff, 2013; Shernoff *et al.*, 2003), goal orientation theory (e.g. Dweck & Leggett, 1988; Pintrich, 2000) and self-determination theory (e.g. Deci & Ryan, 1985, 2002; Ryan & Deci, 2000).

Interest is also an important part of Gardner's socio-educational model, which was developed from a social psychology perspective (Gardner, 1985, 2010). His model was wider in scope than the present one, but some measures have similarities with the model presented here. Gardner's measure of interest in foreign languages is broader because it spans languages in general rather than the single-language domain interest described here. The measures of interest in L2 and passion for L2 learning in the present study align more closely with Gardner's measures of desire to learn English and attitude toward learning English, where only the positively keyed items are considered.

Positive L2 self: Passion

Passion for L2 learning is defined as a strong inclination toward activities that are liked or loved. Where interest theory developed over time from the 'bottom up', based on decades of empirical research, passion theory was created 'top down', from self-determination theory. The model developed by Vallerand *et al.* (2003) posited two types of passions, a more self-determined, harmonious passion and a more un-self-controlled, obsessive passion. Harmonious passions are associated with adaptive behaviours and obsessive passions with maladaptive behaviours. According to Vallerand (2008), interests may or may not be valued, and the time and energy are unspecified. Also, as in self-determination theory, harmonious passions are developed under conditions of autonomy, positive relationships and competence. Vallerand *et al.* (2007) found that harmonious passion predicted mastery goals, which in turn predicted deliberate practice, which in turn predicted higher performance and which was also related to subjective well-being. In this study, the construct 'passion for L2 learning' is defined as harmonious passion for L2 learning; obsessive passion is not part of this study.

Positive L2 self: Mastery goals

Mastery goal orientations, which are also known as learning goal orientations, are based on goal orientation theory or achievement goal theory and are associated with building competence. Mastery goals are defined by the purpose or orientation toward absolute gains in learning within an individual. This is in contrast to performance goals, which are an orientation toward demonstrating competence based on relative normative standards. Kaplan and Maehr (1999) found that mastery goal orientations were positively related to well-being measures and academic achievement. Woodrow (2006) found that mastery goal orientations correlated with speaking proficiency as measured by a section of the IELTS (International English Language Testing System).

Based on the goal orientation literature (Dweck & Leggett, 1988; Elliot, 2005), a mastery goal orientation that is associated with self-improvement, interest, effort, learning and self-efficacy can contribute to a positive self. Hulme *et al.* (2013) found links between mastery goal orientation and being interested in learning. A mastery goal orientation toward learning another language is used as an aspect of a positive L2 self.

L2 Self-efficacy

Bandura's (1997) social cognitive theory of human behaviour relates an individual's actions and cognitions with environmental influences. As a part of social cognitive theory, competence perceptions and control beliefs are important agency components of human development and change. The emphasis of this theory is on competence beliefs or self-efficacy beliefs that one is capable of doing a task in a given situation and domain. It should be noted that although self-efficacy (Bandura, 1977) pre-dates the founding of positive psychology as a movement, it has been adopted as a construct in positive psychology (Bandura, 2008; Maddux, 2002).

Linnenbrink and Pintrich (2002: 315) note that 'Students who have more positive self-efficacy beliefs (i.e., they believe they can do the task) are more likely to work harder, persist and eventually achieve at higher levels'. In the field of foreign language learning, Hsieh and Schallert (2008) found that among self and differing attributional beliefs, self-efficacy was the greatest predictor of achievement. L2 self-efficacy has also been shown to have relationships with L2 achievement and other motivational variables by Mills (2014).

Lake (2013) found that L2 speaking, listening and reading self-efficacy had positive relationships with positive self-concept variables, positive L2 self variables and L2 proficiency. Lake (2014) found that students who read extensively with graded readers gained L2 reading self-efficacy while those who used graded readers but did not read extensively showed no gains. In addition, gains in L2 reading self-efficacy was shown to have a relationship with gains in a positive reading self as measured by an L2 reading interest measure. In another study, with French as a second language, Mills *et al.* found that reading self-efficacy correlated with L2 reading proficiency ($r = 0.29$) and could conclude that the former 'positively influences' the latter (Mills *et al.*, 2006: 284).

The Present Study

Research questions that guide this study are:

(1) Can composite constructs of positive self-concept, L2 positive self and L2 self-efficacy be constructed?
(2) What are the structural relationships between positive self-concept, positive L2 self, L2 self-efficacy and L2 proficiency?

Rasch analysis was used both for the scales and for participant measures. Rasch analysis uses what is known as the Rasch model, sometimes referred to as a one-parameter logistic model, in item response theory, which is based on a probabilistic procedure where a person with a greater quantity of an attribute will have a higher probability of endorsing an item than someone with less of the attribute under consideration, while items that are more endorsable will have a greater probability of being endorsed than those that are less endorsable. The person and item are then put on the same log odds (logit) scale. Rasch analysis returns information on all participants, an individual person, the scale as a whole, or single items, as well as how information is organized through a measure.

Item analysis was done to calculate fit statistics, item difficulties, item standard errors and item–person mapping as depicted in the Wright maps. Item fit statistics and scale structure and dimensionality will be summarized and reported here. Scale analysis was done, including principal components analysis (PCA), of the Rasch residuals for descriptions of unidimensionality given by variance explained by the measures, eigenvalues of unexplained variance in the first contrast and percentage of unexplained variance in the first contrast. Scale structure was examined through category observation counts and ascending orders of endorsability and separation of thresholds. Guidelines suggested by Linacre (2002, 2011) were compared with the empirical values obtained from the Rasch analyses. In addition, Rasch person reliability and separation statistics as well as traditional descriptive statistics are given.

Methods

Participants

The participants in this study were 212 first-year Japanese female students in a four-year private university in western Japan. Most of the students were aged 18–20 years (mean 19.2 years, SD 1.3 years), an age that can be characterized as the developmental period known as emerging adulthood (Arnett, 2004). The selection of these students was based on convenience sampling at an institution where the researcher had access to an adequate pool of participants. However, as wide a range as possible of teachers and students were asked to participate, to more broadly sample from within the institution. The participants were English-speaking classes taught by seven teachers. The students came from a variety of majors, including contemporary culture, expressive arts, psychology, early childhood development and English. The students took a TOEIC Bridge test. TOEIC (Test of English for International Communication) is a test of English proficiency for people whose native language is not English. The TOEIC Bridge is an easier version that measures lower levels of proficiency, with scores ranging from 20 to 180. The mean TOEIC Bridge score was 122.7, with a standard deviation of 18.8. The students were native speakers of Japanese in 25 classes, each of approximately 20–30 students. As is typical for Japanese students, before entering college they had studied English for three years in junior high school and three years in high school.

Instruments

The instruments used in this study were given together in the form of a self-report questionnaire comprising the scales described below. Students also separately took the TOEIC Bridge. Some of the instruments are well established in the general psychology literature, while others were created for this study. The established scales come from a variety of formats, in both English and Japanese, with differing response options; however, for this study, all the scales were given in Japanese with six response options. The scales were developed though previously piloted trials and were modified when necessary by eliminating, rewording, or re-translating items. Additional validity evidence for the scales can be found in Lake (2013).

The instruments are used to develop a model that shows structural relationships with a positive L2 self. In the proposed model, the positive L2 self is an intervening or mediating variable between a 'positive self' independent variable and a dependent or outcome variable of language proficiency, as measured by TOEIC Bridge scores. As mentioned, this model has three levels of specificity. The positive self-concept is global and trait-like. The second level is also dispositional but is more L2 specific in that it centres on a construct of a positive self-concept for learning an L2. This construct relates to positive beliefs about the L2, particular classroom beliefs, and beliefs about learning an L2. The third level of specificity is self-efficacy beliefs in relation to specific language tasks involving the specific skills of reading, speaking and listening.

Measures for the global positive self

The Curiosity and Exploration Inventory – II (CEI-II; Kashdan *et al.*, 2009) is a scale designed to measure trait curiosity. The CEI-II contains five items measuring a dimension of curiosity about seeking new knowledge and experiences (e.g. 'I actively seek as much information as I can in new situations') and five items that measure a dimension of curiosity about a general willingness to embrace the novel, uncertain and unpredictable in life (e.g. 'I am the type of person who really enjoys the uncertainty of everyday life'). Kashdan *et al.* reported alpha reliabilities of 0.85 and 0.86. They also suggested that because the two dimensions strongly correlate ($r = 0.79$), the 10 items can be used together as a single scale. The alpha reliability for the present study was 0.84.

The Hope scale (Snyder, 2000; Snyder *et al.*, 1991) is an eight-item scale that measures trait-level hope. The hope construct consists of two factors. Four items reflect agentic thinking about one's goals (e.g. 'I meet the goals that I set for myself') and four items reflect a 'pathways' thinking about the ways to achieve goals (e.g. 'There are a lot of ways around a problem'). Reported alpha reliabilities have ranged from 0.74 to 0.88. The alpha reliabilities for the present study were for hope (agency) 0.73 and hope (pathways) 0.78.

The Flourishing scale (Diener *et al.*, 2010) consists of eight items describing aspects of positive functioning and human flourishing (e.g. 'I actively contribute to the happiness and well-being of others'). The alpha reliability reported was 0.87, and for the present study it was 0.77.

Measures for the positive L2 self

After creating and piloting items based on the literature on interest as a psychological construct (Harackiewicz *et al.*, 2008; Hidi & Renninger, 2006;

Silvia, 2006) eight items were selected to form an Interested L2 Self scale (e.g. 'English is an interesting field of study'). One item performed poorly and was removed from further analysis. The alpha reliability for the seven items in the present study was 0.92.

For the L2 Mastery Goal scale, three items were adopted from the Mastery-approach Goal subscale of the Achievement Goal Questionnaire – Revised (Elliot & Murayama, 2008; e.g. 'My aim is to completely master the material presented in this class'); one item was adapted from the original Mastery-approach Goal subscale of the Achievement Goal Questionnaire (Elliot & McGregor, 2001; 'I want to learn as much as possible') and four items were created for this study based on the achievement goal literature (e g. 'I like learning difficult things in this class'). One item performed poorly and was removed from further analysis. The alpha reliability for the 2008 study was 0.84 and for the 2001 study it was 0.88. For the seven items in the present study, the alpha coefficient was 0.87.

Items from the Harmonious Passion subscale of the Passion scale (Vallerand *et al.*, 2003) were adapted for English (e.g. 'I am passionate about learning English') to create a Passion for L2 scale. The alpha reliability for the present study was 0.90.

Measures of L2 self-efficacy

The L2 self-efficacy variables are specific to L2 learning, skills and tasks. Variables at this level are more dynamic or less trait-like because of their specificity and the situational nature of the contexts, processes and specific tasks.

The Self-Efficacy in Speaking scale consisted of nine items. Three of these were adapted from Burrows (2009) (e.g. 'I can speak English to order a meal in a restaurant') and six were created for this study (e.g. 'I can give a speech in English'). The alpha reliability for the present study was 0.90.

Three items from the Listening Self-Efficacy scale were adapted from Mills *et al.* (2006) and six were created for this study (e.g. 'I can understand the main ideas when listening to English songs'). Mills *et al.* (2006) reported the alpha reliability to be 0.97. For the present study alpha was 0.89.

Two items from the Reading Self-Efficacy scale were adapted from Mills *et al.* (2006) and five were created for this study (e.g. 'I can read and understand a menu in English'). Mills *et al.* (2006) reported the alpha reliability to be 0.95. For the present study alpha was 0.89.

Procedure

Six teachers participating in the research were given the questionnaire to distribute to participating students to complete during class time. Participants took approximately 20–25 minutes to complete the questionnaire. TOEIC Bridge scores were independently acquired as a part of a school-wide programme evaluation. Data for the different scales were put into Winsteps software (Linacre, 2011) for Rasch analysis.

The Rasch model, as with other item response models, assumes that the scales are unidimensional, that is, differences in the variance of the items is accounted for by a single latent variable. Items are modelled to show a certain amount of randomness or 'noise'. Rasch analysis provides information on data-model fit, indicating how closely the data match the predictions of the model, such as mean-squared (MNSQ) fit statistics. If items are measuring a different dimension beyond that explained by the measure, this will be seen as variance unaccounted for. It is possible to do a principal components analysis (PCA) of the residuals to see if there is any patterning in the residuals that suggests an additional dimension. Linacre (2011) suggests guidelines for detecting the existence of additional dimensions in the data: variance explained by the measure should be at least 50%, eigenvalue units of unexplained variance in the first contrast should be less than 3.0 and the proportion of unexplained variance in the first contrast should be less than 10.0%.

Confirmatory factor analysis and structural equation modelling

Confirmatory factor analysis (CFA) is a statistical technique that shows relationships between latent and measured variables. In CFA, researchers have an *a priori* theory about how variables relate to each other. A model is constructed based on the theory and then the model can be tested against the data. The model is confirmed in the sense of being plausible and consistent with the correlations between observed variables, but is not confirmed as being true or even the best-fitting model.

There are a number of CFA and structural equation modelling (SEM) fit indexes. This study uses the chi-square test, the comparative-fit index (CFI) and the root-mean-square error of approximation (RMSEA). The chi-squared test is an absolute fit index that compares the difference between the expected and actual covariance matrices. An acceptable value for the chi-squared test is a non-significant value ($p > 0.05$). One problem with the chi-squared test is that it is sensitive to sample and model size. The RMSEA is not sensitive to model size. Various values are suggested for model fit, with RMSEA < 0.05 indicating good fit, 0.05 < RMSEA < 0.08 indicating reasonable fit, 0.08 < RMSEA < 0.10 mediocre fit and 0.10 < RMSEA as poor fit (Byrne, 2010; Schumacker & Lomax, 2010). The CFI is based on the comparison of the model with the data while adjusting for sample size. CFI > 0.95 indicate good fit and CFI > 0.90 is considered acceptable (Hu & Bentler, 1999).

There are several assumptions that must be met before conducting CFA and SEM (Kline, 2011; Tabachnick & Fiddell, 2007). The assumptions were met after 24 multivariate outliers were found using the procedure suggested by Bryne (2010) and removed from the analysis, for a final sample of 212 cases.

Analyses

Three analyses were conducted: Rasch analyses, CFA and SEM. First, a Rasch rating scale analysis was carried out for item and scale measures.

At the second stage of this study, CFA was used to determine the relationship of the latent variables with the measured variables and CFA model fit. The third stage of the analysis was to run the full structural model, composed of the two latent constructs and the objective outcome measure of proficiency scores.

Results

The results are presented in two main sections: due to limitations on space, the details of the Rasch analysis cannot be presented here. Interested readers are referred to excellent introductions by Bond and Fox (2007), Boone *et al.* (2014), Engelhard (2013) and Wilson (2005). Rasch analysis results are summarized for items and scales. The respondent values are then used as the measured variables for the CFA and then the full structural model.

Rasch analysis of measured variables

For all measures, item fit statistics fell within the guideline values of 0.5 to 1.5 as suggested by Linacre (2011). As shown in Table 10.1, the results

Table 10.1 Unidimensionality analysis for measured variables

Variable	*Variance explained by measures (%)*	*Eigenvalue of the first contrast*	*Unexplained variance in the first contrast (%)*
Curiosity	50.4	1.7	8.8
Flourishing	49.1	1.5	9.6
Hope (pathways)	60.8	1.5	15.1
Hope (agency)	55.3	1.6	18.1
Interested in L2 Self	64.9	1.7	8.4
Passion for L2 Learning	64.2	1.6	8.1
L2 Mastery Goal Orientation	61.6	1.5	8.2
L2 Speaking Self-efficacy	65.1	1.5	5.9
L2 Listening Self-efficacy	60.7	1.8	8.0
L2 Reading Self-efficacy	60.5	1.5	8.3

of the unidimensionality analysis for all the measures except for flourishing met the guideline value of 50%. As the flourishing scale is an omnibus measure of positive constructs related to overall general positive psychological health, it was expected that very minor dimensions might exist but that they would not be enough to impede measurement. The PCA of the Rasch residuals yielded a first contrast of 1.5 eigenvalue units, well below the guideline value of 3.0. The percentage of unexplained variance in the first contrast was 9.6%, below the 10.0% guideline value. The percentage of unexplained variance in the first contrast was over the guideline value for the two hope subscales. Given the shortness of the scales and the small eigenvalue units, the relatively large amount of variance explained by the hope measures was judged to be acceptable. Across all measures, average values increased monotonically across scale categories. The threshold values between categories also increased monotonically, with all thresholds sufficiently spread apart.

The descriptive statistics and reliability coefficients are given in Table 10.2. The reliability values for the hope subscale were a little low at 0.71 and 0.77 but this may be due to the shortness of these scales. The flourishing scale was also a little low at 0.75 but, as mentioned, this may be due to the omnibus nature of this construct measuring overall positive functioning. The skewness and kurtosis values were all acceptable. Person reliability is done on the Rasch measures and is analogous to Cronbach's alpha of the raw scores and can be interpreted in a similar manner, but it is usually a more conservative estimate of reliability and more generalizable. The person

Table 10.2 Descriptive statistics for measures

Variable	*k*	*M*	*SE*	*SD*	*Skew*	*Kurtosis*	*Alpha*	*PR*	*PS*
Curiosity	10	0.33	0.04	0.87	0.25	0.66	0.84	0.82	2.10
Flourishing	8	0.27	0.04	0.87	0.10	0.76	0.77	0.75	1.72
Hope/Agency	4	0.44	0.06	1.39	0.30	1.00	0.73	0.71	1.57
Hope/Paths	4	0.44	0.07	1.73	0.13	0.62	0.78	0.77	1.81
Interested L2	7	1.42	0.09	2.07	0.13	0.82	0.92	0.87	2.64
L2 Passion	7	0.63	0.07	1.70	0.08	1.15	0.90	0.87	2.62
L2 MGO	7	0.61	0.06	1.50	-0.04	1.07	0.87	0.85	2.34
L2 SSE	9	-0.90	0.06	1.48	-0.34	1.47	0.90	0.87	2.64
L2 LSE	9	-0.19	0.06	1.48	-0.26	1.01	0.89	0.87	2.58
L2 RSE	7	-0.15	0.08	1.76	-0.32	0.98	0.89	0.86	2.47

Note. *k* = number of items; MGO = Mastery Goal Orientation; SSE = Speaking Self-efficacy; LSE = Listening Self-efficacy; RSE = Reading Self-efficacy; standard error of skewness = 0.11; standard error of kurtosis = 0.21; PR = person reliability; PS = person separation.

separation (PS) indicates the sensitivity of the instrument to distinguish or spread out respondents from lower to higher on the measure.

Confirmatory factor analysis and structural equation modelling

Confirmatory factor analysis (CFA) was done based on the interval respondent measures derived from the Rasch analysis using AMOS (Arbuckle, 2007). A CFA was done with positive self-concept, positive L2 self, L2 self-efficacy and the L2 proficiency measure included, for a total of four factors ($n = 212$). The results were acceptable and similar to the fit indexes for the SEM (reported in the following paragraph) so they are not reported here. Measured variables of curiosity, flourishing and hope served as indicators of positive self-concept. Measured variables of interested-in-L2 self, passion for L2 learning and mastery L2 goal orientation served as indicators of positive L2 self. Measured variables of L2 reading self-efficacy, L2 speaking self-efficacy and L2 listening self-efficacy served as indicators of L2 self-efficacy.

Structural equation modelling (SEM) with maximum likelihood estimation (MLE) answered. That is, by assessing the fit of the hypothesized structural model for the relationships between the four latent constructs, it confirmed the structural relationships between positive self-concept, positive L2 self, L2 self-efficacy and L2 proficiency. This model, based on hierarchical constructs of the positive self, proposed that a most stable general positive self-concept would lead to a less stable positive L2 self, which in turn would lead to the least stable L2 self-efficacy and L2 proficiency. The relationships in this three-level hierarchy would be stronger than that

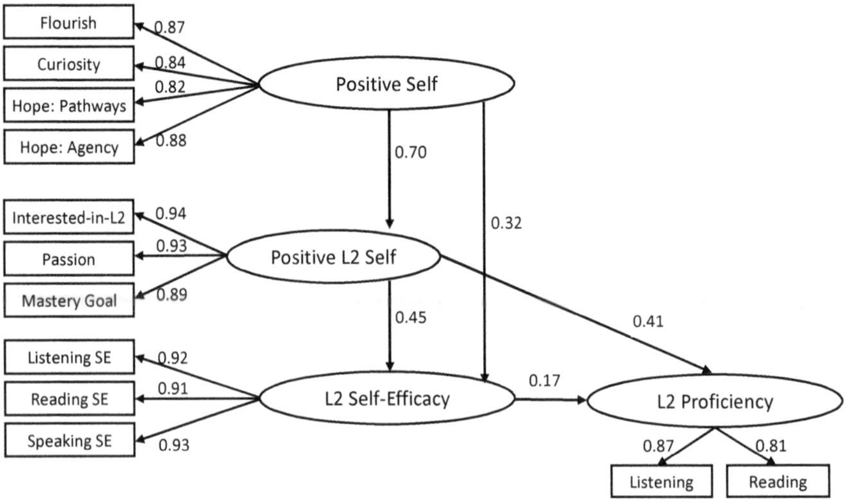

Figure 10.1 Structural equation model with four factors

between the two levels of positive self and L2 motivation. The results of the SEM confirmed that the indicators would load on the latent variables with reasonable fit to the model ($\chi^2(49) = 100.69$, $p < 0.001$, $\chi^2/d.f. = 2.06$, CFI = 0.98, RMSEA = 0.069, 90% CI [0.050, 0.088], AIC = 158.69). The structural component showed that L2 proficiency was influenced by L2 self-efficacy and positive L2 self, and positive L2 self in turn was influenced by positive self-concept. Figure 10.1 illustrates the structural model with loadings of the measured variables and regression paths. All parameters are significant at $p < 0.05$.

Discussion

The results show a successful attempt to build concepts of positive self-concept, positive L2 self, L2 self-efficacy and L2 proficiency, and to assess their structural relations. As discussed at the start of the chapter, positive self-concept is a general view of the total self that is relatively stable and trait-like. This is not to say that it is not changeable, just that change might take time and interventions or treatments might need some degree of frequency and perseverance. Also, like other stable aspects of the self, it does not mean that an individual always behaves in a deterministic and mechanical manner. Thus, positive self-construct refers to general tendencies, not an absolute fixed pattern.

A positive L2 self, as defined in the present study, is specific to the domain of second-language learning. It is less general than positive self-concept but, as a motivational construct, it is distant from language learning behaviour. A positive L2 self requires some degree of developed expertise in order to delineate the domain of second-language learning and this also gives it a degree of stability. In other words, a novice with almost no experience could have a positive language learning experience but until enough of these experiences are strung together they are rather isolated incidents or situations. With enough repeated experience, competence develops and the type of experience is recognized as belonging to a particular domain. Again, as with positive self-concept, this does not mean that it is unchangeable or that it determines behaviour in a direct, absolute fashion.

L2 self-efficacy, in contrast to positive self-concept and positive L2 self, is proximal rather than distant to language learning activity and achievement. The measured variables for the latent construct are specific to language skills and the items to specific situations or activities. The variables reference the self but a highly specific self that is defined by the degree of competence to complete language tasks.

The structural relationship moves from the general to the specific, just as general psychological traits can be conceptualized as leading to a tendency toward particular psychological states. The positive L2 self is in effect a moderating variable between the most general positive self and a highly specific self-efficacy. As the moderating or middle-level variable, the structural relationship would be expected to be stronger between it and the variables it moderates. This is what is shown in the model and supported by the data. It should be emphasized that L2 proficiency is not a self-report measure and is not defined as a self-related concept. Analysis shows a relatively strong path from positive L2 self to L2 proficiency.

This study shows that, at the level of the global positive self, relatively new constructs from positive psychology have direct relationships to a positive L2 self and L2 self-efficacy, and help to confirm the promise of applying positive psychology to motivation and learning. The implications of the two structural models suggest that a global positive self-concept does not necessarily have a direct relationship to L2 proficiency but a direct relationship to a positive L2 self and L2 self-efficacy can be shown. This study has not tested links between the positive self-related concepts defined here and concepts established in the L2 literature more generally. For example, the relationships between the positive L2 self and the three elements of Dörnyei's (2005) L2 self system, or Gardner's (2010) measure of integrative motivation, have not yet been explored. There also is a need to explore the connections between positive L2 self and concepts of both positive and negative emotions in L2. Further research also can explore the pedagogical implications of the model and even whether it is always desirable to have a positive self-concept and a positive L2 self.

This study has a number of limitations. The participants were all female college students, so it is unknown if similar results would be found for males or for younger or older groups. Junior or senior high school students, for example, may not yet have developed stable self-concepts. Also, this study was done cross-sectionally, at a particular point in time and place; a longitudinal study would have provided useful developmental information about the relative changes for the different constructs. For example, it is unknown how quickly L2 self-efficacy changes relative to changes in positive L2 self.

This study relied heavily on quantitative data and used SEM techniques. Qualitative data or a mixed methods study would have provided richness beyond what the numbers alone could supply. It would be useful to explore the reasons why students are strong or weak in particular dimensions. It would also be interesting to learn what particular goals students have for themselves and where they see themselves in relation to the goals. Additional, longitudinal quantitative data would be required to model the reciprocal effects of positive self with positive L2 self, as well as positive L2 self with achievement measures. Over time, successful L2 learning would be expected to build positive competence beliefs and a more stable L2 domain self. The quantitative model also necessarily limits the concepts that can be investigated. Several constructs not discussed here, such as self-control or grit (Baumeister & Tierney, 2011; Duckworth *et al.*, 2007; Lake, 2013), could be used to explore the implications of the model. Future studies could follow the specificity pattern in this study to test additional models.

Conclusion

This study addressed research questions with the overarching aim of demonstrating how constructs from positive psychology can be integrated with second-language learning motivation theory and research. An important principle underlying the study is that the specificity of the constructs and measurement variables need to be clarified and then modelled appropriately. For this study, specificity levels included a general global level, where positive self-concept referenced the whole person; a more specific domain level, where positive L2 self referenced the person within the L2 domain; and even more specific L2 self-efficacy and proficiency.

Learning a second language is a good example of learning a complex skill through much time and effort. Many teachers and administrators tend to focus on how the content, communicating in a second language, is important for current and future academic purposes and career development. The present study shows that the identity processes are also predictive of L2 proficiency and, in addition to academic and career purposes, may help in developing positive identities for personal growth and may contribute to an even greater good in a flourishing self.

Acknowledgements

I would like to express my thanks to the editors for their valuable comments and advice. I would also like to thank Mark Sawyer for comments on an earlier draft.

References

Arbuckle, J.L. (2007) AMOS (Version 16.0). Chicago: SPSS.

Arnett, J.J. (2004) *Emerging Adulthood: The Winding Road from the Late Teens Through the Twenties*. New York: Oxford University Press.

Bandura, A. (1977) Self-efficacy: Toward a unifying theory of behavioral change. *Psychological Review* 84, 191–215.

Bandura, A. (1997) *Self-efficacy: The Exercise of Control*. New York: Freeman.

Bandura, A. (2008) An agentic perspective on positive psychology. In S.J. Lopez (ed.) *Positive Psychology: Discovering Human Strengths* (pp. 167–196). New York: Praeger.

Baumeister, R.F. and Tierney, J. (2011) *Willpower: Rediscovering the Greatest Human Strength*. New York: Penguin.

Bond, T.G. and Fox, C.M. (2007) *Applying the Rasch Model: Fundamental Measurement in the Human Sciences* (2nd edn). Mahwah, NJ: Erlbaum.

Boone, W.J., Staver, J.R. and Yale, M.S. (2014) *Rasch Analysis in the Human Sciences*. Dordrecht: Springer.

Burrows, L. (2009) Assessing speaking self-efficacy: Constructing a scale. *Kinki University English Journal* 4, 1–12.
Byrne, B.M. (2010) *Structural Equation Modeling with AMOS: Basic Concepts, Applications, and Programming* (2nd edn). New York: Routledge.
Csikszentmihalyi, M. (1990) *Flow*. New York: Harper and Row.
Csizér, K. and Magid, M. (eds) (2014) *The Impact of Self-concept on Language Learning*. Bristol: Multilingual Matters.
Deci, E.L. and Ryan, R.M. (1985) *Intrinsic Motivation and Self-determination in Human Behaviour.* New York: Plenum.
Deci, E.L. and Ryan, R.M. (eds) (2002) *Handbook of Self-determination Research*. Rochester, NY: University of Rochester.
Dewey, J. (1913) *Interest and Effort in Education*. Boston, MA: Houghton Mifflin.
Diener, E., Wirtz, D., Tov, W., Kim-Prieto, C., Choi, D., Oishi, S. and Biswas-Diener, R. (2010) New well-being measures: Short scales to assess flourishing and positive negative feelings. *Social Indicators Research* 97, 143–156.
Dörnyei, Z. (2005) *The Psychology of the Language Learn6er: Individual Differences in Second Language Acquisition*. Mahwah, NJ: Erlbaum.
Dörnyei, Z. (2009) The L2 motivational self system. In Z. Dörnyei and E. Ushioda (eds) *Motivation, Language Identity and the L2 Self* (pp. 9–42). Bristol: Multilingual Matters.
Dörnyei, Z. and Ushioda, E. (eds) (2009) *Motivation, Language Identity and the L2 Self.* Bristol: Multilingual Matters.
Dörnyei, Z. and Ushioda, E. (2011) *Teaching and Researching Motivation* (2nd edn). Harlow: Longman.
Duckworth, A.L., Peterson, C., Matthews, M.D. and Kelly, D.R. (2007) Grit: Perseverance and passion for long-term goals. *Journal of Personality and Social Psychology* 92, 1087–1101.
Dweck, C.S. and Leggett, E.L. (1988) A social–cognitive approach to motivation and personality. *Psychological Review* 95, 256–273.
Eccles, J.S. and Wigfield, A. (2002) Motivational beliefs, values, and goals. In S.T. Fiske, D.L. Schacter and C. Zahn-Waxler (eds) *Annual Review of Psychology* (vol. 53) (pp. 109–132). Palo Alto, CA: Annual Reviews.
Egbert, J. (2003) A study of flow theory in the foreign language classroom. *Modern Language Journal* 87 (4), 499–518.
Elliot, A.J. (2005) A conceptual history of the achievement goal construct. In A. Elliot and C. Dweck (eds) *Handbook of Competence and Motivation* (pp. 52–72). New York: Guilford.
Elliot, A.J. and McGregor, H.A. (2001) A 2 × 2 achievement goal framework. *Journal of Personality and Social Psychology* 80, 501–519.
Elliot, A.J. and Murayama, K. (2008) On the measurement of achievement goals: Critique, illustration, and application. *Journal of Educational Psychology* 100, 613–628.
Engelhard, G. (2013) *Invariant Measurement*. New York: Routledge.
Fredrickson, B.L. (2001) The role of positive emotions in positive psychology: The broaden-and-build theory of positive emotions. *American Psychologist* 56, 218–226.
Fredrickson, B.L. (2009) *Positivity: Groundbreaking Research Reveals How to Embrace the Hidden Strength of Positive Emotions, Overcome Negativity, and Thrive*. New York: Crown.
Gardner, R.C. (1985) *Social Psychology and Second Language Learning: The Role of Attitudes and Motivation*. London: Edward Arnold.
Gardner, R.C. (2010) *Motivation and Second Language Acquisition: The Socio-educational Model.* New York: Peter Lang.
Harackiewicz, J.M., Durik, A.M., Barron, K.E., Linnenbrink-Garcia, E.A. and Tauer, J.M. (2008) The role of achievement goals in the development of interest: Reciprocal relations between achievement goals, interest and performance. *Journal of Educational Psychology* 100, 105–122.

Hidi, S. and Renninger, K.A. (2006) The four-phase model of interest development. *Educational Psychologist* 41, 111–127.

Hsieh, P.H. and Schallert, D.L. (2008) Implications from self-efficacy and attribution theories for an understanding of undergraduates' motivation in a foreign language course. *Contemporary Educational Psychology* 33, 513–532.

Hu, L.T. and Bentler, P.M. (1999) Cutoff criteria for fit indexes in covariance structure analysis: Conventional criteria versus new alternatives. *Structural Equation Modeling: A Multidisciplinary Journal* 6, 1–55.

Hulme, E., Green, D.T. and Ladd, K.S. (2013) Fostering student engagement by cultivating curiosity. In P.C. Mather and E. Hulme (eds) *Positive Psychology and Appreciative Inquiry in Higher Education* (pp. 53–64). San Francisco, CA: Jossey-Bass.

Hunter, J.P. and Csikszentmihalyi, M. (2003) The positive psychology of interested adolescents. *Journal of Youth and Adolescence* 32, 27–35.

Kaplan, A. and Maehr, M.L. (1999) Achievement goals and student well-being. *Contemporary Educational Psychology* 24, 330–358.

Kashdan, T.B. (2004) Curiosity. In C. Peterson and M.E.P. Seligman (eds) *Character Strengths and Virtues: A Handbook and Classification* (pp. 125–141). New York: Oxford University Press.

Kashdan, T.B. (2009) *Curious? Discover the Missing Ingredient to a Fulfilling Life*. New York: William Morrow.

Kashdan, T.B. and Silvia, P. (2009) Curiosity and interest: The benefits of thriving on novelty and challenge. In S.J. Lopez and C.R. Snyder (eds) *Handbook of Positive Psychology* (2nd edn) (pp. 367–374). New York: Oxford University Press.

Kashdan, T., Gallagher, M.W., Silvia, P.J., Winterstein, B.P., Breen, W.E., Terhar, D. and Steger, M.F. (2009) The curiosity and exploration inventory – II: Development, factor structure, and initial psychometrics. *Journal of Research in Personality* 43, 987–998.

Keyes, C.L.M. (2007) Promoting and protecting mental health as flourishing. *American Psychologist* 62, 95–108.

Kikuchi, K. (2013) Demotivators in the Japanese EFL context. In M.T. Apple, D. Da Silva and T. Fellner (eds) *Language Learning Motivation in Japan* (pp. 206–224). Bristol: Multilingual Matters.

Kline, R.B. (2011) *Principles and Practice of Structural Equation Modeling* (3rd edn). New York: Guilford.

Lake, J. (2013) Positive L2 self: Linking positive psychology with L2 motivation. In M.T. Apple, D. Da Silva and T. Fellner (eds) *Language Learning Motivation in Japan* (pp. 225–244). Bristol: Multilingual Matters.

Lake, J. (2014) Curious readers and interesting reads: Developing a positive L2 reading self and motivation through extensive reading. *Journal of Extensive Reading* 2, 13–27. Retrieved from http://jalt-publications.org/access/index.php/JER/article/view/1150/63 (accessed November 2015).

Linacre, J.M. (2002) Optimizing rating scale category effectiveness. *Journal of Applied Measurement* 3, 85–106.

Linacre, J.M. (2011) *A User's Guide to WINSTEPS: Rasch-Model Computer Program*. Chicago, IL: Winsteps.com.

Linnenbrink, E.A. and Pintrich, P.R. (2002) Motivation as an enabler for academic success. *School Psychology Review* 31, 313–327.

Lopez, S.J. (2013) *Making Hope Happen: Create the Future You Want For Yourself and Others*. New York: Atria.

Lopez, S.J. and Snyder, C.R. (eds) (2003) *Positive Psychological Assessment: A Handbook of Models and Measures*. Washington, DC: American Psychological Association.

MacIntyre, P.D. (1999) Language anxiety: A review of literature for language teachers. In D.J. Young (eds) *Affect in Foreign Language and Second Language Learning* (pp. 24–43). New York: McGraw Hill.

MacIntyre, P.D. and Mercer, S. (2014) Introducing positive psychology to SLA. *Studies in Second Language Learning and Teaching* 4 (2), 153–172.
MacIntyre, P.D., MacKinnon, S.P. and Clément, R. (2009) From integrative motivation to possible selves: The baby, the bathwater, and the future of language learning motivation research. In Z. Dörnyei and E. Ushioda (eds) *Motivation, Language Identity and the L2 Self* (pp. 43–65). Bristol: Multilingual Matters.
Maddux, J.E. (2002) Self-efficacy: The power of believing you can. In C.R. Snyder and S.J. Lopez (eds) *Handbook of Positive Psychology* (pp. 277–287). New York: Oxford University Press.
Marsh, H.W. (2007) *Self-concept Theory, Measurement and Research into Practice: The Role of Self-concept in Educational Psychology*. Leicester: British Psychological Society.
Marsh, H.W. and Craven, R.G. (2006) Reciprocal effects of self-concept and performance from a multidimensional perspective: Beyond seductive pleasure and unidimensional perspectives. *Perspectives on Psychological Science* 1 (2), 133–163.
Marsh, H.W. and Shavelson, R.J. (1985) Self-concept: Its multifaceted, hierarchical structure. *Educational Psychologist* 20, 107–125.
Marsh, H.W., Craven, R.G. and McInerney, D.M. (eds) (2000) *International Advances in Self Research*. Greenwich, CT: Information Age.
Marsh, H.W., Craven, R.G. and McInerney, D.M. (eds) (2005) *New Frontiers for Self Research*. Greenwich, CT: Information Age.
Marsh, H.W., Craven, R.G. and McInerney, D.M. (eds) (2008) *Self-processes, Learning, and Enabling Human Potential: Dynamic New Approaches*. Greenwich, CT: Information Age.
Mercer, S. (2011) *Towards an Understanding of Language Learning Self-concept*. Dordrecht: Springer.
Mercer, S. and Williams, M. (eds) (2014) *Multiple Perspectives on the Self in SLA*. Bristol: Multilingual Matters.
Mills, N. (2014) Self-efficacy in foreign language acquisition. In S. Mercer and M. Williams (eds) *Multiple Perspectives on the Self in SLA* (pp. 6–22). Bristol: Multilingual Matters.
Mills, N., Pajares, F. and Herron, C. (2006) A reevaluation of the role of anxiety: Self-efficacy, anxiety, and their relation to reading and listening proficiency. *Foreign Language Annals* 39, 276–295.
Mischel, W. and Morf, C.C. (2003) The self as a psycho-social dynamic processing system: A meta-perspective on a century of the self in psychology. In M. Leary and J. Tangney (eds) *Handbook of Self and Identity* (pp. 15–43). New York: Guilford.
Ong, A. and Van Dulmen, M.H.M. (eds) (2007) *Oxford Handbook of Methods in Positive Psychology*. New York: Oxford University Press.
Pintrich, P.R. (2000) Multiple goals, multiple pathways: The role of goal orientation in learning and achievement. *Journal of Educational Psychology* 92, 544–555.
Reschly, A.L., Huebner, E.S., Appleton, J.J. and Antaramian, S. (2008) Engagement as flourishing: The contribution of positive emotions and coping to adolescents' engagement at school and with learning. *Psychology in the Schools* 45, 419–431.
Ryan, R.M. and Deci, E.L. (2000) Self-determination theory and the facilitation of intrinsic motivation, social development, and well-being. *American Psychologist* 55, 68–78.
Ryff, C.D. and Singer, B. (1998) The contours of positive human health. *Psychological Inquiry* 9, 1–28.
Ryff, C.D. and Singer, B. (2008) Know thyself and become what you are: A eudaimonic approach to psychological well-being. *Journal of Happiness Studies* 9, 13–39.
Schlegel, R.J. and Hicks, J.A. (2011) The true self and psychological health: Emerging evidence and future directions. *Social and Personality Psychology Compass* 5, 989–1003.
Schumacker, R.E. and Lomax, R.G. (2010) *A Beginner's Guide to Structural Equation Modeling* (3rd edn). New York: Routledge.
Seligman, M.E.P. (2002) *Authentic Happiness: Using the New Positive Psychology to Realize Your Potential for Lasting Fulfillment*. New York: Free Press.

Seligman, M.E.P. (2011) *Flourish: A Visionary New Understanding of Happiness and Well-being.* New York: Free Press.
Seligman, M.E.P. and Csikszentmihalyi, M. (2000) Positive psychology: An introduction. *American Psychologist* 55, 5–14.
Shavelson, R.J., Hubner, J.J. and Stanton, G.C. (1976) Self-concept: Validation of construct interpretations. *Review of Educational Research* 46, 407–441.
Sheldon, K.M. (2002) The self-concordance model of healthy goal-striving: When personal goals correctly represent the person. In E.L. Deci and R.M. Ryan (eds) *Handbook of Self-determination Research* (pp. 65–86). Rochester, NY: University of Rochester Press.
Shernoff, D.J. (2013) *Optimal Learning Environments to Promote Student Engagement.* New York: Springer.
Shernoff, D.J., Csikszentmihalyi, M., Schneider, B. and Shernoff, E.S. (2003) Student engagement in high school classrooms from the perspective of flow theory. *School Psychology Quarterly* 18, 158–176.
Silvia, P.J. (2001) Interest and interests: The psychology of constructive capriciousness. *Review of General Psychology* 5, 270–290.
Silvia, P.J. (2006) *Exploring the Psychology of Interest.* New York: Oxford University Press.
Silvia, P.J. and Kashdan, T.B. (2009) Interesting things and curious people: Exploration and engagement as transient states and enduring strengths. *Social and Personality Psychology Compass* 3, 785–797.
Snyder, C.R. (1994) *The Psychology of Hope: You Can Get There From Here.* New York: Free Press.
Snyder, C.R. (2000) *Handbook of Hope*. San Diego, CA: Academic Press.
Snyder, C.R., Harris, C., Anderson, J.R., Holleran, S.A., Irving, L.M., Sigmon, S.T., Yoshinobu, L., Gibb, J., Langelle, C. and Harney, P. (1991) The will and the ways: Development and validation of an individual-differences measure of hope. *Journal of Personality and Social Psychology* 60, 570–585.
Snyder, C.R., Shorey, H.S., Cheavens, J., Pulvers, K., Adams, V.H. and Wiklund, C. (2002) Hope and academic success in college. *Journal of Educational Psychology* 94 (4), 820–826.
Swann, W.B. and Bosson, J. (2010) Self and identity. In S.T. Fiske, D.T. Gilbert and G. Lindzey (eds) *Handbook of Social Psychology* (5th edn) (pp. 589–628). New York: McGraw-Hill.
Swann, W.B., Chang-Schneider, C. and McClarty, K.L. (2007) Do people's self-views matter? Self-concept and self-esteem in everyday life. *American Psychologist* 62 (2), 84–94.
Tabachnick, B.G. and Fidell, L.S. (2007) *Using Multivariate Statistics* (5th edn). Boston, MA: Pearson.
Vallerand, R.J. (2008) On the psychology of passion: In search of what makes people's lives most worth living. *Canadian Psychology* 49, 1–13.
Vallerand, R.J., Blanchard, C.M., Mageau, G.A., Koestner, R., Ratelle, C., Léonard, M., Gagne, M. and Marsolais, J. (2003) Les passions de l'âme: On obsessive and harmonious passion. *Journal of Personality and Social Psychology* 85, 756–767.
Vallerand, R.J., Salvy, S.J., Mageau, G.A., Elliot, A.J., Denis, P., Grouzet, F.M.E. and Blanchard, C.B. (2007) On the role of passion in performance. *Journal of Personality* 75, 505–533.
Wigfield, A. and Eccles, J.S. (2002) The development of competence beliefs, expectancies for success, and achievement values from childhood through adolescence. In A. Wigfield and J.S. Eccles (eds) *Development of Achievement Motivation* (pp. 91–120). San Diego, CA: Academic Press.
Wilson, M. (2005) *Constructing Measures: An Item Response Modeling Approach*. Mahwah, NJ: Erlbaum.
Woodrow, L. (2006) A model of adaptive language learning. *Modern Language Journal* 90 (3), 297–319.

11 Affect in Directed Motivational Currents: Positive Emotionality in Long-Term L2 Engagement

Zana Ibrahim

Directed motivational current (DMC) is a newly conceptualized phenomenon which applies to relatively long-term, sustained and heightened motivational engagement (Dörnyei *et al.*, 2014, 2015). DMCs organize and combine prominent concepts from positive psychology (such as eudaemonic happiness, engagement and flow) into a goal-directed process that covers a potential timescale of some months or even years. Although only recently presented as an independent theoretical framework, DMCs are believed to have occurred in virtually everybody's life. Examples of DMCs include sticking to a strict diet for a while, or when a group of campaigners get together to work passionately toward a shared cause in which their collective energy creates a sense of momentum. In the second language (L2) learning arena, an example might be someone who has been deeply involved in improving their L2 skills for a time in pursuit of reaching a certain level of proficiency. A particular DMC example collected for this research is a student who became frustrated because she could not understand her brother and uncle, who spoke in English, and they further irritated her by saying 'who does not understand, does not deserve to know'. This incident gave rise to her almost two-year motivational journey, which she described as not only intense, but also 'the happiest days' in which, not satisfied with her school's English lessons, she started learning on her own, mainly through watching TV shows late at night to develop her listening skills.

The conceptualization of DMCs has been discussed in recent work by Dörnyei and colleagues (Dörnyei *et al.*, 2014, 2015). DMCs are goal-directed engagement and hence they function by allowing the individual to invest a substantial amount of their energy toward a final goal which needs to be perceived as personally valuable and deserving to be heartily sought after. Although a personally meaningful and precious goal is not in itself sufficient to generate such a uniquely powerful amount of motivational energy, the maintenance of such sustained and intense motivation is indeed in part the function of the presence of such a goal along with a matching DMC structure. For the generation of a DMC, a number of time and contextual conditions need to coexist, but once a DMC journey has started, it will almost automatically maintain its progress through utilizing a salient structure comprising habitual routines, sub-goals and affirmative feedback (Dörnyei *et al.*, 2016). The pursuit of the goal is then kept alive and intensified through a psychological process called *vision* (Dörnyei & Kubanyiova, 2014), through which people experience *sensory* imagining of the moment they achieve their goal.

Since the goal of engagement in a DMC is not the intrinsic pleasure of the engagement itself, as in the *flow* experience (Csíkszentmihályi, 1988) for example, one's progress towards the final goal – incarnated in the form of imaginative sensory envisioning – is postulated to generate positive emotionality (Muir & Dörnyei, 2013). This positive emotionality can be in part a by-product of the delightful sense that one is making progress toward a *self-concordant* goal, that is, a goal that truly represents one's interests and values (Sheldon & Elliot, 1999). As this happens and further steps along the DMC path are taken, one also feels happy due to the sense that one has been capable of maintaining one's motivation, which in turn leads to further self-esteem and even self-admiration. Also, as new skills are acquired as a result of the heightened motivational energy associated with DMCs, individuals develop a sense of *eudaemonic happiness*, which 'refers to quality of life derived from the development of a person's best potentials and their application in the fulfilment of personally expressive, self-concordant goals' (Waterman *et al.*, 2010: 41).

DMCs and Positive Emotionality

According to Dörnyei *et al.* (2014), a DMC has three main components: goal-orientedness, a salient facilitative structure, and positive emotional loading. The issue of positive emotionality in DMC experiences is worth investigating in its own right – that is, separately from the holistic study of the DMC as a motivational experience – for two main reasons. First, it enables us to learn more about the operation of this kind of emotionality and hence its structure. Second, it gives us a better understanding of how positive emotionality within DMCs affects motivational behaviour, especially whether positive affect plays *any* role in promoting motivated action within the DMC framework. This is crucial in understanding how positive emotionality might impact motivation in long-term L2 learning.

Based on these two areas of enquiry, the main aims of this study are: first, to obtain a thorough understanding of the affective aspects of experiencing

DMCs (that is, what is it like to be experiencing a DMC?); and second, to investigate the mechanism by which positive emotionality can impact learning behaviour in the context of a DMC experience. The latter point is particularly important. Whereas the focus on, and hence the link between, negative emotion and L2 learning is relatively well researched, knowledge about the mechanism of the impact of positive emotion on behaviour, including learning behaviour, is scarce (MacIntyre & Gregersen, 2012).

This chapter does not address the prevalence of DMCs among students or the frequency with which they occur for an individual. Rather, this study is one of the first attempts to understand the positive emotions involved in a DMC, as described by learners who have reported experiencing at least one DMC. The research question guiding this project can be phrased as: what are the themes underlying the positive emotions described by people who experienced a DMC during language learning?

Method

Phenomenology

A qualitative phenomenological method was utilized in all the data collection and data analysis phases of this project. This method was considered to be appropriate because rather than focusing on differences between individuals, building theories or documenting case studies, a phenomenological method provides grounds for investigating a phenomenon as *lived* and *experienced* by a number of individuals (Creswell, 2007). In order to gain rich data, this method allows participants the opportunity to narrate their experiences with as much detail as possible, including their subjective reflections and judgements (Smith *et al.*, 2009).

Procedure

The sampling was based on recruiting individuals (potential DMC cases) who had experienced a period of intense involvement in L2 learning. On a recruiting visit to his home country (Iraqi Kurdistan), the researcher asked friends to survey anyone they knew who would reflect back on their L2 experiences for any periods of extraordinarily intense engagement. The same recruiting procedure was applied at a British university, where the researcher asked some postgraduate students for such experiences.

Upon receiving responses about the occurrence of such an intense involvement and consent to participate, structured interviews were conducted with over 20 individuals, and a set of questions was sent electronically to further voluntary participants. However, based on the criteria as conceptualized by Dörnyei and colleagues, only 10 individuals were identified as having had DMCs, and of these 10 only seven were selected for this particular study because the other three had not provided sufficiently elaborate answers (for example they had given a general answer like 'I was feeling good' in the 'feelings' section of the interview questions). After a month, the seven participants were invited either to provide *written accounts* (Finlay, 2011) electronically or to be interviewed for a second time to answer specific questions about their affective states during their DMCs. Four participants did so. Thus, the entire corpus comprised data taken from three participants interviewed once, and another four participants interviewed twice.

Four of the participants were interviewed in English and three in Kurdish. All the interviews were transcribed verbatim and the Kurdish interviews and written accounts were then translated into English by the researcher. Despite the advantage of being a Kurdish native and thus grasping the cross-cultural meanings, to avoid issues with translation of data, the researcher later went through the English versions and checked their accuracy against the recordings. In the second round, the interviews were semi-structured and the questions centred on how participants felt, what influenced their moods and what they thought at the time of their experiences about their affective states. An interview protocol was used for all the interviews conducted that included a brief introduction to the research, the study objectives and all the potential interview questions. An ethics application was made to and approval was obtained from the University of Nottingham's Research Ethics Committee. All the participants signed an informed consent form which explained that participation was voluntary and the respondents were not required to answer any of the questions.

Research participants

Of the seven participants, four of them were Kurdish working professionals from and living in Kurdistan, working at multinational organizations and firms, and the other three were studying towards a PhD at a British university, but originally from the Middle East and Eurasia (see Table 11.1). All the participants held university degrees.

Data analysis

A *phenomenological* approach was deployed for the data analysis in order to capture the 'universal essence' and meaning of the phenomenon in question as lived and experienced by the participants (Creswell, 2007: 58). This method was seen as particularly useful in understanding affect in DMCs with regard to *what* emotions the participants experienced and *how* and *why* they experienced them (Moustakas, 1994). A modified approach as described by Colaizzi (1978) and Moustakas (1994) was used. First, all the interviews and written accounts were merged together and both individual

Table 11.1 Background overview of the participants

Participant	*Gender*	*Age when experienced DMC*	*Age at the time of interview*	*How long their DMC lasted*	*DMC goal*
Suzan	Female	16–18	26	1.5–2 years	To prove to brother and uncle that she could also understand L2
Sahar	Female	18–20	25	About 2 years	To understand media content in L2
Shokhan	Female	25–27	27	About 2 years	To use L2 for research and teaching career
Omed	Male	28–33	37	About 5 years	To use L2 for work-related communication
Ali	Male	29–31	34	About 1.5 years	To be successful at job interviews in L2
Kardo	Male	18–20	23	About 2 years	To prove that he is talented in L2 use
Louise	Female	23	26	3 months	To prepare for studying a post-graduate degree involving L2

transcriptions and the whole data-set were read several times to obtain a general feel for it. Then, the researcher went through the entire data-set and extracted a non-overlapping list of the significant phrases and statements, treating them as of equal worth (Table 11.2). The criteria used for selecting these statements were: a statement needed to be around a DMC experience (e.g. not giving a general opinion on how to best learn an L2); and

Table 11.2 Examples of how raw data were developed into formulated meanings

Significant statements (140 total)	*Formulated meanings*
Suzan Q8 So you were not very interested in showing or telling people that 'I am using TV for learning'? No, because they said, I thought that they would say that to watch more TV [laughter], so as an excuse for watching TV not learning. So, this is why I didn't tell them the way I use it, for learning English	Participant feared people might ridicule her for saying she relied on TV to learn L2 and was an excuse for watching more TV
Q17 So even sometimes especially, especially yeah at the beginning of the academic yeah it was actually very exhausting because you know, changing time changing school, it is, but I was yeah, I have this routine for actually yeah for two years, almost two years yeah	Despite exhausting times, participant kept her L2 learning routines

Table 11.3 Example of how formulated meanings were developed into theme-clusters and themes.

Formulated meanings	*Theme clusters*	*Themes*
Time spent with family was seen as unproductive because nothing useful was achieved (**Suzan Q27**)	Other life engagements were seen as barriers	
Engagement was not seen as extra effort, or forceful self-regulation, but rather a total immersion (**Louise Q3**)	Big or biggest agenda	**Effort as not effort**
Participant felt she was getting better at English just by watching TV and movies at her free times which was not perceived as that much of extra effort (**Suzan Q12**)	No need for self-regulation	
Learning L2 was seen as fun and not as tiring hard work (**Shokhan Q18**)	Studying as not homework	

they had to provide a new piece of information (not repeated information). Formulated meanings, that is, interpretive meanings, were developed for each statement, and then clusters of themes and finally independent themes were produced (see Table 11.3; for more detail on this approach, see Sanders, 2003).

This study utilized a number of strategies to achieve validity. First, participants were given the example of an overweight person going through a regimen for a while in pursuit of losing weight and, instead of being given too much detail on the theoretical components of DMCs, they were asked to describe how they experienced their long-term engagement and what their feelings were like throughout. In the process of data collection, they were mainly asked to *describe* and narrate their experiences. The semi-structured interviews also centred on the issue of *what* happened, rather than relying extensively on the participants' perceived reasons for their experiences.

Results

After analysing the interpretive formulated meanings developed from the raw significant statements in the data, the researcher produced a number of themes and theme clusters representing *what* was dominant in the data, based on the frequency of the formulated meanings; close attention was paid to covering all the areas of the data-set which were thought to be relevant or to contribute to the participants' affect. After combining similar theme clusters, six major themes and a number of related sub-themes were extracted. In doing so, rather than generating statements that explicitly described an emotion or affective state, attempts were made to develop themes that would best reflect the data and hence explain why the participants experienced the emotions they reported.

In the sections below describing these themes, emphasis (italics) has been added by the researcher, and quotations of the participants (which are reproduced verbatim and essentially uncorrected) are numbered (Suzan Q1 etc.) for ease of cross-referencing.

Theme 1: Unique experience

In response to the interview question asking them to describe their feelings during the DMC period, the participants mostly compared it to other times in order to demonstrate its uniqueness:

> **Interviewer**: How was your feeling inside?
> **Suzan**: Actually, when I remember these days, these days I thought that, even I *can't describe* it because I never felt that feeling again. (Suzan Q1)

This uniqueness was described in terms of a number of aspects, most dominantly productivity, intensity of engagement and positive affect. Ali, for example, whose intense motivational experience was triggered by a failed interview conducted in English, described his newly acquired capacity during his DMC as being unprecedented:

> I was feeling happy but also that I have an outstanding ability, honestly. This feeling of *outstanding capability* is something I can't really understand what it is. When I say outstanding, I mean it is *above your regular human ability*.... So I mean I was much better than any time before. (Ali Q1)

For Louise, studying Old Norse for three months (in preparation for a postgraduate degree involving that language) was comparable only to when she was preparing for a university entrance exam:

> I think it is one of my *most intense periods in my life in studying languages*. So I could only compare it with how I studied English when I was at the end of my school studies because I was going to take an entrance exam to the university. (Louise Q1)

Despite this comparison, it seemed that her motivation to learn Old Norse was not similar to that to study English, as she never thought she had displayed particularly high motivation toward English:

> Well, you know, I had different situations with my other languages, because I studied English for my whole life and I can't say if I was motivated, because I lived a large part of my life in English. (Louise Q2)

In addition to Old Norse and English, Louise had studied three other second languages, but she considered only her study of Old Norse to be a unique experience. Whereas 'other languages were just languages' (Louise Q3), her study of Old Norse was more than simply learning an L2:

> **Interviewer**: Now, does this mean that in that summer you made a transformation?
>
> **Louise**: Yes, absolutely so, but I think it was more *psychological than linguistic* because it was the better part of my life starting from that. And there was something personal to this as well, because my husband was doing a PhD here, and I was quite unhappy that he left. And I was still finishing my MA and I didn't know what to do next. So it was like *two goals achieved spontaneously*, so I was going to live with my important other and do something I really wanted to do. (Louise Q4)

As can be seen, one reason why Louise's DMC experience was unique was a combination of internal (studying what she wanted to study) and external (going to live with partner) motives associated with learning Old Norse. A similar case was Omed's passion for improving his English for his ideal career:

> **Omed**: It had occupied a *major part* of my life. I am actually a graduate of the Farsi department, but my English is much better. I don't really know much Farsi.... My passion for English was *so powerful* that I am now better in English than my own major.
>
> **Interviewer**: What do you mean by passion? Was it a hobby?
>
> **Omed**: No it was not a hobby. If you interpret the term passion, it means *a goal for which you make a lot of effort*. Hobby doesn't need any effort.... Mine was passion which requires effort and also changes your life. (Omed Q1)

Both the sense of doing what one wants to do (e.g. Louise) and passion for a life-changing career (e.g. Omed) might have had a major role in making their L2 experiences unique. However, as Louise stated (Q4), it seemed that this uniqueness was mainly perceived in psychological or *affective* terms rather than how they prioritized the L2 in their daily schedule. When asked about how important it was in comparison with other engagement, the L2 learning was not always the first priority (although two participants were full-time students studying in the L2 at the time). For Sahar, for example, despite being constantly on her mind even during 'lectures', the L2 learning would come after schoolwork and mainly when she had free time:

> **Interviewer**: Did you study it every day or...?
> **Sahar**: When time allowed I think, so it was like I go for free time as soon as like the *more important things* are out of the way then I could just have that time for myself and learn. (Sahar Q1)

Theme 2: L2 learning as lifestyle

None of the participants reported any strict schedules for their L2 learning, and only two of them took language courses to support their own learning. For all of them, learning seemed to be a personal and autonomous undertaking with minimum external regulation. As such, they engaged in their L2 learning the way they chose to and at times that suited them best.

Louise, for example, used flashcards as the main learning method and took them with her when going out:

> So I carried those small pieces of paper *everywhere* with words, because *I saw that vocabulary is very important* when you are trying to learn a language very quickly. And even when I was a party like with my friends or going somewhere, I was *just looking at those flashcards all the time.* (Louise Q5)

There were two main mechanisms used to accommodate the L2 learning. First, older routines were utilized and directed in the furtherance of the L2 learning:

> **Interviewer**: Was the learning done as homework or how was it?
> **Ali**: Actually, I was so into it that *I had changed my everything into English*, so not just as homework to get to it at home, no. I mean, on radio it was English, even *if it was songs*, I would put it on English songs. I would watch TV in English, when I had time, for example. I would watch documentaries.... At work, as I said, if I needed to search on a topic..., I would go to an English one, even though I knew it was taking me more time, and more effort, but I would do it *anyway.* (Ali Q 2)

As can be seen, Ali made a conscious change from Arabic into English in how he performed some of his daily activities, and whereas changing what he listened to on radio might have been easier, he also accepted the extra effort of reading materials in the L2. Additionally, he became more aware of resources available to him and incorporated new habits, some of which seemed unusual for him, such as befriending foreigners and (as a Muslim) visiting a church:

> Before that interview event [the failed job interview that led to his DMC], I was *hiding from those foreigners* and never wanted to speak with them.... So the first step was to get benefit from the resources available to me *which I didn't feel they existed before*.... So I approached him [Jerry, one of the foreign expats], and asked him if he could help me with my English and he agreed. He also told me that he was giving some lectures on learning English and I attended some of his classes. His lectures were not public and were given at a hall in a church.... He told me it was in a church and if this was OK with me, *and I agreed right away.* (Ali Q3)

Theme 3: Enjoyment/happiness

All seven participants remembered their DMC experiences as happy, exciting and enjoyable periods. Enjoyment was reported in the data at two different levels: task level and experience level. First, at the L2-task level, all the participants described enjoyment while engaged in the L2 learning tasks; however, whereas *flow* was reported by some participants, involvement was equally, or more so, due to a sense of learning, not merely interest in the task at hand itself:

> **Interviewer**: When you were in a session learning Japanese, what was your feeling?
>
> **Sahar**: I was quite happy I think and, I was *enjoying my time*, it was kind of a hobby and a pastime but at the *same time improving myself* so, it was, it was an interesting time for me yeah. (Sahar Q2)

For Omed, who used translation as a way of improving his L2 skills, a similar pattern was identified in which enjoyment would increase with a sense of learning new L2 skills:

> **Interviewer**: What was the quality of your time while learning?
>
> **Omed**: I would be obsessed and occupied with the material and was very enjoyable while translating, *especially when I was learning new words or new phrases*, for example, that was more enjoyable.... (Omed Q2)

Enjoyment from the L2 tasks was in part related to what the participants used as a method of learning. Omed chose *'pleasurable'* stories for translation, Louise used flashcards, Kardo used YouTube and novels, Ali listened to the radio while going to work, and Sahar, Shokhan and Suzan all made use of media for their learning. As none of them mentioned any strict or arduous studying structure, it seemed to them that learning was more about *'fun'* than a self-regulatory measure:

> **Suzan**: I am exercising on something particular, then I find myself *get more than what, I paid*, you understand what I am saying? Yeah, I

> [am] just *having fun watching TV and at the same time I am learning English*, so.
>
> **Interviewer**: When you say, 'I am getting more than I've paid', can you elaborate?
>
> **Suzan**: Yeah, because I watch TV, it is fun, *it is enjoyable, it is free time*, and at the same time, I am getting better in school, in English module, and also I am *having this satisfaction* of being superior than my brother…, because, because actually *studying is difficult*, but when it is done by for example by TV, watching movies, it is *fun and learning at the same time.* (Suzan Q2)

Despite this, the L2 activities were not always perceived as fun and pleasurable. All the participants were asked if they experienced feelings of boredom or lack of interest, and although negative affect did not emerge as a dominant theme, three of them did report exhaustion and sometimes boredom (see also the section below):

> **Interviewer**: So was it boring in any way?
>
> **Suzan**: No, actually, no I like spending time like that because it is *productive*, it's not I am using dictionary … so, if I learn it in the context, it is worth it, because I know how to use the word, it is not a meaning the main issue, I want to communicate in English. So even sometimes especially in, especially yeah at the beginning of the academic yeah it was *very exhausting* because you know, changing time changing school, it is, but I was yeah, I have *this routine* for actually yeah two years, almost two years yeah.
>
> **Interviewer**: Was it not, were you not tired that you had to stay up that late and have to go to school in the morning?
>
> **Suzan**: Actually sometimes I just *fall asleep* before the beginning of the movie but still waiting, but because *I just want to learn this conversation*, maybe I need it someday. I thought it is important, so yeah, it was exhausting (Suzan Q3)

As can be concluded from her account, Suzan did not feel bored, because engagement was perceived as productive and particularly useful for her L2 goal: improving communicative skills. Further, both developing regular learning routines and linking involvement to a future end goal ensured sustained engagement even at times when the going was tough, even exhausting.

At the experience level, the participants described the whole DMC experience as happy and positive:

> [T]his two years was from *the happiest days in whole my life* actually, I am, when I think about it, I think I relate it to *satisfaction because I am satisfied with what I am doing and succeeding in what I am doing*, whatever I

> try, it succeeds, I thought I was *lucky* at that period, then I am not lucky again [laughter], again when I try it again. But as I said the experience, yeah, it was very, very yeah, *enlightenment experience*, I was yeah. (Suzan Q4)

Being satisfied with what one was doing (learning an L2) was a dominant theme, but so was satisfaction with oneself. It seemed that contentment was not specific to the times when the participants were engaged in the L2 learning activities but extended to other times:

> At that period, I had a sort of happiness and even excitement as they say, but *it was not just because I was travelling to another country* to study, but it was the fact that *I had finally found the mechanism and way which would enable me to achieve one of my life's big dreams.* (Shokhan Q1)

Shokhan's intense L2 learning started when she realized she could travel to an English-speaking country for a master's degree, but her major goal was to improve her English skills. She had tried to improve her English earlier but she did not know how to do it or if making effort would be beneficial: 'Previously, even though I wanted to learn English, *I didn't know how* or *didn't believe that making an effort* on my own would be *useful*' (Shokhan Q2).

Enjoyment was not experienced only due to the sense that they were learning a valuable second language even though their experiences were triggered by this specific goal. Later in the process, all the participants felt happy because of other, far greater ambitions than merely learning an L2. In describing their enjoyment at both task and experience levels, they reported feelings not directly associated with improvement in their L2s:

> **Interviewer**: Would you wish to repeat that experience?
> **Louise**: Oh absolutely, because it *makes you happy*, you know. So you [are] really *productive*, but what I like about it is more *the process than the result. You feel everything has a meaning* when you are doing something. And when you are just simply working, you wonder what it is about and in such periods you have this question, you are just *burning* with that. And I really like this feeling. (Louise Q6)

Thus, at the task level, it was the process of learning and the positive emotions associated with being productive that provided Louise with these unique feelings. It was not simply learning a set of linguistic skills but a perception of meaning and personal productivity. Similarly, at the experience level, feelings of personal achievement and growth were mostly reported:

> I felt like, as if a door of *life's doors, a positive one*, has just been open to me, like, as I said before, it was like a big door, a *big barrier that I can't*

> *exceed*, so imagine, you're now getting better at a language which is a global language, it is a great feeling, I mean. (Ali Q4)

As a result, these individuals felt happy beyond the times of learning an L2, and their happiness was due to a sense of achievement beyond the fact that they were learning an L2:

> Honestly, I was listening to English podcasts five to eight hours a day. It looks a bit of *hyperbole*, but this is a reality. Beside this, I was reading interesting novels, articles surfing on YouTube watching *motivational and inspirational videos* made me on cloud nine and I was enjoying *every second of my life* that time. This is because it was a *transitional period* for me. It was about holding my hand and taking me to *another world*. Truthfully, I became a little *narcissist* because I was seeing a great *achievement* every day! Even, my grades boosted up from C and D, to A and A+! That was *crazy* to me! (Kardo Q1)

From his description, it is clear that in addition to spending time on materials in the L2, Kardo also watched '*motivational and inspirational videos*' which did not seem to be part of the linguistic aspects of the L2 learning, but perhaps one way of making sense of his unexpected, '*crazy*' transformation which seemed '*hyperbole*' to him.

As a consequence, experiencing this positive affect had a direct motivational empowerment: not only did they not feel bored or uninterested, but they used almost all their free time for learning and made the L2 learning a great agenda of their daily lives, as made clear from this excerpt:

> I would love to point out that listening to English podcasts, reading novels and articles, writing essays ... not only became a daily mundane, they became a *part of me, part of my life*, or, to be more precise, the *all things in my life*. That period, there was a day that I was reading *10 to 13* hour[s] whereas we were told from our instructors that the reading hour is seven hour[s] per week, which was thoroughly *meaningless* to me! (Kardo Q2)

The feeling that specifying a certain number of hours for learning is '*meaningless*' makes sense in light of the unique positive affect experienced throughout the DMC period, especially because these individuals no longer perceived their L2 engagement as studying; rather, learning the L2 was seen as being about oneself, one's endorsed goals, interests and values. Therefore, time spent on learning became more enjoyable than free time or even time spent with family:

> **Interviewer**: And how do you compare the time that you spent on watching the movie and other times...¿

Suzan: Actually as I said, it is *productive*, the time spent watching TV was productive, and also it is something *related to me*, because we're a large family so there is no something, there is no privacy as you like it, but when I turn on the TV, it is *my area*, my room yeah, so no one annoying me. (Suzan Q5)

Although enjoyment seemed to be the dominant affective state for all the participants while in their DMCs, the level of enjoyment was not unchanging throughout. All the participants referred to some instances of fluctuations in their emotionality. Throughout the data-set, two main factors were identified to have a direct influence on the participants' affective states: sense of progress and vision.

Progress

Progress seemed to be the most dominant factor in the data in generating feelings of either happiness or frustration. The participants reported increased feelings of happiness when they were making progress, either through their own sense of actual learning or through accomplishing tangible task-level goals.

Three of the participants felt that time spent with family was not as productive, and therefore they preferred studying. However, the underlying reason was that they saw other engagements as barriers to their progress in learning. As discussed above, Suzan preferred her L2 learning to spending time with family, but she also considered learning through movies to be of a higher quality and more effective than her English subject lesson at school, because she perceived that little learning was taking place.

On the other hand, not only did the participants feel happy when a sense of progress was perceived, but they also actively sought affirmative feedback signalling progress:

For example, once … this friend … said I can say you have *now learnt English*. I said why. He said you used a word in your speech, which is 'minority' …, he said, if this guy is able to use these kinds of vocabulary … he has almost learnt English. So when I would see these things *in the eye of people* around me on a daily basis, so these situations were very happy moments. They would make me *super happy*. (Ali Q5)

When the participants were asked to describe any negative feelings such as frustration or boredom, three of them did so, and the feeling of not making progress was the major reason for the participants' reported negative emotions. Sahar, for example, felt frustrated because she could not find enough time to invest in her L2 learning, and Suzan felt bored when the films she was watching did not contain much conversation, as she did not find them useful for her communicative improvement goal:

Interview: Did you ever feel bored while...?
Suzan: I feel bored only when it is *kids' movies* about dogs, and there is *no[t] much conversation.* (Suzan Q6)

Similarly, Louise reported negative emotions at two circumstances:

Interviewer: So does this mean in that period when you were doing this, was that the most enjoyable engagement kind of thing?
Louise: Depends on the engagement, because well *I really enjoyed going out with my friends*; I took *my flashcards with me*, so if we were sitting somewhere in the evening, *I'd be reading my flashcards*, but I still enjoyed talking to them. But when we had those you know *family meetings* or something and I'm usually at them anyway, and I was just *mad* at them, like they were *interrupting my studies*. And sometimes I was reading something secretly [laughter]. (Louise Q7)

As such, going out with friends was still enjoyable because it did not represent a barrier to Louise's L2 progress as she could continue reading her flashcards, whereas family gatherings were perceived as an obstacle to her learning. Secondly, she reported frustration when the difficulty level of the material increased, which was also seen as a major barrier to her progress:

Interviewer: Did you ever feel bored, frustrated?
Louise: Yeah, especially with *theoretical grammar* and all those paradigms I always feel I can't remember them, it was *too much information.* (Louise Q8)

Whereas a sense of making/not making progress produced either increased enjoyment or boredom, vision was seen to be working by only increasing positive affect and sometimes motivational tendency as a result.

Vision

Visualizing the moment of achieving L2 proficiency had powerful but varying effects on inducing and increasing enjoyment. Four participants reported moments of visualizing the time of achieving their goals, although they displayed disparities in terms of the exact envisioning and what they envisioned. Examples of clear and tangible visualization were provided by two participants:

Sometimes *I imagine that I'm at the University of Cambridge* ... I was imagining myself going abroad, studying, majoring in science but in English country. (Suzan Q7)

A second example was reported by Sahar:

> So, that is one thing I always thought oh one day someone will need my help, and I will help them in Japanese and speak it fluently, and *they will be surprised* that they found someone to help them. (Sahar Q3)

To her, visualizing these imaginative situations induced feelings of excitement:

> I would *get excited* thinking about meeting my favourite pop star and just asking them oh what is your favourite foods and things like that. (Sahar Q4)

These cases of visualization were also associated with experiencing positive affect in the imagined future: 'I imagined that *I would be very happy* once I mastered the language and can read an untranslated manga on my own' (Sahar Q5).

Not all participants, however, discussed using visualization. Two participants discussed experiencing vision without providing further details. Another participant talked about deliberately avoiding visualizing as an emotional-regulation trait: 'Well maybe it is just a psychological trait, just my own trait that I don't really like imagining the future because *I know it was going to be different anyway*' (Louise Q9).

Theme 4: Effort as not effort

As a result of pursuing L2 learning as part of one's newly modified lifestyle, learning was less seen as self-regulatory homework or a tedious daily task. The participants were asked to describe their regular engagement in their L2 learning tasks and how they perceived that engagement, and they all seemed to have engaged in their L2 tasks almost spontaneously, rather than seeing them as a chore:

> I did not feel that learning English and English vocabulary and speaking was something I needed *to sit down or and fall asleep on*. I mean, these days it was nice that I didn't look at study as *a tough task or homework*.... For example, when I was watching TV, it was not a difficult thing to do, and when I was reading, instead of reading it in Kurdish or Arabic, I would read it in English. (Shokhan Q3)

Being the owner of one's autonomous and customized method of learning was identified as another major factor in how the participants perceived effort. For Suzan, for example, studying English at school was boring but watching a TV show of her own choice at home was not:

> Actually I thought the time, I was watching a series, it was called Ally McBeal, she was a lawyer, I thought the time I spent watching Ally

> is *better than the time I spent at learning English at school*, because ... so boring, yeah, yeah *it is boring studying English in school.* (Suzan Q8)

On the other hand, seeing her L2 as something she would *'think about all the time'* made one participant perceive effort as not requiring self-regulation but nonetheless with the achievement *'great'* results in a short period of time: 'Well, to tell the truth, I was *not really pushing myself*. Well, *when you think about something all the time*, it is not really like I have to finish this text but I don't want to or I can't' (Louise Q10).

Theme 5: Sense of change

As discussed above, engagement along the process was no longer only about learning/improving a second language and the positive affect reported was more than short-lived excitement or joy at succeeding at a language learning task; indeed, a deeper look into the data-set suggested that positive affect was not even only about a future L2 goal, despite the fact that specific L2 future goals provided both framework and direction to the L2 learning behaviour. What seemed to underlie the participants' rather subdued happiness was a sense of change they witnessed in their perceptions and skills.

First, the participants expressed their acquired confidence with regard to learning the L2 as a result of improvement:

> It also created self-confidence in me that what appeared to be so difficult and challenging, I was about to achieve it *almost easily*. And it made me feel that this thing was *not impossible*. (Shokhan Q4)

Further, not only did they find a mechanism that helped them learn the L2, but they also reported changes in how they perceived effort as discussed earlier.

Second, the feeling of change was of a much wider scope than learning an L2. In almost all the cases, it seemed that seeing change in their L2 abilities led to change in other aspects of their lives:

> When people were talking about the need for *growth and development* I could see that development in myself. I could see that on a daily basis, especially when I was *using new vocabulary*, words that I even myself could not understand how I was able to use these words.... These cases would make me very happy, especially when I could talk to a foreigner in English, and reflect later and say, how could I make this happen.... So to be honest, this feeling of being capable made me *push even further*, to continue learning on a daily basis, and at the same time feel great about it. (Ali Q6)

As can be clearly seen, as a consequence of making outstanding progress in his L2 skills, Ali felt changes in his own abilities toward which he developed a sense of admiration. This in turn led him to be further motivated to continue his engagement but also, and perhaps more significantly, *'feel great about it'*. As such, positive affect due to skill development was utilized again in the service of pushing *'even harder'*.

Theme 6: Sense of being lucky

The participants described the DMC period as productive, as they achieved beyond their own expectations and often beyond merely acquiring language skills. Therefore, four of them felt they were lucky in that period:

> Actually as I said I can't even get the word *even in Arabic, it is something special*. I was very *lucky* to have this period of my life actually because it changed my life *in other ways*. (Suzan Q9)

As such, they felt proud of their achievement and saw themselves as success stories:

> And in the evenings, when we would gather with friends, I would talk about these situations, you know like a *hero* who's just come back from an adventure.... This was very nice because it would *encourage me again* towards more. I mean, in these gatherings, I would *lead the discussion* and talk about my achievement. (Ali Q7)

Sharing happiness seemed to be utilized as a motivational tool, as discussed by Ali. Similarly, Sahar and a group of classmates who studied Japanese together used to share their learning and become more encouraged to use the L2 when speaking to one another:

> **Interviewer**: Did you try to share this happiness with...?
> **Sahar**: Yeah definitely, like when you would learn a new word or figure out a sentence, we would just *tell each other* or sometimes *call each other and talk in Japanese.* (Sahar Q6)

Also, some of the participants were asked if they would like to go through the same experience or if they had tried to repeat it, and they all expressed a longing for that period. Whereas only one of them said she was partially successful in repeating the same experience in L2 learning, others felt a similar experience might not happen to them again:

> **Interviewer**: Have you tried to repeat that experience?
> **Ali**: *Tried too much*. I think if I can repeat this experience, that would be

> the advanced level and that would be very good. But as I said, I don't know, this is not exaggeration, *no exaggeration, that this feeling will not happen again.* (Ali Q8)

Discussion

All seven participants reported a considerable amount of positive emotionality, leading to a general description of DMCs as happy and enjoyable experiences. The prevalence of positive emotionality compared with very limited negative affect might also be interpreted in light of the participants' partial bias toward evaluating their overall L2 experiences in these specific periods. Since the data were collected long after the experiences had occurred, it is possible that the participants were at least partially under the effect of the *remembering self* (Kahneman, 2011), versus the *experiencing self*, which assumes that people's judgement of a particular experience is greatly influenced by how the peak or end of that event was experienced. With that limitation in mind, it is important to note that all the participants shared their strong and often explicit desire to go through the same experience again, and they narrated their stories with zealous enthusiasm and pride. In the current thinking of psychology, personal narratives are viewed as essential in the scientific study and understanding of human behaviour and motivation (McAdams, 2001). In the L2 acquisition field, they can also provide us with 'deep insights into learners' psychological thinking and can serve as a useful tool both for teachers and learners in bringing to the surface beliefs and agentic thinking which may be facilitative or hindering for learners' ongoing and future learning' (Mercer, 2013: 180).

The main goal of this research has been to not only understand positive affect within a DMC experience, but more ambitiously to investigate the mechanism by which positive emotionality may influence behaviour. Although emotions have long been thought to be 'processes which arouse, sustain, and direct activity' (Leeper, 1948: 17), the nature of the relationship between positive emotion and motivation has rarely been clearly made and the 'motivational properties of emotion have been severely underestimated in the language learning literature' (MacIntyre, 2002: 61). That state of affairs has not changed much recently, and so this study, then, is probably a first attempt to make that link.

Positive emotionality in DMCs

While the data clearly suggest the dominance of positive emotionality in the DMC cases reported, the exact mechanism by which DMCs make use of positive emotionality is far from being straightforward. As all the DMC cases studied here were triggered by specific (Latham & Locke, 1991) and self-concordant (Dörnyei *et al.*, 2016) goals, merely having an initial goal on its own accounted for little positive emotionality. However, for the duration of their DMCs and in order to maintain their elevated motivational levels, the individuals made use of a sophisticated combination of emotional resources.

One of these resources used by some of the participants was the utilization of *anticipatory* (current experience of an emotion because of an event in the future) and *anticipated* (imagined emotions in the future) emotions (Baumgartner *et al.*, 2008) in respect of the formation of possible future selves (Dörnyei, 2009; MacIntyre & Gregersen, 2012), evident from not only instances of envisioning sensory moments in the future (Dörnyei & Kubanyiova, 2014), but also imagining how proud and successful one would be upon the completion of the L2 goal.

Positive affect and motivation

Despite the fact that DMCs are not particularly frequent occurrences, they may nevertheless provide us with significant insight into how positive affect contributes to the motivational intensity of the DMC experience. First, even though keeping a vision alive and frequent use of envisioning the final goal seemed to be important in arousing certain positive emotions, such as excitement, which in some ways motivated them further, envisioning was not frequent or vivid for all the participants. However, all the participants described and focused more on enjoyment within the process of L2 learning versus being consciously goal-oriented at all times. As can be seen from the results, the participants mostly associated enjoyment and, more so, satisfaction with making tangible progress toward their goals. On the other hand, the only instances in the data-set where the participants reported experiencing negative emotions, such as frustration and boredom, were when their perception of progress was thwarted; thus, one can conclude that DMCs make use of mainly positive but also negative emotionality, and thus regulate the whole emotional entity to maintain engagement. This is consistent with other research findings that making progress in meaningful work not only activates the sense of accomplishment, but perhaps is also the most powerful stimulant to the major psychological processes – perception, emotion and motivation (Amabile & Kramer, 2011).

Sense of growth

Even though the participants experienced short-lived but repeated instances of positive emotions such as excitement whenever they made tangible progress, they all rated their experience and the whole life period as happy, unique and exceptionally enjoyable, not only because of learning a valuable second language, but predominantly due to experiencing a sense of *change*, which they interpreted as an indication of personal growth and improvement. They described these feelings explicitly but also through reporting feelings of satisfaction with not only what they were doing, but also in *themselves*, such as being what they wanted and having an image of themselves they liked. They reached these judgements mainly through a constant feeling of acquiring new personal value and meaning in relation to discovering one's potential, developing important life skills, and becoming a different, unique and better person.

The participants were not only concerned with learning a language, but through an initial L2 learning goal, they, later in the process, developed other personal agendas, such as expanding their potential, discovering and aiming for higher life opportunities and perhaps acquiring a new identity. As such, learning was not restricted to specific times; it was, rather, incorporated into the participants' lifestyles. In such circumstances, engagement in the L2 learning activities becomes more than just fun, providing 'a break from focused study' (Tomlinson & Masuhara, 2009: 646), or even an authentic undertaking (Henry, 2013); it constantly dominates one's emotional, motivational and cognitive attention. Therefore, rather than being seen as taking an extra spot in one's schedule which one *needs* to do and then feels bored or loses interest, one actively looks forward to the learning times and, most importantly, one's perception of effort changes to seeing learning as not homework (Waterman, 2005).

Thus, the source of enjoyment and positive emotionality in DMCs in considerable part seems to come in the form of *eudaemonic happiness* (Ryan & Deci, 2001), which, unlike hedonistic happiness and worldly pleasure, is concerned with feelings of self-actualization, developing potential and finding meaning in life (Waterman, 1993). Eudaemonia seems to explain well the participants' mostly indescribable, unique and unprecedented happiness and well-being. It also helps in understanding how positive affect worked almost implicitly to generate deep happiness when the participants felt they were developing valuable life skills, and in explaining their constant desire for L2 engagement.

This happiness originated from progress, and increased every time progress was made and growth perceived. Therefore, DMCs may not be distinguished by frequent short-lived emotions of excitement and joy, but by a prolonged good mood and an almost constant, subdued sense of happiness, contentment, pride and interest. This collection of positive emotions all function together, according to Fredrickson's broaden-and-build theory, to 'broaden people's momentary thought-action repertoires, which in turn serves to build their enduring personal resources, ranging from physical and intellectual resources to social and psychological resources' (Fredrickson, 2001: 218).

The notion of 'broadening and building' personal resources seems to partially account for the mechanism by which DMCs make use of positive affect to produce their powerful motivational stamina. Fredrickson (2001) proposes that certain positive emotions broaden one's thought-action repertoire. Among these emotions, *interest* produces the urge to explore and develop the self; *contentment* generates the urge to savour life events and incorporate them into new self and world views; and *pride* urges people to share their achievements. The occurrence of these emotions and their resulting tendencies in the data, such as the constant tendency to develop one's potential, having newly acquired perspectives on the self, L2 and life, and a strong desire to share personal achievements seem to indicate the 'durable' impact of positive emotions on long-term engagement in DMC experiences. Therefore, positive emotions 'are not merely the absence of negative emotions; they have a place of their own' in L2 learning (MacIntyre & Gregersen, 2012: 208).

While outstanding stamina for L2 engagement can be considered as the broadening power of *physical* resources, the tendency to remain involved in a task despite its challenges is an example of expanding psychological resources to fight negative emotions such as boredom, lack of interest and anxiety. DMCs can thus be an effective framework through which L2 engagement and feeling happy about it becomes the norm, reflecting the human tendency toward optimal psychological functioning (Ryan & Deci, 2001). The same tendency also implies that while caught in a DMC, an individual no longer requires constant self-regulatory strategies to sustain engagement. In DMCs, learning becomes part of one's daily routines, automatized habits or even the most preferred involvement that one will engage in, with little conscious self-regulation. In other words, once a DMC goal or sub-goal is perceived as emotionally rewarding, one would engage in goal-directed behaviour unconsciously by simply activating a stimulant signalling such positive affect (Papies & Aarts, 2010; see Al-Hoorie, 2015, for a review). As such, among the three major components of the DMC construct – self-concordant goal, salient structure and positive emotional loading – the last might be the most crucial in generating the DMC's intense and unique motivational properties.

Conclusion

The individuals who experienced DMCs in this study reported enjoyment for a variety of reasons, including *vision*, a reactional feeling of excitement and joy because of positive feedback signalling progress, and sometimes *flow*. However, what accounted for most of the positive affect and a subdued sense of happiness was not the pleasure of engagement itself or feelings associated with merely learning a second language. Rather, happiness was felt to be due to the sense that one was going through a transformational process in which one's image and identity, level of operation and skills, and one's entire personal entity were being developed. This somewhat indirect link between personal growth and happiness through L2 learning is a new, promising, but challenging area of research. Further studies of positive emotionality in DMCs are needed to unveil the potential of DMCs in generating not only positive affect but also a less arduous path for L2 acquisition.

References

Al-Hoorie, A.H. (2015) Human agency: Does the beach ball have free will? In Z. Dörnyei, P.D. MacIntyre and A. Henry (eds) *Motivational Dynamics in Language Learning* (pp. 55–72). Bristol: Multilingual Matters.

Amabile, T. and Kramer, S. (2011) *The Progress Principle*. Boston, MA: Harvard Business Review.

Baumgartner, H., Pieters, R. and Bagozzi, R. (2008) Future-oriented emotions: Conceptualization and behavioral effect. *European Journal of Social Psychology* 38 (4), 685–696.

Colaizzi, P.F. (1978) Psychological research as the phenomenologist views it. In R.S. Valle and M. King (eds) *Existential-Phenomenological Alternatives for Psychology* (pp. 48–71). Oxford: Oxford University Press.

Creswell, J.W. (2007) *Qualitative Inquiry and Research Design: Choosing Among Five Approaches* (2nd edition). Thousand Oaks, CA: Sage.

Csíkszentmihályi, M. (1988) Introduction. In M. Csikszentmihalyi and I.S. Csikszentmihalyi (eds) *Optimal Experience: Psychological Studies of Flow in Consciousness* (pp. 3–14). Cambridge: Cambridge University Press

Dörnyei, Z. (2009) The L2 motivational self system. In Z. Dornyei and E. Ushioda (eds) *Motivation, Language Identity and the L2 Self* (pp. 9–42). Bristol: Multilingual Matters.

Dörnyei, Z. and Kubanyiova, M. (2014) *Motivating Learners, Motivating Teachers: Building Vision in the Language Classroom*. Cambridge: Cambridge University Press.

Dörnyei, Z., Muir, C. and Ibrahim, Z. (2014) 'Directed motivational current': Energising language learning through creating intense motivational pathways. In D. Lasagabaster, A. Doiz and J.M. Sierra (eds) *Motivation and Foreign Language Learning: From Theory to Practice* (pp. 9–29). Amsterdam: John Benjamins.

Dörnyei, Z., Ibrahim, Z. and Muir, C. (2015) 'Directed motivational currents': Regulating complex dynamic systems through motivational surges. In Z. Dörnyei, P. MacIntyre and A. Henry (eds) *Motivational Dynamics in Language Learning* (pp. 95–105). Bristol: Multilingual Matters.

Dörnyei, Z., Henry, A. and Muir, C. (2016) *Motivational Currents in Language Learning: Frameworks for Focused Interventions*. New York: Routledge.

Finlay, L. (2011) *Phenomenology for Therapists: Researching the Lived World*. Chichester: Wiley-Blackwell.

Fredrickson, B.L. (2001) The role of positive emotions in positive psychology: The broaden-and-build theory of positive emotions. *American Psychologist* 56 (3), 218–226.

Henry, A. (2013) Digital games and ELT: Bridging the authenticity gap. In E. Ushioda (ed.) *International Perspectives on Motivation: Language Learning and Professional Challenges* (pp. 133–155). Houndmills: Palgrave Macmillan.

Kahneman, D. (2011) *Thinking, Fast and Slow*. London: Penguin.

Latham, G.P. and Locke, E.A. (1991) Self-regulation through goal setting. *Organizational Behavior and Human Decision Processes* 50 (2), 212–247.

Leeper, R.W. (1948) A motivational theory of emotion to replace 'emotion as disorganized response'. *Psychological Review* 55 (1), 5–21.

MacIntyre, P.D. (2002) Motivation, anxiety and emotion in second language acquisition.

In P. Robinson (ed.) *Individual Differences and Instructed Language Learning* (pp. 45–68). Amsterdam: John Benjamins.

MacIntyre, P. and Gregersen, T. (2012) Emotions that facilitate language learning: The positive-broadening power of the imagination. *Studies in Second Language Learning and Teaching* 2, 193–213.

McAdams, D.P. (2001) The psychology of life stories. *Review of General Psychology* 5 (2), 100–122.

Mercer, S. (2013) Working with language learner histories from three perspectives: Teachers, learners and researchers. *Studies in Second Language Learning and Teaching* 3 (2), 161–185.

Moustakas, C. (1994) *Phenomenological Research Methods*. Thousand Oaks, CA: Sage.

Muir, C. and Dörnyei, Z. (2013) Directed motivational currents: Using vision to create effective motivational pathways. *Studies in Second Language Learning and Teaching* 3 (3), 357–375.

Papies, E.K. and Aarts, H. (2010) Nonconscious self-regulation or the automatic pilot of human behavior. In K.D. Vohs and R.F. Baumeister (eds) *Handbook of Self-regulation: Research, Theory, and Applications* (pp. 125–142). New York: Guilford Press.

Ryan, R.M. and Deci, E.L. (2001) On happiness and human potentials: A review of research on hedonic and eudaimonic well-being. *Annual Review of Psychology* 52 (1), 141–166.

Sanders, C. (2003) Application of Colaizzi's method: Interpretation of an auditable decision trail by a novice researcher. *Contemporary Nurse* 14 (3), 292–302.

Sheldon, K.M. and Elliot, A.J. (1999) Goal striving, need satisfaction, and longitudinal well-being: the self-concordance model. *Journal of Personality and Social Psychology* 76 (3), 482–497.

Smith, J.A., Flowers, P. and Larkin, M. (2009) *Interpretive Phenomenological Analysis: Theory, Method and Research*. London: Sage.

Tomlinson, B. and Masuhara, H. (2009) Playing to learn: A review of physical games in second language acquisition. *Simulation and Gaming* 40 (5), 645–668.

Waterman, A.S. (1993) Two conceptions of happiness: Contrasts of personal expressiveness (eudaimonia) and hedonic enjoyment. *Journal of Personality and Social Psychology* 64 (4), 678–691.

Waterman, A.S. (2005) When effort is enjoyed: Two studies of intrinsic motivation for personally salient activities. *Motivation and Emotion* 29 (3), 165–188.

Waterman, A.S., Schwartz, S.J., Zamboanga, B.L., Ravert, R.D., Williams, M.K., Bede Agocha, Kim, S.Y. and Donnellan, M.B. (2010) The Questionnaire for Eudaimonic Well-Being: Psychometric properties, demographic comparisons, and evidence of validity. *Journal of Positive Psychology* 5 (1), 41–61.

12 Project Perseverance: Helping Students Become Self-Regulating Learners

R. Kirk Belnap, Jennifer Bown, Dan P. Dewey, Linnea P. Belnap and Patrick R. Steffen

Perseverance appears to be a key factor in determining long-term success (Duckworth *et al.*, 2007, 2010). Language students who persevere succeed because they refuse to give up. They possess or develop positive psychological traits such as self-efficacy, intrinsic motivation and positive emotion regulation, which empower them to work through difficulties and frustration (Dörnyei, 2009; Ehrman & Dörnyei, 1998; Gregersen & MacIntyre, 2014; Hart & Sasso, 2011; Seligman & Csikszentmihalyi, 2000; Seligman *et al.*, 2006). Attaining higher levels of proficiency in a second language, especially a language not cognate with one's own, is a significant long-term undertaking. Project Perseverance (ProjP) began as an effort to help students maximize their engagement during study abroad by focusing on the development of their self-regulatory skills. In this chapter, we describe the key interventions employed by the ProjP team, including coaching, group processing sessions, journaling and peer role models, as well as students' perception of their effectiveness. We also report on their overall satisfaction with their speaking experiences and how this relates to their proficiency gains. This chapter considers the experiences of 52 English-speaking students of Arabic, who participated in an intensive Arabic semester abroad in the autumn of 2011. It does not present a formal program evaluation; rather, it represents one in a series of mixed-method studies to better understand the learners' experiences. The primary data sources reported on in this chapter is a program exit survey, daily student ratings of their speaking satisfaction and standardized measures of language proficiency. We conclude the chapter with two illustrative case studies to provide a more holistic view of the student experience.

In order to lessen the effects of culture shock and other psychological forms of distress, a number of researchers (e.g. Brislin & Yoshida, 1994;

Trentman, 2012; Vande Berg *et al.*, 2009) have documented the value of training and other interventions to help learners make more of their study abroad experience. For example, Trentman (2012: 353) concluded that 'sustained, program-facilitated access [to level-appropriate opportunities to use the target language] is a crucial program contribution to the study abroad experience particularly for short-term programs'. Even an optimal program is, of course, no guarantee of student success. Ultimately, students are responsible for choosing to engage and remain engaged, but programs can do much to help students learn to manage their affective responses, as well as cope with the cultural differences they encounter (Bennet, 2008; Pusch & Merrill, 2008).

Why one student chooses to persevere and another does not is a complex issue. Perseverance, as Oxford notes in Chapter 2 of the present volume, has rarely been studied in connection with second language learning. She includes it as one of the eight dimensions of her 'EMPATHIC' vision for a psychology of language learning. However, it does feature in positive psychology work. For example, it is also repeatedly mentioned as a core virtue in Seligman and Csikszentmihalyi (2000) and is included as one of the 24 character strengths in Peterson and Seligman (2004). In his overview of 20 years of self-efficacy research, Pajares (1997) cites a number of studies indicating that perseverance increases as students grow in self-efficacy. More recently, research has looked at 'grit' as consisting of 'perseverance of effort and consistency of interests over time' (Von Cullin *et al.*, 2014: 306).

We have been running and reviewing intensive study abroad programs since 1989 (Belnap & Abuamsha, 2015). Years of observation and interviewing students have led us to believe that perseverance is a key to making the most of study abroad. The experience can engender a significant amount of stress, 'involving both confrontation and adaptation to unfamiliar physical and psychological experiences and changes' (Cushner & Karim, 2004: 292). Most students go abroad with the hope of making new friends, but limited linguistic and cultural proficiency often hinder them from forming meaningful relationships with locals (Dewey *et al.*, 2013). Far too many turn away from the host culture and instead spend more time strengthening ties with co-nationals than they planned (Citron, 2002; Pitts, 2009).

Pellegrino Aveni's (2005) study of a group of Americans studying in Russia provides a telling account of the difficulties as well as possibilities. In spite of previous study of the language, most began with neither the culture or language skills to feel confident – and they may also have been feeling the effects of jet lag. Many had experiences with their host family or other interlocutors that made them feel stupid. Worse yet, they began to compare themselves to other students whom they perceived to be much more proficient. Summarizing the work of Pozo *et al.* (1991) and others, Pellegrino Aveni observed: 'Negative expectations and perceived negative reactions of others have been shown to create cycles of poor performance and withdrawal, thus perpetuating a sense of failure and inadequacy' (2005: 70). These intense negative emotions often challenge one's identity. Not surprisingly, some students, who only weeks before had looked forward to immersing themselves in the culture, were instead seeking to avoid the opportunities for practice that they needed in order to build their skills and their confidence.

The study abroad literature indicates that pre-departure orientation and training can help to ease the transition and thus improve learning outcomes (Citron, 2002; Kruse & Brubaker, 2007; Ryan & Twibell, 2000; Vande Berg *et al.*, 2009). Students who begin their study abroad experience with realistic expectations and awareness of the challenges they will likely encounter are believed to be in a much better position to persevere and thus subsequently thrive.

Project Perseverance: An Overview

Each individual brings a unique history to what would appear to be the same learning task or environment. In the end, learning is the result of what an individual thinks and does. In his chapter on 'the dynamic interplay of learner characteristics and the learning environment', Dörnyei (2009: 183) observed that 'we need to shift our focus ... to the learner's self-regulating capacity, that is, the extent of the learner's proactiveness'. In response to this call as well as student priorities and needs identified through research conducted largely between 2002 and 2008, the National Middle East Language Resource Center (NMELRC) launched ProjP[1] in 2010 with the aim of empowering students to become effective self-regulating language learners, particularly in intensive in-country study settings. The ProjP website (http://nmelrc.org/Pathways) provides students with online training materials in the form of video of training sessions, biofeedback resources, summaries of relevant research and learner success stories.

ProjP builds on the results of a detailed NMELRC survey of 1055 students that indicated that most students of Arabic in the US are studying it in order to acquire 'professional level proficiency' (Belnap & Nassif, 2011: 5). The survey report (Belnap & Nassif, 2011) confirms that student proficiency gains in Arabic vary considerably. Even allowing for individual learner differences, NMELRC has found that student engagement during study abroad and thus their linguistic progress leaves much room for improvement. NMELRC partners have worked to address the need for higher-quality learning experiences through sharing research results with program administrators and teachers in conferences and workshops in the US and abroad, and in publications such as Al-Batal and Belnap (2006) and on its website (http://nmelrc.org/making-most-study-abroad).

Two recent studies in particular have looked at anxiety as a significant impediment to students making the most of their in-country experience (Hunley, 2008; Pellegrino Aveni, 2005). Largely as a result of how well Pellegrino Aveni's findings matched our own experience, we decided to stress the development of mindfulness in our project. Mindfulness training prior to or during study abroad is now increasing (Pryor *et al.*, 2014). However, to the best of our knowledge, ProjP is the only concerted effort to do so within the language teaching field. Mindfulness is a technique that pre-dates the positive psychology movement and is now frequently used in conjunction with positive psychology approaches. The use of mindfulness as part of a series of psychological interventions began to be relatively commonplace with the work of Jon Kabat-Zinn (2003) and his mindfulness-based stress reduction (MBSR) programs used in medical settings and the creation of mindfulness-based cognitive therapy (MBCT). MBSR and MBCT help participants learn to tolerate distress and develop effective stress coping skills, both of which are important in helping students learn to persevere. Garland and Fredrickson (2013) note that psychotherapies such as MBCT help to moderate emotion and increase ability to pay attention to things that are useful for them. For example, in a controlled experimental study, Ramsburg and Youmans (2013) found that students who engaged in mindfulness meditation for 15 minutes prior to an academic lecture, compared with a control group who merely sat quietly for 15 minutes, scored significantly higher on a quiz about the material at the end of the lecture.

Becoming aware of negative emotions and dealing with them before they become crippling is critical. Early work in positive psychology had not much good to say about negative emotions, as Oxford notes in Chapter 2, but she concludes that 'there is potentially a bright side to negative emotions' (p. 15); for example, they can serve as a wake-up call that something needs to change. Developing mindfulness skills helps students to draw on positive strengths while accepting that language learning can be difficult and frustrating at times. Negative emotions can be viewed as information about how things are going.

Awareness and acceptance of their current state guide students in their self-regulation efforts and help them to balance the positive and the negative. Oettingen *et al.* (2013) conclude that fantasizing about exclusively happy outcomes saps energy and can make people feel worse in the long term. They suggest that it is better to engage in 'mental contrasting', which entails visualizing one's goal, then evaluating current realities that stand in the way of achieving it and how to move forward. The value of cognitive dissonance is widely heralded in educational psychology as a critical stimulus that motivates learners to consider new options (Adcock, 2012) and is likewise acknowledged as a key component that sets the stage for transformational learning in study abroad contexts (Brockington & Wiedenhoeft, 2009).

The Study Abroad Program

Fifty-two students (20 females and 32 males) participated in a 16-week intensive Arabic program hosted at a private language institute in Amman, Jordan, in the autumn of 2011. All had completed at least four semesters (16 credit hours) of rigorous study prior to departure (for details on the ProjP program and its place in the curriculum, see Belnap & Abuamsha, 2015). Students were accompanied by two full-time faculty from their home university, as well as three teaching assistants (TAs), whose primary purpose was to provide support to the participants. The TAs also helped to document the students' experience as part of ProjP.

The students' typical five-day-a-week routine consisted of two hours of classes in the morning, led by Jordanian teachers. A one-hour current events course focused on issues regularly covered by local newspapers and a one-hour Jordanian Arabic class consisted largely of student presentations and discussion of the topic of the day. A typical class consisted of about 10 students with similar linguistic proficiency. Students also spent two hours a day reading newspaper articles assigned by the faculty. They received vocabulary lists and detailed instructions on which articles to read intensively (for total comprehension) and which to read extensively (either searching for a specific piece of information or to get the gist of a text or individual paragraphs). In the afternoon, students all met together for an hour, during which one of the faculty members from the home institution typically addressed linguistic and some cultural details from the readings and administered regular quizzes. The faculty members and TAs used part of this time to provide strategy and other training that helped students to understand and acquire aspects of the language and culture. This often included 5–10 minutes and occasionally more of ProjP-related training.

Students were required to spend two hours a day (five days a week) speaking Arabic with native speakers. They also met with Jordanian tutors to go over the week's writing assignment; another 30-minute appointment was devoted to speaking. All of the students were invited to sit in on a political science class at the University of Jordan, but only a handful persisted in attending every week. Most took advantage of the opportunity to be on campus, which was a good place to meet and talk with peers. They lived in apartments near the institute with other program participants or a spouse.

Students' oral proficiency was measured with the official Oral Proficiency Interview (OPI) immediately prior to or during their first two weeks and then again during their last two weeks in Jordan. Reading and listening proficiency gains were similarly assessed using NMELRC online tests, which have been developed in cooperation with the American Council on the Teaching of Foreign Languages (ACTFL).

Preparation class and follow-up training

Prior to traveling to Jordan, students were required to take a seven-week preparation course, meeting weekly for approximately 90 minutes. Topics included an overview of the program, Jordanian culture and history, challenges that the students would likely encounter, and strategies for making the most of their time in country, including the importance of cultivating mindfulness. In Jordan, the program directors and TAs, who had been students on the program previously and therefore served as role models, continued to provide training in class, in periodic email messages and in weekly interviews (mandatory during the first half of the program, optional thereafter).

Journaling and reporting

Students were required to report online five days a week about their speaking and reading experiences. Students were asked to provide information on: how much time they spent finding people to talk with; how well they were able to understand; and their overall satisfaction with their speaking experiences (the latter two rated using a seven-point Likert scale). In addition, students were required to write a weekly journal entry; guidelines encouraged them to reflect on their speaking experiences that week and plan for the coming week. Suggestions to help them reflect included: 'What did you do that went well?' 'What things did I do to encourage speaking, and what things did I do to shut off opportunities that may have presented themselves?' 'What did I do to encourage getting beyond pleasantries?' 'Did I find ways to separate from my American colleagues and have one-on-one conversations with Jordanians?' This journaling and reporting encouraged students to become more mindful of what they do when speaking Arabic and to evaluate and make specific plans as to how they could improve.

Group processing sessions

As a result of a site visit to the program the previous year, Madeline Ehrman (1996; Ehrman & Dörnyei, 1998), a member of the ProjP team and clinical psychologist by training who founded the Foreign Service Institute School of Language Studies' Learning Consultation Service (Ehrman, 2001), recommended a weekly group processing session with the goal of helping students deal with unrealistic expectations, culture shock and other sources of stress. This session was held for 20–30 minutes toward the end of each school week. It often began with the program directors offering insights from their own experiences or from students who had previously participated in a study abroad program, in order to provide encouragement to students and to help them be more mindful and stay motivated to persevere through their challenges. Students were given time to share their own challenges with the class, volunteer suggestions and celebrate successes. This open group discussion was intended to help students feel that they were not alone in facing their challenges, as well as to encourage them to reflect on and re-evaluate their goals and expectations for their study abroad experience. These sessions, along with reporting, journal entries and interviews, helped the program directors and TAs respond to student needs. For example, journal entries and interviews helped program directors realize that learners had difficulty finding speaking partners, and that their interactions were often limited to pleasantries. As a result, ProjP arranged for students to meet with trained speaking partners in order to enhance the learners' access to quality input and opportunities for pushed output.

Skill-building training

Each week during the afternoon class, one or more TAs provided training on building a specific skill. A TA would prepare a presentation on a potentially useful skill, often one assessed in the OPI, such as describing future plans or narration of a past event. The students would often practice this skill or strategy in their Jordanian Arabic class. For example, one of the first strategies taught was the acronym FORTE, which stands for Family, Occupation, Recreation, Travel and Education. Students were encouraged to remember this acronym so that they could think of topics to discuss when introducing themselves.

Data collection and analysis

The purpose of this chapter is to report on participants' perceptions of the effectiveness of the various interventions that comprise ProjP, as well as the relationship between their daily speaking satisfaction reports and their OPI gains. The ProjP team followed established standards of research ethics, including maintaining the confidentiality of the students who participated in the study by using pseudonyms and securely storing the data.

An anonymous exit survey administered during the students' last week in Jordan asked them to rate ProjP interventions on a seven-point Likert scale, from 'very ineffective' (scored 1) to 'very effective' (scored 7). The survey also invited students to provide open-ended answers regarding the effectiveness of the program interventions that they had just rated, as well as to make suggestions as to how to improve the program. Almost all (47 of the 52 students who took the survey) commented in the open-ended section on the interventions, but not at length, given that only one text box was provided for comment on any of 10 response items. The research team calculated the average and standard deviation for each item. Quotes provided below are given to illustrate the range of student perspectives. We chose both positive and negative comments for each intervention in order to convey the considerable differences in individual students' feelings about these interventions. There were too few comments for each intervention for any to be deemed representative of the majority. They merely provide some context for the ratings.

Findings: Student Perceptions of the Effectiveness of ProjP Interventions

Every intervention was rated at least 'somewhat effective' by a majority of the students in the exit survey, with 25 of the 52 students rating all eight of the interventions at least 'somewhat effective'. The average of the responses for each intervention ranged from well above 6 to almost 4 ('neither effective nor ineffective') on the seven-point scale, as can be seen in Table 12.1. In this section, we report on the students' perspectives on the various interventions and illustrate with quotes from their open-ended responses.

Encouragement from language teachers

The most positively rated survey item was 'encouraging words from language teachers'. As Student 50[2] observed:

> I think the most important thing which helped me really progress in my language learning is the constant encouragement and confidence given to me by my teachers. A positive, encouraging environment is invaluable.

Table 12.1 Results of the exit survey ($n = 52$)

	Average	*Standard deviation*
Encouragement from language teachers	6.44	0.83
Daily coaching from faculty/staff	6.02	1.04
Interviews with faculty/staff	5.27	1.51
Interviews with TAs in Jordan	4.77	1.44
Group processing sessions	4.71	1.46
Pre-departure orientation class	4.62	1.61
Emails of encouragement	4.21	1.87
Submitting regular journal entries	4.10	1.72

Student 42 also commented:

> the most effective thing as far as motivating me to keep going was hearing positive feedback from teachers. It always gives such a boost of confidence to hear the people who have been teaching me and working with me one on one confirm that I am improving.

Social or verbal persuasion may significantly enhance learner self-efficacy (Mills, 2014); the high rating given to this particular intervention and this data extract suggests it could have helped to enhance students' sense of self-efficacy and, therefore, their ability to persevere. Bandura (1997: 104–105) stressed that for such persuasion to be effective, the source must be deemed credible. Atticus, one of the program's best speakers and later a ProjP research assistant, shared an experience by email during the analysis of the exit survey data in which he reported on his experience with a TA and verbal persuasion and how it gave him added motivation:

> However, I do remember an experience in an interview with [TA2] that was insightful. He started talking to me about the OPI and what I expected to get. The OPI didn't really mean much to me because I wasn't planning to use it in applying for a job or anything. Also, I really didn't think that I was that good at Arabic, but when I told [TA2] that I thought Advanced Low was probably what I was pushing for he told me that he thought I could get Advanced High or Superior. Now, I got Advanced Mid but his belief in me and encouragement really took me back and then motivated me to keep trying because he obviously thought I was succeeding. Or in other words he was perceiving my success as greater than what I saw it as which, coming from a leader like [TA2], was very encouraging to keep going. (3 April 2013)

Daily coaching from faculty/staff

The second highest rated item was 'daily coaching' in the afternoon classes from TAs and/or faculty. This coaching included encouraging the students to recognize the progress they had made. It also contributed to greater mindfulness. As Student 16 wrote, it 'kept people aware of what they were going through', helping them keep 'track of how [they are] feeling and what is and is not effective'.

Well designed programs seek both to provide a safe and encouraging environment and to challenge students appropriately so that they are able to feel a sense of accomplishment as they add one relevant skill to another (Gregersen & MacIntyre, 2014; Mills, 2014). Graham (2007) also indicates that strategy training can boost student self-efficacy. In their speaking journals, many of the students mentioned that they appreciated the regular skills training they received in the afternoon class, especially FORTE. The main benefit appeared to be that these strategies helped them to be better prepared to converse with locals. For example, Marshal reported that using FORTE was helpful for him because he often felt that that he did not know what to talk about when he met new speaking partners. FORTE allowed him to feel confident about introducing himself to random strangers, because he had a plan for what to say.

Interviews with faculty/staff and with TAs in Jordan

Students also rated the weekly interviews as one of the more beneficial ProjP interventions, especially those with the faculty. This was confirmed at least in part by the responses of seven students who explained in their open-ended responses that the interviews helped them discover how to make the most of their strengths and overcome the challenges they faced. Student 18's full response to the invitation to comment on the program intervention was:

> I thought that it was all very beneficial, especially the interviews while in Jordan. Getting any frustrations out and acknowledging them really helped me to knock down any emotional barriers.

Additionally, Student 20 reported that interviews with faculty 'were the best tools to motivate me to perform my best'.' Student 34 noted: 'I really enjoyed the weekly interviews.... I think they were really effective, especially as a way to vent frustration.'

Some students found the interviews less useful. For example, Student 21, who reported having an 'independent personality', felt that the interviews 'got old'. Two students complained about their interview experiences because they felt that the TAs did not provide advice they needed, perhaps because the TAs were trained in reflective listening and were thus explicitly instructed to refrain from offering advice. This practice was followed in order to encourage students to come to their own conclusions and increase their metacognition and self-regulation ability. However, it seems that at least some students were unaware of the purpose of the interviews.

TAs are selected with an eye to their serving as near-peer role models who provide the kind of vicarious experiences that can lead to increased self-efficacy (Mills, 2014). Though not all students responded positively to the formal interviews (especially with TAs), informal interaction with the TAs was appreciated. As Atticus reported:

> From my personal experience with other students: I never heard anyone really complain and I know for some they looked forward to the opportunity to sit down with the TAs. For me, the formal interviews were a little awkward although I didn't mind them. I will say that ... just talking with [TA1] on the bus ... I think was really beneficial to me because he would share his experiences and his general positive attitude would rub off on me. (3 April 2013)

Group processing sessions

Most students found the weekly group processing session to be at least somewhat effective; the average for this intervention was 4.71. Only one person, Student 45, gave this intervention the highest possible rating, adding that the experience 'always cheered me up and taught me that other people struggle with Arabic too'. Student 43 realized 'after a Thursday pep session' that his/her expectations were unrealistic, causing feelings of discouragement. He/she was then able to step back and re-evaluate, enabling him/her to stay positive and appreciate progress. Student 32 observed:

> I felt that many of the activities that required me to reflect on my learning process and progress (TA/leader interviews, Thursday discussion, etc.) were very effective in pushing me and keeping my spirits high.

Of the 12 students who disliked the group processing sessions, Student 9 reported that hearing about others' experiences led to discouraging comparisons, and Student 10 felt that the sessions were not as effective as they could have been because some of the same people spoke every week about the same things. Student 33 said:

> I also question a little bit the timing ... so many people are so tired at the end of the day that they just want to go home and think it might be better to have the sessions on a different day than the last day of the week when people may be more focused and more willing to participate.

Pre-departure orientation class

Survey responses indicate that the preparation class worked well for some but not for others, as is evident from its average of 4.62. Only three students gave it the highest possible rating. Another, who rated it a point lower, commented:

> I did my best to pay attention in the prep class, so I felt like I got exactly what I expected from the program. [The program directors] did a great job of telling us all the little things which might make us uncomfortable.

For those who found the preparation class ineffective, five complained that it did not provide sufficient program detail, such as packing lists and more on Jordanian culture. Four students, including one who gave the class the highest possible rating, were put off by the experiences shared by two former students, who, as Student 10 observed, 'gave poor responses and were unable to leave us with any faith in the program or in the Middle East as a whole'.

Emails of encouragement

One of the program directors regularly wrote email messages to the students as a group. These consisted of insights from past experience and research and excerpts from student reports or email messages. These messages were often long and for some students repetitive. This item had the largest standard deviation of any item. Student 8 wrote:

> emails were always a long read, and I ended up skimming them at best. It is comforting to know that he cares and I appreciate all … he does for us. With that said, I never complained about the length and frequency…. They weren't necessarily important for me, so I would set them aside. But I do know that they acted to help a lot of people here.

Weekly journaling

'Submitting regular journals entries' received the lowest rating of all interventions (4.1) and had a high standard deviation (1.72). Students who found journaling beneficial reported that they appreciated the opportunity to reflect on their progress, both linguistically and emotionally. Student 41 compared it to 'a weekly doctor's appointment', because the 'reports helped ensure that I was aware of my mental and spiritual health'. Previous research has indicated the benefits of writing in a journal regularly, particularly for developing self-awareness (Burton & Carroll, 2001; Casanave, 2011).

Six of the 52 students rated the weekly journal requirement as 'very ineffective', with Student 27 commenting that 'I found it to be busy work and a waste of time for me although I was happy to do it if it benefits research or the teachers'. Helping resistant students to see the value of journaling is a challenge. Sharing experiences such as the following may help to open their eyes:

> For a while, I experienced problems with competition and comparing myself to others. I was too worried about how I was doing compared to others rather [than] just having fun learning the language. I experienced a turning point through writing in my journal and reflecting on my progress. I discovered that my competitive feelings and negative feelings about others were my way of coping with difficulties in language learning. I was having difficulty going to the university and having to find new people every day. I changed the way that I found people – I found more steady partners that would be more patient with me. This helped relieve my stress, and it also helped me focus more on my own progress rather than on others. (Student 38)

The program faculty members are considering the possibility of expanding the options for students. Some might enjoy similar benefits by reflecting in a different way, such as recording their thoughts in an audio report or in a discussion with a friend, but helping students to embrace contemplative writing remains a high priority. As Barbezat and Bush note:

> Writing benefits from the capacities that mindfulness, mindful listening, and other contemplative practices cultivate: seeing and hearing things as they are, bearing witness to life; being in the moment, even when remembering the past or imagining the future; no judging others and oneself yet exercising discriminating wisdom; holding multiple perspectives while being open to the new; and practicing kindness, compassion and patience. (Barbezat & Bush, 2013: 123)

Satisfaction and speaking progress

Figure 12.1 plots learners' reported satisfaction with speaking versus their linguistic progress, measured by gains from pre- to post-OPI tests. Satisfaction data are from students' daily speaking reports and were averaged. Using a seven-point Likert scale ranging from 'not very satisfying' to 'very satisfying', they were asked to respond to the prompt: 'Mark your level of satisfaction with this day's speaking; your ranking should

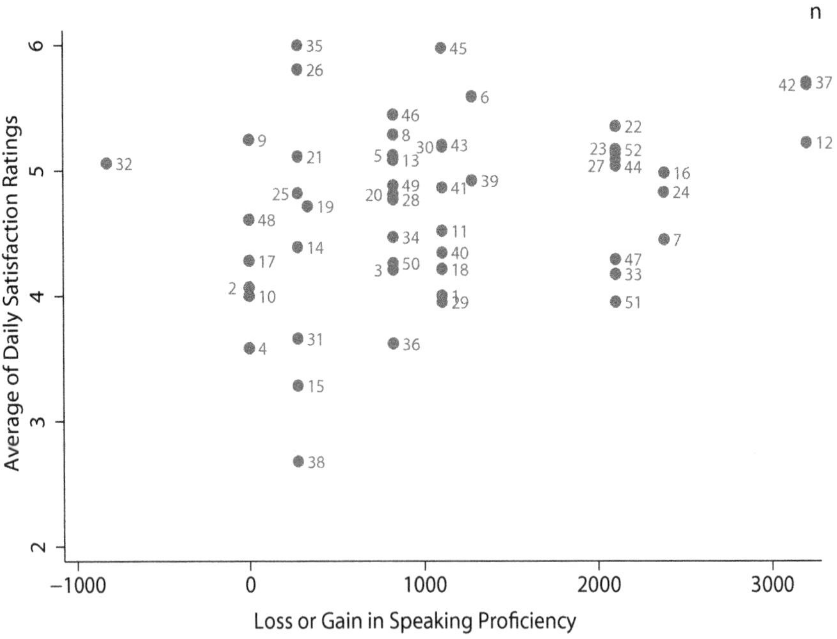

Figure 12.1 Student self-assessment of speaking satisfaction and oral proficiency gains

reflect your level of frustration or happiness with your own performance, and with your success in finding people to talk to'. Their gains in oral proficiency are represented in Figure 12.1 using a logarithmic scale developed by Meredith (1990) to account for the unequal intervals between the ACTFL proficiency levels (the further up the scale one goes the greater the interval). For example, Student 22 in Figure 12.1 advanced from Intermediate Mid to Advanced Low, which results in a lower score than Student 24, who moved from Intermediate High to Advanced Mid, even though both progressed two sub-levels. The correlation between OPI progress and speaking satisfaction is $r = 0.29$, $p < 0.05$.

Figure 12.1 clearly indicates that some learners were quite satisfied with their speaking experiences even though they made little progress, as measured by the OPI.[3] An interesting finding was that the students most satisfied with their speaking experiences did not make as much progress in their educational pursuits as those who were moderately satisfied, and this confirms what has been observed in other studies (Oishi *et al.*, 2007). Some dissatisfaction with one's ability to perform appears to be a potential catalyst for improvement. What is striking about Figure 12.1 is that very few students who regularly felt dissatisfied (whose average was less than 4 on the Likert scale) were able to make significant progress, as measured by the OPI.

Discussion and Illustrative Case Studies

Our ProjP data underscores the importance of interventions for helping students develop self-efficacy and self-regulatory strategies that will help them to persist in their efforts despite the obstacles typically encountered during study abroad, including culture shock and the frustration of not being able to express oneself adequately. The empty lower right quadrant of Figure 12.1 underscores the importance of students' finding joy in the journey if they are linguistically to make the most of their study abroad experience. The interventions in ProjP center around helping the learners to feel efficacious and to recognize their own agency in the learning process. Two unlikely success stories illustrate the importance of grit, of mindfulness and of finding joy in the journey, and provide a holistic perspective on the study abroad experience. We chose them as case studies because: both made more progress in learning Arabic than could have been predicted from their pre-program in-class performance and proficiency scores; they wrote in detail about the challenges they faced in Jordan and how they were able to persevere; and the ProjP team felt that they were exemplary in their use of ProjP skills.

Kylie was a political science major. While not a 'natural' at language learning, at least not at first, she had vision, discipline and a high degree of self-awareness. She excelled in positive self-talk. She was confident in her ability to take on significant challenges and succeed. She was patient with herself and balanced. She viewed the time that she took each weekend to reflect and plan as sacred. She wrote a great deal about her thoughts and feelings, in her weekly journals and in her personal blog. She commented in a post-program telephone interview that one key to her success was a TA who had helped her before she left for Jordan to begin the program with more realistic expectations. Student number 7 in Figure 12.1, Kylie went from Intermediate Low to Advanced Low as measured by the OPI. Extensive excerpts from journal entries she made in her weekly reports can be found at: http://nmelrc.org/pp/arabic-success-stories/kylie.

Heidi was a Middle East studies/Arabic major with far more experience in analyzing complex political or historical issues than in learning languages. Like Kylie, she came to Jordan with a lot of discipline and self-awareness; but unlike her, she had a specific vision for how Arabic would fit into her professional plans. She excelled in self-evaluation and goal setting. She did not write as much as Kylie in the reflection section of her weekly speaking reports (1851 versus 4387 words), but she did plan her days out down to the minute and followed her plan quite strictly. She demonstrated that she was evaluating and making necessary adjustments when she concluded later in the program that she needed to be more flexible. She recognized her weaknesses and strategically sought to make the most of both the Arabic and the personality resources at her command. She frankly acknowledged what she felt she needed to work on the most in order to improve and made a specific plan to do so, with little or no negative self-judgment. Number 43 in Figure 12.1, she went from Intermediate Low to Intermediate High. Extensive excerpts from her journal can be found at: http://nmelrc.org/pp/arabic-success-stories/heidi.

Both Kylie's and Heidi's experiences underscore the importance of self-awareness and mindful self-regulation. Both exhibited a high degree of grit. Kylie took her journaling seriously and, as a result, felt she was better able to cope with negative feelings and experiences, as well as to better analyze her progress. Heidi's ability to set goals, work her plan, reflect on her performance and revise her goals without self-recriminations appeared to help her to have a positive experience. Both made significant progress in speaking (and also reading) and found the study abroad experience meaningful and transformative.

Conclusion

A host of factors affect an individual's linguistic progress, at home or abroad. Self-efficacy and the ability to self-regulate are likely to play a major role in determining whether students persevere in learning a language. Our findings indicate that program interventions and design features designed to promote both of these things appeared to make a difference for at least some of the students. The interventions that helped the greatest number of students in this study came from coaching and encouragement from the program staff. Weekly speaking journals and group processing sessions had more mixed reviews: highly effective for some, but apparently not for others. Additionally, the program was able to help those students struggling to overcome the challenges of finding quality speaking opportunities by providing trained speaking partners (Bown *et al.*, 2015) and by facilitating mastery experiences (Belnap *et al.*, 2015).

The findings of this study have implications for the design of future study abroad programs and language programs generally. The most important implication is that program directors must communicate with their participants and be in tune with their needs. Specifically, sincere encouragement seems to go a long way to helping learners persevere by improving self-efficacy, if the person offering the encouragement is perceived positively by the recipient (Bandura, 1997). Strategy training is also helpful and excellent resources are available to support this (Murphey, 2006; Paige *et al.*, 2009). Near-peer TAs can also provide the vicarious experiences that facilitate the development of self-efficacy (Mills, 2014: 13–14). While reflection is a critical component of self-regulation, journaling may not be the most effective means of reflection for all students. Therefore, program directors may want to consider additional methods of reflection, including oral recordings or face-to-face interviews. Recent research on grit suggests that this characteristic can be more important for achievement even than intelligence or aptitude (Duckworth *et al.*, 2007). An important component of grit is self-efficacy; in order to persevere, learners must believe that they are capable of achieving a particular goal. Mills (2014) gives a useful overview of self-efficacy and ways to help learners grow in their language learning self-efficacy beliefs about themselves and their learning community. The goal of ProjP is to support learners in their efforts to manage their learning and persevere through challenges. Ideally, the program will empower students to become more joyful and effective learners, starting with their self-efficacy and belief that they can improve and grow.

The program interventions mentioned here are only the tip of the iceberg. Many more practical suggestions for helping learners flourish can be found elsewhere (e.g. Dörnyei, 2009; Dörnyei & Kubanyiova, 2014; Gregersen & MacIntyre, 2014). We feel that we are only at the beginning of understanding what types of interventions inspired by research in positive psychology could be useful in empowering learners and enhancing their self-efficacy in study abroad contexts. As the student feedback on our project has shown, this is a complex undertaking that requires the designers of study abroad programs to reflect on the preferences and needs of individual students. We continue to fine-tune the preparation class and various aspects of the program, but our experience has made it clear that change takes time, especially when it comes to mindfulness and effective self-regulation, and can also be a very unique and varied experience. We are convinced that this training should begin as early as possible, preferably no later than the first day of first-year Arabic. We, too, will continue to persevere and design interventions that we believe offer the most positive foundations from which to enjoy and profit from intensive study abroad.

Notes

(1) We thank Andrew Cohen, a founding member of the ProjP team and expert on strategies training (Paige *et al.*, 2009), for suggesting the name. We also thank the College of Humanities of Brigham Young University for its generous support of the ProjP research team. Finally, we express our gratitude to taxpayers for the Title VI Language Resource Center funds that have made ProjP possible.

(2) The student number indicates the order in which they responded to the survey. All student names reported in this chapter are pseudonyms.

(3) The program directors and staff observed noticeable progress in speaking among all of the learners. A few tested unusually high (Intermediate High or Advanced Low) before the program began and received the same rating at the end, which is common in the literature because it typically takes more time to move from Advanced Low to Mid than from Intermediate Low to Mid (see, for example: Brecht *et al.*,1995;Vande Berg *et al.*, 2009). Some of the 2011 students did make less progress than would likely have been expected, such as a student who experienced the tragic death of a close friend back home. Another, who also showed no progress according to the OPI, later returned to Jordan on a Critical Language Scholarship and made considerable progress toward achieving her linguistic and cultural proficiency goals. One student lost ground, according to the OPI, scoring Intermediate Mid in December after being rated Intermediate High in August. She later reported that she felt a good deal of anxiety about what she took to be a high-stakes test. Our experience with various methods of evaluation has underscored the need to avoid over-reliance on one or two measures.

References

Adcock, A. (2012) Cognitive dissonance in the learning process. In N. Seel (ed.) *Encyclopedia of the Sciences of Learning* (pp. 588–590). New York: Springer.

Al-Batal, M. and Belnap, R.K. (2006) The teaching and learning of Arabic in the United States: Realities, needs and future directions. In K.M. Wahba, Z.A. Taha and L. England (eds) *Handbook for Arabic Language Teaching Professionals* (pp. 389–399). Mahwah, NJ: Lawrence Erlbaum.

Bandura, A. (1997) *Self-efficacy: The Exercise of Control*. New York: Freeman.

Barbezat, D.P. and Bush, M. (2013) *Contemplative Practices in Higher Education: Powerful Methods to Transform Teaching and Learning*. Somerset, NJ: Wiley.

Belnap, R.K. and Abuamsha, K. (2015) Taking on the 'ceiling effect' in Arabic. In T. Brown and J. Bown (eds) *To Advanced Proficiency and Beyond: Theory and Methods for Developing Superior Second-Language Ability* (pp. 105–116). Washington, DC: Georgetown University Press.

Belnap, R.K. and Nassif, M.N. (2011) *Middle East Language Learning in U.S. Higher Education*. National Middle East Language Resource Center. Retrieved from. http://

nmelrc.org/middle-east-language-learning-us-higher-education-ten-years-after-911-0 (accessed 23 November 2014).

Belnap, R.K., Bown, J., Dewey, D., Dean, E., Schouten, L.J., Smith, A., Smith, R. and Taylor, J. (2015) Project perseverance and study abroad. *Al-'Arabiyya: Journal of the American Association of Teachers of Arabic* 48, 1–21.

Bennett, J.M. (2008) On becoming a global soul: A path to engagement during study abroad. In V. Savicki (ed.) *Developing Intercultural Competence and Transformation: Theory, Research and Application in International Education* (pp. 13–31). Sterling, VA: Stylus.

Bown, J., Dewey, D. and Belnap, R.K. (2015) Student interactions during study abroad in Jordan. In R. Mitchell, N. Tracy-Ventura and K. McManus (eds) *Social Interaction, Identity and Language Learning During Residence Abroad* (pp. 199–222). Eurosla Monographs Series, vol. 4.

Brecht, R.D., Davidson, D.E. and Ginsberg, R.B. (1995) Predictors of foreign language gain during study abroad. In B.F. Freed (ed.) *Second Language Acquisition in a Study Abroad Context* (pp. 37–66). Amsterdam: John Benjamins.

Brislin, R.W. and Yoshida, T. (1994) *Intercultural Communication Training: An Introduction*. Thousand Oaks, CA: Sage.

Brockington, J.L. and Wiedenhoeft, M. (2009) The liberal arts and global citizenship: Fostering intercultural engagement through integrative experiences and structured reflection. In R. Lewin (ed.) *The Handbook of Practice and Research in Study Abroad: Higher Education and the Quest for Global Citizenship* (pp. 117–132). New York: Routledge.

Burton, J. and Carroll, M. (eds) (2001) *Journal Writing*. Alexandria, VA: Teachers of English to Speakers of Other Languages.

Casanave, C.P. (2011) *Journal Writing in Second Language Education*. Ann Arbor, MI: University of Michigan Press.

Citron, J.L. (2002) U.S. students abroad: Host culture integration or third culture formation? In W. Grünzweig and N. Reinhart (eds) *Rockin' in the Red Square: Critical Approaches to International Education in the Age of Cyberculture* (pp. 43–56). Münster: LIT Verlag.

Cushner, K. and Karim, A. (2004) Study abroad at the university level. In D. Landis, M. Bennett and J. Bennett (eds) *Handbook of Intercultural Training* (3rd edn) (pp. 289–308). Thousand Oaks, CA: Sage.

Dewey, D.P., Ring, S., Gardner, D. and Belnap, K. (2013) Social network formation and development during study abroad in the Middle East. *System: An International Journal of Educational Technology and Applied Linguistics* 41, 269–282.

Dörnyei, Z. (2009) *The Psychology of Second Language Acquisition*. Oxford: Oxford University Press.

Dörnyei, Z. and Kubanyiova, M. (2014) *Motivating Learners, Motivating Teachers: Building Vision in the Language Classroom*. Cambridge: Cambridge University Press.

Duckworth, A.L., Peterson, C., Matthews, M. D. and Kelly, D. R. (2007) Grit: Perseverance and passion for long-term goals. *Journal of Personality and Social Psychology* 92 (6), 1087–1101.

Duckworth, A.L., Kirby, T., Tsukayama, E., Berstein, H. and Ericsson, K. (2010) Deliberate practice spells success: Why grittier competitors triumph at the National Spelling Bee. *Social Psychological and Personality Science* 2, 174–181.

Ehrman, M.E. (1996) *Understanding Second Language Learning Difficulties*. Thousand Oaks, CA: Sage.

Ehrman, M.E. (2001) Bringing learning strategies to the learner: The FSI language learning consultation service. In J.E. Alatis and A. Tan (eds) *Language in Our Time: Bilingual Education and Official English, Ebonics and Standard English, Immigration and the Unz Initiative* (pp. 41–58). Washington, DC: Georgetown University Press.

Ehrman, M.E. and Dörnyei, Z. (1998) *Interpersonal Dynamics in Second Language Education: The Visible and Invisible Classroom*. Thousand Oaks, CA: Sage.
Garland, E.L. and Fredrickson, B.L. (2013) Mindfulness. In T.B. Kashdan and C. Joseph (eds) *Mindfulness, Acceptance, and Positive Psychology: The Seven Foundations of Well-Being* (pp. 30–67). Oakland, CA: Context Press/New Harbinger Publications.
Graham, S. (2007) Learner strategies and self-efficacy: Making the connection. *Language Learning Journal* 35, 81–93.
Gregersen, T. and MacIntyre, P. (2014) *Capitalizing on Language Learners' Individuality: From Premise to Practice*. Bristol: Multilingual Matters.
Hart, K. and Sasso, T. (2011) Mapping the contours of contemporary positive psychology. *Canadian Psychology* 52, 82–92.
Hunley, H.A. (2008) The impact of mental health on the decision to study abroad and on students' functioning while studying abroad. PhD thesis, Loyola University, Chicago.
Kabat-Zinn, J. (2003) Mindfulness-based stress reduction (MBSR). *Constructivism in the Human Sciences* 8 (2), 73–107.
Kruse, J. and Brubaker, C. (2007) Successful study abroad: Tips for student preparation, immersion and postprocessing. *Teaching German* 40 (2), 147–152.
Meredith, R.A. (1990) The Oral Proficiency Interview in real life: Sharpening the scale. *Modern Language Journal* 74 (3), 288–296.
Mills, N. (2014) Self-efficacy in second language acquisition. In S. Mercer and M. Williams (eds) *Multiple Perspectives on the Self in SLA* (pp. 6–19). Bristol: Multilingual Matters.
Murphey, T. (2006) *Language Hungry! An Introduction to Language Learning Fun and Self-Esteem*. London: Helbling Languages.
Oettingen, G., Wittchen, M. and Gollwitzer, P.M. (2013) Regulating goal pursuit through mental contrasting with implementation intentions. In E. Locke and G. Lantham (eds) *New Developments in Goal Setting and Task Performance* (pp. 523–548). London: Routledge.
Oishi, S., Diener, E. and Lucas, R.E. (2007) The optimum level of well-being: Can people be too happy? *Perspectives on Psychological Science* 2, 346–360.
Paige, R.M., Cohen, A.D., Kappler, B., Chi, J.C. and Lassegard, J.P. (2009) *Maximizing Study Abroad: A Student's Guide to Strategies for Language and Culture Learning and Use* (2nd edn). Minneapolis, MN: Center for Advanced Research on Language Acquisition, University of Minnesota.
Pajares, F. (1997) Current directions in self-efficacy research. In M. Maehr and P.R. Pintrich (eds) *Advances in Motivation and Achievement* (vol. 10, pp. 1–49). Greenwich, CT: JAI Press.
Pellegrino Aveni, V. (2005) *Study Abroad and Second Language Use: Constructing the Self*. Cambridge: Cambridge University Press.
Peterson, C. and Seligman, M.E.P. (2004) *Character Strengths and Virtues: A Handbook and Classification*. Oxford: Oxford University Press.
Pitts, M.J. (2009) Identity and role expectations, stress and talk in short-term sojourner adjustment: An application of the integrity theory of communication and cross-cultural adaptation. *International Journal of Intercultural Relations* 33, 450–462.
Pozo, C., Carver, C., Wellens, A.R. and Scheier, M. (1991) Social anxiety and social perception: Construing others' reactions to the self. *Personality and Social Psychology Bulletin* 17, 355–362.
Pryor, R., Clark, M., Cope, D. and Robinson, J. (2014) The role of mindfulness training in intercultural education. Panel at the Forum on Education Abroad, 4 April, San Diego, CA.
Pusch, M.D. and Merrill, M. (2008) Reflection, reciprocity, responsibility and committed relativism: Intercultural development through international service-learning. In V. Savicki (ed.) *Developing Intercultural Competence and Transformation: Research, Theory and Application in International Education* (pp. 297–321). Sterling, VA: Stylus.
Ramsburg, J.T. and Youmans, R.J. (2013) Meditation in the higher-education classroom:

Meditation training improves student knowledge retention during lectures. *Mindfulness* 5 (4), 431–441.
Ryan, M.E. and Twibell, R.S. (2000) Concerns, values, stress, coping, health and educational outcomes of college students who studied abroad. *International Journal of Intercultural Relations* 24 (4), 409–435.
Seligman, M.E.P. and Csikszentmihalyi, M. (2000) Positive psychology: An introduction. *American Psychologist* 55, 5–14.
Seligman, M.E.P., Parks, A.C. and Steen, T. (2006) A balanced psychology and a full life. In F. Huppert, B. Keverne and N. Baylis (eds) *The Science of Well-Being* (pp. 275–283). Oxford: Oxford University Press.
Trentman, E.G. (2012) Study abroad in Egypt: Identity, access and arabic language learning. PhD thesis, Michigan State University.
Vande Berg, M., Connor-Linton, J. and Paige, M.R. (2009) The Georgetown Consortium Project: Interventions for student learning abroad. *Frontiers: The Interdisciplinary Journal on Study Abroad* 18, 1–75.
Von Cullin, K.R., Tsukayama, E. and Duckworth, A.L. (2014) Unpacking grit: Motivational correlates of perseverance and passion for long-term goals. *Journal of Positive Psychology* 9 (4), 306–312.

Part 3
Applied

13 Happiness in ESL/EFL: Bringing Positive Psychology to the Classroom

Marc Helgesen

Just over a decade after the positive psychology movement was launched, Seligman (2011) released *Flourish*, a book that presented a new model for positive psychology, PERMA. The acronym stands for the elements of positive psychology: Positive emotion, Engagement, positive Relationships, Meaning and Accomplishment. One can think of PERMA as 'Happiness 2.0' or, more accurately, 'Well-being 2.0' since it looks at happiness as one part of a larger, more complete picture.

This chapter looks at ways to incorporate PERMA into ESL/EFL classes in ways that incorporate positive psychology strategies and clear language teaching/learning goals. In short, it looks at combining happiness and the language classroom. Many positive psychologists/researchers avoid the word 'happiness', preferring terms like 'positive emotion' and 'subjective well-being'. The word 'happiness' does trigger unscientific images, like yellow smiley faces. It can be, as Fredrickson (2009: 37) said, 'murky and overused'. Kahneman (2010) said, 'the word "happiness" is just not a useful word anymore because we apply it to too many things.' Why, then, does this writer not only use the term but include it in this chapter's title? Simply because the word is comprehensible. Learners understand it. Everyone wants it. As with all tasks in the language learning classroom, the promise of positive results makes most learners willing to try the activities, even if they are different from some they usually associate with studying English.

Why should ESL/EFL teachers add positive psychology tasks to our classes? Teachers are, after all, busy. We are already responsible for listening, speaking, reading and writing. We worry about vocabulary, grammar and functions. We think about assessment, record keeping and a host of other things. Do we really need more responsibility? Perhaps we should think of positive psychology tasks as more of an opportunity than a responsibility. Of course, all teachers deal with educational psychology, whether with awareness or by default. Awareness would seem to be a preferred strategy.

There are other reasons as well. Happy students learn more. Oishi *et al.* (2007) reported that happy students have higher grade point averages, miss fewer classes and report higher levels of conscientiousness. The same paper reported on an international survey of over 118,000 people that found that higher levels of life satisfaction correlated positively with the desire to continue one's education. Seligman *et al.* (2009) connected positive mood to broader attention as well as enhanced creative, analytical and critical thinking. Achor suggested that positive emotion 'primes' people, making them better learners. He explained the neuroscience behind this, saying,

> positive emotions flood our brains with dopamine and serotonin, chemicals that not only make us feel good, but dial up the learning centers of our brains to higher levels. They help us organize new information, keep that information in the brain longer, and retrieve it faster later on. (Achor, 2010: 44)

Those neurotransmitters increase focus, memory and motivation (Willis, 2010), elements that every teacher wants to see in students.

Positive Emotion

Although the five aspects of PERMA are all important, positive emotion is probably the one that most teachers will find useful in the classroom most frequently. It contains concrete elements that are easily connected to specific functions, grammar points, topics and lexical sets.

Lubomirsky (2005) identified eight types of cognitive and personal behaviour that lead to a more satisfying life. Those items, which I have paraphrased to make them more accessible to the learners, are as follows.

(1) Remember good things in your life. (Count your blessings.)
(2) Do kind things.
(3) Say 'thank you' to people who help you.
(4) Take time for friends and family.
(5) Forgive people who hurt you.
(6) Take care of your health and body.
(7) Notice good things when they happen.
(8) Learn to work with your problems and stress.

Language teachers will notice that many of these are things that we already work with in our classes. 'Remembering' requires grammar, the past tense. 'Noticing good things when they happen' requires the present. 'Thanking' and 'forgiving' are functions and imply the use of related language routines.

'Friends', 'family' and 'health' are typical topics in many beginning-level English classes. If we are already broaching these topics anyway, framing them as 'working with happiness' can be a useful way of introducing positive psychology into the ESL/EFL class. One simple way is via a 'sentence strip dictation' (Davis & Rinvolucri, 1988: 13). Simply copy the above eight sentences. Make one copy for every seven students, cut the strips into sentences and distribute the sentence strips. Keep the first one for yourself to use as the example. Dictate this first sentence, 'Remember good things in your life'. Students write it. They also copy the sentence strip you have given them. Then learners stand, circulate and collect and write the remaining sentences while dictating their own to their classmates.

Once everyone has written all eight, have learners work in small groups, discussing the ideas and thinking of ways they do – or could do – them. The dictation activity gets the information to the students but, of course, it is at the level of individual sentences. It takes the discussion or expansion to get them thinking about the real meaning and how to apply the ideas to their lives.

One way to do meaning-based review of the ideas is to have learners write 'happiness haiku'. In pairs or small groups they write a haiku poem about one of the ideas. In haiku poems, the first line has five syllables, the second has seven syllables and the final line has five. Writing such structured poems can be challenging but, as Maley (2014) pointed out, constraints such as syllable counts are actually a form of scaffolding that make success possible. Noticing English syllable counts can also be a useful exercise for learners whose native language is syllable-timed, which makes the prosody of stress-timed English difficult. Here are examples of 'happiness haiku' written by first-year Japanese university students:

Whatever happens,
don't be afraid. Keep going.
We are living now.

The day won't come back.
Think about today's good things.
Open a new door.

We have many friends.
If you feel sad, they will help.
We must savor friends.

Just breathe air slowly.
It will calm your angry mind,
and you can forgive.

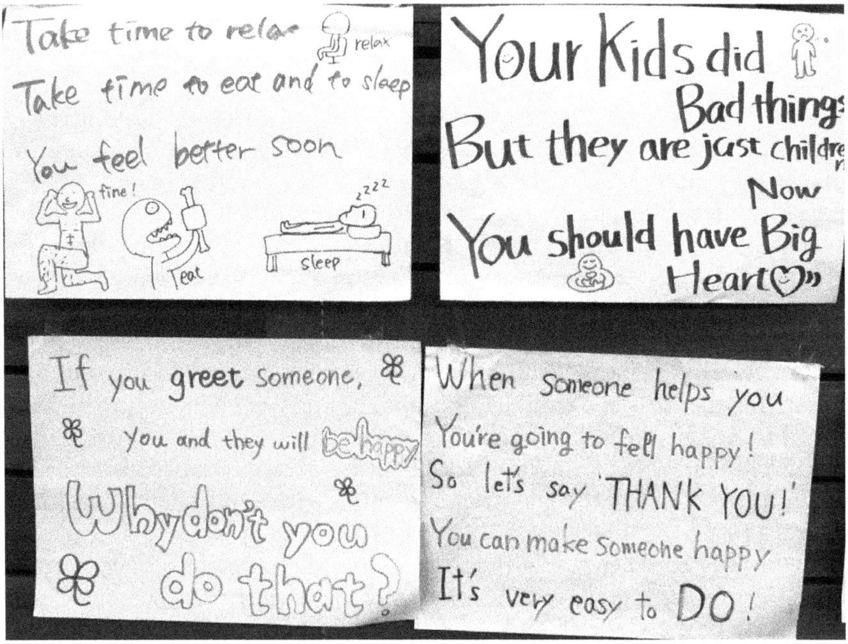

Figure 13.1 Student haiku posters decorating the classroom wall

The class that wrote these haiku poems made illustrated posters and took turns sharing their poems with their classmates. See Figure 13.1.

As teachers, we know the importance of spaced repetition (Tokuhama-Espinosa, 2014: 132) for reviewing new language and concepts over time. For learners to gain the benefits of the ideas above, teachers may want to regularly include activities that combine language goals with the contents of the ideas.

Eight activities

The following are examples of ways to bring each of the eight ideas into the language classroom. Since it is generally easier to raise the level of activities than to lower it, elementary level tasks are used. Grammar targets, functions or topic areas are identified in parentheses.

1. Remember good things in your life: Gratitude list *(past and present tenses, fluency practice)*

Students make one oval on a piece of paper for each year of their age. In each, they write one thing they are thankful for. In groups, they explain the most interesting items. Note that this activity usually includes thanking, friends and family as well. This is based on Pink (2006: 236).

2. Do kind things: Compliments *(complimenting, reported speech)*

Write eight or so compliment phrases such as 'That's a great jacket' or 'You've got a beautiful smile' on the board. In groups of four or five, each learner gives one true compliment to each person. At the end, they try to remember all the compliments, using indirect speech ('She told me…', 'He said I…').

3. Say 'thank you' to people who help you: Thank you to the world *(giving reasons with* because*)*

On the board, write: 'I want to say (thank you) to (country) because…'. In pairs, students see how many different languages they can say 'thank you' in and why they want to thank that country or culture. ('I want to say *kop kun kha* to Thailand because of wonderful green curry'. 'I want to say *shukran* to Arab countries because they gave us math. I don't like math but it is important'.)

4. Take time for friends and family: Toothpick family *(family vocabulary, positive adjectives)*

Write model sentences on the board: 'This is my [*mum, dad, etc.*]. Her/His name is ____. She/he is a [*job*]. She/he is very [*adjective*].'

Brainstorm positive adjectives (happy, energetic, smart, hard-working, creative, etc.) and write them on the board. Students work in groups of four or five. Give each group some toothpicks. Students use the toothpick to introduce their family, laying the toothpicks on the desk while using the target and other sentences. They can break the toothpicks to represent different heights. After everyone has had a turn, partners see how much they can remember. If toothpicks aren't available, they can draw simple pictures.

5. Forgive people who hurt you: Forgiveness metaphor *(listening, following instructions, imperatives)*

Tell the students to think of someone who did something bad whom they have not forgiven. Tell them that this is a listening activity. They will not be asked to talk about it. The information is private. Everyone needs a small object like a water bottle, cell phone or pencil case. Read this script to them:

> Pick up the small object. Hold it in front of you. [Pause] Someone did something bad to you. Forgiveness does *not* mean the bad thing was okay. [Pause] Forgiveness does *not* mean that person can do the bad thing

> again. Forgiveness is important for things that must *not* be done again. [Pause] When you do not forgive, who is hurt? The person who did the bad thing usually doesn't know. Or doesn't remember. Or doesn't care. [Pause] The anger is in your heart. You carry the weight. [Pause It does not help to know why the person did the bad thing. Usually that person doesn't know. [Pause] It is heavy, isn't it? Long pause] You carry the weight. You have the power to – let – it – go.

Afterwards, you might want to discuss how metaphors are useful to talk about things that are hard to discuss directly. Proverbs from the learners' countries/languages are one way into the topic.

6. Take care of your health and body. Our health/our habits *(modal auxiliary verbs for obligation/permission, likes/dislikes)*

Each student divides a piece of paper in half and writes 'I like these' on one side and 'I don't like these' on the other. In groups of four or five, they think of health-related rules and customs using words like 'should/shouldn't', 'must/must not', 'have to/don't have to', 'can/can't'. They write the sentences on the side of the paper that reflects what they think. Then they compare where they wrote the ideas. As a variation, they can divide them according to how well they follow the rules (always, usually, never) (see Figure 13.2).

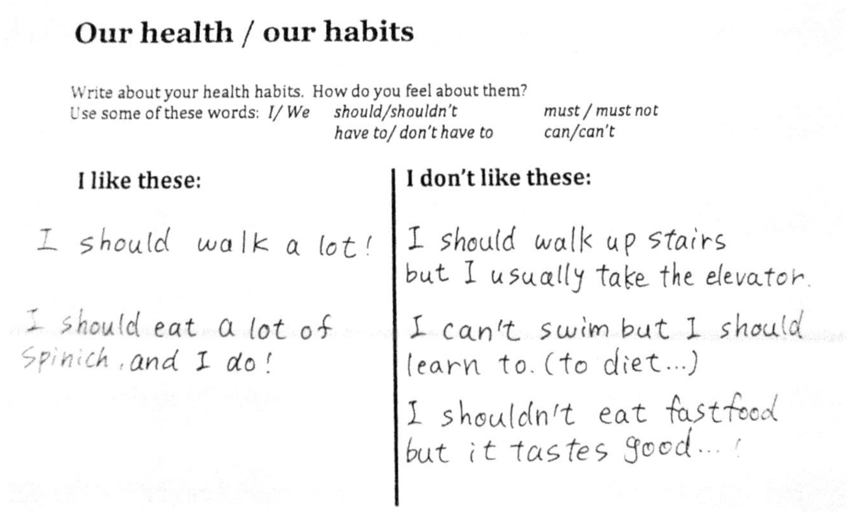

Our health / our habits

Write about your health habits. How do you feel about them?
Use some of these words: *I/ We* *should/shouldn't* *must / must not* *have to/ don't have to* *can/can't*

I like these:	I don't like these:
I should walk a lot!	I should walk up stairs but I usually take the elevator.
I should eat a lot of Spinich, and I do!	I can't swim but I should learn to. (to diet...)
	I shouldn't eat fastfood but it tastes good...!

Figure 13.2 Student example of 'Our health/our habits'

7. Notice good things when they happen: Happiness chains *(present simple, present progressive)*

Give each student three strips of paper about 3 cm × 15 cm (1 inch × 6 inches) long. Each group of four or five students will need a stapler, glue stick or paper clips. They each write sentences about good things in their lives right now on the strips. In their groups, they take turns reading their sentences and adding their strip to a group 'paper chain', pasting or stapling the strips together. Each strip makes a link. Encourage partners to ask questions and make comments about other people's ideas.

8. Learn to work with your problems and stress. Working with stress *(habitual present, past tenses)*

In small groups, students brainstorm ways in which they deal with problems and stress. They suggest ideas. Partners ask 'what, when, who, where, how' questions (What do you do? How often? When do you do this? How do you do that? etc.). Ideas often include exercise, prayer, meditation, eating chocolate or going for a walk.

Three further useful activities

In addition to the eight exercises described above, positive psychology researchers have developed other ways of introducing important concepts to various audiences. Three additional activities that teachers might choose to use with their students are 'positive emotion sentences', 'guided journeys' and 'three good things'.

Positive emotion sentences

As mentioned above, the term 'happiness' is avoided by some positive psychologists as too simplistic. Fredrickson (2009: 39–48) identified 10 distinct forms of positive emotion, listed below, along with 'sentence starter cues' that can help learners understand and get started talking or writing about each.

- Joy. *I was really happy when...*
- Gratitude. *I was thankful for...*
- Serenity. *I felt peaceful when...*
- Interest. *Sometimes I'm so interested in something, I don't even notice the time. I was very interested, alert and focused when...*
- Hope. *Even when things are difficult, I felt they would get better. For example...*
- Pride. *I felt good about something I did when...*
- Amusement. *It was fun and funny when...*
- Inspiration. *Sometimes I see people doing wonderful things for other people. For example...*

- Awe. *Some things are so wonderful, I almost cannot believe them. For example, when…*
- Love. *This can include all of these feelings. It can be romantic love, family love or caring about friends. I really knew I was loved when…*

The sentence starter cues above are written to elicit past tense examples and stories from the students. They can easily be modified to encourage present or present habitual tenses, by changing the verbs to the present simple.

There are many ways to use these ideas in the classroom. Some teachers copy them, ask students to write answers to at least seven of the sentence starter cues, and then talk or write about one or more that interests them. It can be useful, before they write or talk about the topics, to spend a few minutes of 'thinking time' to clarify both what they want to communicate and how they will do so in English (Helgesen, 2003b). Other teachers lead a 'guided journey' (Berman & Brown, 2000).

Guided journeys

A 'guided journey' is sometimes called a 'guided visualization' but the term 'journey' is used here because it often involves more senses than vision alone. After introducing the types of positive emotion and sentence starter cues, the students choose one they want to talk or write about. They close their eyes. The teacher, speaking in a calm voice, mentally leads them through the situation in a way that helps them re-experience the positive time. The teacher pauses frequently to give the learners time to imagine and to re-experience the event.

> Think about the time you felt very happy. In your mind, visit that time and place again. Where are you? When did this happen? Who are you with? Look around. Notice the place. Notice the colours. Notice what things are made of. Notice the people. What do they look like? Who are they? What are they saying? What are you saying? What else do you hear? Notice what you are feeling. Is it warm? Cool? Is there a breeze? Notice the feeling in your heart – your emotion. What happens next? Notice everything that happens.

The teacher allows about 30 seconds of quiet time for students to imagine the story. Then they write or tell about it in pairs or small groups. If they are telling the stories aloud, it is useful to encourage partners to ask 'WH' questions (who, what, where, how, etc.) or other kinds of questions. This is, of course, a useful discourse strategy to help the learners practise keeping a conversation going. It also leads to what Seligman (2011: 48) called 'active, constructive responding'. This type of response not only shows one is paying attention and leads to better communication, it also helps the main speaker mentally recreate the positive event, taking their own re-experience of the event deeper.

Some teachers have learners change partners, retelling their stories one or more times. This not only provides fluency practice (Mazgutova, 2013), it also gives the speaker an additional experience of the positive emotion, since by re-experiencing the event mentally the student is reflectively savouring (Bryant & Veroff, 2007). Fredrickson (2009) suggested that it is the experiences of positive emotion, including those that happen through remembering and savouring, rather than just the actual occurrence of positive events that contributes to a person's feeling of positivity.

Three good things

Most of the classroom activities mentioned in this chapter are ways of modifying positive psychology ideas and interventions to make them useful for language learning. Interestingly, the final classroom task in the section, 'Three good things', requires no modification. It is used directly as reported in Seligman *et al.* (2005). For one week, the participants keep a daily log. They write down three good things that happen each day and why. For example, a student might write, 'Dinner was great tonight'. The 'why' can be 'why it happened' or 'why it was good'. Here are some possible reasons dinner why was great:

- My mum/dad is a good cook.
- I was really hungry.
- Pizza is my favourite.
- I helped make dinner.

Note that while the good things will usually be remembering something good that happened, the reasons can touch on some of the other positive emotion items identified at the beginning of this section. Identifying someone as a good cook is similar to thanking, in this case a family member. Recalling the experience of being hungry and then eating is like recalling something good as it happened. Helping make dinner is doing an act of kindness.

The activity goes on for one week. It doesn't take long, perhaps five minutes a day. The significant thing is the results. Seligman *et al.* (2005) found that this one-week task connected to six months of positive emotion. The activity correlated with a rise in positive emotion scores and a decline in depressive symptoms. Although the participants were explicitly told to do the activity for only one week, follow-up interviews showed that they continued to notice good things in their lives. It is as if the one-week training had produced a mentally healthy habit of noticing and remembering good things in their lives.

Engagement

In experimental studies, increased learner engagement has been shown to be connected with 'improved ... curiosity, love of learning, and creativity' (Seligman, 2011: 85). Engagement is a challenge. If activities are too easy, learners get bored. If they are too difficult, learners give up. According to Sousa and Tomlinson (2011: 114), 'Work that interests students will necessarily be at an appropriate challenge level'. To encourage engagement, Seligman encouraged creating *flow*, the 'experience of complete absorption in the present moment' (see Nakamura & Csikszentmihalyi, 2009: 195). Tardy and Snyder (2004: 118) stated that 'flow tends to occur when the level of challenge in a task is high, but manageable given the person's skills in completing the task'. In flow experiences, attention becomes ordered and fully invested, leading to a loss of self-consciousness and a distorted sense of time. In the classroom, cooperative learning and scaffolded autonomy tasks can lead to flow (Nakamura & Csikszentmihalyi, 2009).

Flow requires a balance between challenge and skill. The goal must be challenging but achievable. Mazgutova (2013) suggested that fluency tasks that include task repetition and time limits can be useful in building fluency. One such task that works well for this is 4–3–2 (Nation, 1989), also known as 'fluency workshop' (Maurice, 1983). In the task, students are assigned or choose a topic. Any topic can be used but to make use of positive psychology in ESL/EFL classes, personalized items related to the positive behaviours identified at the beginning of this chapter work well. Normally, learners have a minute or two of 'thinking time' to consider what they want to say. Then they work with a partner. The first partner has four minutes to talk about the topic. At the discretion of the teacher, this can either be a dialogue, with the other partner asking questions for clarification or more information, or it can be a monologue, with questions coming after the four minutes. Then the other partner has a four-minute turn. Next, the learners change partners and repeat the task, this time with a three-minute time limit. Finally, they change partners again and do the task in two minutes. The first time, the task is fairly challenging. They are thinking about what to say and how they will say it. The challenge is high and, since they have not said this content before, their skill level is low. The second time, they have said it before. They are clearer about what they want to say. The first round provided a rehearsal for the second. They are becoming more fluent. By the third round, many learners experience flow. They are focused on their meaning and are often not thinking much about language itself.

Other fluency frames which feature this 'task recycling' include: 'poster carousel' (Lynch & Maclean, 2001), where students work in pairs to make a poster, then take turns presenting it while the partner goes off to see and hear other students' poster presentations; 'line-up' (Helgesen, 2003a), which is similar to 4–3–2 but the times are shorter and don't change; and 'mouth marathon', where students speak as long as they can each round – the round is over when they pause for five seconds or say a word not in the target language. All of these classroom activities provide for task repetition, which can lead to challenge, flow and engagement.

Relationships

Positive psychology pioneer Christopher Peterson was asked to explain, in one or two words, the essence of positive psychology. He responded, 'Other people' (see Seligman, 2011: 20). Haidt (2006: 223) shared a similar sentiment when he rewrote the adage 'Happiness comes from within' to 'Happiness comes from *between*'. Layard (2005: 63) identified human relationships (family and friends) as two of the five most important factors affecting happiness. All of these ideas point to the importance of relationships. In the classroom, of course, we are concerned primarily with student–student and student–teacher relations. As Hamre and Pianta (2006: 71) pointed out, good student–teacher relationships 'are fundamental to [students'] success in school, and as such, these relationships should be explicitly targeted'.

For teachers, this often starts with learning the students' names. This sounds obvious but in many parts of the world, classes have large numbers of students – 40 or 50 or more is not unusual and each teacher may have many classes meeting only once a week. As Viney (2009) pointed out, 'learning names takes work'. One way to facilitate learning names in large classes is to have students make name cards with index cards (see Figure 13.3).

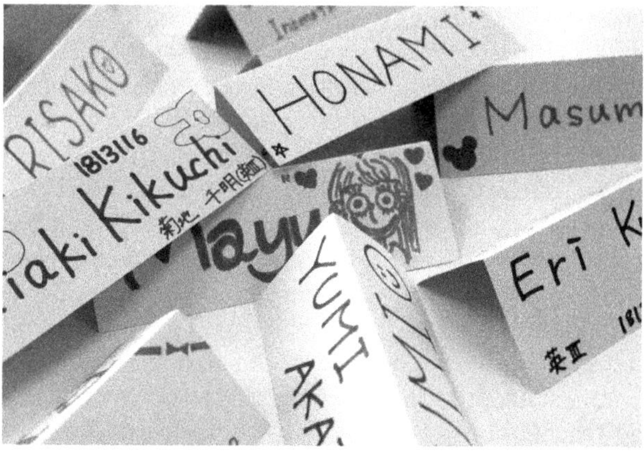

Figure 13.3 Student name cards

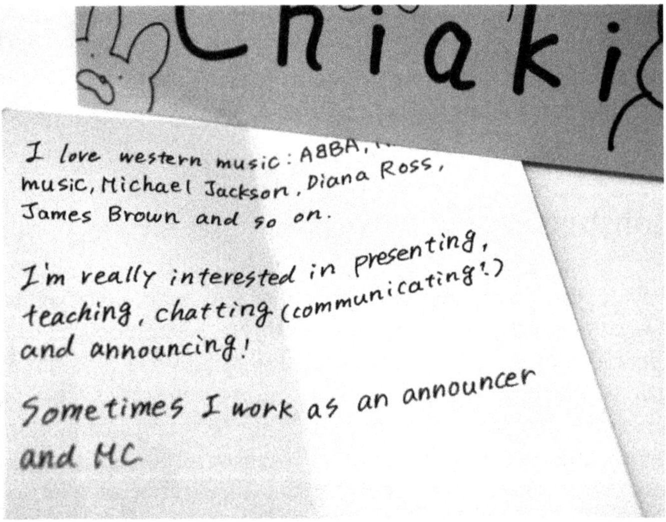

Figure 13.4 Student self-introduction on the inside of the card

Students fold the cards in half so they stand up in an inverted 'V'. They write their names with a magic marker on both the front and back of the card. During class, students place it on their desks. The name is written on both sides so the teacher can see it from most viewpoints. Some teachers invite the students to decorate and personalize the cards, which makes it easier to associate the card with its owner. In the sample in Figure 13.3, they wrote given and family names on the outside side of the card and whatever they wanted to be called by the teacher on the inside. Alternatively, on the inside of the card, the student writes a short self-introduction. It is helpful if the students write something about something unique to themselves – something that is not true about most of the other students (see Figure 13.4 for an example). Although it is easier to have each learner keep their own card, it is better for learning names for the teacher to collect them at the end of each class. In the subsequent class, the teacher spends a few minutes reading the student biographies, trying to associate the information with the names. The teacher arrives a few minutes early for each class and passes the cards to their owners. Just as challenge is useful for learner engagement, the positive pressure of remembering which card goes with which person is useful in helping the teacher learn the students' names.

In trying to establish rapport between learners as well as with themselves, many teachers begin courses with name-related activities to help learners get to know each other. Wiltshier (2014) suggested four 'mini-tasks' that encourage learners to talk about and learn partners' names. Students

Figure 13.5 Name poem

write their name in the middle of a piece of paper. In the four corners of the paper, they write or make notes about the following:

- What their name means.
- Why they were given that name.
- What they like or dislike about their name.
- If they had a different name or a nickname, what they would want it to be.

The teacher designates one corner of the room for each of the items; students choose the one they want to talk about, go to that corner, find a partner and talk about the topic. They change partners several times, trying to remember each partner's name.

A final name-learning activity is 'name poem'. Students write their name vertically on a large (A3 or B4) sheet of paper with a marker. With a different-coloured marker, they write one phrase that includes a word that starts with one of the letters in their name. Then they circulate their sheets, reading other learners' poems and asking about interesting items. An example by the present author appears in Figure 13.5.

Modern language teaching methodology emphasizes student-to-student communication. This, of course, builds social relationships, which Hefferon and Boniwell (2011: 56) called 'one of the greatest predictors and facilitators of SWB [subjective well-being]'. Most of the classroom activities suggested in the 'positive emotion' section of this chapter included learner interaction. Hadfield (1997: 10, 40) suggested an activity called 'Medals' at the mid-point or end of a course. Learners receive copies of a paper with an award-type medal printed on them. They cut them out, and decide on qualities of classmates that deserve recognition – good listener, interesting partner, helpful friend, cool fashion award and so on. They give the awards to each other, building their relationships as they practise English.

Meaning

It may surprise language teachers that 'meaning' and 'meaningfulness' need to be listed. Language teaching saw a shift away from mechanical, strictly form-focused pedagogy in the 1970s, toward more meaning-based communicative and task-based methodologies. In positive psychology, however, 'meaning' takes on a special nuance. Seligman (2011: 17) defined it as 'belonging to and serving something that you believe is bigger than the self'. Incorporating this idea, Lyubomirsky expanded her suggestions to 'learn to deal with problems and stress' and 'take care of your health and body' to 'Take care of your body and soul' (Lyubomirsky, 2007). In the category she includes religion and spirituality, meditation and physical activity. Like many positive psychologists, Lyubomirsky (2013) and Fredrickson (2013) suggest practising meditation, with Fredrickson focusing on *metta* meditation. *Metta* is a Pali word usually translated as 'loving kindness'. Pali is the language of the Buddha but, although derived from Buddhist tradition, 'loving kindness meditation' is not particularly connected to religion. To do it, one sits quietly, initially focusing on one's breathing. Then the person mentally repeats a series of items, while imagining his or her own compassion flowing to the person who is the object of their thought. There are many variations on the sentences but they are usually similar to the following series, which has been simplified to make it comprehensible to language learners:

- May I be healthy.
- May I be happy.
- May I be peaceful.
- May I be loved.

Initially, learners focus on the self, wishing these gifts of compassion for themselves. Then the cycle is repeated, with the focus on someone they love, often a family member or close friend, changing 'I' to 'you'. Mentally repeating the phrases, they visualize their own loving kindness compassion flowing from their heart to the other person. Next they think about someone they feel neutral about. Often students choose someone like a school bus driver or the office staff. These are people who are part of their lives but the learners do not have a strong emotional attachment to them, positive or negative. Finally, they think about someone they do not really like. Even though they do not like the person, they can still wish them compassion. Many people end their loving kindness meditation with general, inclusive thoughts of compassion for their whole community, area, country and even people all over the world. To use this in the classroom, the teacher can either use the meditation as a listening task, leading the learners through the ideas, or make use of one of the many versions available on YouTube or the free audio on Fredrickson's website, http://positivityresonance.com.

Another standard positive psychology intervention with direct ELT application is the 'gratitude letter'. The teacher teaches students the conventions of English letter-writting, then asks the students to think of someone who really helped them. It is often a parent, a special teacher, a coach or someone who has given them useful advice. They write a letter to the person, explaining specifically what that person did that helped them and how it made a difference in the student's life. In many or most cases with language learners, they need to write the letter twice, one in English for the class assignment and once in the language the person who helped them uses. Once they have written the letter, the teacher gives each student an envelope and, if it is not practical for the student to give the letter directly to the person, stamps so the student can mail the letter. The ideal way to deliver the letter is for the student to read it to the recipient.

In one study of the gratitude letter being used in a compulsory second-year university writing class in Japan, 95% of the students writing and reading the letters reported experiencing positive emotions. They reported that 85% of the recipients reacted in positive ways, ranging from 'fairly surprised' to 'astonished' (Harada, 2014).

The gratitude letter was developed by Seligman and Peterson (see Peterson, 2006: 31–36). Peterson reported never having an experience of one parent being jealous when the letter is given to the other parent. There may be, however, cultural considerations. The present author teaches in Japan, where such direct statements of emotion are unusual. To make it easier, the students use a form that gives the following explanation, in Japanese:

> in my English class, we have been talking about important people and events in our lives. My teacher asked me to write a 'gratitude letter' to someone who had helped me. I decided to write to you.

People in other cultures may have different reactions. When Peterson was explaining the activity to now-prominent positive psychologist Nansook Park, she responded, 'Do you mean that your students have never done this before?' In Korea, where Park grew up, every child writes an appreciation letter to their teacher every year (Peterson, 2006: 17).

Accomplishment

Accomplishment or achievement can play an important role in positive emotion. The pursuit of winning – playing the game well – can be as important as the actual rewards of winning. Seligman (2011) used examples as varied as athletes, bridge players and tycoons like John D. Rockefeller and Andrew Carnegie and their current counterparts Bill Gates and Warren

Buffett, who made huge fortunes which they later gave away. Synder *et al.* (2011) describe the idea as 'agency' when describing the pursuit of goals. It involves 'pathway thinking' – deciding on goals and finding alternative routes to those goals when initial paths are blocked – and 'agency thinking' – taking action to move along those alternative routes. Lyubomirsky (2007) identified six psychological benefits of pursuing goals: giving the person a sense of purpose; bolstering self-esteem in the case of meaningful goals; adding structure and meaning to one's life; helping people prioritize in order to achieve higher-order goals; learning to cope with roadblocks and to replace unfeasible goals; and, when the goals involve engaging with other people, the pursuit of those goals become its own reward.

Wingate (2000: 52–53) brings goal-setting to the classroom with an activity called 'Future Dreams'. Students are invited to think about their dreams, then identify the problems or challenges to achieving each goal, find ways to overcome those problems and, most importantly, break those ways down into small steps that they can actually accomplish. For example, many EFL students have a vague dream of studying in an English-speaking country. Of course, that is very expensive and out of reach to most. Lack of money is the first problem to be overcome. Studying abroad can cost thousands. It is difficult to save that much money. However, it is relatively easy to save a small amount. The learner can identify how much he or she can save in a month and then commit to actually saving that much, perhaps putting it in a 'tin can' bank – the kind that can be opened only once with a can opener, to make it harder to break one's goals.

Another example of breaking goals into small, achievable steps for learners relates to improving scores on tests like the IELTS, TOEIC, TOEFL or Cambridge English Exams. 'I want to improve' is vague. A goal such as 'I will spend 15 minutes every day practising for the test' is much more concrete and achievable.

Two caveats about goal-setting: Snyder *et al.* (2011: 397) urged teachers to make class goals relevant to learners' lives, ideas that fit into the 'engagement' and 'meaning' aspects of the PERMA model. When good grades are emphasized as goals, it can 'turn students into grade predators who are more fascinated with their performances and with doing better than their peers than they are with learning'. Also, Sivers (2010) cautioned against telling goals to others lest it create a 'social reality' in which we feel we are closer to the goal than we really are and thus less motivated to do the necessary work to achieve it.

Snyder *et al.* (2011) endorsed positive self-talk statements like 'I will keep going' to encourage people to keep working on their goals. Lyubomirsky (2007: 220) contended that such statements can help create 'self-fulfilling prophecies'. However, Wood *et al.* (2009) stated that repeating positive affirmations such as 'I am a lovable person' may actually lower self-esteem in people with a weak sense of self-worth to begin with. It is as if they start feeling, 'I am not really a lovable person and now I'm a liar, too'. Kross *et al.* (2014) offered a more complex view of self-talk, suggesting that the grammar of it makes a difference. When, instead of talking to oneself in the first person ('I need to relax') before a stressful situation like a big test or giving a speech, subjects change it to the second person ('You need to relax') or the third person, including their name ('[name] needs to relax'), they experience 'linguistic self-distancing', which makes the advice to themselves stronger. The point of bringing up these issues is to note the complexity. A search for affirmations for students on Google brings up over a half million hits. The research, however, clearly demonstrates that it is not as simple as telling students to say positive things to themselves. Teachers should be aware of the complexity and, perhaps, share some of those issues with students, encouraging them to say positive things they actually believe.

Conclusion

Positive psychology has matured. We have moved beyond 'happiness' to looking at the bigger area of well-being. It is also impacting a broader range of fields, including language teaching. We know that happy, engaged students learn more. As ESL/EFL teachers, we all deal with educational psychology and related issues like motivation and learner interest. Attention to developments in positive psychology such as PERMA – Positive emotion, Engagement, Relationships, Meaning and Accomplishment – provides tools to let us teach more than grammar, functions and the like. They allow us to truly engage in humanistic language teaching. They let us teach people.

Acknowledgments

Thank you to Miyagi Gakuin Women's University, Sendai, Japan, and to Kazuyoshi Sato and Nagoya University of Foreign Studies MATESOL Program, Nagoya, Japan, and Hugh and Alastair Graham-Marr of ABAX ELT Publishing for supporting my work. Thanks to Joanne Sato for the photographs. Thanks also to the editors of this volume both for their valuable feedback and for organizing such a worthwhile project.

References

Achor, S. (2010) *The Happiness Advantage: The Seven Principles of Positive Psychology that Fuel Success and Performance at Work.* New York: Crown Business.

Berman, M. and Brown, D. (2000) *The Power of Metaphor.* Carmarthen: Crown House Publishing.

Bryant, F. and Veroff, J. (2007) *Savoring: A New Model of Positive Experience*. Mahwah, NJ: Lawrence Erlbaum Associates.

Davis, P. and Rinvolucri, M. (1988) *Dictation: New Methods, New Possibilities.* Cambridge: Cambridge University Press.

Fredrickson, B. (2009) *Positivity*. New York: Crown.

Fredrickson, B. (2013) *Love 2.0: How Our Supreme Emotions Affects Everything We Feel, Think, Do, and Become.* New York: Hudson Street Press.

Hadfield, J. (1997) Medals. In P. Watcyn-Jones (ed.) *Top Class Activities* (pp. 10–40). London: Penguin English.

Haidt, J. (2006) *The Happiness Hypothesis: Finding Modern Truth in Ancient Wisdom.* New York: Basic Books.

Hamre, B. and Pianta, R. (2006) Student–teacher relationships. In G. Bear and K. Mink (eds) *Children's Needs III: Development, Prevention, and Intervention* (59–71). Washington, DC: National Association of School Psychologists.

Harada, N. (2014) Gratitude project: Writing, reading and reporting. Paper presented to the Japan Association for Language Teaching 2014 Conference, Tsukuba, 23 November.

Hefferon, K. and Boniwell, I. (2011) *Positive Psychology: Theory, Research and Applications.* Milton Keynes: Open University Press/McGraw-Hill Education.

Helgesen, M. (2003a) One more time with feeling: Bringing task recycling to the classroom. *English Connection* 7 (3), 6–7.

Helgesen, M. (2003b) Plan ahead: A do-it-yourself guide to helping your students think about what they will say. *English Teachers in Japan Journal* 4 (2), 1–7.

Kahneman, D. (2010) The riddle of experience vs. memory. Video file retrieved from http://www.ted.com/talks/daniel_kahneman_the_riddle_of_experience_vs_memory (accessed 17 December 2014).

Kross, E., Bruehlman-Senecal, E., Park, J., Burson, A., Dougherty, A., Shablack, H., Bremner, R., Moser, J. and Ayduk, O. (2014) Self-talk as a regulatory mechanism: How you do it matters. *Journal of Personality and Social Psychology* 106 (2), 304–324.

Layard, R. (2005) *Happiness: Lessons from a New Science.* New York: Penguin.

Lynch, T. and Maclean, J. (2001) A case of exercising: Effects of immediate task repetition on learners' performance. In M. Bygate, P. Skehan and M. Swain (eds) *Researching Pedagogic Tasks: Second Language Learning, Teaching and Testing* (pp. 141–162). Harlow: Longman (Pearson Education).

Lyubomirsky, S. (2005) Eight steps toward a more satisfying life. *TIME – Asia Edition* 165 (8) 32–33.

Lyubomirsky, S. (2007) *The How of Happiness.* New York: Penguin.

Lyubomirsky, S. (2013) *The Myths of Happiness.* New York: Penguin.

Maley, A. (2014) Putting creativity into writing. Paper presented to Japan Association for Language Teaching Conference, Sendai, Japan, 30 November.

Maurice, K. (1983) The fluency workshop. *TESOL Newsletter* 17 (4), 1–29.

Mazgutova, D. (2013) Focus on fluency. *English Teaching Professional* 85, 34–35.

Nakamura, J. and Csikszentmihalyi, M. (2009) Flow theory and research. *The Oxford Handbook of Positive Psychology* (pp. 195–206). New York: Oxford University Press.

Nation, P. (1989) Improving speaking fluency. *System* 17 (3), 377–384.

Oishi, S., Diener, E. and Lucas, R.E. (2007) The optimum level of well-being: Can people be too happy? *Perspectives on Psychological Science* 2 (4), 346–360.

Peterson, C. (2006) *A Primer in Positive Psychology.* New York: Oxford University Press.

Pink, D. (2006) *A Whole New Mind.* New York: Riverhead Trade.

Seligman, M.E.P. (2011) *Flourish: A Visionary New Understanding of Happiness and Well-Being.* New York: Free Press.

Seligman, M.E.P., Steen, T., Park, N. and Peterson, C. (2005) Positive psychology progress: Empirical validation of interventions. *American Psychologist* 60 (5), 410–421.

Seligman, M.E.P., Ernst, R., Gillham, J., Reivich, K. and Linkins, M. (2009) Positive education: Positive psychology and classroom interventions. *Oxford Review of Education* 35 (3), 293–311.

Sivers, D. (2010) Keep your goals to yourself. Video file retrieved from http://www.ted.com/talks/derek_sivers_keep_your_goals_to_yourself#t-61540 (accessed December 2014).

Snyder, C., Lopez, S. and Pedrotti, J. (2011) *Positive Psychology: The Scientific and Practical Explorations of Human Strengths* (2nd edn). Thousand Oaks, CA: Sage.

Sousa, D. and Tomlinson, C. (2011) *Differentiation and the Brain.* Bloomington, IN: Solution Tree Press.

Tardy, C.M. and Snyder, B. (2004) That's why I do it: Flow and EFL teachers' practice. *ELT Journal* 58 (2), 118–126.

Tokuhama-Espinosa, T. (2014) *Making Classrooms Better: 50 Practical Applications of Mind, Brain and Education Science.* New York: Norton. 132–134.

Viney, P. (2009) Think tank: What are some ways to start a class off right. Retrieved from the blog http://www.eltnews.com/columns/thinktank/2009/04/what_are_some_ways_to_start_a.html (accessed 17 December 2014).

Willis, J. (2010) The current impact of neuroscience on teaching and learning. In D. Sousa (ed.) *Mind, Brain and Education: Neuroscience Implications for the Classroom* (pp. 47–67). Bloomington, IN: Solution Tree Press.

Wiltshier, J. (2014) Speaking activities with principles. Paper presented to the Japan Association for Language Teaching 2014 Conference, Tsukuba, 23 November.

Wingate, J. (2000) *Knowing Me, Knowing You.* Guildford: Delta Publishing.

Wood, J., Perunovic, W.Q.E. and Lee, J. (2009) Positive self-statements: Power for some, peril for others. *Psychological Science* 20 (7), 860–866.

14 Teaching to Learn and Well-Become: Many Mini-Renaissances

Tim Murphey

Introduction

Most teachers realize that when sharing positive content in their lessons, students seem to prosper and flourish (Seligman, 2011; Seligman & Czikszentmihalyi, 2000). Pushing the envelope somewhat, this chapter proposes that getting students to teach others outside of class spreads the benefits to the wider info-sphere (networks), and also embeds the ideas even more deeply in the students themselves, due to the hypothesized well-becoming through teaching/giving effect (Murphey, 2014). Teachers themselves recognize this 'high' when they have delivered significant ideas in their classrooms that they notice makes significant differences in their students' lives. This chapter looks briefly at how 206 students over a five-year period taught affirmation songs to people in their social networks and how they reported teaching 'rushes' in their published case studies when doing so. Then I look more in depth at the outcomes of 56 students, in a later course, who began teaching a variety of 'well-becoming' material in their networks.

Extrapolating from the early song case studies, I began asking students in a variety of classes to teach a variety of valuable information from their courses to others in their social networks (significant split-story narratives, eight ways to reduce stress, the power of sleep, ground-breaking neuroscience information for learning, etc.) and noticed similar 'highs' being reported by the students, thus supporting the 'well-becoming through teaching' hypothesis, or what I have more recently conceptualized as *mini-renaissances*. Thus, in a more focused manner, I report on data from one class in the spring of 2014 in which students started doing weekly teaching reports describing out-of-class teaching in their action logs (Murphey, 1993, 1995; Murphey *et al.*, 2014) and carrying it further in the second semester with 56 short case studies for a final writing project, in other words, potentially negotiating *many mini-renaissances* in students' environments through expansive learning (Sannino & Ellis, 2014).

Background: Mini-Renaissances

In SLA it has been proposed for a long time that task-based learning is effective for language learning (Ellis, 2003; Samuda & Bygate, 2008), and in general education for a century, since Dewy (1910, 1963), yet with little buy-in from many practicing teachers who seem addicted to PPP (present, practice, produce). Positive psychology, however, is offering a host of ways to live more healthy, happy and intellectually stimulating lives that people actually wish to share with their social networks to make them healthier, happier, stimulated and stimulating. Recasting task-based learning as student task-based teaching in their networks provides students with a way to see the value of what they are learning and a way to ensure that teachers themselves are teaching something worth paying forward.

In Csikszentmihalyi's 1996 iconic book *Creativity: The Psychology of Discovery and Invention*, he mentions and describes several periods in human history when humans were particularly creative. Describing the great 25-year renaissance period between 1400 and 1425 in Florence, he supports his systemic view of creativity (social conditions plus individuals) showing how wealth and competitions enhanced individual possibilities:

> Thus the sociologist of art Arnold Hauser rightly assesses this period: 'In the art of the early Renaissance … the starting point of production is to be found mostly not in the creative urge, the subjective self-expression and spontaneous inspiration of the artist, but in the task set by the customer. (Csikszentmihalyi, 1996: 36; quoting Hauser, 1951)

Here I equate the *customer* with the *teacher* who sets a task for artists (students) and then gives them time to complete the task (out of class). For a mini-renaissance to occur, the task needs to be well thought out but with enough leeway to give the artists (students) room to create. (Creating a mini-'renaissance' in their students could be a goal for every teacher. Below, I will describe more directly how I equate renaissance with 'expansive learning'.)

In Csikszentmihalyi's note 36, at the back of his book, he states:

> A similar conclusion is reached by Heydenreich, who writes about the same historical period (1974, p. 13): 'the patron begins to assume a very important role: in practice, artistic production arises in large measure

> from his collaboration.' The same argument holds for creative production in other domains as well. (Csikszentmihalyi, 1996: 408)

I contend that the teacher 'begins to assume a very important role' as she or he learns to collaborate with students through task-based learning in and out of class. Teaching can be one of those 'other domains' that Csikszentmihalyi mentions and we do not have to wait for any higher authority to give us permission to give tasks to start a renaissance. We just do it!

Robinson and Tamir's chapter 'A task-focused mind is a happy and productive mind: A processing perspective' in *Designing Positive Psychology* (Sheldon *et al.*, 2011) contrasts the task-focused mind with the self-focused mind and the authors see (as does the supporting literature they cite) the 'preoccupation with the self as a source of problems rather than benefits' (Robinson & Tamir, 2011: 161; cf. their Figure 11.1, p. 163). Their chapter shows how too much self-focusing produces lesser task success, psychopathology and negative affect, while task-focusing tends to create greater task success, mental health and positive affect.

The tasks that Robinson and Tamir (2011) describe have to do basically with self-regulation in one's environment, studying for a test, writing a report and so on. It is fairly easy to imagine how students might slip out of task-focus and into self-focus, lamenting and doubting their 'poor' abilities. Those who report that they can sustain a task-focus rather than a self-focus obviously do better and accomplish more.

The tasks of teaching others out of the classroom, however, take the task-focus to another level, in which interaction with another person perhaps allows them to remain more task-focused, as well as altruistic in their goals. Tomasello writes, 'Teaching is a form of altruism, founded on a motive to help, in which individuals donate information to others for their use' (Tomasello, 2009: xiv). Thus, I would hypothesize that when students are given tasks which involve helping/teaching others, rather than just learning themselves, they can move to a deeper level of involvement and are able to interact more with the material and others, which keeps them much more task-focused and less likely to slip into negative self-focusing. And they learn the material better as well! Leary and Guadagno say, 'quieting the self can increase prosocial action' (Leary & Guadagno, 2011: 140). I would contend the inverse as well, that the tasks of teaching/helping others learn are prosocial tasks, and that by increasing the prosocial tasks, 'the quieting of the self' is more likely; that is, when we are concerned mainly with others succeeding at a task, we forget ourselves, in states of flow (Csikszentmihalyi, 1990). Thus, there seems to be another level of task that is beneficial for humans, that is, those tasks which help others. As the literature already states, task-focus is better for us than self-focus, and we might extend this by saying that teaching/helping others to learn enhances our own learning tasks and provides us with an altruistic teaching rush (as in

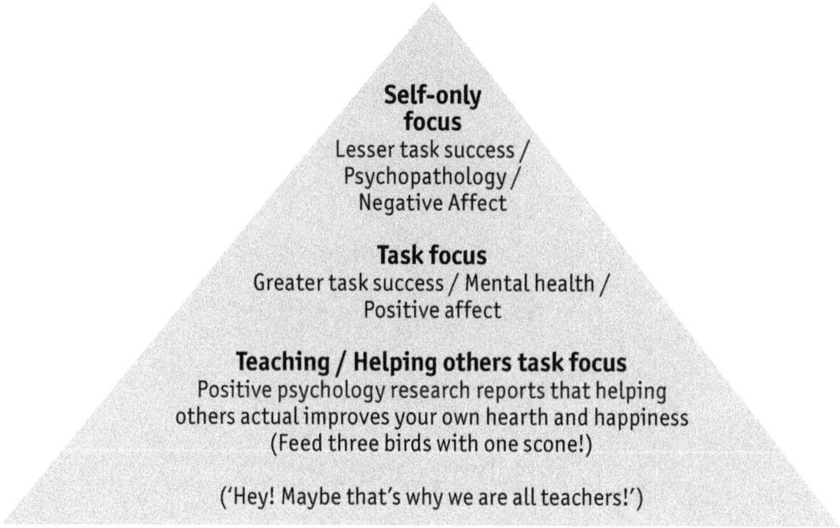

Figure 14.1 Levels of focus pyramid (partially derived from Robinson & Tamir, 2011)

Figure 14.1), which not only quiets the self but engages us with interaction and potentially a teaching rush.

Figure 14.2 presents some popular conceptions of the same idea (popularly attributed to the National Training Laboratories, Bethel, Maine, and other medical training centers) that are easily found on the internet. Although the actual data-sources and precise numbers are disputed by some writers online, many admit that they seem reasonable, although seldom enacted in general education, where the factory model of information delivery and banking (Friere, 1970) are most dominant. The basic idea is that the people who do the most (teachers usually), learn the most. Thus, if we want students to learn more we could organize their work in terms of teaching others, which helps not only them but potentially their whole social network. That the data in Figure 14.2 have their origin in medical institutions, where it matters most that young interns really learn, should be no surprise.

Milton Erickson, known mainly for his hypnotherapy success, reportedly much preferred giving people real-world tasks to perform outside of therapy, as they seemed to work much better than anything he could do with them in therapy and the tasks were more convincing because they happened in the real world, providing a real experience for clients that they could not just attribute to the place of therapy or the therapist (Rosen, 1991), that is, the clients did it themselves and had to realize they had some agency and were

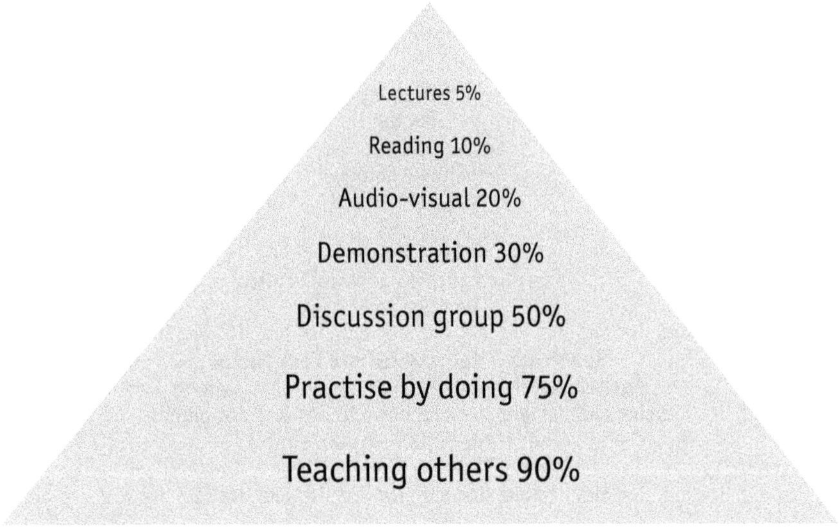

Figure 14.2 Learning pyramid

not dependent on the therapist or the therapy. Perhaps teachers could also follow this model more explicitly by getting students to perform teaching/helping tasks out of the classroom more regularly.

Murphey (2014) reported on 155 folk musical therapy case studies (MTCSs, hereafter) in which students taught an array of 'songlets' (short song lines to well known melodies) (cf. *kaeuta*; Dorsey, 2013), usually tied to a call and response (e.g. call: 'How are you?' Response: 'Super happy optimistic joyful and prodigious', sung to the tune of Walt Disney's Mary Poppins' 'Supercalifragilisticexpialidocious'). Since that article, he has added two more class publications to the database, bringing the number to 206 case studies over a five-year period. Most songlets benefit from the melodies of well known iconic folk and Christmas tunes, as well as gestures and the generation of positive emotions.

In this chapter, I wish to generalize this procedure from simply songlets to students' sharing and teaching *whatever* they might be learning in class. To do so, I report particularly on one large 'Ways of Learning' class's responses to weekly assignments to teach what they learned in class to others, as reported in their action logs (Murphey, 1993, 1995; Murphey *et al*., 2014), and more specifically on short reports at the end of the autumn semester 2014, about teaching selected material in slightly more depth, which was also made into a class publication available online (Murphey, 2015). First, below, I describe the 'well-becoming through teaching/giving' hypothesis in more detail.

The 'Well-Becoming Through Teaching/Giving' Hypothesis

> Before I did this Case Study, I read a booklet of case studies from a previous class. Many students wrote: 'After I taught songs to friends or family, they really looked happy, and I also became happy.' Somehow, I did not believe their words. I changed my mind after my experience. It is true. I can't explain exactly why, but my sister and I laughed a lot and felt happy during the activity. *Though I hesitated to do this and thought that we might quarrel doing this, I could enjoy teaching and my sister enjoyed it.... It has been a few days since I taught her, but I still hear her singing 'Do it again' in the house.* (Ito, cited in Murphey, 2014)

I cited Ito in my 2014 article to show that just reading about something does not really convince us. Ito said she had read previous MTCSs but had not really believed them. But when she did it herself, that is, when she had the experience herself, she recognized that it was indeed an enriching activity. Thus, while we can learn a lot from reading others' experiences, it is immensely more impressive to us to enact it ourselves, to do it (Dewey, 1910, 1938). This is what I call a *teaching rush*! (At the meta-level of your reading of this chapter, you might indeed understand and become motivated to do similar things that I describe, but I assure you, it will be much more convincing when you actually enact them and see for yourself how these concepts help learners learn through teaching.)

The basics of the 'well-becoming through teaching/giving' hypothesis are the positive feelings at 'seeing someone learn' that came to many of the students as they taught. The following quotes are from the songlets data:[1]

> ...watching someone's skill improve was *very exciting*. (M. Yonaha)

> *the most important thing is how much I could enjoy teaching! While I was teaching songs, I could enjoy it and my mother seemed to enjoy singing new songs. Our enjoyment made it a successful project!* (M. Sekine)

> *It is an effective way to teach that mixes study with happy things.* (Tsubasa Sato)

> *We laughed many times. We almost forgot that this was studying.* (Y. Omagari)

> It was really nice opportunity for me to communicate with my father. I thought *sharing good songs makes us happy*. I will keep teaching songs and things that I learned in this class to everyone. (A. Yamamoto)

While the above quotes show directly the changes in emotions of the teacher, many more show the exciting changes in the learners, implying a teaching rush as well:

> After a week, I decided to call ... she said suddenly, *'I can change my own mind by singing a song a little bit. I try to change my mind positively more from now*. Thank you for your teaching! Please teach me more...'. In conclusion, when we sing a song that includes happiness and meaningfulness, people tend to create positive thinking as above ... singing a song is a tool to give good effects for mental and physical health. (Y. Koge)

> *I manage my stress by singing this song* ['What do you love¿']…. The laughing part was too embarrassing to sing at class. However I didn't feel embarrassed at home with my mother. Rather I enjoyed singing it with her.... That went beyond my imagination ... I appreciate my mother. (S. Enomoto)

> from 6pm–midnight ... I sang it and showed the gestures during a pause in our work.... Two hours later when we cleared the tables I started singing the song and she joined me.... *We worked humming it for the rest of this work time and enjoyed it ... our hard working time changed to an enjoyable working time. The song made us happy. She told me that she wanted to sing more English songs.... I really enjoyed doing this case study because now I have someone to sing with at my part-time job. Now, we are happier.* (Arisa Sato)

> I found this teaching interesting and difficult. I was interested in how *he changed*. I could see *the changing of his singing and attitude*. At first he was not interested in singing an English song, but after he could sing 'Why do you smile¿' he wanted to learn another song. This changing was *really an interesting point*. (F. Kobayashi)

Preliminary Results from Action Logs: Regular Teaching Reports and Newsletters

I have been doing action logs for over 20 years (Murphey, 1993), getting students to report on how they felt about each activity in class, and to evaluate the activities so that I might teach better and they might communicate better with me about how they want the class to be run. Action logging has become a great resource to enact student-centered teaching. During the spring semester 2014 in Japan (April–July) I experimented with giving students small assignments out of class to teach various sets of material to others in their particular networks (friends, classmates, family, co-workers, etc.). They were free to use any of the material I gave them (stories, songlets, ideas, strategies, videos, etc.) or what partners may have given them (e.g. vocabulary). I regularly take comments from students' action logs and put them on a short newsletter to share with the whole class. The comments below were initially in their action logs and shared in the class newsletters anonymously (with slight spelling and grammar editing). The newsletters are regularly used in class in pair work, for one to read out loud and the other to shadow (from just listening) and then to summarize and discuss.

> I taught 'Eight Ways [to Reduce Stress]' to my mother. She is so busy she fell asleep while I was talking.
>
> I taught to my brother who seems to be overly stressed by exams.
>
> I taught The Girl Effect to my mom who teaches English in our house. We discussed education in foreign countries after that.
>
> We laughed learning 'Ten Idioms' together. 'We laugh a lot, WHEN we talk a lot!'
>
> I taught my brother the 'Five Ways to Happiness' and the 'Seven Ways of Improvisation'! He was surprised about it. I will teach the 'Ten Idioms' soon.

And some students were already expressing some of the main ideas in this chapter in their action logs that I also added to the newsletters:

> I taught the Wise Person story to my friend and she agreed. I think that *teaching and learning have a very important relationship with each other.*
>
> I want to know *how to learn and teach better and help other people like a wise person. I want to be always learning.* I told my father & he enjoyed it & agreed!
>
> My boyfriend is doing teaching practice so I taught him the 'Eight Ways to Reduce Stress' and I think it will help him. *It makes me happy to help someone.*
>
> I taught my mother the 'Ten Idioms'. She liked them and showed me the gestures always. *I could remember them well by teaching her!*
>
> *'If you really want to learn something, just TEACH!'* I did it with the idioms!

And some started thinking like teachers and occasionally I responded myself ('TM', below):

> *Are there any treats or strategies to keep people interested and motivated while I am teaching the things we learn in class?*
>
> **TM**: It often is more engaging if you start with a question? Or a scene: e.g. Do you know how they say 'goman osuri' in English? Would you like to know good ways to reduce your stress? I saw a super video today, would you like to watch it with me? When a wise person talks to a fool, who learns the most? Did you know that writing can actually make you healthier, if you write in certain ways?

Some displayed 'teaching highs' and seemed to learn expansively from the procedure. Some examples from that spring semester, shared with the students, allowed me to see the greater potential for this activity that engaged students' social networks outside the classroom:

> In this time, the person who I taught 'Eight Ways [to Reduce Stress]' was my mother. She always looks exhausted because of hard work every day. Therefore, I thought this is my duty and feel responsible to teach her 'Eight Ways'. I did not teach her in English but in Japanese. After that, I made a copy of the paper and gave it to her.
>
> My poor brother again became a target of teaching 'Girl Effect.' He showed that he got the idea with his facial expression, but said nothing! This has to be beneficial for him! I am going to teach these ideas again and again.
>
> I taught how to use 'We both' for my cousin. She is 1 year younger than me so she is studying for the entrance exam of university. She understood the role of 'both' and she made some good example sentences. I hope it was good lecture for her.

Thus, I gradually began appreciating more and more students' connections with out-of-class networks as being potentially great resources for remediation (re-telling, re-learning) of what they were learning in class. In the autumn semester 2014, the 'teaching report' became a mainstay of the action logs homework and students were requested to report after every class on their out-of-class teaching of something that we did or learned in class. Students did a good job and convinced me that they were indeed learning, as the above quotes show. However, to push the envelope a bit further, I wanted them to reflect a bit deeper and teach a bit more in depth. So I devised the short case study project, described below.

The Present In-depth Study

The present study describes results stemming from the specific assignment to teach material we had been learning in class and to do follow-up checks to see if it had indeed been learned. Students were free to select the material, the people they wished to teach, and the other procedures. Fifty-six students completed the assignment in December 2014, and their 'teaching to learn' descriptions were put into a class publication available online (Murphey, 2015); paper copies were distributed to all students in the final class in January 2015.

The class

The name of the class was 'Ways of Learning'. It was an elective open to all four years and all departments (English, Asian Languages, International Communications Department, and Iberian Languages), with usually about two-thirds of the students being first- and second-year students and the rest composed of third- and fourth-year students. It met twice a week for a 90-minute class, September through to January for a total of 15 weeks, or a total of 30 classes, each of 90 minutes. The number of students in the class usually ranged from 45 to 85, and in the semester in question it was 62.

The final writing assignment

Students were given the handout reproduced in Box 14.1 on 2 December 2014.

The materials taught by students

In Murphey (2014), short songlets were the main material in the language classes[2] focusing on music and song and attended by third- and fourth-year students only. In this Ways of Learning class, students were looking more holistically at their foreign language learning endeavors in terms of strategies, beliefs, motivations and attitudes. My personal feeling that health and happiness add greatly to the more strictly SLA materials provokes me into openly showing and promoting better health and happiness habits to ensure better learning and living through English. Because many first- and second-year students were involved and because of the large class size, 250 words were required (rather than 400 words, as in the folk music case studies). Students were allowed to choose the material they wanted to teach (from a short suggested list) and the procedures. Briefly let me describe some of these materials (listed in the Appendix to this chapter).

The 'Ten Idioms' are simply fun idioms that are coded along with 10 gestures that make them easier to remember. Additionally, the initial

Box 14.1 Student information handout for the case study 'Ways of Learning' project

Final Writing Assignment: Ways of Learning Class Dec 2, 2014: Teaching Case Study

You need to teach one of the following: Ten Idioms / Eight Ways to Reduce Stress / Seven Ways of Improvisation / Five Ways to Happiness and the reasons they are five ways to happiness (optional to also teach another song or two also for fun). You need to write a paper (at least 250 minimum words – put a word count at the bottom of your paper – see below). Send it to Tim by email by Dec. 15 **mits@kanda.kuis.ac.jp** or earlier.

Sample Paper

Title: **Teaching My Dear Mother!** Author: **Hiro Kasegawa**

1. Initial Teaching
I chose my XXXXX to teach xxxxxxxx to. She is .... years old and works .... I taught after dinner on Dec 5th 2014 at about 8 pm in the kitchen. First I taught.... Then I taught....She had some troubles with .... So we repeated that part many times. She seemed to like/dislike/ xxx and was frustrated sometimes. I wrote down a complete version at the end and gave it to her to read and use. I also taught her 'How do you succeed?' because I think she is afraid of making mistakes.

2. Follow up!
After working about 30 minutes, I told her I would come back and give her a quiz every hour for 3 hours and to help her remember it. Before I left her she could say it all perfectly.
The first time I came back she had trouble remembering XXXX . The second time 2 hours later she really forgot a lot. The third time, it seems she really got it. Two days later, I asked her again and she could still say the whole thing. I am happy and I think she is too. She wanted to learn more. So I taught her my favorite song....

3. Conclusion
I have never taught anyone anything before this class. I think .... (220 words to here already)

handout had four sets of the idioms with Japanese translations that the students could cut up and paste on their mirrors, refrigerators, doors, or the back of their iPhones.

The 'Eight Ways to Reduce Stress' piece was copied from an orange juice carton but is information from the highly respected Mayo Clinic. We brainstormed for several semesters different acronyms that would help us remember them and the winner seemed to be COPS BEES, which stands for being Connected with friends and family, being Organized, being Positive, and Simplifying your life. Then there is a break between the words that reminds us to take Breaks. And the last three are all physiological: Eat well, Exercise appropriately and Sleep enough. (It was noted also that seeing 'cops and bees' can often increase our stress, thus making it easier to remember the acronym.)

The 'Seven Ways of Improvisation' also benefited from a strange acronym (PLLYARF) and Dave Morris's great TEDx talk: Play, Let yourself fail, Listen, say Yes, say And, follow the Rules, and relax and have Fun.

Finally, the 'Five Ways to Happiness' (Murphey, 2013b) is a *kaeuta* (a borrowed melody with new words) that I wrote to the tune of the '12 Days of Christmas' and which originally was 12 ways to happiness, but it was too long and hard to remember, so we shortened it to five and added some fun gestures: smile from ear to ear, breathe in deep, look up at the sky, sing a melody, and dare to show your love.

These four sets of material were suggested and done by the great majority, but a few students took the initiative to teach several other songs and materials. Several also taught one of the above and added a song in for fun.

Quantitative and qualitative data

In the 2014 autumn semester of the 'Ways of Learning' class, 56 students did the final writing assignment and turned it in on time (Table 14.1).

There is ample qualitative data to see that students learned this material better through teaching it.[3] One student said:

> I also think teaching is very enjoyable for me because I also learn a lot from teaching and I can make someone happy. So I will try to teach a lot to many people from now on! (Kanda Mio)

Another said:

> This experience is really useful for me and more than that, I realized, through this activity that teaching someone is effective for me to remember clearly.' (Satake Miki)

Table 14.1 Students' selection of material to teach that they described in their case studies

Teaching material	*No. of students (out of 56)*	*Facilitators*
Eight Ways to Reduce Stress	29 (52%)	Acronym COPS BEES
Ten Idioms	12 (21%)	Gestures
Five Ways to Happiness	9 (16%)	Song (familiar tune) and gestures
Seven Ways of Improvisation	4 (7%)	Acronym PLLYARF
Other material	2 (4%)	Songs, shadowing, etc.

The 'teaching to learn' process obviously allowed students themselves to learn the material better.

However, much more was happening than merely learning the material. Teaching information that you value also creates greater affordances beyond the material and it creates opportunities that do not seem probable within classrooms alone. This out-of-class teaching to others creates 'expansive learning' or mini-renaissances:

> At the beginning of a process of expansive learning the object is only abstractly mastered as a partial entity, separated from the functionally interconnected system of the collective activity. By ascending to the concrete, an abstract object is progressively cultivated into concrete systemic manifestations and transformed into a material object that resonates with the needs of other human beings as well. These phases often require the subject to struggle and break out of previously acquired conceptions in conflict with new emerging ones. (Sannino & Ellis, 2014: 8)

Some students struggled with being teachers and often expanded previous conceptions of themselves as they developed emerging new identities, new insights, better relationships, and agency and well-becoming, among other things! Gregersen and MacIntyre (2014: 111) note, 'As language learners interact in their TLs [target languages], they are engaged in ongoing identity construction'. Asking them to take on the role as a teacher seems to create an even greater, and yet usually beneficial, shift in their identity constructions.

Evidence of the 'Well-becoming Through Teaching/Giving' Hypothesis

As with the songlets in Murphey (2014), most of the students in the 'Ways' class also wrote about the joys of teaching, often with surprise and a wish to do it more often. Whether they were helping parents, siblings or friends, the same types of 'teaching rushes' seems to overtake them:

> I felt happy about teaching this to my young sister because I could see her happy face. She was able to think about her future. So she could reduce her stress. After I taught it to her, she said, 'I'll teach these to my friends!' (Asuka Hori)

> Helping others learn is no less important than learning by oneself. I gave him what I could teach. In the end, he was successfully able to express

> the 'Eight Ways to Reduce Stress'. We became very happy. (Naoki Suzushika)

> I think the style of this homework is so good because we can share good information to learn English. (Mayuko Oka)

> he said thank you for teaching me them because these are very useful to reduce daily stress and I will try these from now on! I felt great because I could help my dear father. (Mio Kanda)

And some students waxed altruistically:

> I realized that teaching what I've got is helpful for not only me but also the others and remains stuck in my head. I'm spending productive days after taking this class because [it] teaches us to have a better life and encourages us to teach others. The best information in the world cannot help people unless we tell them about it. Our actions make better lives for others. (Shohei Okubo)

Thoughts on student selection of material to teach

Most of us know the old urban legend that 'We teach what we need to know most!' Well, maybe it is not really a legend but a truth. I want to understand how to live better and thus I seek out information that can help me and my students live better. It seems that the majority of them do the same, since 52% (29) chose the 'Eight Ways to Reduce Stress' and another 16% (9) chose the 'Five Ways to Happiness'. The 12 (21%) who chose to teach the 'Ten Idioms' may have chosen them because they were the first on the list or the latest that we needed to learn in the class before the assignment, or perhaps they are simply more focused on language learning than happiness and well-being – maybe they are already happy and well enough and thus can choose other goals.

Discussion

Getting students to teach what they are learning is like putting a young person in the driver's seat of a car for the first time and saying 'Go!' When they drive, they learn amazingly fast – they have to! (Fortunately, teaching others is not as dangerous as driving.) If they stay continually riding in another seat in the car (sitting passively in the classroom) they do not really learn to drive – and that unfortunately is what is happening in most schooling around the world – students are merely along for the ride, not driving. This is one of the main problems of education. How do you get all those people in front of you to drive? To do it! The 'flipped classroom' (Iswanti & Murphey, 2014; Jackson, 2013) is a good idea which I think will increase interaction in the regular classroom, but will cause other problems outside of the class if students just passively read and watch video lectures without interacting (discussing and teaching) with others at the same time as they read and watch.

I was a sports teacher in my younger years and there are no long lectures in sports – you demonstrate something and then the 'students' try to 'do it' in real time, with real results. They either make a layup in basketball or they don't, and they get quick feedback and try again, and again. They are in the driver's seat. In tennis, skiing and most other sports the same procedure is followed. However, in classroom learning we too often assume that an abstraction or model is sufficient without any actual 'doing'.

The repercussions for classroom teaching

Re-conceptualizing our teaching jobs as getting students to actually do something (drive and teach others to drive – doing something that increases their agency and that can increase the agency of others) also gets teachers to look twice at the material they are using in the classroom and ask, 'Is this really useful for my students? Is this something that is so useful that they might want to teach it to others, out of class? At least to others who are interested in the same topic? At least to each other?' Much of the information in positive psychology is making a big difference in the lives of those who study it and is excellent material for students to share beyond the classroom, in their own info-spheres. I love teaching about flow (Csikszenmihalyi, 1990), Love 2.0 (Fredrickson, 2013) and other positive psychology concepts and each time I realize it is a chance for me to re-learn and improve my understanding and integration of the concepts into my own psyche. I love teaching songs about smiling, laughing and enjoying life because I feel they develop the spirit of positive psychology without having to understand it all at the abstract level, which seems to come easier after experiencing singing the songs together.

Conclusion

Firstly, the 'well-becoming through the teaching/helping' hypothesis states that certain tasks that help others can get people out of self-focus. And thus the teaching/helping may even help in cures for certain mental illnesses. Secondly, I am convinced that teaching creates better learning and that usually it is the teacher in the classroom who is actually learning the most. Thus, if we want students to learn more, we need to spread that teaching time among them, giving them time to teach each other, and then invite them to take it out of the classroom and to teach others. It will be successful if the materials meet the basic health, happiness and social needs of the students, and those they teach. In any case, one teacher cannot really adjust to every individual in a large group at once in the ways they need in order to learn (Murphey, 2013d). But we can teach our students to adjust to their partners and they can learn naturally to adjust when they take the material out of class. And once teachers have a collection of case studies from one term, the next term's set of students can read the case studies and have near-peer role models (Murphey & Arao, 2001) to guide them.

In terms of language study, I call this value-added English (Murphey, 2013a). My students certainly do not always stay in English when teaching outside the classroom (or even in it) but the source material comes from English and thus they tend to think of it in those terms and the positive concepts give more value to learning the language because they are sharing life-promoting information that can make them and their networks healthier and happier.

Let me return for a moment to Robinson and Tamir (2011), who showed clearly that task-focused behaviors outperform self-focused behaviors and were seen as much healthier. I would like to suggest, that an *interactive-helping* task-focus approach might help people who are overly self-focused to break out of their negative affect and pychopathology and do a lot of good for others at the same time! When teachers report a state of 'flow', it is most likely because they feel they have been helping others to learn well. The 'teaching/helping rush' hypothesis holds that when you are successful at teaching and helping someone learn, you lose your self-focus and you have entered the territory of shared task-based joy and wonder. And like any dopamine rush, you want more! I believe that when teachers 'dare greatly' (Brown, 2012) and risk asking students to teach people in their networks the valuable things they are learning in their classes, and when teachers can read how students are 'paying it forward' in their case studies, then teachers will understand a greater good that deepens and widens the purpose of education.

Appendix. Optional materials taught by students

Eight Ways to Reduce Stress

Teacher-made handout originally from a Minute Made orange juice container, but information attributed to http://www.MayoClinic.com/nutrition.

Class-facilitated with the acronym **COPS BEES** for easier memorization:

Connect	Stay connected to family and friends
Organize	Organize so that you know where things are
Positive	Talk to yourself positively. Spend time with positive people.
Simplify	Prioritize and pace yourself.
Breaks	Take time to relax, stretch, or take a walk during the day.
Eat well	When you eat well and you're healthy you are better able to handle stress.
Exercise well	Some people find exercise not only healthy but also an outlet for stress.
Sleep well	Make enough time to sleep enough. Take power naps if they help.

Seven Ways of Improvisation

Facilitated by the acronym **PLLYARF**, and the Tedx talk by Dave Morris): **P**lay, **L**et yourself fail, **L**isten, say **Y**es, say **A**nd, follow the **R**ules (play the game), relax and have **F**un

Five Ways to Happiness!

English: Tim Murphey. Facilitated with gestures and the well known Christmas tune '12 Days of Christmas'.
When you want to be happy, there's (#) thing(s) you can do…
(#: one, two, three, four, five) (Tune: '12 Days of Christmas')

(1) Smile from ear to ear.
(2) Breathe in deep.
(3) Look up at the sky.
(4) Sing a melody.
(5) Dare to show your love.

Ten Idioms

Facilitated with gestures.

(1) my lips are sealed
(2) sweet talker
(3) bad mouth
(4) sharp mind
(5) take my hat off to …

(6) lend an ear
(7) lend (give) a hand
(8) show your face
(9) hard headed
(10) apple polishing

Other songs that some students used

- 'How Do You Succeed¿'
- 'Young and Strong and Beautiful'
- 'How Do You Have a Good Life¿'
- 'Why Do You Smile¿'

Notes

(1) This section of the chapter draws on the following student contributions to the various volumes of the *Music Therapy Case Studies* publication, edited by T. Murphey (available at https://sites.google.com/site/folkmusictherapy):
M. Ito (2013) The joy of laughing and singing. In vol. 4, p. 13.
S. Enomoto (2012) In vol. 3, pp. 8–9.
F. Kobayashi (2014) In vol. 7, p. 10.
Y. Koge (2012) In vol. 3, p. 11.
Y. Omagari (2013) Five ways friend. In vol. 5, p. 28.
Arisa Sato (2013) Singing while we work. In vol. 4, p. 12.
Tsubasa Sato (2013) How do you write¿ In vol. 5, p. 27.
M. Sekine (2014) Teaching songs project. In vol. 6, p. 17.
A. Yamamoto (2014) In vol. 8, p. 4.
M. Yonaha (2013) Doi Ta Ga. In vol. 4, p. 8.
(2) These were CBI/CLIL (content-based instruction/content and language integrated learning) classes.
(3) This section and the next of the chapter draws on the following student contributions to the *Teaching to Learn* publication, edited by T. Murphey (2015), produced from the Ways of Learning classes (available at http://issuu.com/luciusvonjoo/docs/waysfall2014teachingtolearn):
Kanda Mio, p. 13.
Satake Miki, p. 12.
Okubo Shohei, p. 14.
Hori Asuka, p. 7.
Suzushika Naoki, p. 8.
Oka Mayuko, p. 11.

References

Brown, B. (2012) *Daring Greatly*. New York: Gotham Books.
Csikszentmihalyi, M. (1990) *Flow: The Psychology of Optimal Experience*. New York: Harper Collins.
Csikszentmihalyi, M. (1996) *Creativity: The Psychology of Discovery and Invention*. New York: Harper.
Dewey, J. (1910) *How We Think*. Boston, MA: D.C. Heath.

Dewey, J. (1938) *Experience and Education.* New York: Collier.
Dorsey, J. (2013) Breaking records: Media, censorship, and the folk song movement of Japan's 1960s. In J. Lent and L. Fitzsimmons (eds) *Asian Popular Culture: New, Hybrid and Alternate Media* (pp. 79–107). New York: Lexington Books.
Ellis, R. (2003) *Task-Based Language Learning and Teaching.* Oxford: Oxford University Press.
Fredrickson, B. (2013) *Love 2.0.* New York: Hudson Street Press.
Friere, P. (1970, 1993) *Pedagogy of the Oppressed.* New York: Continuum.
Gregersen, T. and MacIntyre, P. (2014) *Capitalizing on Language Learners' Individuality.* Bristol: Multilingual Matters.
Hauser, A. (1951) *The Social History of Art.* New York: Vintage.
Heydenreich, L.H. (1974) *Il Primo Rinascimento.* Milan: Rizzoli.
Iswanti, S.N. and Murphey, T. (2014) Flipped student-activity videoing for expansive learning at home. In N. Sonda and A. Krause (eds) *JALT 2013 Conference Proceedings.* JALT: Tokyo.
Jackson, T. (2013) 'Flipped classroom' model shows proven progress in addressing broken educational experience in the US. Press release 19 November, retrieved from http://www.marketwatch.com/story/flipped-classroom-model-shows-proven-progress-in-addressing-broken-educational-experience-in-the-us-2013-11-19 (accessed November 2015).
Leary, M. and Guadagno, J. (2011) The role of hypo-egoic self-processes in optimal functioning and subjective well-being. In K. Sheldon, T. Kashdan and M. Steger (eds) *Designing Positive Psychology* (pp. 135–146). Oxford: Oxford University Press.
Murphey, T. (1993) Why don't teachers learn what learners learn? Taking the guesswork out with action logging. *English Teaching Forum* 31 (1), 6–10.
Murphey, T. (1995) Action logging. In R. White (ed.) *New Ways in Teaching Writing* (pp. 213–214). Alexandria, VA: TESOL.
Murphey, T. (2013a) Value added English learning. *Journal of the Saitama Educators* 3 (5), 1–8. Retrieved from http://issuu.com/saitamacityeducators/docs/vol.3__issue_5 (accessed November 2015).
Murphey, T. (2013b) Know happy, know life! *Journal of Saitama City Educators* 3 (5), 18–21, 30–32. Retrieved from http://issuu.com/saitamacityeducators/docs/vol.3__issue_5 (accessed November 2015).
Murphey, T. (2013c) The impact of self-information given to socially intelligent dynamic systems (SINDYS) i.e. classes! *'Scuola e Lingue Moderne' ANILS* 1 (5), 6–9.
Murphey, T. (2013d) Adapting ways for meaningful action: ZPDs and ZPAs. In J. Arnold and T. Murphey (eds) *Meaningful Action: Earl Stevick's Influence on Language Teaching* (pp. 172–189). Cambridge: Cambridge University Press.
Murphey, T. (2014) Singing well-becoming: Student musical therapy case studies. *Studies in Second Language Learning and Teaching* 4 (2), 205–235.
Murphey, T. (ed.) (2015) *Teaching to Learn!* 'WaysFall2014TeachingToLearn'. Retrieved from https://sites.google.com/site/folkmusictherapy/home (accessed November 2015).
Murphey, T. and Arao, H. (2001) Changing reported beliefs through near peer role modeling. *TESL-EJ* 5(3), 1–15. Retrieved from http://tesl-ej.org/ej19/a1.html (accessed November 2015).
Murphey, T., Barcelos, A. and de Moraes, R. (2014) Narrativizing our learning lives through action logs and newsletters. *Revista Contexturas* 23, 99–111.
Robinson, M. and Tamir, M. (2011) A task-focused mind is a happy and productive mind: A processing perspective. In K. Sheldon, T. Kashdan and M. Steger (eds) *Designing Positive Psychology* (pp. 160–174). Oxford: Oxford University Press.
Rosen, S. (1991) *My Voice Will Go With You: The Teaching Tales of Milton H. Erickson.* New York: W.W. Norton.

Samuda, V. and Bygate, M. (2008) *Tasks in Second Language Learning.* New York: Palgrave Macmillan.
Sannino, A. and Ellis, V. (eds) (2014) *Learning and Collective Creativity: Activity-Theoretical and Sociocultural Studies*. New York: Routledge.
Seligman, M. (2011) *Flourish.* New York: Free Press.
Seligman, M. and Czikszentmihalyi, M. (eds) (2000) Positive psychology. *American Psychologist*, 55 (special issue).
Sheldon, K., Kashdan, T. and Steger, M. (eds) (2011) *Designing Positive Psychology*. Oxford: Oxford University Press.
Tomasello, M. (2009) *Why We Cooperate*. Cambridge, MA: MIT Press.

15 Why and How to Use Positive Psychology Activities in the Second Language Classroom

Candy Fresacher

Introduction

In the second or foreign language classroom, a variety of themes or topics are used in order to teach the language and provide opportunities for students to practice it. In this chapter, I suggest that positive psychology (PP) activities could be used as content topics for language learning with the additional benefits of teaching PP strategies, which can also help students with other aspects of their education and lives, such as reducing inhibitive anxiety or increasing coping skills and positive learning attitudes. New research in PP provides specific interventions which can increase people's resilience and thus make it easier for them to cope with difficult situations (such as with anxiety) and which help people to be more productive (Seligman, 2002, 2006), creative (Fredrickson, 2011) and healthy (Diener & Biswar-Diener, 2008; Fredrickson, 2013). So the question then is, how can language teachers use PP interventions to support a more positive climate within the language classroom?

What is Positive Psychology?

Positive psychology is the scientific study of what goes right in life and looks at the optimal experiences people have when they are doing their best. It does not deny that there are negatives in the world, but the focus of this strand of psychology is on concentrating on how humans flourish. PP research has therefore been conducted to examine the effects of positive subjective experiences, successes, positive individual traits and positive relationships or groups. Interventions used in PP are meant to help anyone to lead more fulfilling lives, irrespective of whether they have psychological problems or not. Interventions are very often designed with the idea of offering resilience to those with issues such as depression or anxiety (Park & Peterson, 2008).

Since 1998, when Martin Seligman became President of the American Psychological Society, more research into the positive side of psychology has been done to establish the parameters necessary for people to 'flourish'. The research is focused on topics such as: positive emotions, engagement, interest, meaning, purpose, self-esteem, optimism, resilience, vitality, self-determination and positive relationships. Seligman (2011) uses the acronym PERMA to organize these aspects of PP and Oxford expands this approach to EMPATHICS (see Chapter 2 of this volume).

With respect to emotions, Barbara Fredrickson (2011, 2013) has done a considerable amount of research on positivity with her 'broaden-and-build' hypothesis. By this, she means that experiencing positive emotions broadens our awareness and ability to creatively explore opportunities around us. For learners of a second language, this is an important function of positive emotions, when the language itself opens new worlds and positivity allows them to focus on this new world more fully. MacIntyre and Gregersen (2012) have focused on these positive emotions in the second language classroom. Ed Diener and his son Robert Biswas-Diener have also done research seeking the universals in life satisfaction (Biswas-Diener, 2010; Diener & Biswas-Diener, 2008). Sonja Lyubomirsky (2007, 2013) has written more specifically about how positive activities can be useful in daily life. Together, these researchers, and many more, have shown that engaging in various activities can increase an individual's well-being. Against this background, the question arises as to whether using such activities in the second language classroom can enhance learners' well-being in a productive and positive way to improve their language-learning experiences.

Educational Uses of PP

Park and Peterson (2008) believe that the basic premise of PP is that the happiness and fulfillment of children and youth need more than just the identification and treatment of their problems. They suggest activities that rely on oral and written work which could be adapted to reflect the requirements of the language learner as well as offer positive energy to assist students in other areas of their lives. Their strengths-based approach uses the VIA (Values in Action) Strengths Survey developed by Peterson and Seligman to help students identify their strengths and use them when confronted with difficult tasks. This approach is described in more detail under 'Activity 2: VIA strengths', below.

In an eight-week seminar on stress management done with depressed college freshmen in the US, the Penn Resiliency Program (PRP), helped these students with positive education and the identification of their VIA signature strengths. The seminar raised optimism, lowered the depression and anxiety of the participants over a period of 30 months (Seligman, 2011). The PRP also introduced 'positive education' in an entire school in Australia and found that both students and teachers used the results of this positive education in ways the researchers had not anticipated (Seligman *et al.*, 2009). PP activities were used within all classrooms (music, sports, language instruction, etc.). Teachers who had received training from the PRP representatives used PP activities to reinforce PERMA in their students. This program has been used in schools for over 20 years and in various countries (including the US, the UK, Australia, China and Portugal) and a summary of the findings has shown: a reduction in and prevention of symptoms of depression, a reduction in the feeling of hopelessness, a prevention of clinical levels of depression and anxiety, and that it works equally well for children of different racial/ethnic backgrounds (Seligman *et al.*, 2009).

Fritz-Schubert (2011), with the approval of the German Ministry of Education, also integrated the special subject of 'happiness' into a school in Germany to find ways to promote social connectedness between students and classes, hoping to give students more self-confidence, trust and social connectivity as well as to reduce stress. After the first year, the 'happy' groups of students were compared with a similar group of students who had not participated in such a course. In the 'happy' group 80% of the students found their own actions meaningful, whereas only 33% of the students in the control group felt the same. The 'happy' students also found their classroom situation and the overall school atmosphere to be better. Therefore, at least in the short term, all of the sought-after qualities of the students in the test school were found to be higher than those in a school without the core subject 'happiness'.

These programs show that PP activities can be used with good effect in schools. I would argue that the same or similar activities applied in the second language classroom offer our students opportunities to increase their optimal experiences also in the second language. Through written and oral work, some of which can be corrected by the teacher for language and content as appropriate, students develop a positive attitude toward their second language, which can make them more willing to communicate and less anxious and more socially connected to their peers. An additional bonus is that the PP skills they learn in the language class can also be applied in their lives beyond the classroom.

How Malleable is Happiness?

For the classroom context, an especially important question to consider is whether interventions can in fact enhance learners' positivity. Research by Lyubomirsky and others has shown that everyone has a set range of 'happiness' or life satisfaction from their genetic makeup that accounts for anywhere between 25% and 50% of how a person approaches life (Lyubomirsky, 2007). Between 10% and 20% of our 'happiness quota' is made up of life circumstances, which might include: the country lived in, marital state, number of social connections, and religious beliefs/meaning in life. Areas that make less difference to personal happiness than perhaps might be expected include: youth, health, education level, race, and even a better climate (Seligman, 2002).

The important point is that an additional 40–50% of a person's happiness quota can be established through voluntary control – people can make themselves more or less happy. This means that life satisfaction can be increased within the set range that is part of a person's genetic background (Lyubomirsky, 2007).

The amount of happiness or life satisfaction can change over time. We cannot be happy every moment of every day. However, with more positive moments within our days, we not only increase our level of overall life satisfaction but can go from languishing to flourishing once we have passed the tipping point (which is usually considered three positives to one negative). Increasing our positivity through voluntary control offers us the chance to become more resilient for times when events may make life difficult. While the Losada line, which described the three-to-one phenomenon, has been critically examined and found wanting, the research behind the principle of more positive to negative interaction has withstood rigorous research testing (Fredrickson, 2014). This means, as Fredrickson (2011) indicates, we can broaden and build our emotional resources through positivity.

The findings from these studies offer good reasons why educators should seek to add more positive moments to the classroom. 'Optimism is not simply a matter of inborn temperament, but is also a skill that can be learned by recognizing unhelpful thinking strategies and replacing them with more positive ones' (Diener & Biswar-Diener, 2008: 193). We want our students to flourish, and this suggests that being optimistic can help them. Especially with respect to foreign language learning, it can be expected that the associated lower anxiety levels will increase their willingness to communicate (WTC) and so increase their class participation (see, e.g. MacIntyre *et al.*, 1998).

However, the word 'happiness' in English is really too general for the overall definition of what we want to accomplish in our second language classrooms. Some people might think that happiness is simply a momentary feeling, whereas what we want for our students is an increase in the moments of positivity that will then enable them to achieve the best possible results they can and 'flourish' within our learning environments. PP researchers refer to this as eudemonic happiness, which captures the deeper meaning of the concept of well-being, which includes growth, virtue and self-actualization. It is an added bonus if we can affect our students' lives positively beyond the classroom by generally enhancing their life satisfaction, resilience and flourishing as a result of PP interventions. This can be done by offering them the chance to be more positive in their attitudes toward their second language learning and by increasing their resilience, which helps them to bounce back from small defeats they might feel, such as when confronted with criticism. A hedonistic concept of happiness emphasizes enjoyment of the moment, but does not include the ideas of meaning and growth that are necessary for flourishing. Although here-and-now events are important, the striving to accomplish a goal, the helping of others and the belief in meaning outside of the self are also intricate parts of the concept of living a life of satisfaction. These goals can be achieved in the second language classroom using the second language, not only increasing ability in the language, but also contributing to other goals as well.

In this chapter, I would like to suggest ways in which this can be done from my experiences working with EFL learners in Hungary. The PP activities outlined in this chapter are thus twofold. Firstly, they are intended to help students find more satisfaction in their lives generally, but they are also intended to transfer the positive experiences and outlooks specifically to the task of second language learning. When students increase their attention to positive moments in learning, less importance will be given to the anxiety they might feel at times in the classroom, which in turn will give them more self-confidence. Further, an increase in self-confidence should increase their WTC and use the language according to the pyramid model of WTC (MacIntyre *et al.*, 1998). Resilience will also help learners to bounce back from any feedback that they may see as negative with regard to their language skills. Rather than ruminating about their deficiencies and showing signs of helplessness, resilience should help them to be open to exploring strategies to improve their language competencies and regulate their own learning.

Activities in the Classroom

The PRP (Penn Resiliency Program) team, which has done extensive work with young people in schools throughout the world using PP activities, has shown many benefits to students. However, training of group leaders is essential. In other words, the teachers need to understand the background of PP, be positive themselves and practice what they preach in order to be effective. 'Training and supervision of group leaders is critical.... Program effects were strongest when group leaders were members of the PRP team, or trained by the PRP team and closely supervised by the PRP team' (Seligman *et al.*, 2009: 298).

I decided some years ago to integrate PP activities into a four-day block course I teach at a university in Hungary entitled 'Improving Management

Communication Skills'. I chose to do this because I felt that the research was convincing in terms of the value of such activities, especially with regard to reducing stress, lowering anxiety and enhancing well-being. In total, the PP activities represent about one hour of class time within a 27-hour course. Although students are not required to do homework involving the activities, they do submit a feelings journal in which they often indicate whether and how they have used the activities outside the classroom.

In the following sections, I will outline a number of activities I have used with my classes, explaining the rationale behind them and issues involved in their use. The settings in which the following activities might be appropriate depend on the age and level of proficiency of the learners as well as the context in which the teaching takes place. These activities may therefore need to be adapted. From my experience, I have found that it is beneficial to try a number of activities, as not every individual – whether teacher or learner – responds positively to every exercise: variety means finding the right activity for each individual.

Activity 1: Three gratitudes

Lyubomirsky (2007) explains that there are eight ways that gratitude increases happiness. First, it means you savor the positive in your life. Second, expressing gratitude adds to self-worth and self-esteem, making you feel more confident. Gratitude also helps people cope with stress (by reframing negative life experiences). Fourth, being grateful means more moral behavior through an awareness of kindliness and caring. Fifth, gratitude builds social bonds and relationships. Sixth, appreciating what you have makes you less likely to want what others have. Seventh, gratitude dissolves negative emotions. And, finally, gratitude prevents – to some extent – hedonic adaptation (which means that when you experience something positive you get used to it quickly and so do not appreciate it as much as you could). With all these good reasons to think about what you are grateful for and pinpoint times of gratitude, the 'three blessings' or 'three gratitudes' activity is a powerful, easy and effective activity to establish positive emotions. Since we want our students to communicate in our classrooms and use their second language skills in a variety of ways, we want them to feel self-confident and have less anxiety, and this exercise provides that support while offering them opportunities to write in an informal manner.

The activity

Students write down three things for which they are grateful before they go to bed at night. Typically, this is done for any area of their own lives and opportunities they have. In this context, I have focused the gratitude on aspects of their second language learning. This could be specific actions or ideas or thoughts that occurred to the student that day about their second language or in their second language. It means that each day produces different areas of thankfulness specific to that day. This reflection also includes how the student believed this good thing came to be. How were they responsible for this happy event? Examples could be the fact that the student understood a YouTube video in the second language or wrote a translation that went smoothly or simply realized that they are fortunate to have the opportunity to learn a foreign language. In this exercise, it is important to find three new and different areas of thankfulness each day. While the exercise can be done at any time of the day, doing it before going to bed at night has an added advantage: it means that the student is likely to fall asleep thinking of the positive events in the second language rather than any negative thoughts.

In the first three weeks of class, the teacher can provide students with time to start their journals of gratitude. They can be creative in choice of notebook, but in the beginning it will be useful if the instructor can go around and help them formulate their three sentences in their second language. They should be encouraged to include at least one second language incident each time they consider their three gratitudes. Depending on how often the teacher sees the class each week, once they have understood the concept, the task can be done as homework. They do not need to share their journals with others in the class, but as their teacher you might wish to collect them to ensure the task is being done and the content is being expressed correctly. However, I believe that grades should not be given for tasks like this.

In the summer of 2014, a Facebook challenge spread through social media asking participants to list these gratitudes on their Facebook page for a week and nominate two others to do the same. This approach has an added impact of making others aware of the good things happening in their friends' lives. A friend sent me the following comment: 'I can feel the difference with the gratitudes – and, noticed it before someone else pointed out the health benefits. Even today when I am relatively down – it makes me at least remember all I do have to be grateful about.' While common sense tells us that concentrating on the positive rather than the negative is good, studies first done by Emmons and McCullough (2003) now substantiate this concept. Naturally, one could also encourage students to do this Facebook exercise too. However, the exercise needs to start only when the class feels comfortable with each other and there is an atmosphere of trust, otherwise they might not want to share what they are thankful for with classmates they do not know so well.

Activity 2: VIA strengths

The Value In Action (VIA) strengths test was designed to help individuals discover which of 24 character strengths best represent themselves. These 24 strengths were chosen by 55 scientists over a period of three years and include such traits as: honesty, curiosity, kindness, love of learning, and spirituality. When used with depressed individuals, the VIA strengths test helps uncover personal strengths and helps individuals become aware of the resources they have. They are encouraged to use this knowledge of their strengths actively. In a 14-session program in positive psychotherapy, Rashid and Seligman (2011) found that using this method relieved depressive symptoms better than other treatment, including drugs, in 55% of patients, as opposed to only 20% in 'treatment as usual' and 8% in 'treatment as usual plus drugs'.

In the second language classroom, there are many ways to use these strengths profiles, not only as individuals, but one could also form a class strengths profile as well. According to Linkins *et al.* (2015), when students identified and applied their signature strengths within a school program, students' social skills, engagement in school and learning strengths improved, although it was reported to have no effect on their symptoms of anxiety or depression. As a general statement, they conclude: 'the emerging research presents a compelling case for character strengths-based practices. Youth participants in VIA programs have demonstrated benefits related to achievement, engagement and wellbeing' (Linkins *et al.*, 2015: 66).

The activity

In class, we start with a general discussion of our strengths, imagining that we are brainstorming for a job interview. The type of job the teacher selects as the one being applied for will depend on the type of school in which they teach. However, general entry-level positions often require the same type of skills, and students are usually good at recognizing some of their own strengths. These might include: being organized, communicative, helpful, loyal, trustworthy, reliable, ambitious or competitive. Then I suggest to the students that, as homework, they try the VIA strengths test, which is available free online (at https://www.authentichappiness.sas.upenn.edu). This test can be found in English, German, French and Chinese, and it is part of an ongoing research program carried out by the Values-In-Action (VIA) Institute. Because there are over 200 questions and the test can be taken in selected languages, and because the results are given in that language, discussion can also be done in that same language. The 24 character strengths are listed and the test then lets the students know which of these strengths represent their top eight. There are two other versions of the test, one in a shorter format and the other for children. However, it must be noted that to do the test, students must register. After completing the test, students can be encouraged to speak to one another about their strengths, with examples showing how they have been used in the past. A next step could be to ask students to write a short letter to a potential employer about how they plan to use their strengths to help with difficult tasks in the future, since this is useful both for language building and for positivity.

To extend the activity, one can also discuss the strengths of characters in literature (Romeo and Juliet) or films (the musical/movie Grease) to see what character strengths are revealed. However, sometimes a strength can be overused as well as underused (Rashid, 2014) and so it is advisable for the teacher to guide a critical discussion about this possibility. For example, students might know someone who uses humor (one of the 24 VIA strengths) too often or inappropriately. They might also find that too much curiosity leads to frequent risk-taking activities that could have negative impacts. Students thus discuss the various strengths of the characters in literature or films in class and then later write about how the strengths were an advantage or disadvantage to the characters within the realm of the play, novel or movie.

Activity 3: Active constructive dialogs

This activity addresses a key concern in communication, one which lies at the core of language teaching, namely interpersonal dynamics. There are many ways to respond to someone who is relating a positive moment in their life. If we value their friendship, the best way to respond would be by sharing the joy and positivity of whatever event occurred to that friend. Gable *et al.* (2004) found that the way we react to good news actually predicts the quality of the relationship and can add to the relationship if the response is actively constructive; they went on to suggest a fourfold categorization of the types of responses people could give – active constructive, passive constructive, active destructive and passive destructive – which could be constructed as a simple table or matrix (Gable *et al.*, 2004).

An active constructive response to a good event would be to ask leading questions. The news: 'I just got a job promotion!' would lead the respondent to say: 'Wow, that's great news. Tell me more. What is the new job? Why did they give it to you? How does that make you feel?' A passive constructive response to the same news could be: 'Oh gee, that's pretty good … glad it happened', with no strong emotional connection or eye contact and therefore soon a change of subject. An active destructive response to the good news of 'I just got a job promotion!' would be: 'Oh no, does that mean you'll be staying late at the office every night now? I guess you'll be under a lot more stress. It surely isn't worth the extra money is it?' 'Why on earth did they choose you?' So the respondent is negatively active, looking for all the bad parts of the good news. A passive destructive response to the same good news of 'I just got a job promotion!' would be to interrupt the person telling the good news, or a change of subject to a concern of the respondent's own life, with little eye contact and no show of interest.

Active constructive dialogues promote flourishing and enhance interpersonal communicative contexts and so in classes students should participate in dialogs with this form of response (Achor, 2011; Froh & Parks, 2013). In this exercise, the teacher needs to explain the four ways one can react to any conversation involving a positive event as shown above. Indeed, students could be given a summary of the research to explain this rationale as a pre-speaking activity or watch the YouTube explanation given by Martin Seligman (https://www.youtube.com/watch?v=MU3y2ApnG7Y).

Learning the difference between these language forms can have an impact on relationship building and increases both parties' well-being. Active constructive dialog means dynamic listening to one another, with questions that ask the person to recount the details of their success and their feelings during the successful event. During a workshop with Rashid in Graz (April 2014), remarks made from participants who experienced the passive destructive or active destructive dialog in a role-play showed that both parties in the exercise were pulled down in mood by the experience.

This form of the exercise is also suggested by Froh and Parks (2013) in their book *Activities for Teaching Positive Psychology*.

The activity

I have used this activity in the following way. After the teacher has presented and explained the four possible responses to a good event, students work in pairs. Before they start, the teacher should brainstorm with all students about what body language is involved in dynamic listening: leaning forward, nodding the head, good eye contact, maybe taking notes if appropriate, saying 'yes, I understand' or 'I see', or asking for more information. One student is then assigned to tell the other student about a successful event or moment that they had recently. The second student should use active constructive dialog as well as positive body language to make the experience a positive one for both parties. After five minutes, the students should change roles and start again. Afterwards, the class can have a guided reflection on how it felt, what one needs to attend to in either role and how this could be important for them as communicators in a foreign language. A homework assignment can ask the students to keep a journal of their responses in their daily lives both as givers and receivers.

Activity 4: Loving-kindness meditation

Fredrickson's research (2013) shows that loving-kindness meditation is most effective in increasing well-being, as it produces physical changes in the vagus nerve that connects brain and heart. Her studies involved checking the emotional connectivity and capacity for positive resonance of the participants, depending on whether they had learned loving-kindness meditation or not. The vagus nerve, among other functions, checks that your breathing is in sync with your heart – ensuring that when you breathe in, your heart beats a little faster (to help propel oxygenated blood around the body) and when you exhale your heart slows down, so that the oxygenated blood is expelled less quickly. Fredrickson found that a better vagus tonality makes people more flexible across the physical, mental and social domains. Although generally the values measured for the vagus nerve are stable throughout a lifetime, with less than an hour a week of loving-kindness meditation they can be positively changed when checked months later. As an increase in this tonality leads to both better mental function and better social connectivity, and these are both important in the second language classroom, it would be good to do such exercises.

It is difficult to incorporate this type of meditation in the classroom, so in my class I use a form of meditation called visualization for students to control or manage their emotions by finding a place of calmness. We use it under the segment of the course in general stress reduction, and we talk about the possibility of using it when one is anxious before giving a presentation or before taking an exam or at other times in life. I repeat this exercise a number of times throughout the four-day period. Generally, I have the impression that I can see the amount of relaxation in the bodies of the students increase as they do this activity again and again. Although studies have shown that loving-kindness meditation is most effective for increasing positivity, other types of meditation can be used. Diener and Biswas-Diener (2008: 198) state that 'a promising body of new research shows that, with a little mental effort, recalling good events from the past can boost well-being'. Visualization is a form of this recall which can be seen as a 'savoring' of good events through visualizing a place where the person has felt safe and calm. When 'savoring',

> the subjects report feeling happier than those in a control group. The key component to effective savoring is focused attention. By taking the time and spending the effort to appreciate the positive, people are able to experience more well-being. (Diener & Biswas-Diener, 2008: 198)

As we can have students write descriptive paragraphs about their place of calmness, we can also effectively use second language skills of writing to reinforce the visualization's effects.

The activity

Explain to the students that visualization exercises can be very useful at times of stress and that the first step will be for them to think about a place in which they feel safe and calm. Students can be encouraged to discuss in groups places that are special to them. Once they have 'found' their 'safe' place, they write a short description of what it looks like. When that is done, they add the various other senses to their vision. What smells do they smell in this special place? What can they hear? What can they touch or what touches them? What do they taste?

I give them my own example of the ocean. The visual picture can be put up on a screen or brought into class. I describe the smells to them: salty air, seaweed, clear, fresh-smelling air on the wind. I add the sounds: seagulls in the air, waves against the shore, the wind. I then add what I can feel: the wind on my cheeks, the wet sand between my toes, or the warm sand under my body. Finally, I describe what I can taste: the salt in the air. The more details that are incorporated in the 'picture' one is building of this safe space, the better and deeper the students can enter into the scene in their imagination and become calm.

When each segment is completed, a final text could be handed in and corrected for language use. We then use this text as the basis for a three-minute visualization exercise that can take place in class. During these three minutes, the teacher instructs the students to find a comfortable position in their chairs, close their eyes and only then start playing some relaxing music. When the music starts, they should again think about the place that they have described in their writing, in all its detail. Ideally, students will do this at home as well and if continued over a two-week period twice a day this visualized place will bring calmness very quickly in stressful situations (Palmer & Cooper, 2008). Such affective strategies for controlling and managing their emotions can be especially important for second language learners to have at their disposal, given the anxiety generated for some by having to interact and speak in the language (e.g. Horwitz *et al.*, 1986).

Activity 5: Positivity portfolios

Research continues to be conducted into the value of collecting symbols of positive emotions, especially for later review in more difficult times. These studies are based on the experience of James Pawelski, who created such a portfolio to help his self-confidence when applying for a job. He is now the director of education at the Positive Psychology Center at the University of Pennsylvania (see Fredrickson, 2011). Fredrickson (2011) also encourages the making of different portfolios in the 10 areas of positivity: awe, amusement, gratitude, hope, inspiration, interest, joy, love, pride and serenity. Such an activity requires the person doing it to go on a 'treasure hunt' looking for items that symbolize when they experienced a particular positive emotion and gathering these items together. They need to think about when they experienced the emotion, what triggered it, when they last felt it and what was happening then, what they were doing: perhaps listening to music, watching a video, smelling a particular smell or tasting something. Collecting such symbols in a place that can be accessed in future challenging times offers the possibility of again experiencing those positive emotions when they are needed most. As an increase in remembering positive moments in our lives helps our overall positivity, this activity should be done mindfully and over a longer period of time. When reviewed, the portfolio should be savored and kept close at hand. When more than one portfolio is made, only one should be examined at any one point in time.

Lyubomirsky (2007) reminds us that when using any of these interventions one needs to always consider variety, timing, motivation, effort, person–activity fit and the cultural aspect. In terms of second language learning, portfolios represent an opportunity for students not only to collect and talk about positive emotions generally, but also to collect positive symbols of their language learning in one place, to look back on with pride and/or interest and/or amusement and/or hope. Indeed, the creation of portfolios has this inherent in their design, although the focus and purpose may vary. In this context, the focus is to concentrate on the positive experiences related to language learning and use.

The activity

Building a portfolio is a longer activity that progresses through an entire course. Explain to the students that this activity will give them a chance to savor the good things happening in their lives and/or specifically related to their second language use, as well as keep those things as memories to enliven future periods. The students can choose to make a portfolio of general positivity or of any one of the 10 areas of positivity mentioned above, whichever they feel most comfortable with in respect of their language learning. Also, the medium or method they use should be whatever they feel most comfortable with: an electronic album, a scrapbook or a photo album. The album itself needs to have captions and written sections which explain the significance of what is included, to use the language alongside visuals. It may be especially useful to discuss the items within the portfolio in class, enabling students to talk about positive impulses in their second language if they feel comfortable doing so. This may also mean that they will associate those positive feelings with that second language acquisition in the future, when they reopen the portfolios. Teachers could also show students their own portfolio, as an example, to show that they have also done such a project and explain some of the elements involved. Perhaps this could be a positive portfolio showing one of the various roles a teacher or the teacher as a language learner might have. This will also allow for a feeling of connectedness between the teacher and the students. Encourage them to be creative, include music, tickets to events they attended, actual pieces of material they may have appreciated (fallen leaves from a trip abroad, for example). Instructors could have students hand in their portfolios at various times throughout the semester (and talk about new items) in order to ensure that this is a continuing activity and not one done only in one long session before it is due. Such a portfolio offers students a chance to be creative, with the added benefit of having something to look back upon when positivity is needed, with second language use embedded into the process.

Conclusion

These are only a few of the activities that can be used effectively in the second language classroom. My experiences with working with these and other activities from PP suggest that there is a great value to increasing students' positivity. The exercises also give them vocabulary for discussing the positive in their lives as well as recognizing when positive moments occur. Students' comments from their feelings journals in my courses reinforce my belief that they acknowledge that these issues are important.

More research is needed to answer questions about why some language learners 'flourish' more than others (MacIntyre & Mercer, 2014) and whether the amount of engagement on the part of learners can be increased in the context of using activities such as those presented in this chapter. Other questions might be more readily answerable when results are collected from classes that have incorporated PP activities in contrast to those that have not.

As the present volume attests, interest is growing in how PP can be integrated into research and teaching in the second and foreign language classroom. I believe we will find that PP and its adapted pedagogical activities can offer our language learners an increased potential for learning their respective languages positively and flourishing in the endeavor, as well as also promoting positivity in their lives beyond the classroom.

References

Achor, S. (2011) *The Happiness Advantage: The Seven Principles That Fuel Success and Performance at Work*. New York: Virgin Books.

Biswas-Diener, R. (2010) *Practicing Positive Psychology Coaching: Assessment, Activities, and Strategies for Success*. Hoboken, NJ: Wiley.

Diener, E. and Biswas-Diener, R. (2008) *Happiness: Unlocking the Mysteries of Psychological Wealth*. Boston, MA: Blackwell.

Emmons, R.A. and McCullough, M.E. (2003) Counting blessings versus burdens: An experimental investigation of gratitude and subjective well-being in daily life. *Journal of Personality and Social Psychology* 84, 377–389.

Fredrickson, B. (2011) *Positivity: Groundbreaking Research to Release Your Inner Optimist and Thrive*. Oxford: Oneworld Publications.

Fredrickson, B. (2013) *Love 2.0: How Our Supreme Emotion Affects Everything We Feel, Think, Do, and Become*. New York: Hudson Street Press.

Fredrickson, B. (2014) Die Macht der guten Gefühle und der Liebe: Wie eine positive Haltung Ihr Leben dauerhaft verändert. [The power of good feelings and love: How a positive attitude can permanently change your life.] Positive Psychology Tour, Graz, Austria, 26–28 June.

Fritz-Schubert, E. (2011) *Schulfach Glück: Wie ein neues Fach die Schule verändert. [School Subject Happiness: How a New Subject Changes the School.]* Freiburg im Breisgau: Verlag Herder GmbH.

Froh, J.J. and Parks, A.C. (eds) (2013) *Activities for Teaching Positive Psychology: A Guide for Instructors*. Washington, DC: American Psychological Association.

Gable, E.L., Reis, H.T., Impett, E.A. and Asher, E.R. (2004) What do you do when things go right? The intrapersonal and interpersonal benefits of sharing positive events. *Journal of Personality and Social Psychology* 87 (2), 228–245.

Horwitz, E., Horwitz, M. and Cope, J. (1986) Foreign language classroom anxiety. *Modern Language Journal* 70 (2), 125–132.

Linkins, M., Niemiec, R.M., Gillham, J. and Mayerson, D. (2015) Through the lens of strength: A framework for educating the heart. *Journal of Positive Psychology* 10 (1), 64–68.

Lyubomirsky, S. (2007) *The How of Happiness: A Practical Guide to Getting the Life You Want.* London: Piatkus.

Lyubomirsky, S. (2013) *The Myths of Happiness: What Should Make You Happy, But Doesn't, What Shouldn't Make You Happy, But Does.* New York: Penguin.

MacIntyre, P. and Gregersen, T. (2012) Emotions that facilitate language learning: The positive-broadening power of the imagination. *Studies in Second Language Learning and Teaching* 2 (2), 193–213.

MacIntyre, P. and Mercer, S. (2014) Introducing positive psychology to SLA. *Studies in Second Language Learning and Teaching* 4 (2), 153–172.

MacIntyre, P., Dornyei, Z., Clément, R. and Noels, K. (1998) Conceptualizing willingness to communicate in a L2: A situational model of L2 confidence and affiliation. *Modern Language Journal* 82 (4), 545–562.

Palmer, S. and Cooper, G. (2008) *How to Deal with Stress.* London: Kogan Page.

Park, N. and Peterson C. (2008) Positive psychology and character strengths: Application to strengths-based school counseling. *Professional School Counseling* 12 (2), 85–92.

Rashid, T. (2014) Workshop on positive psychotherapy. Positive Psychology Tour, Graz, Austria, 29 June.

Rashid, T. and Seligman, M. (2011) *Positive Psychotherapy: A Treatment Manual.* New York: Oxford University Press.

Seligman, M.E.P. (2002) *Authentic Happiness: Using the New Positive Psychology to Realize Your Potential for Lasting Fulfillment.* New York: Free Press.

Seligman, M.E.P. (2006) *Learned Optimism: How to Change Your Mind and Your Life.* New York: Vintage Books.

Seligman, M.E.P. (2011) *Flourish: A Visionary New Understanding of Happiness and Well-Being.* New York: Free Press.

Seligman, M.E.P., Ernst, R.M., Gillham, J.E., Reivich, K. and Linkins, M. (2009) Positive education: Positive psychology and classroom interventions. *Oxford Review of Education* 35 (3), 293–311.

16 Music and Language Learning: Emotions and Engaging Memory Pathways

M. Carmen Fonseca-Mora and
Francisco Herrero Machancoses

... you know what music is¿ ...
It's God's little reminder that there's somethin' else out there other than us....
The Wizard, *August Rush*

Introduction

Two major theoretical issues that have dominated the field of applied linguistics for many years concern the type of linguistic content and the strategies learners need to become successful language learners. However, less has been said about learners' willingness to learn the target language (TL). Affect – that is to say, learners' beliefs, attitudes, interest, motivation, creativity, anxiety, among other factors – is the driving force that supports the sustained deep learning crucial for language development (Arnold, 1999). In addition, teachers' selection of appropriate tasks and materials can impact on learners' approaches to language learning. In fact, teachers can 'organize a variety of contexts that offer learners a variety of ways to engage meaning and strengthen memory pathways' (Arnold & Fonseca-Mora, 2004a: 119). One of the ways of engaging learners that will be considered in this chapter is musical input. Of all the multiple intelligences described by Gardner (1983, 1999), musical intelligence is the first to develop in humans. In their basic form, multiple intelligences are present to some extent in everyone, although a person will generally be more talented in some than in others. They interact to facilitate the solution of daily problems (Arnold & Fonseca-Mora, 2004a).

Musical intelligence begins when we are in the womb, from our conception (Deliège & Sloboda, 1996). Our musical perceptions of the melodies of the voice or of the sounds of musical instruments start very early and remain in our memory. Vocalized affection teaches us the emotions (Loui *et al.*, 2013) and at the same time, these vocal melodies are the basis of the acquisition of language, as they have been defined by Wermke and Mende (2009). Their findings state that melody functions as a framework and scaffolding during early L1 acquisition, from infant cries to the first spoken words and beyond, as intonation is an essential prosodic feature (Fonseca-Mora *et al.*, 2011).

Research also suggests that students' willingness to learn a foreign language (Fonseca-Mora *et al.*, 2011) and their cognitive skills (Fonseca-Mora *et al.*, 2015; Schön *et al.*, 2008) can be modified by the use of melodies and rhythm. Melodies and rhythm are key instruments for language learning that take advantage of the emotional and cognitive elements provided by music and songs. Musical activities have been found to influence attention and effort as a result of their physiological properties: they can alter blood pressure, posture, respiratory rate, pulse rate and general activity (Benenzon, 1997).

Tapping into learners' musical intelligence in the second language classroom can have the benefits of helping students to concentrate and connect with their inner selves, as music can create a balanced-noise environment by blocking out any distracting sounds. Music also stimulates and unlocks creative writing processes and, above all, it fosters a relaxed and safe but motivating and productive classroom atmosphere (Fonseca-Mora *et al.*, 2011). Many language students believe that musical resources such as songs and karaoke can improve their language learning skills, as they feel that these musical activities help them to remember grammatical structures and lexical items, improve their pronunciation and fluency while singing and reading the lyrics, and, at the same time, make learning more enjoyable. Listening to songs can become a beyond-the-classroom activity that can be done anywhere, at any time, reinforcing language learning and students' autonomy (Kerekes, 2015). Singing also helps develop auditory perception and aids two central language aptitude components: phonological and verbal memory (Ludke *et al.*, 2014).

Working with certain language learning skills, mainly the oral ones, can lead to anxiety-provoking situations, where some students feel a sense of fear at sounding ridiculous in front of their teacher and classmates. Our main hypothesis is that musical activities can help to produce positive emotions in the language classroom and reduce negative ones, such as anxiety. Therefore, the central aims of this chapter are: first, to reflect on the emotions that can commonly be found in the language classroom; secondly, to describe the effects of music on human well-being; and thirdly, to highlight how music and songs can be used as an effective way of connecting learners with the TL. Music and songs in the language classroom can be appraised positively and trigger changes in cognitive activity, as well as engaging learners in using these resources to increase 'self-discovery of knowledge' and their personal well-being.

Emotions in Language Learning

There is consensus about the importance of achieving a positive classroom atmosphere, where the student may want to communicate. Obviously, the success or failure of approaches to teaching second languages seeking to develop communicative competence depends largely on the participation of students in tasks where they practice their oral skills. If learners do not perceive the tasks proposed as having personal relevance and feel resistant to participating actively in the classroom, this will seriously reduce their chances of achieving communicative competence (Arnold & Fonseca-Mora, 2004b).

Several useful models have been developed to conceptualize what in communication studies has been called willingness to communicate (WTC), which has to do with the tendency of an individual to initiate communication when there is an opportunity to do so (McCroskey & Richmond, 1987). MacIntyre and colleagues developed a model related to the learning of second languages. MacIntyre and Clément (1996) incorporated Gardner's socio-educational model and found that WTC was a factor that predicted the frequency of communication in the second language. A more highly developed model (MacIntyre *et al.*, 1998) includes various emotional variables that influence WTC in the TL, such as the personality of the student, the climate of the classroom, intergroup attitudes, motivation and self-confidence. In this pyramid model, the top level, communicative behavior (use of the L2), rests on the level of intent (willingness to communicate), which in turn relies on these designated affective variables.

Obstacles or negative emotions: Reluctance to talk

Learners who convey their normal thoughts with transitional language competence may sometimes experience negative emotions, such as fear, insecurity, inefficacy and shame, among others, which reduce the possibility of becoming successful language learners. In general, research suggests that learners' self-concept can be negatively affected by having to reduce their expression of mature ideas to a child-like level, causing anxiety and frustration that lead the student to avoid communication (Horwitz, 2001; MacIntyre *et al.*, 1998; MacIntyre & Gregersen, 2012).

Positive emotions in language learning

Recent studies advocate the centrality of positive emotions in language learning (Oxford, 2014; Rahimi & Bigdeli, 2014; Swain, 2011) and the need to create a comfortable classroom atmosphere that depends on teachers' and learners' positive emotions. The effect of these positive emotions is well explained through Fredrickson's (1998, 2000) broaden-and-build model, based on the hypothesis that negative and positive emotions provoke different action tendencies. Fredrickson states that 'positive emotions have an undoing effect on negative emotions [...] positive emotions seem instead to spark changes primarily in cognitive activity' (Fredrickson, 2000: 264). In fact, Frederickson (2003) analyzes five positive emotions: joy, interest, contentment, pride and love. Rahimi and Bigdeli (2014) apply the broaden-and-build theory to second language learning and add that teachers 'should encourage students to pursue a wider range of thoughts and actions, such as playing, exploring, and enjoying, aimed at providing the learning environment for optimal motivation, engagement, and learning' (Rahimi & Bigdeli, 2014: 799).

Furthermore, Barrett and Bond (2014) state that a positive classroom atmosphere can be more easily created if teachers consider the 'Five Cs approach to positive youth development', which involves working on learners' *Competence* (social, academic, cognitive, and vocational), *Confidence* (sense of self-efficacy and positive self-worth), *Connection* (positive bonds with people and places), *Character* (integrity and moral centeredness and respect for societal and cultural rules), and *Caring* (humane values, sympathy and empathy, and social justice). It implies careful lesson planning, where teachers sequence the different steps needed to empower language learners and pay special attention to group dynamics and learning engagement. More concretely, our proposal is that the use of music – instrumental or vocal – can easily elicit positive emotions in the language classroom.

The following example may illustrate how to motivate learners to participate in activities ranging from non-verbal communication to oral interaction. The teacher selects some very short musical extracts. Students are instructed to stand up and turn to their right or to their left if they like or dislike it (it may help to post on the respective walls of the classroom the statements 'I like this music' and 'I don't like this music'). Students may stand looking toward the blackboard if they are indifferent to them. From this silent body response, the teacher invites students to participate with a (silent) written verbal response on the blackboard with other things they like or dislike. Then, students find at least three classmates who agree with them on the things chosen, by asking them orally. Finally, they negotiate a name for their group and report to the class (for example, 'We like chocolate. We're the chocolate group').

Melodies and rhythm can create an attractive and enjoyable environment fostering learners' willingness to participate in the language classroom, similar to the effects on human well-being of music and songs in everyday life.

Music and Human Well-being

The effect of music is so very much more powerful and penetrating than is that of the other arts, for these others speak only of the shadow, but music of the essence.
Arthur Schopenhauer. *The World as Will and Representation* (1819: vol. I, ch. II)

Schopenhauer's words emphasize the essential objective of this chapter: to explore the power of music beyond the pleasure and enjoyment it causes. Indeed, Darwin (1871) proposed that music has an adaptive function,[1] as if it were a pre-linguistic way of communication that evolved to what today we understand as human language. The fact that music is so deeply rooted in humanity can be seen in archeological findings which show that music has accompanied humans since the dawn of mankind. Conard *et al.* (2009) affirm that the existence of complex musical instruments is an indication of fully modern behavior and advanced symbolic communication. At sites in south-east Germany, the discovery of flutes made with bones demonstrates 'the presence of a well-established musical tradition at the time when modern humans colonized Europe, more than 35,000 calendar years ago' (Conard *et al.*, 2009: 737). So, if musical behavior has been present throughout our evolutionary development, we can accept that it must be useful for our survival, since otherwise it would have been discarded (Bispham, 2006). Even today, music still plays a key role in our everyday lives. It is currently very difficult to go through a whole day without hearing music, either involuntarily, for example music played over loudspeakers in shops, or voluntarily, by listening to the radio or by switching on our iPods. Many marketing professionals understand that music affects people in multiple ways, so it is used in radio and television advertisements (Bruner, 1990). Film-makers introduce music in scenes that they want to emphasize; a soundtrack consistent with a given scene increases the transmission of emotion (Boltz *et al.*, 2009). Therefore, music often functions as a catalyst of intentional messages and emotions.

The effects of music have also been studied from a neurobiological perspective. Chanda and Levitin (2013) and Tarr *et al.* (2014) explain that neurochemical systems, including the dopamine system, the hypothalamic–pituitary–adrenal axis and sympathetic nervous system, and the serotonergic system, react when humans are exposed to music. The dopamine system is involved in our sensations of reward, motivation and pleasure, while the hypothalamic–pituitary–adrenal axis and the sympathetic nervous system regulate stress and arousal. Finally, the serotonergic system acts on our immune system. Chanda and Levitin (2013) observe that levels of the hormone oxytocin can be modulated by music, which can thus affect social bonding. Therefore, music and songs can act as a regulator of emotional and cognitive processes, with both social and socializing effects. Brown (2000), Fitch (2006), Mithen (2005) and Richman (1993) suggest that group music, singing or playing instruments together, as well as the coordination among the people involved, could serve to promote group cohesion and stability.

Curiously, all the neurochemical elements mentioned above also are involved in one way or another in language learning (Schumann, 1998). This indicates a neurochemical basis for arguing for a possible role of music specifically in language learning.

Melodies and Rhythm in Language Learning: Cognitive and Emotional Benefits

Many researchers affirm that there is a connection between musical abilities and language acquisition. Slevc and Miyake (2006) describe musical ability as an individual difference in second language proficiency. Their study examined the relationship between musical ability and competence in adult second language (L2) learners. They analyzed L2 competence in relation to lexical knowledge, productive phonology, syntax and receptive phonology. They also evaluated other factors that may explain individual differences in L2 acquisition, such as the age of L2 immersion, patterns of use, period of exposure to the language and phonological short-term memory. According to their results, musical abilities predict both receptive and productive L2 phonological abilities, that is, they affect listening comprehension and pronunciation. Similarly, Chobert and Besson (2013) proposed that musical training may reduce phonological deficits in L2 learning.

From a neurocognitive perspective, Patel (2011) explains why instrumental musical training affects brain plasticity and shared speech processing networks. He refers to the overlap in acoustic features of instrumental music and speech, and he identifies emotions present while playing. Furthermore, he defines repetition and focused attention as core features of instrumental music training that develop learners' auditory precision, due to the high demands of music. In this vein, Fonseca-Mora, Avila and Segador analyzed the relationship between instrumental musical training and TL learning in a group of 454 Spanish learners of English in compulsory secondary education (Fonseca-Mora *et al.*, 2015). The academic success of the students enrolled in a pilot musical program combining secondary and musical studies were compared with those of students in the same institution following the standard secondary education curriculum. Results showed a statistically significant difference between students attending instrumental musical classes and those without this musical training. The success in language learning of the music students was also explained by a higher level of self-efficacy and willingness to keep on studying English.

Not all school curricula include musical training, but it could be of interest to use musical input in the language classroom as, to a certain degree, 'all normal (non brain-damaged) people possess some musical intelligence'

(Gardner, 1983: 285). This means that, in general, humans have the ability to perceive and enjoy music, although not all can produce it properly. Using music with lyrics in the language classroom may be of benefit to learners because 'songs bridge the [brain's] hemispheres, strengthening retention due to complementary functions as the right hemisphere learns the melody, the left, the words' (Guglielmino, 1986: 20). For example, the teacher organizes the class into small groups and hands them a phrase of a song or allows each group to select one (it is better if they are not repeated, but if different groups show interest in the same fragment, they can negotiate it and, when necessary, two groups may have the same). All students write their phrase in capital letters on a sheet of paper. A video clip with lyrics is displayed and each group shows its fragment to the others when they hear it, and read it. The selection of songs with strong rhythm and repetitive texts makes the activity especially fun. Some students begin to sing their fragment, but there is no obligation to do so. This joint group task favors recognition of sounds, words and structures, and is a warming-up activity where group success is ensured.

In a broad sense, neural activities provoked by listening to music work deeper in the auditory cortex, influencing the frontal, temporal, parietal and subcortical areas which connect to attention (Schellenberg *et al.*, 2007). They also affect semantic and syntactic processing, memory and motor functions (Koelsch *et al.*, 2004), and the limbic and paralimbic system of emotions (Koelsch *et al.*, 2006).

Talented language learners have been described as those with an unusual verbal memory (Swanson *et al.*, 2015). Skehan (1998: 201) defined language aptitude as a triarchic concept based on 'auditory ability, linguistic ability and memory ability'. According to Skehan (1998), memory ability refers to the capacity for the retention of verbal material in such a way that retrieval takes minimal time and effort and thus furthers fluency in oral communication. Singing songs may provide all learners, even the ones who are struggling with language, with easily memorized expressions or lexical phrases, mainly due to the repetition of expressions in the chorus of a song, which might help to increase their oral fluency.

Memorized expressions, also called *lexicalized chunks*, are one of the core components of effective communication. Memorized expressions help learners to become more fluent speakers, as these expressions work as 'islands', providing the speakers with more time to activate their referential knowledge and to generate their message.

Music influences the attention individuals pay to the tasks to be carried out. For example, research on runners listening to music through headphones demonstrates that music improves athletic performance (Barwood *et al.*, 2009). Features such as tone and tempo can modulate our spatial skills and as well as attention and executive control. The emotional valence and activation produced while listening to music generate changes in our attention network (McConnell & Shore, 2011). This attention network is composed of three neural networks with differentiated functions, distinct neural anatomy and diverse neurotransmitters. The alert network and the orienting network are involved in achieving and maintaining a state of alertness and orientation in the presence of sensory events, and the executive attention network regulates any conflicts between the other two (Rothbart *et al.*, 2011), promoting concentration and focus on the task. For instance, de Groot (2006) found that more foreign language vocabulary was learnt when background music was played than in the silent condition, and Parbery-Clark *et al.* (2009) affirmed that musical experience limits the negative effects of background noise, although the degree of concentration and focus on the task is determined by the intensity and tempo of the melody (Bishop *et al.*, 2013).

In addition, self-regulation has also been studied to explain the positive effects of music. The concept of self-regulation can be defined, in general, as behavior directed at a target in a given period of time (Bandura, 1991). The importance of self-regulation is clearly observed in behaviors where performance, personal effort and the control of goals are essential, as well as in the processes of self-control or rejection of unwanted impulses. Self-regulation helps maintain positive emotional states, motivation and the cognitive activation required for adjustment or personal adaptation. Additionally, it aids in the development of positive social relationships, productivity and success management, and in the development of accurate self-perception (Blair & Diamond, 2008; Hofmann *et al.*, 2012). Murphey (2014) illustrates these socio-emotional benefits of singing and includes results related to individual self-regulation. His longitudinal study analyses the effect on adult Japanese English-language learners of teaching short affirmation songlet routines to their relatives or friends, that is to say, to people outside the language classroom (see also Chapter 14 of the present volume). The qualitative data of this study includes quotes such as this:

> I can't explain exactly why, but my sister and I laughed a lot and felt happy during the activity. Though I hesitated to do this and thought that we might quarrel doing this, I could enjoy teaching and my sister enjoyed it.... It has been a few days since I taught her, but I still hear her singing 'Do it again' in the house. (Murphey, 2014: 208)

Students reported their relatives and friends having acquired certain self-regulation abilities; for instance, one of them said: 'I can change my own mind by singing a song a little bit. I try to change my mind positively more from now. Thank you for your teaching!' (Murphey, 2014: 213). They also reported enjoyment while sharing their songs with their relatives and/or friends, as this gave them the opportunity to feel more connected to them.

Self-regulation has also been described as being important for very young language learners. Kindergarten teachers frequently mention very young learners' problems in concentrating and following instructions, both essential components of self-regulation (Blair & Diamond, 2008). Music may be very beneficial at this stage to avoid boredom and direct students' attention. Songs help children follow instructions and increase their attention span while at the same time songs leave deeper traces in their memories. Child development includes self-regulatory mechanisms that are produced in conjunction with social norms, and emotional and behavioral control increases during the first three to four years of life (Posne & Rothbart, 2000; Rothbart *et al.*, 2011). Self-confidence and empathy also influence self-regulation and take shape at early ages. Intervention in social and emotional learning at early ages favors students' skills, attitudes and behaviors (Durlak *et al.*, 2011; Rothbart *et al.*, 2011).

The effects of music on language learning need to be considered from a sociocultural perspective as well. Murphey's study (2014) reports on the social bonding effects of singing. He found that singing and teaching with movements and sharing a musical classroom activity produced positive emotions and had an effect on participants' well-being, as they felt more connected to each other. Singing with others (choral singing) is a social routine where students need to pay attention to others, which can produce enjoyment. In fact, when taking on the teacher role for their friends and relatives, as indicated in the instructions given in Murphey's study, Japanese students commented on great enjoyment while singing with their relatives (Murphey, 2014: 216; and see Chapter 14). Student teachers felt the joy of helping others grow – a positive experience that enhances teacher motivation and it also reminds us of one of Stevick's well known quotations: 'Success [in language learning] depends less on materials, techniques and linguistic analyses and more on what goes on inside and between the people in the classroom' (Stevick, 1980: 4).

The aspects of culture that often are embedded in songs may be relevant in language acquisition. Abbott (2002: 10) suggests that 'cultures have musical traditions because of the enjoyment people receive from creating rhythms and expressing their feelings, ideas, thoughts, and cultural values through lyrics'. Music and songs provide both cultural and linguistic elements with respect to TL learning. Clearly, songs offer an important way to introduce culture and help motivate students who are not living in the target country (Murphey, 2010). In fact, music helps to create mental images in our students' minds as 'a result of the interaction between what we have in storage and what is going on at that moment' (Stevick, 1986: 16). The well known tune of 'Happy birthday' can bring to our minds the picture of celebrating with our relatives or friends, while the main tune of the movie *The Hobbit* can place us mentally in a nature setting (Fonseca-Mora, 2005). Instrumental music can, for instance, unlock learners' potential for creative writing because melodies can evoke images based on common cultural references that belong to our collective identity or personal experiences while learners simultaneously connect to their inner selves (Fonseca-Mora *et al.*, 2011).

From a cognitive perspective, Christiner and Reiterer consider singing to be 'a good indicator of the ability to remember new and unintelligible utterances' (Christiner & Reiterer, 2013: 9) and to be a better indicator of the ability to imitate speech than is instrumental musical training. They affirm that singing speeds up the rate at which speech is acquired and conclude that the ability to sing improves the memory span of the auditory working memory. Ludke *et al.* (2014) add that, in language learning, singing shows better results than rhythmic speaking, suggesting that listening plus singing can facilitate verbatim memory for spoken TL phrases.

Furthermore, Murphey (2014) reports on linguistic outcomes of singing. Students 'learned about rhyming, blending, vowel changes, as well as assonance, alliteration, and rhythm' (Murphey, 2014: 210). Singing is considered a subcategorization of speaking where correct pronunciation seems to be an easier task for language learners. Listening to songs can facilitate the development of the auditory capacity, while singing improves word articulation. In fact, 'there probably isn't a better or quicker way to teach phonetics than through songs' (Leith, 1979: 540). The 'song-stuck-in-my-head' phenomenon (Murphey, 1990) has the power to mentally produce an involuntary rehearsal that activates our capacity for language acquisition.

Although not all students enjoy singing aloud, video clips where students listen to the song and read the subtitles with their 'inner voices' may have an effect on their TL reading fluency. Fitzgerald (1994) found that the 23 Spanish students enrolled in an English bilingual program where they had to sing significantly improved their participation, pronunciation and reading skills. Furthermore, Moreno *et al.* (2009) concluded that using musical tasks for an eight-week period positively influenced young learners' ability to perceive and distinguish individual phonemes of the language. Other language areas such as vocabulary and grammatical structures can also be learnt more easily with melodies, rhythms, timing and measurement of sentences in songs because 'the new structures that may seem isolated or out of context in pattern drills, are seen in a different perspective when they are part of a song' (Failoni, 1993: 101). The internet offers numerous video clips containing appropriate songs with their lyrics, adverts or short films with subtitles that include the targeted structures on which teachers may want to focus.

Finally, music also can act as a transmitter or catalyst of messages and emotions that may be included in class to indicate the different parts of a lesson. For example, a good class can be organized around musical routines. Greeting songs are routines that welcome and acknowledge learners at the beginning of a lesson. A typical example for younger learners is the jazz chant by Carolyn Graham (1978) 'Hi, how are you?', which she accompanies with rhythmic clapping, feet stomping and gestures while involving all learners in chanting and doing the same movements. Instrumental music may also be used to specify a transitional phase whereby students prepare for another type of activity or as a means to create a particular classroom atmosphere while learners are working in groups. Furthermore, music can be an effective classroom management tool to maintain pace: lively music can energize students, whereas soothing music can help them to calm down. Hallam and Price (1998) analyzed the effects of background music on students with behavioral and emotional problems, and observed an improvement in mathematics, increased cooperation and a decrease in the levels of aggressive behavior.

Conclusions

In addition to being a pleasant component in the classroom, music possesses characteristics that make it an important vehicle for adaptation and learning. Additionally, music creates a favorable classroom atmosphere and is a useful tool to manage the different rhythms of active and passive energy that formal learning requires. Melodies and rhythm have the effect of creating positive emotions, encouraging and reassuring, and, therefore, affect students' predisposition toward learning.

Learning a TL is a highly complex cognitive, affective and social activity that can be facilitated by the use of musical elements that promote the development of motivation, verbal memory and language skills. Instrumental music and songs may also build social bonds and be an excellent resource for self-regulation. As these processes are dynamically interconnected, their effects on TL learning must be studied with this caveat in mind. TL teaching and learning could be exponentially more dynamic and motivating with the inclusion of music and positive emotions. Considering the value added by the cognitive benefits that melodies and rhythm can enhance, what are we waiting for¿

Note

(1) Adaptive function refers to humans' capacity for independently handling the common demands of life.

References

Abbott, M. (2002) Using music to promote L2 learning among adult learners. *TESOL Journal* 11, 10–17.

Arnold, J. (ed.) (1999) *Affect in Language Learning*. New York: Cambridge University Press.

Arnold, J. and Fonseca-Mora, M.C. (2004a) Multiple intelligence theory and foreign language learning: A brain-based perspective. *International Journal of English Studies* 4 (1), 119–136.
Arnold, J. and Fonseca-Mora, M.C. (2004b) Reflexiones sobre aspectos del desarrollo de la competencia comunicativa oral en el aula de español como segunda lengua. In S. Ruhstaller and F. Lorenzo Berjillos (eds) *El desarrollo de la competencia lingüística y comunicativa en el aprendizaje de español como L2* (pp. 45–60). Madrid: Edinumen.
Bandura, A. (1991) Social cognitive theory of self-regulation. *Organizational Behavior and Human Decision Processes* 50 (2), 248–287.
Barrett, M.S. and Bond, N. (2015) Connecting through music: The contribution of a music programme to fostering positive youth development. *Research Studies in Music Education* 37 (1) 37–54.
Barwood, M.J., Weston, N.J.V., Thelwell, R. and Page, J. (2009) A motivational music and video intervention improves high-intensity exercise performance. *Journal of Sports Science and Medicine* 8 (3), 435–442.
Benenzon, R. (1997) *Music Therapy Theory and Manual: Contributions to the Knowledge of Nonverbal Contexts. Music Therapy Perspectives* (2nd edn). Springfield, IL: Charles C. Thomas.
Bishop, D.T., Wright, M.J. and Karageorghis, C.I. (2013) Tempo and intensity of pre-task music modulate neural activity during reactive task performance. *Psychology of Music*. doi:10.1177/0305735613490595
Bispham, J. (2006) Rhythm in music. What is it? Who has it? And Why? *Music Perception* 24 (2), 125–134.
Blair, C. and Diamond, A. (2008) Biological processes in prevention and intervention: The promotion of self-regulation as a means of preventing school failure. *Development and Psychopathology* 20 (3), 899–911.
Boltz, M.G., Ebendorf, B. and Field, B. (2009) Audiovisual interactions: The impact of visual information on music perception and memory. *Music Perception* 27 (1), 43–59.
Brown, S. (2000) The 'musilanguage' model of music evolution. In N.L. Wallin, B. Merker and S. Brown (eds) *The Origins of Music* (pp. 271–300). Cambridge, MA: MIT Press.
Bruner, G.C. (1990) Music, mood, and marketing. *Journal of Marketing* 54 (4), 94–104.
Chanda, M.L. and Levitin, D.J. (2013) The neurochemistry of music. *Trends in Cognitive Sciences* 17 (4), 179–191.
Chobert, J. and Besson, M. (2013) Musical expertise and second language learning. *Brain Sciences* 3 (2), 923–940.
Christiner, M. and Reiterer, S.M. (2013) Song and speech: Examining the link between singing talent and speech imitation ability. *Frontiers in Psychology* 4 (November), 1–11.
Conard, N.J., Malina, M. and Münzel, S.C. (2009) New flutes document the earliest musical tradition in southwestern Germany. *Nature* 460, 737–740.
Darwin, C. (1871) *The Descent of Man and Selection in Relation to Sex*. London: John Murray.
De Groot, A. (2006) Effects of stimulus characteristics and background music on foreign language vocabulary learning and forgetting. *Language Learning* 56 (3), 463–506.
Deliège, I. and Sloboda, J.A. (eds) (1996) *Musical Beginnings: Origins and Development of Musical Competence*. New York: Oxford University Press.
Durlak, J.A., Weissberg, R.P., Dymnicki, A.B., Taylor, R.D. and Schellinger, K.B. (2011) The impact of enhancing students' social and emotional learning: A meta-analysis of school-based universal interventions. *Child Development* 82 (1), 405–432.
Failoni, J.W. (1993) Music as means to enhance cultural awareness and literacy in the foreign language classroom. *Mid-Atlantic Journal of Foreign Language Pedagogy* 1, 97–108.
Fitch, W.T. (2006) On the biology and evolution of music. *Music Perception* 24 (1), 85–88.
Fitzgerald, L.A. (1994) *A Musical Approach for Teaching English Reading to Limited English Speakers*. Chicago, IL: National Louis University.

Fonseca-Mora, M.C. (2005) Individual characteristics of secondary school students. In N. McLaren and D. Madrid (eds) *TEFL in Secondary Education* (pp. 79–110). Granada: Editorial Universidad de Granada.

Fonseca-Mora, M.C., Toscano-Fuentes, C. and Wermke, K. (2011) Melodies that help: The relation between language aptitude and musical intelligence. *Anglistik International Journal of English Studies* 22 (1), 101–118.

Fonseca-Mora, M.C., Jara-Jiménez, P. and Gómez-Domínguez, M. (2015) Musical plus phonological input for young foreign language readers. *Frontiers in Psychology* 6 (March), 1–9.

Fonseca-Mora, M.C., Avila-López, J. and Segador, A. (2015) Beneficios del entrenamiento musical para el aprendizaje de una lengua extranjera. *Revista Electrónica Complutense de Investigación en Educación Musical* 12, 29–36.

Fredrickson, B.L. (1998) What good are positive emotions? *Review of General Psychology* 2 (3), 300–319.

Fredrickson, B.L. (2000) Cultivating positive emotions to optimize health and well-being. *Prevention and Treatment* 3 (1), 260–280.

Fredrickson, B.L. (2003) The value of positive emotions. *American Scientist* 91, 330–335.

Gardner, H. (1983) *Frames of Mind: The Theory of Multiple Intelligences.* New York: Basic Books.

Gardner, H. (1999) *Intelligences Reframed: Multiple Intelligences for the Twenty-First Century.* New York: Basic Books.

Graham, C. (1978) *Jazz Chants*. New York: Oxford University Press.

Guglielmino, L.M. (1986) The affective edge: Using songs and music in ESL instruction. *Adult Literacy and Basic Education* 10 (1), 19–26.

Hallam, S. and Price, J. (1998) Can the use of background music improve the behaviour and academic performance of children with emotional and behavioural difficulties? *British Journal of Special Education* 25 (2), 88–91.

Hofmann, W., Schmeichel, B.J. and Baddeley, A.D. (2012) Executive functions and self-regulation. *Trends in Cognitive Sciences* 16 (3), 174–180.

Horwitz, E. (2001) Language anxiety and achievement. *Annual Review of Applied Linguistics* 21, 112–127.

Kerekes, E. (2015) Using songs and lyrics in out-of-class learning. In D. Nunan and J.C. Richards (eds) *Language Learning Beyond the Classroom* (pp. 33–42). New York: Routledge.

Koelsch, S., Kasper, E., Sammler, D., Schulze, K., Gunter, T. and Friederici, A.D. (2004) Music, language and meaning: Brain signatures of semantic processing. *Nature Neuroscience* 7 (3), 302–307.

Koelsch, S., Fritz, T., Cramon, D.Y.V., Müller, K. and Friederici, A.D. (2006) Investigating emotion with music: An fMRI study. *Human Brain Mapping* 27, 239–250.

Leith, W.D. (1979) Advanced French conversation through popular music. *French Review* 52, 537–551.

Loui, P., Bachorik, J.P., Li, H.C. and Schlaug, G. (2013) Effects of voice on emotional arousal. *Frontiers in Psychology* 4, 675.

Ludke, K.M., Ferreira, F. and Overy, K. (2014) Singing can facilitate foreign language learning. *Memory and Cognition* 42 (1), 41–52.

MacIntyre, P.D. and Clément, R. (1996) A model of willingness to communicate in a second language: The concept, its antecedents and implications. Paper presented at the World Congress of Applied Linguistics (AILA), Jyväskylä, Finland, 4–9 August.

MacIntyre, P.D. and Gregersen, T. (2012) Affect: The role of language anxiety and other emotions in language learning. In S. Mercer, S. Ryan and M. Williams (eds) *Psychology for Language Learning: Insights from Research, Theory and Practice* (pp. 103–118). Basingstoke: Palgrave Macmillan.

MacIntyre, P.D., Dörnyei, Z., Clément, R. and Noels, K.A. (1998) Conceptualizing

willingness to communicate in a L2 A situational model of L2 confidence and affiliation. *Modern Language Journal* 82 (4), 545–562.
McConnell, M.M. and Shore, D.I. (2011) Mixing measures: Testing an assumption of the Attention Network Test. *Attention, Perception and Psychophysics* 73, 1096–1107.
McCroskey, J.C. and Richmond, V.P. (1987) Willingness to communicate. In J.C. McCroskey and J.A. Daly (eds) *Personality and Interpersonal Communication* (pp. 129–156). Newbury Park, CA: Sage.
Mithen, S. (2005) *The Singing Neanderthals: The Origins of Music, Language, Mind, and Body*. London: Weidenfeld and Nicolson.
Moreno, S., Marques, C., Santos, A., Santos, M., Castro, S.L. and Besson, M. (2009) Musical training influences linguistic abilities in 8-year-old children: More evidence for brain plasticity. *Cerebral Cortex* 19 (March), 712–723.
Murphey, T. (1990) The song stuck in my head phenomenon: A melodic din in the lad? *System* 18 (1), 53–64.
Murphey, T. (2010) Gracias a la vida – musica que me ha dado tanto: Songs as scaffolded-languaging for SLA. In A. Hermont, R. Esprito Santo and S. Cavalcante (eds) *Linguagem e Cognição* (pp. 241–255). Belo Horizonte: PUC Minas.
Murphey, T. (2014) Singing well-becoming: Student musical therapy case studies. *Studies in Second Language Learning and Teaching* 2 (2), 205–235.
Oxford, R. (2014) What we can learn about strategies, language learning, and life from two extreme cases: The role of well-being theory in second language learning and teaching. *Studies in Second Language Learning and Teaching* 4 (4), 593–615.
Parbery-Clark, A., Skoe, E. and Kraus, N. (2009) Musical experience limits the degradative effects of background noise on the neural processing of sound. *Journal of Neuroscience: The Official Journal of the Society for Neuroscience* 29 (45), 14100–14107.
Patel, A.D. (2011) Why would musical training benefit the neural encoding of speech? The OPERA hypothesis. *Frontiers in Psychology* 2 (June), 1–14.
Posne, M.I. and Rothbart, M.K. (2000) Developing mechanisms of self-regulation. *Development and Psychopathology* 12, 427–441.
Rahimi, A. and Bigdeli, R.A. (2014) The broaden-and-build theory of positive emotions in second language learning. *Procedia – Social and Behavioral Sciences* 159, 795–801.
Richman, B. (1993) On the evolution of speech: Singing as the middle term. *Current Anthropology* 34, 721.
Rothbart, M.K., Sheese, B.E., Rueda, M.R. and Posner, M.I. (2011) Developing mechanisms of self-regulation in early life. *Emotion Review* 3 (2), 207–213.
Schellenberg, E.G., Nakata, T., Hunter, P.G. and Tamoto, S. (2007) Exposure to music and cognitive performance: Tests of children and adults. *Psychology of Music* 35, 5–19.
Schön, D., Boyer, M., Moreno, S., Besson, M., Peretz, I. and Kolinsky, R. (2008) Songs as an aid for language acquisition. *Cognition* 106 (2), 975–983.
Schumann, J.H. (1998) The neurobiology of affect in language. *Language Learning: A Journal of Research in Language Studies*, 48 (supplement).
Skehan, P. (1998) *A Cognitive Approach to Language Learning* (Oxford Applied Linguistics). Oxford: Oxford University Press.
Slevc, L.R. and Miyake, A. (2006) Individual differences in second-language proficiency: Does musical ability matter? *Psychological Science* 17, 675–681.
Stevick, E.W. (1980) *Teaching Languages: A Way and Ways*. Rowley, MA: Newbury House.
Stevick, E.W. (1986) *Images and Options in the Language Classroom*. Cambridge: Cambridge University Press.
Swain, M. (2011) The inseparability of cognition and emotion in second language learning. *Language Teaching* 46 (2), 1–13.
Swanson, H.L., Orosco, M.J. and Lussier, C.M. (2015) Growth in literacy, cognition, and working memory in English language learners. *Journal of Experimental Child Psychology* 132, 155–188.

Tarr, B., Launay, J. and Dunbar, R.I.M. (2014) Music and social bonding: 'Self–other' merging and neurohormonal mechanisms. *Frontiers in Psychology* 5 (September), 1–10.
Wermke, K. and Mende, W. (2009) Musical elements in human infants' cries: In the beginning is the melody. *Musicae Scientiae* 13 (suppl. 2), 151–175.

17 Conclusion

Peter D. MacIntyre, Tammy Gregersen and Sarah Mercer

In some ways, the emergence of positive psychology in SLA is overdue. Successful language learning requires an integration of the learner's emotional experiences and characteristics (traits, emotions, etc.) with the features of the learning situation, including formal institutions that provide language training (schools, universities, study-abroad programs, etc.). These also are the pillars of positive psychology (Seligman & Csikszentmihalyi, 2000). A full list of the goals of language pedagogy would include, among other things, positive self-development of the learner, enjoyment of the learning process, and positive interactions with speakers of the language. Self-development, enjoyment and positive interactions are also the topics of positive psychology.

This anthology was designed to explore ways in which positive psychology might be applied in SLA, combining theory, research and practice. Looking over the chapters that are included here, we see expanded theory and new concepts ready for future research, along with new techniques for language teaching and learning, inspired by positive psychology. In many ways, we view this volume as a step toward expanding upon a new collection of topics and ideas for study in SLA, including EMPATHICS, empathy, well-being, love, social capital, hope, flow, enjoyment, positive L2 self, directed motivational currents, and perseverance, among other concepts. MacIntyre and Mercer argued that advancing the study of positive psychology

> helps to ensure that the literature covers the full range of positive and negative experience with languages, communication, and the learning processes. The introduction of PP opens up a broad, rich collection of under-researched themes and directions for further exploration in an SLA field that is perhaps in a particularly strong position to engage with PP to generate innovative thinking and research. (MacIntyre & Mercer, 2014: 167)

The SLA field currently has a diversity of well accepted research approaches that allows for flexibility in devising new research questions. In proposing an expanded role for positive psychology in SLA, however, we understand that there will be critics. Authors who are critical of positive psychology, such as Barbara Ehrenreich (2009), note that the complexity of the situation interacts with personal attributes in ways that have to be actively negotiated. In articulating her negative reactions to both a diagnosis of breast cancer and what she encountered as a relentlessly upbeat culture surrounding it, Ehrenreich wrote: 'You can get so busy comparing attractive head scarves that you forget to question whether chemotherapy is really going to be effective in your case' (Ehrenreich, 2009: 29). Scholarly critics, such as Lazarus (2003), contend that positive psychology has oversimplified the conceptualization and measurement of emotion, for example ignoring the positive side of what might be considered negative emotion and the negative side of what might be considered positive emotion.

Every scholarly endeavor does have and should have its critics. But it takes no scholarly effort at all to dismiss a topic as irrelevant or silly. It is a lazy reader who argues 'that can't possibly work' in place of the question 'can that possibly work?' There has been plenty of received wisdom that has proven incorrect or even dangerous over the years, but we see no defensible reason for a smug dismissal of positive psychology. If there is an overarching message from positive psychology that even its critics can accept, it might be this: 'it's not that simple'. The aim of this collection is to seriously engage with the concepts and perspectives it offers and consider their validity and relevance for the domain of foreign and second language learning.

Contributions to Positive Psychology

In this anthology, we have tried to find a balance among the theoretical, empirical and practice-oriented dimensions of positive psychology in SLA, while showing the complexity of the area. Indeed, it is possible to suggest that this anthology contributes both to the field of SLA and to the development of positive psychology. Among the 16 preceding chapters, readers will find a long list of concepts and theories, novel arguments and findings, as well as a variety of research and practice-oriented approaches. To address the development of the field, we turn to a seminal article by Linley, Joseph, Harrington and Wood (2006) which was the first article ever published in the *Journal of Positive Psychology*. Linley *et al.* discussed issues and directions for the future of the burgeoning field of positive psychology. Given that a decade has passed since the publication of that article, it might be instructive to consider the five issues that Linley *et al.* raised under the heading 'Issues and directions for the future of positive psychology' with regard to the present anthology.

(1) Synthesize the positive and the negative

Linley *et al.* address the ways in which positive psychology can be used to approach traumatic events and similar occurrences, taking a novel and positive approach to such topics as post-traumatic stress. In the chapters that are present in this anthology, we see some of the integration of positive and negative that is already happening in SLA. For example, in Chapter 9 Dewaele and MacIntyre treat anxiety and enjoyment as the right foot and left foot of the learner, bringing forward some of the complexity in emotion also demanded by Lazarus (2003). In Chapter 12 Belnap *et al.* discuss the ways in which Project Perseverance produces both positive and negative outcomes among the learners studying abroad. Hiver in Chapter 7 discusses the ways in which hope is both lost and regained among new language teachers. In this anthology, we are seeing the integration rather than polarization of positive and negative, and we view this is a constructive development for both SLA and positive psychology.

(2) Build on historical antecedents and existing knowledge

Linley *et al.* discussed the advantages of revisiting humanistic and existential ideas; we see authors in this anthology doing so. Oxford's encyclopedic masterpiece outlining the EMPATHICS vision (Chapter 2) has articulated well the connections between prior research/theory in SLA and current views of positive psychology. Oxford's chapter clearly connects historical antecedents, including roots in humanistic psychology and other areas, with new directions inspired by positive psychology. Chapter 5, by Barcelos and Coelho, draws on theories of love that are both very recent, such as Fredrickson's, as well as established, cross-cultural ideas of love. In addition, Mercer's discussion of empathy (Chapter 3) draws its inspiration from a long line of humanistic thinking, integrated with more modern conceptions, including those developed from neuroscience.

(3) Integrate across levels of analysis

Linley *et al.* discussed some of the ways in which a holistic approach would be beneficial to understanding the topics of positive psychology. In this anthology, we see multiple levels of analysis being used. In their respective chapters (4 and 10), both Falout and Lake elaborate on the role of the self in language learning, creating a more comprehensive conceptualization of the L2 self than has previously been offered. In Chapter 6 we also see Gregersen *et al.* taking a holistic approach to language learning that includes social capital and interpersonal context; the authors show how positive psychology exercises affect language learning and communication. The idea of a holistic approach, integrated across levels of analysis, is consistent with the modern direction of SLA as a discipline that is emphasizing the learner-in-context. One of the key points in Lazarus's (2003) critique of positive psychology, applicable to psychology more generally, was the use of a limited range of methods. As a collection, the diversity of methods and approaches used in this anthology places the SLA field in an advantageous conceptual and methodological position.

(4) Build constituency and reach out to powerful stakeholders

Linley *et al.* discussed ways in which positive psychology might become a constructive force for social improvement through positive institutions and collaborations. Several of the authors in this volume, especially the ones who are dealing with the practicalities of language classrooms and language programs in Part 3 – Helgesen, Murphey, Fresacher, Fonseca-Mora and Herrero Machancoses – are forging the links between SLA and tenets of positive psychology in action. Making overt connections to Seligman's PERMA model, Helgesen demonstrates means by which teachers can implement language strategies and learning goals (Chapter 13). To help language learners concentrate and connect with their inner selves, Fonseca-Mora and Herrero Machancoses use music to unlock learners' creative processes and foster relaxed and productive classrooms (Chapter 16). Murphey uses tenets from positive psychology to offer ways of healthier and happier living via teaching language to members within their social networks (Chapter 14). Finally, in Chapter 15 Fresacher has described a series of established activities from the positive psychology literature that, in her experience, her learners are finding valuable. As Lindley *et al.* recognized, positive institutions have been the least well studied of the three main pillars of positive psychology (the other pillars being positive emotions and positive personality traits). Indeed, there is a considerable amount to be gained by considering ways in which language teaching can be made more positive by orienting to the needs of the individuals and groups served by teaching institutions. In doing so, it is crucial to consider the effect of positive psychology on the language teacher as well as the learner.

(5) Description or prescription?

Linley *et al.* reminded readers that we must be mindful of the difference between describing and prescribing. As editors of this volume, we have noted the same tension among the topics discussed here. When language teachers and language learners are going about their business, they are embedded in social, cultural and historical traditions that impact on the language learning experience. For this reason, it can be very difficult to prescribe a particular course of action that would be universally beneficial. Indeed, many of the interventions that are recommended by authors in this volume are tailored to the specific, local circumstances and the individuals with which the authors were working. For example, Gregersen *et al.* suggest that individualizing positive psychology exercises to the conversation partners in their study was responsible for at least some of the positive effects of the program. Dewaele and MacIntyre report that students enjoy classroom activities that language teacher trainers likely would never recommend. Further, the specific pedagogical activities discussed by Murphey, Fonseca-Mora and Herrero Machancoses, Fresacher and Helgesen also can be tailored to the identified needs of specific learners, operating in particular contexts. One example is Fresacher, who provides language teaching tips that incorporate specific positive psychology interventions that increase learners' resilience and facilitate each individual's coping strategies. We agree with Lindley *et al.* when they say 'positive psychology ought to be very mindful of carrying into the trap of prescription without the necessary critical reflection, and assuming that a positive psychological position would ever be right for all of the people, all of the time' (Lindley *et al.*, 2006: 14). Perhaps this is one area in which the study of language is more sensitive to context and culture than positive psychology would be in general.

Final Thoughts

There is good reason to engage with positive psychology in SLA. The theories, concepts, methods and research findings already available provide powerful ways to study important aspects of experience that have not yet been widely studied. Positive psychology has an added dimension of practice and applications that can further inform both the teaching and learner development sides of SLA. Whether this anthology makes small ripples or a big splash in the field will depend on the ideas that are contained herein and the ways in which teachers and researchers receive them. We are hopeful that this anthology will provide both tangible evidence of the potential for positive psychology to inform the field of SLA and inspiration for new theory, research and practice in the years to come.

References

Ehrenreich, B. (2009) *Bright-Sided: How Positive Thinking Is Undermining America*. New York: Metropolitan Books.

Lazarus, R.S. (2003) Target article: Does the positive psychology movement have legs? *Psychological Inquiry* 14 (2), 93–109.

Linley, P.A., Joseph, S., Harrington, S. and Wood, A.M. (2006) Positive psychology: Past, present, and (possible) future. *Journal of Positive Psychology* 1, 3–16.

MacIntyre, P.D. and Mercer, S. (2014) Introducing positive psychology to SLA. *Studies in Second Language Learning and Teaching* 4, 153–172.

Seligman, M.E.P. (2011) *Flourish: A Visionary New Understanding of Happiness and Well-Being*. New York: Free Press.

Seligman, M.E.P. and Csikszentmihalyi, M. (2000) Positive psychology: An introduction. *American Psychologist* 55 (1), 5–14.

Index

Lightning Source UK Ltd.
Milton Keynes UK
UKHW021835281122
412984UK00028B/382

9 781783 095346